Give to the Heart

Vol.2

WANN

NETCOMICS

Give to the Heart Vol. 2

Story and Art by WANN

Produced by Ecomix Media Company

Translator Jeong Lee

Editor Philip Daay

Cover Designer purj

Graphic Designer Jihye Kim

Publisher Heewoon Chung

5405 Wilshire Blvd. Suite 269
Los Angeles, CA 90036
info@netcomics.com
www.NETCOMICS.com

ISBN: 978-1-60009-953-3
First Printing: November 2014
10 9 8 7 6 5 4 3 2 1
Printed in Korea

Give to the Heart

Vol.2

WANN

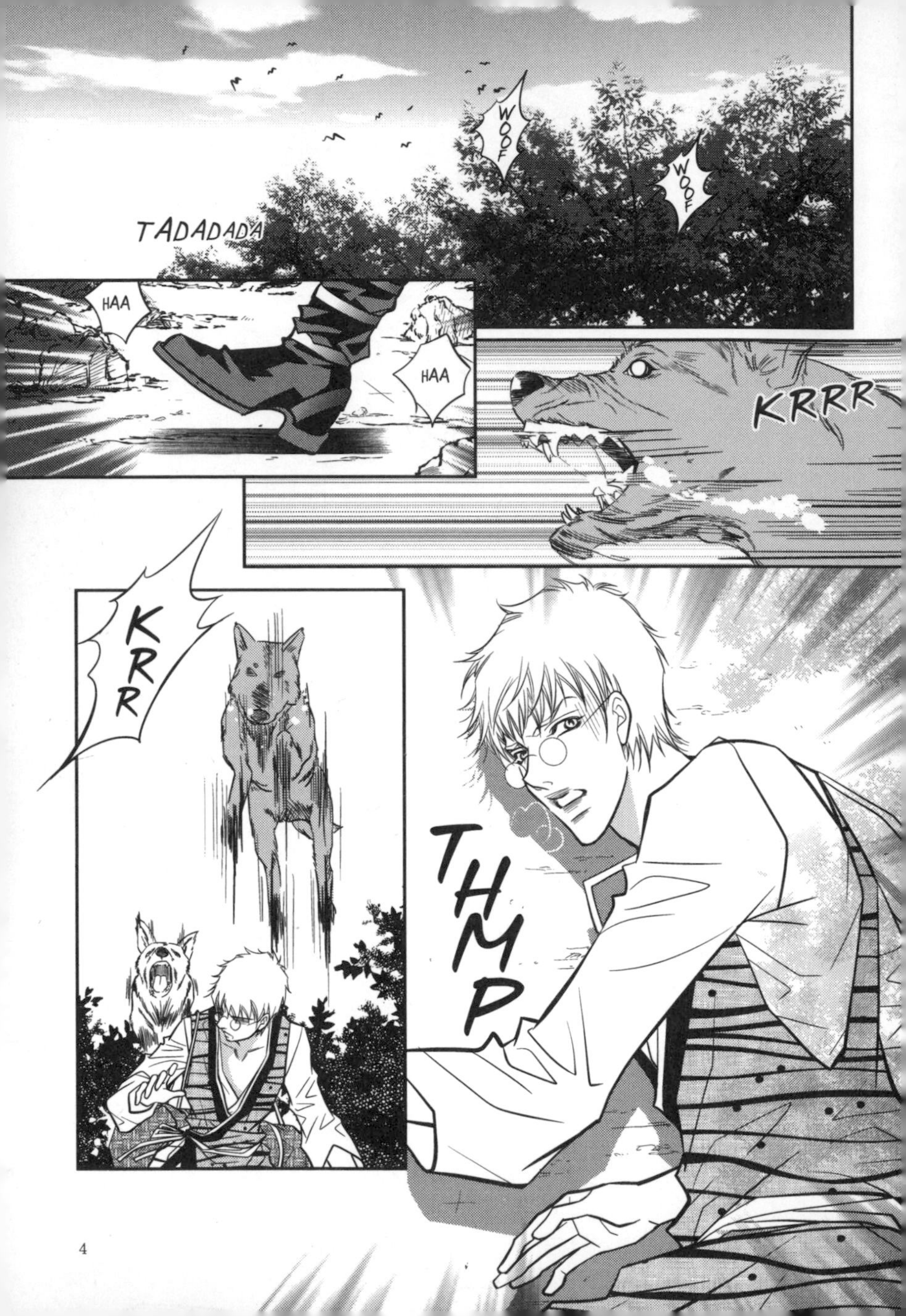
TADADADA
WOOF
WOOF
HAA
HAA
KRRR
KRR
THMP

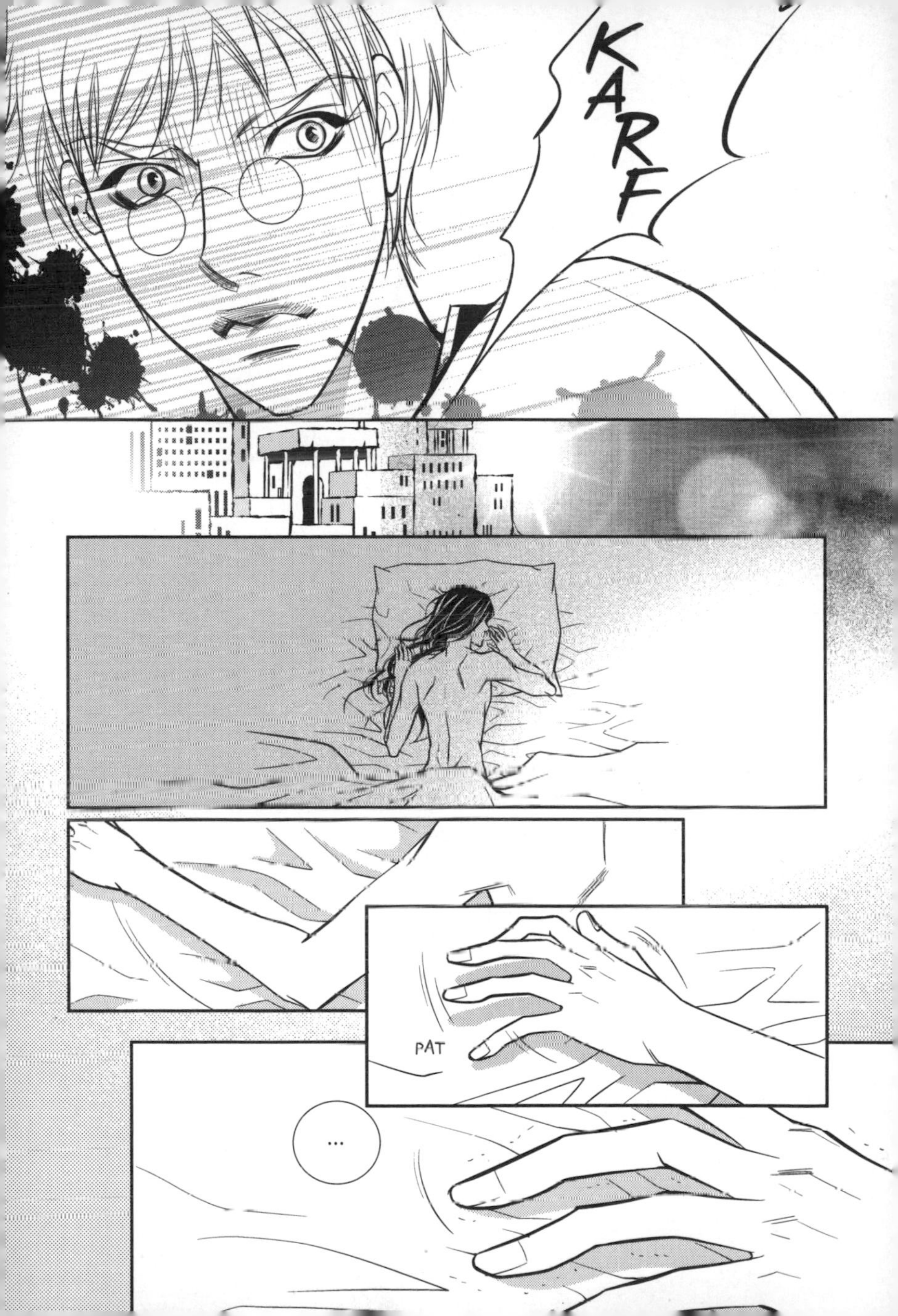
KARF
PAT
...

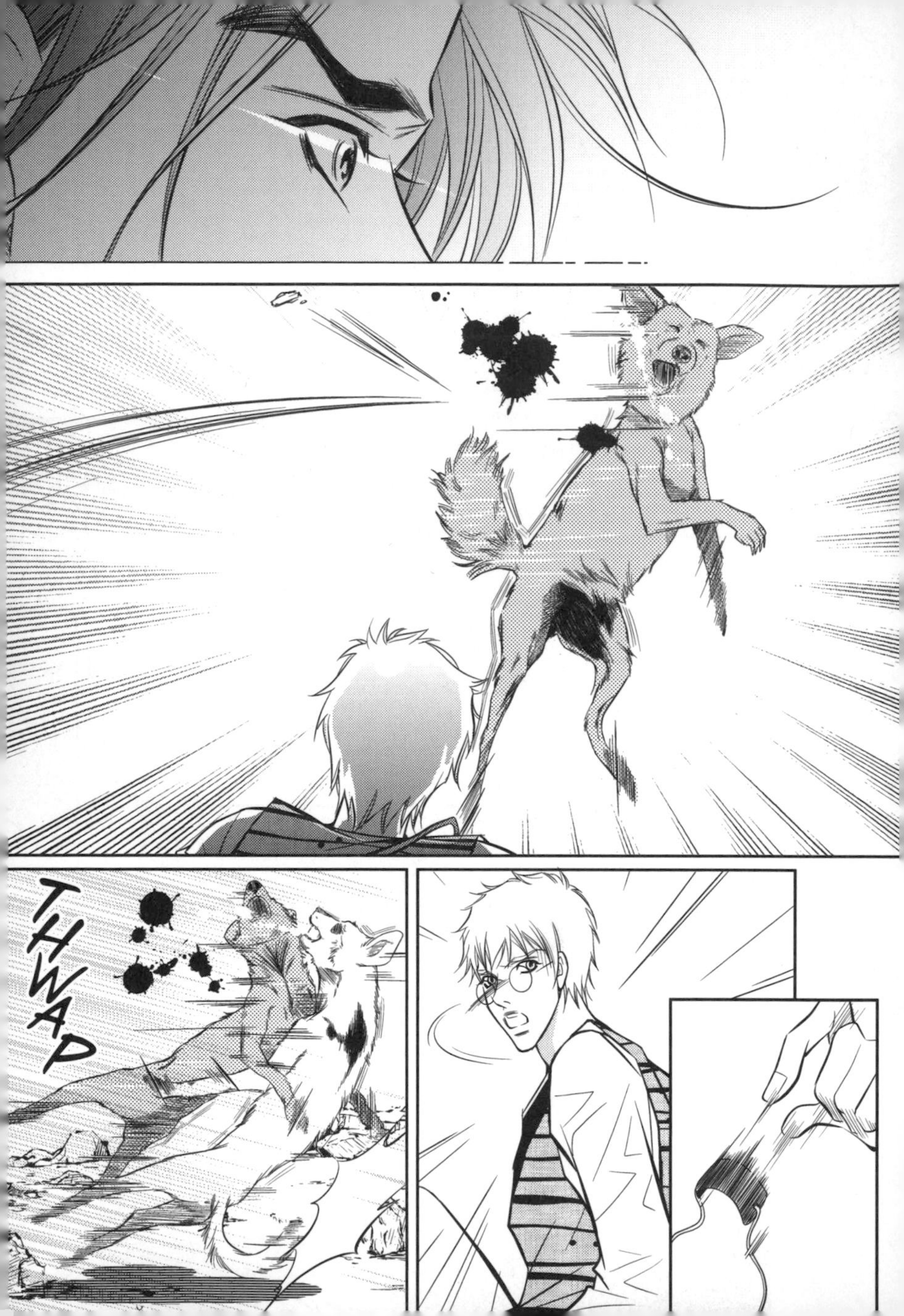
THWAP

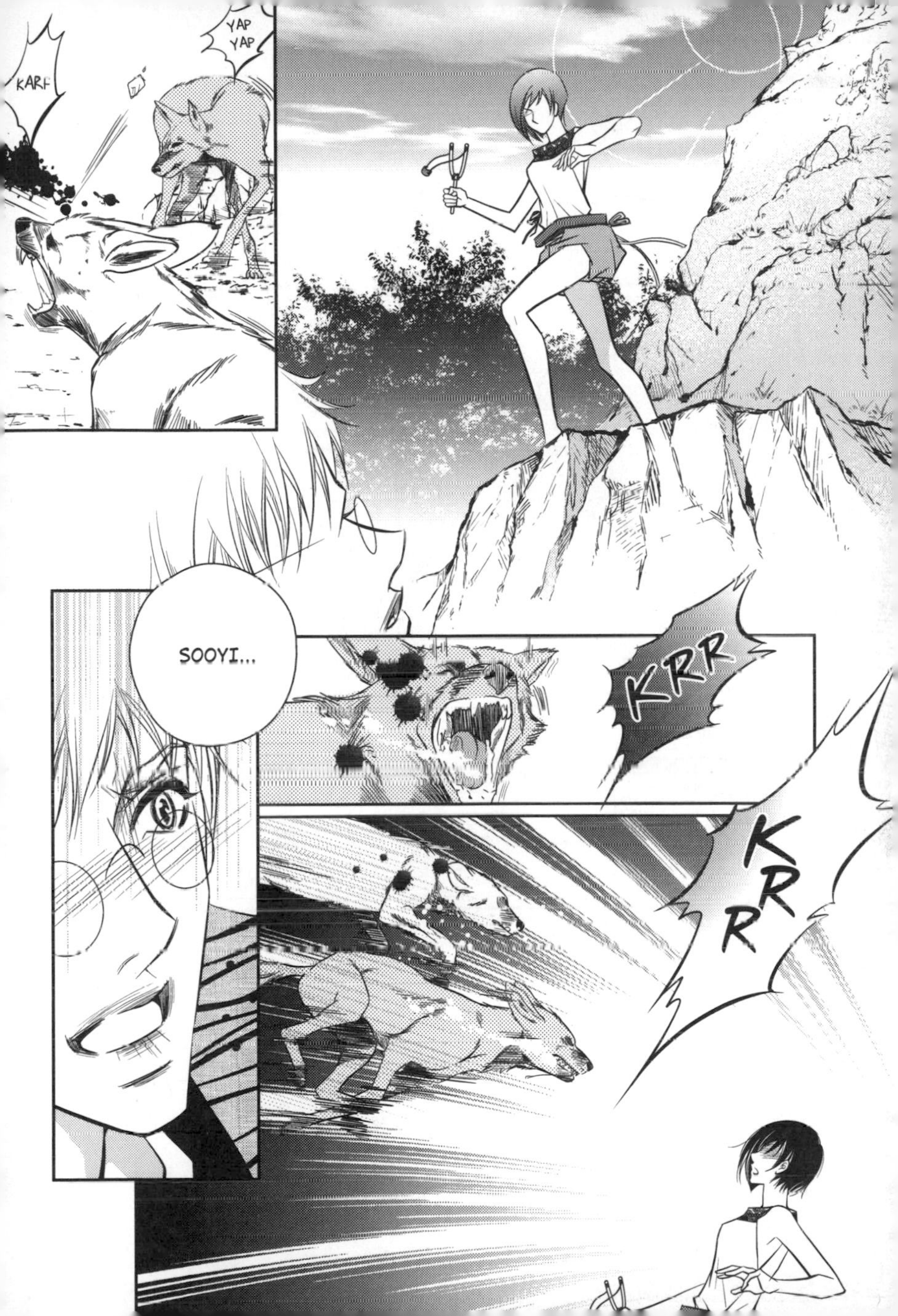
KARF
YAP YAP
SOOYI...
KRR
KRRR

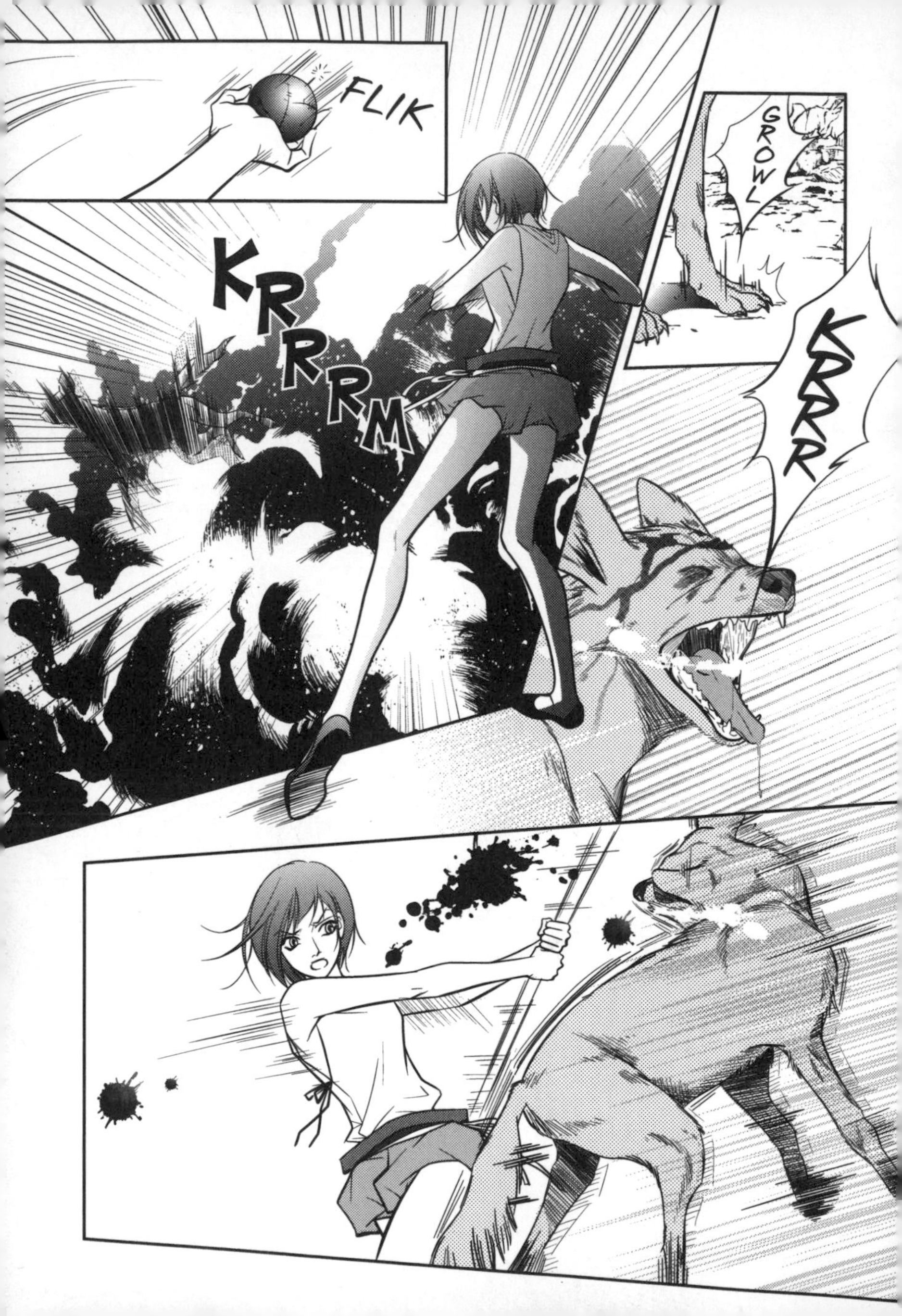
FLIK
GROWL
KRRRM
KRRR

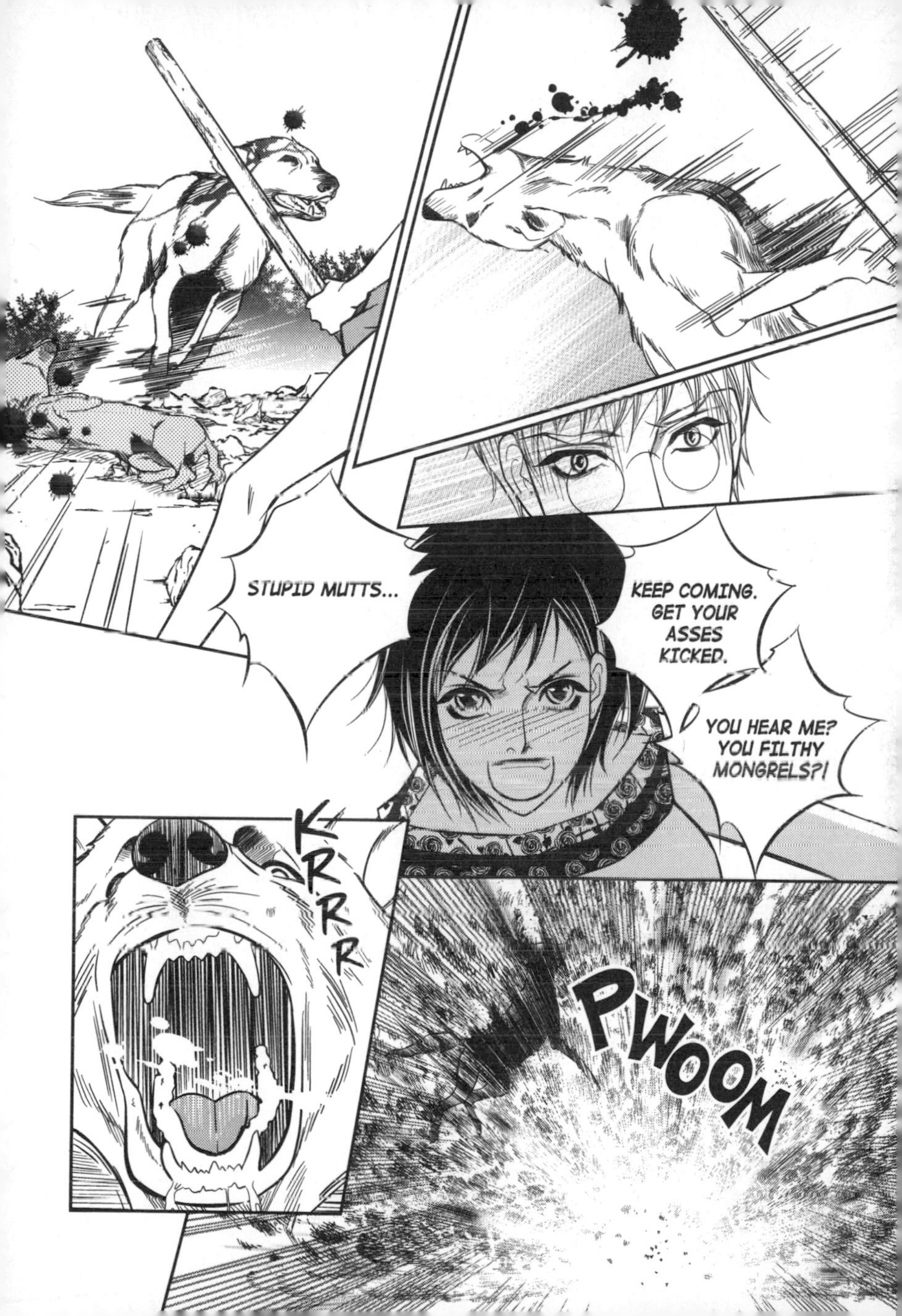
STUPID MUTTS...
KEEP COMING. GET YOUR ASSES KICKED.
YOU HEAR ME? YOU FILTHY MONGRELS?!
KRRRR
PWOOM

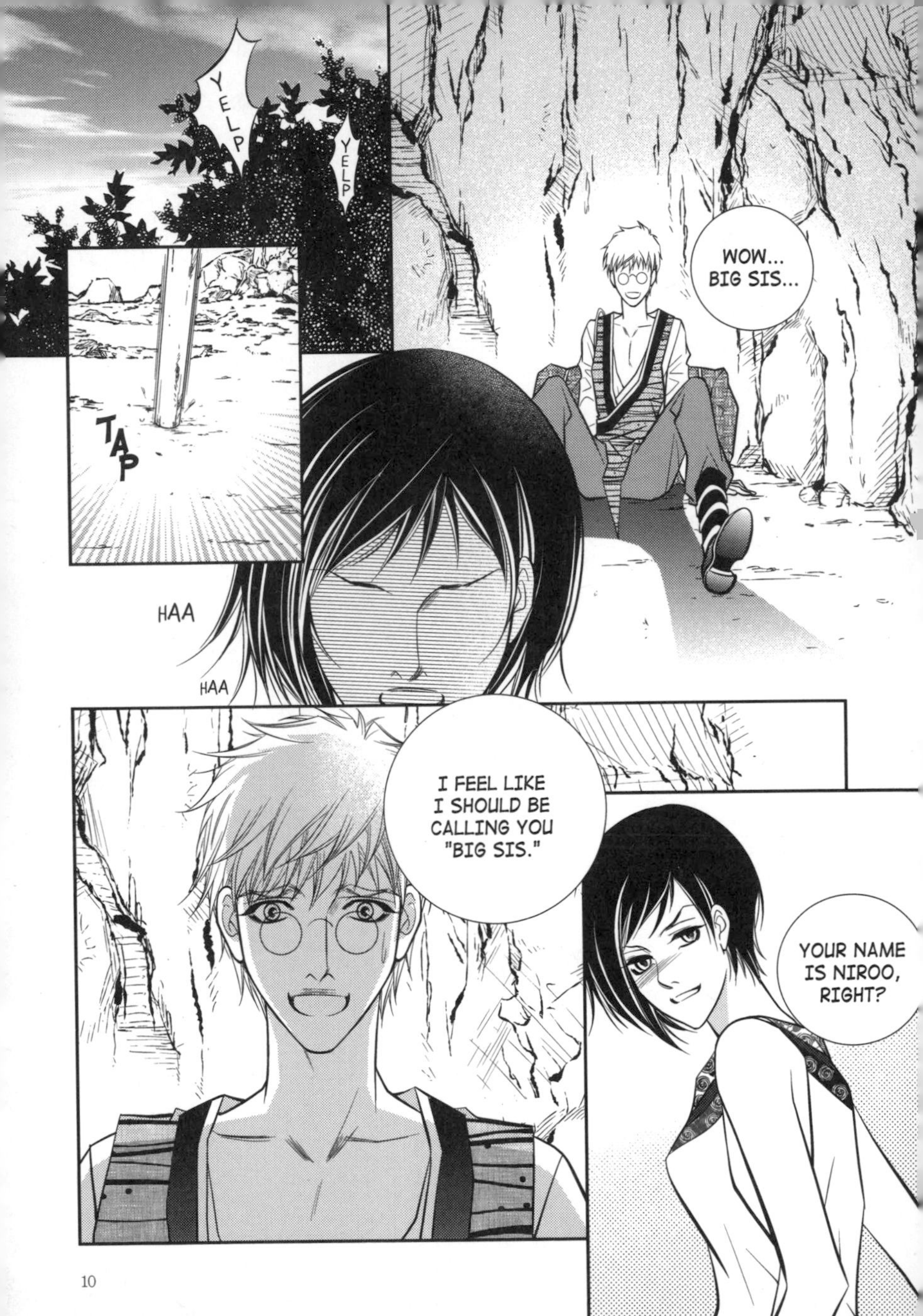
YELP
YELP
WOW... BIG SIS...
TAP
HAA
HAA
I FEEL LIKE I SHOULD BE CALLING YOU "BIG SIS."
YOUR NAME IS NIROO, RIGHT?

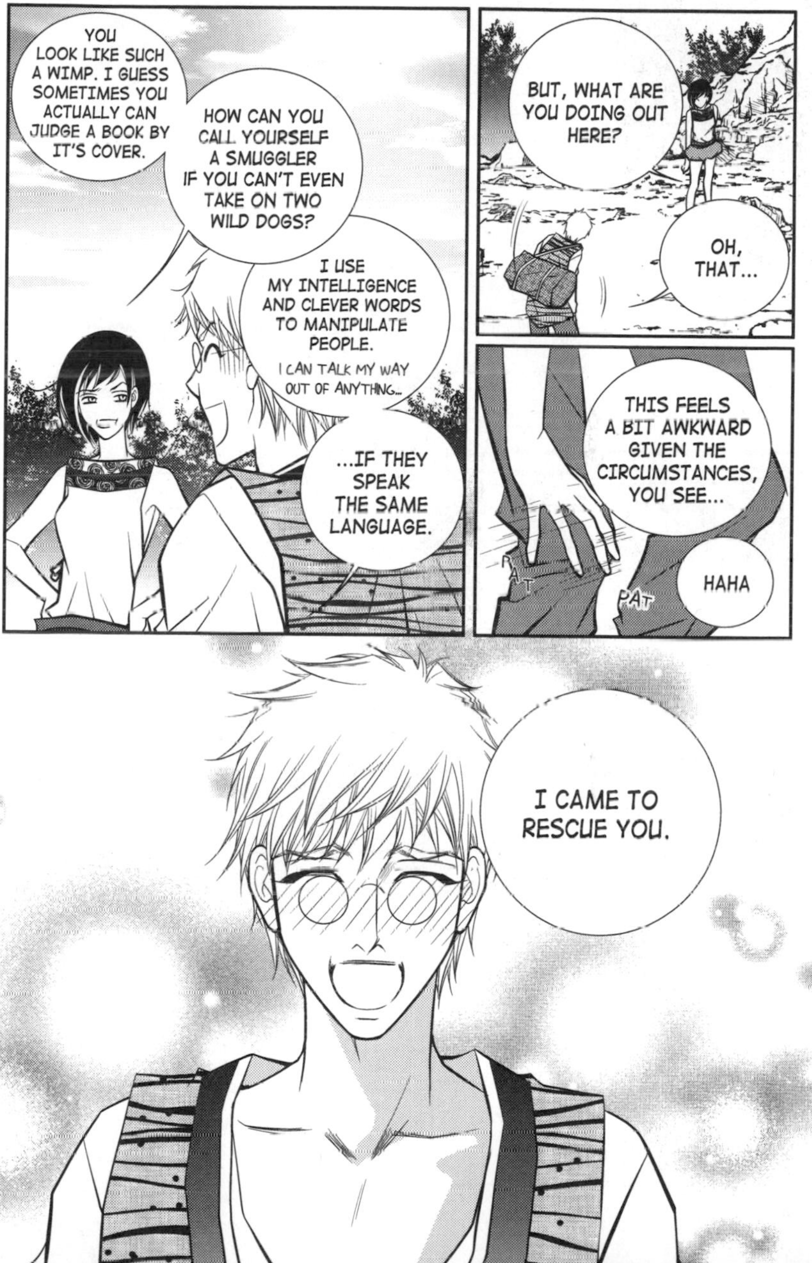
YOU LOOK LIKE SUCH A WIMP. I GUESS SOMETIMES YOU ACTUALLY CAN JUDGE A BOOK BY IT'S COVER.
HOW CAN YOU CALL YOURSELF A SMUGGLER IF YOU CAN'T EVEN TAKE ON TWO WILD DOGS?
I USE MY INTELLIGENCE AND CLEVER WORDS TO MANIPULATE PEOPLE.
I CAN TALK MY WAY OUT OF ANYTHING...
...IF THEY SPEAK THE SAME LANGUAGE.
BUT, WHAT ARE YOU DOING OUT HERE?
OH, THAT...
THIS FEELS A BIT AWKWARD GIVEN THE CIRCUMSTANCES, YOU SEE...
PAT
PAT
HAHA
I CAME TO RESCUE YOU.

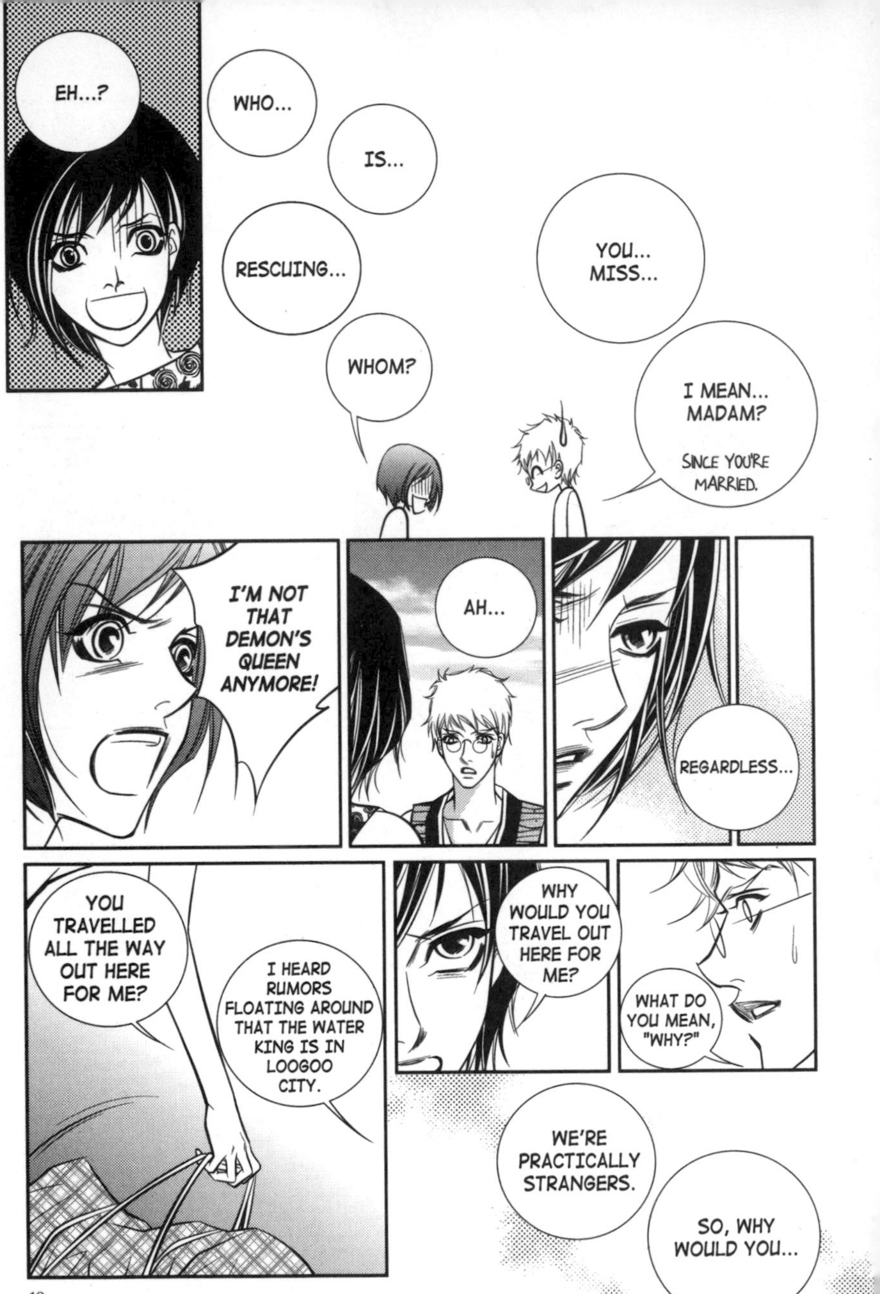
EH...?
WHO...
IS...
RESCUING...
WHOM?
YOU... MISS...
I MEAN... MADAM?
SINCE YOU'RE MARRIED.
I'M NOT THAT DEMON'S QUEEN ANYMORE!
AH...
REGARDLESS...
YOU TRAVELLED ALL THE WAY OUT HERE FOR ME?
I HEARD RUMORS FLOATING AROUND THAT THE WATER KING IS IN LOOGOO CITY.
WHY WOULD YOU TRAVEL OUT HERE FOR ME?
WHAT DO YOU MEAN, "WHY?"
WE'RE PRACTICALLY STRANGERS.
SO, WHY WOULD YOU...

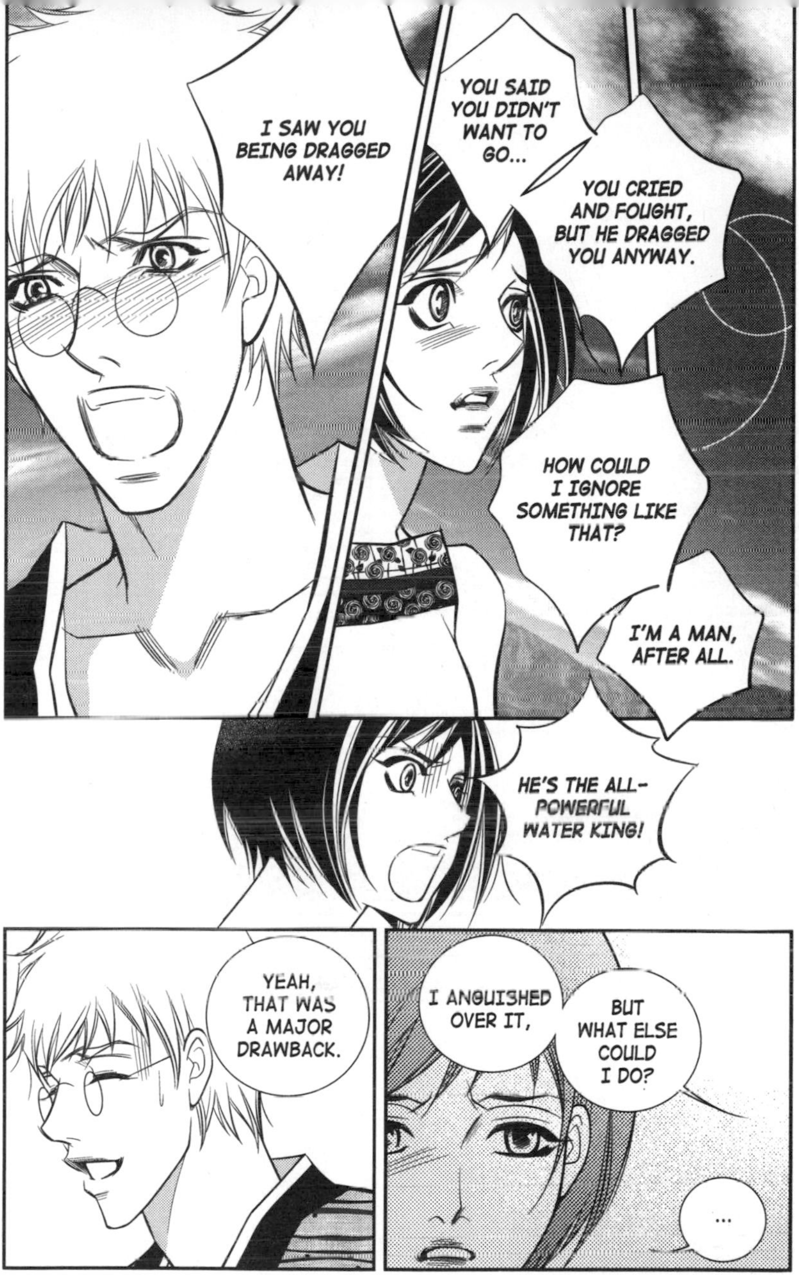
I SAW YOU BEING DRAGGED AWAY!
YOU SAID YOU DIDN'T WANT TO GO...
YOU CRIED AND FOUGHT, BUT HE DRAGGED YOU ANYWAY.
HOW COULD I IGNORE SOMETHING LIKE THAT?
I'M A MAN, AFTER ALL.
HE'S THE ALL-POWERFUL WATER KING!
YEAH, THAT WAS A MAJOR DRAWBACK.
I ANGUISHED OVER IT,
BUT WHAT ELSE COULD I DO?
...

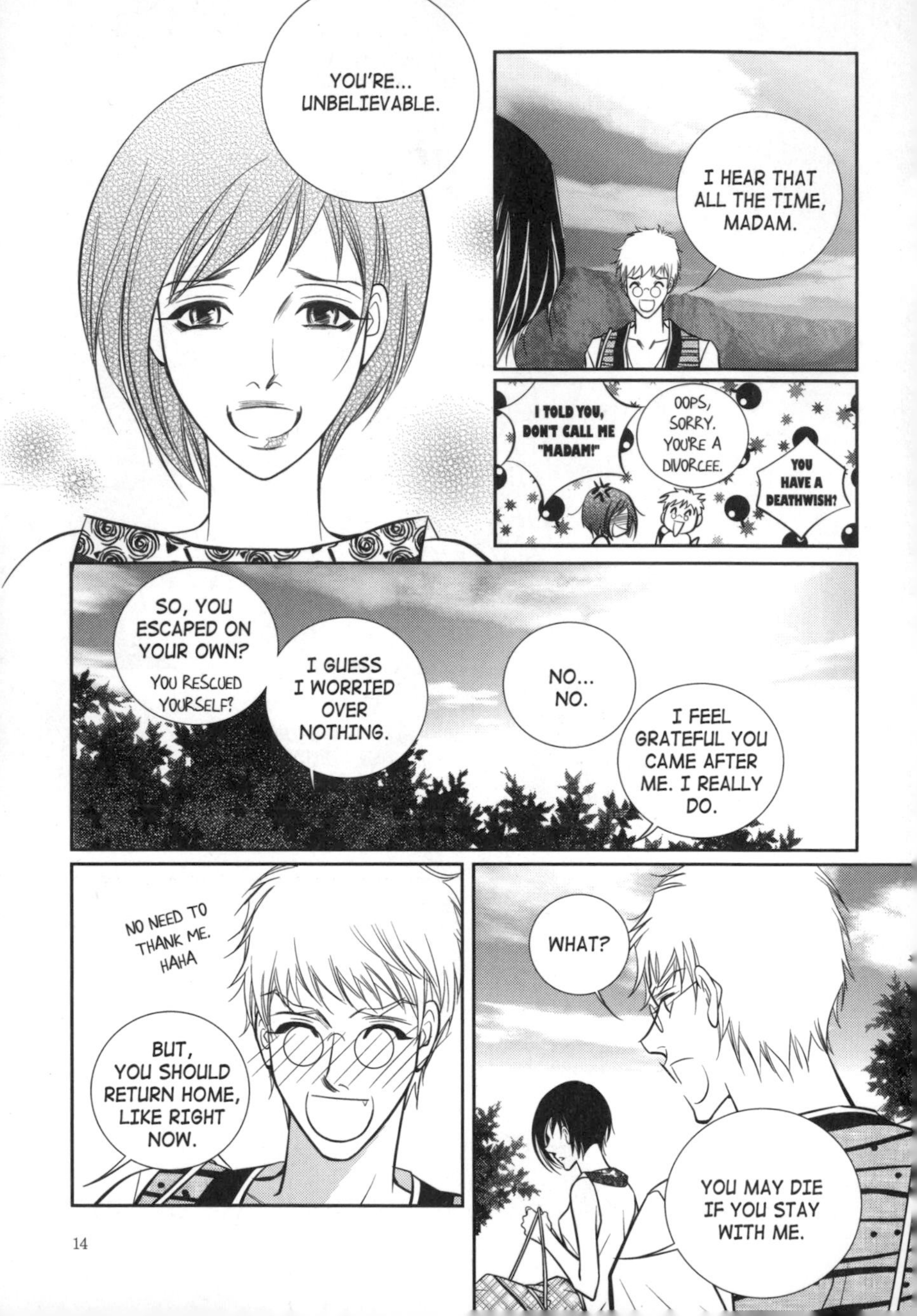
YOU'RE... UNBELIEVABLE.
I HEAR THAT ALL THE TIME, MADAM.
I TOLD YOU, DON'T CALL ME "MADAM!"
OOPS, SORRY. YOU'RE A DIVORCEE.
YOU HAVE A DEATHWISH?
SO, YOU ESCAPED ON YOUR OWN?
YOU RESCUED YOURSELF?
I GUESS I WORRIED OVER NOTHING.
NO... NO.
I FEEL GRATEFUL YOU CAME AFTER ME. I REALLY DO.
NO NEED TO THANK ME. HAHA
BUT, YOU SHOULD RETURN HOME, LIKE RIGHT NOW.
WHAT?
YOU MAY DIE IF YOU STAY WITH ME.

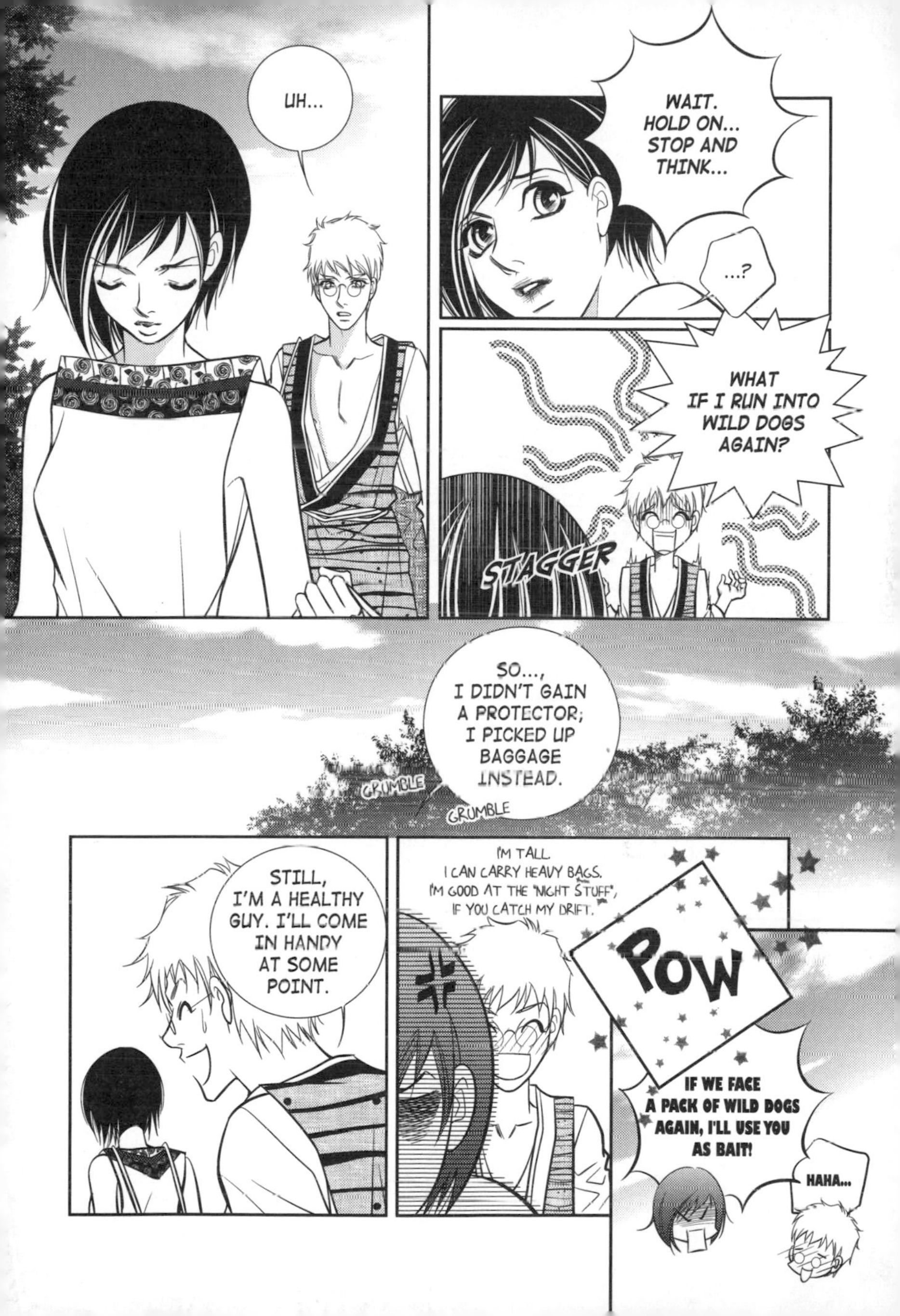
UH...
WAIT. HOLD ON... STOP AND THINK...
...?
WHAT IF I RUN INTO WILD DOGS AGAIN?
STAGGER
SO..., I DIDN'T GAIN A PROTECTOR; I PICKED UP BAGGAGE INSTEAD.
GRUMBLE
GRUMBLE
STILL, I'M A HEALTHY GUY. I'LL COME IN HANDY AT SOME POINT.
I'M TALL. I CAN CARRY HEAVY BAGS. I'M GOOD AT THE "NIGHT STUFF", IF YOU CATCH MY DRIFT.
POW
IF WE FACE A PACK OF WILD DOGS AGAIN, I'LL USE YOU AS BAIT!
HAHA...

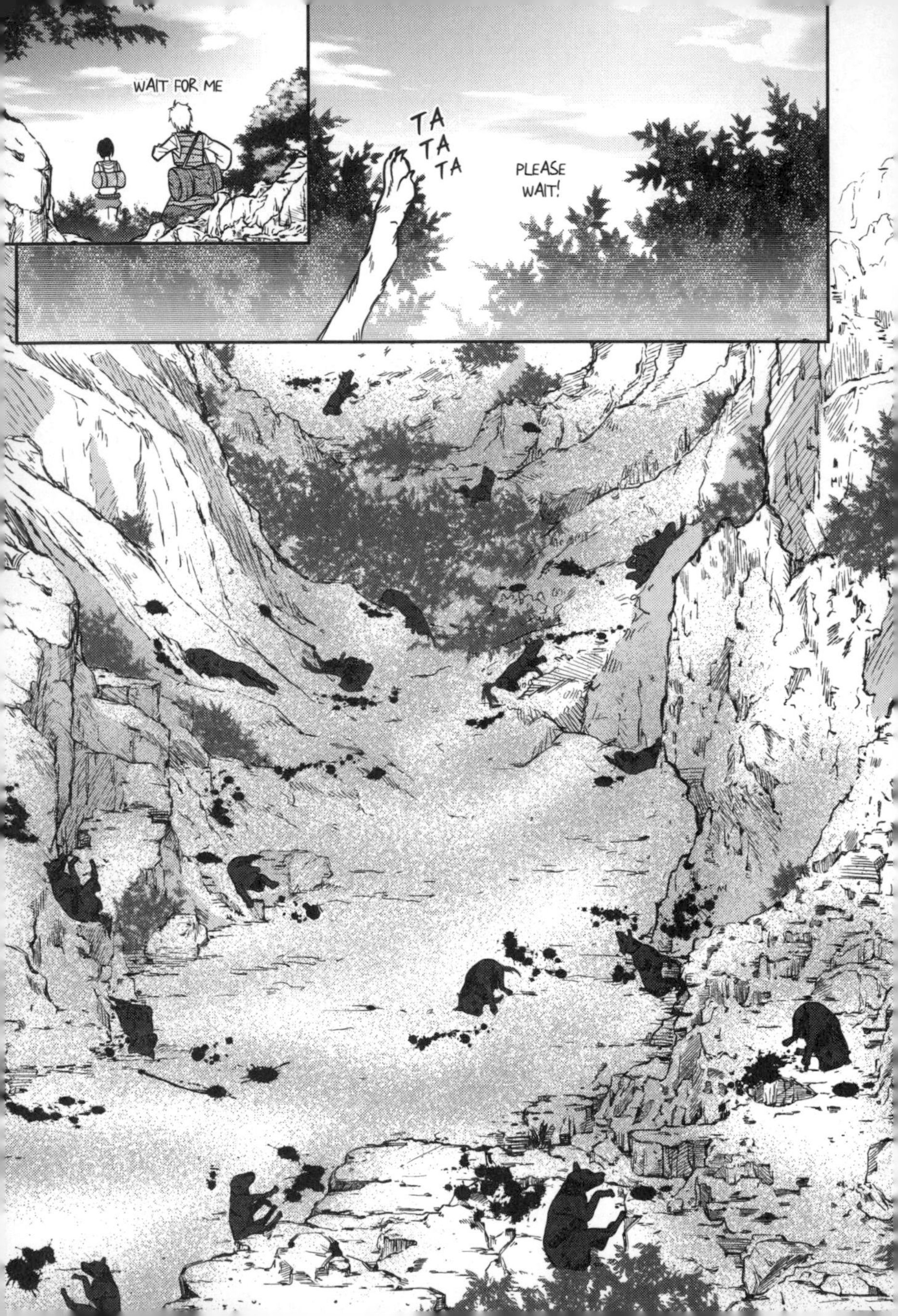
WAIT FOR ME
TA TA TA
PLEASE WAIT!

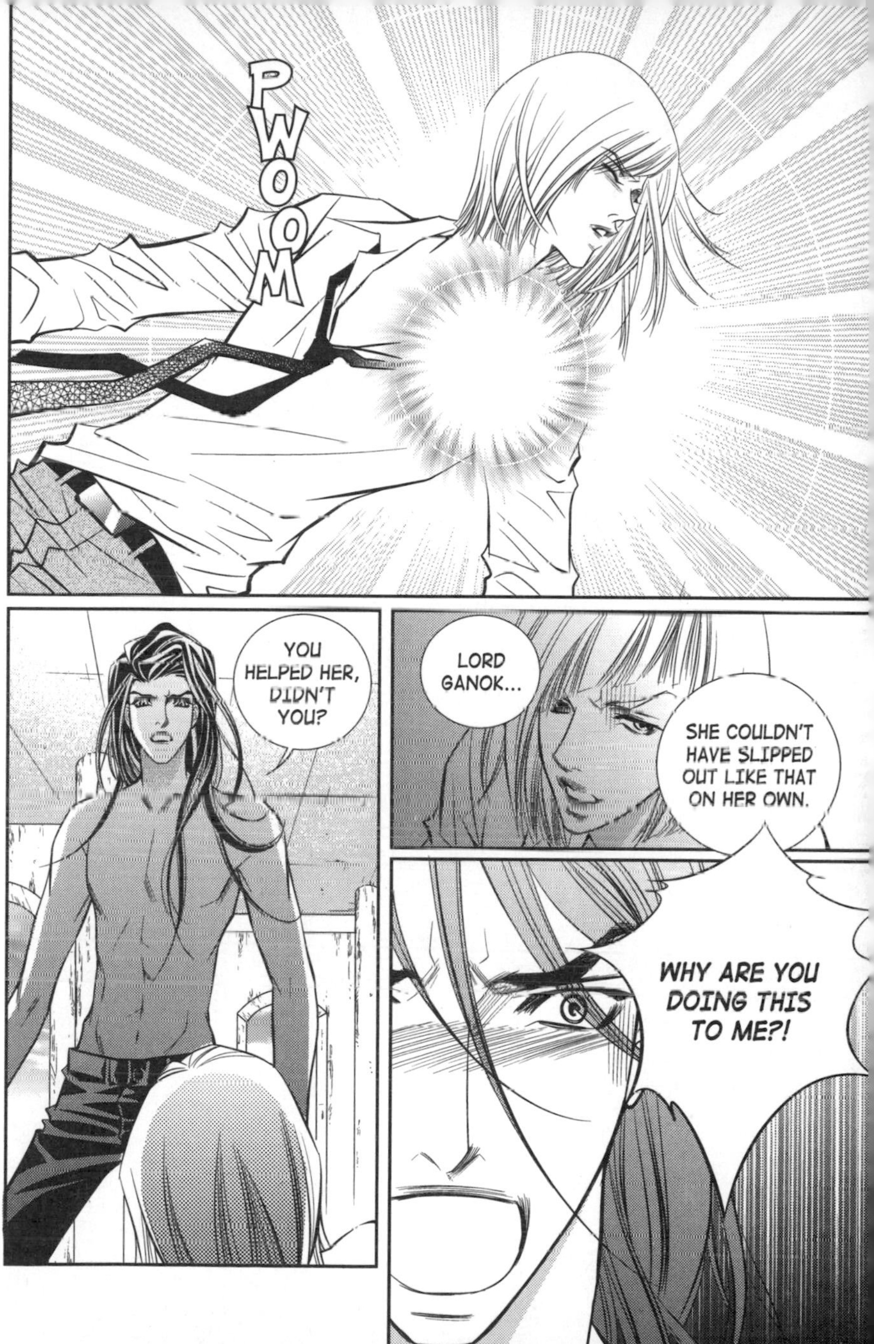
PWOOM
YOU HELPED HER, DIDN'T YOU?
LORD GANOK...
SHE COULDN'T HAVE SLIPPED OUT LIKE THAT ON HER OWN.
WHY ARE YOU DOING THIS TO ME?!

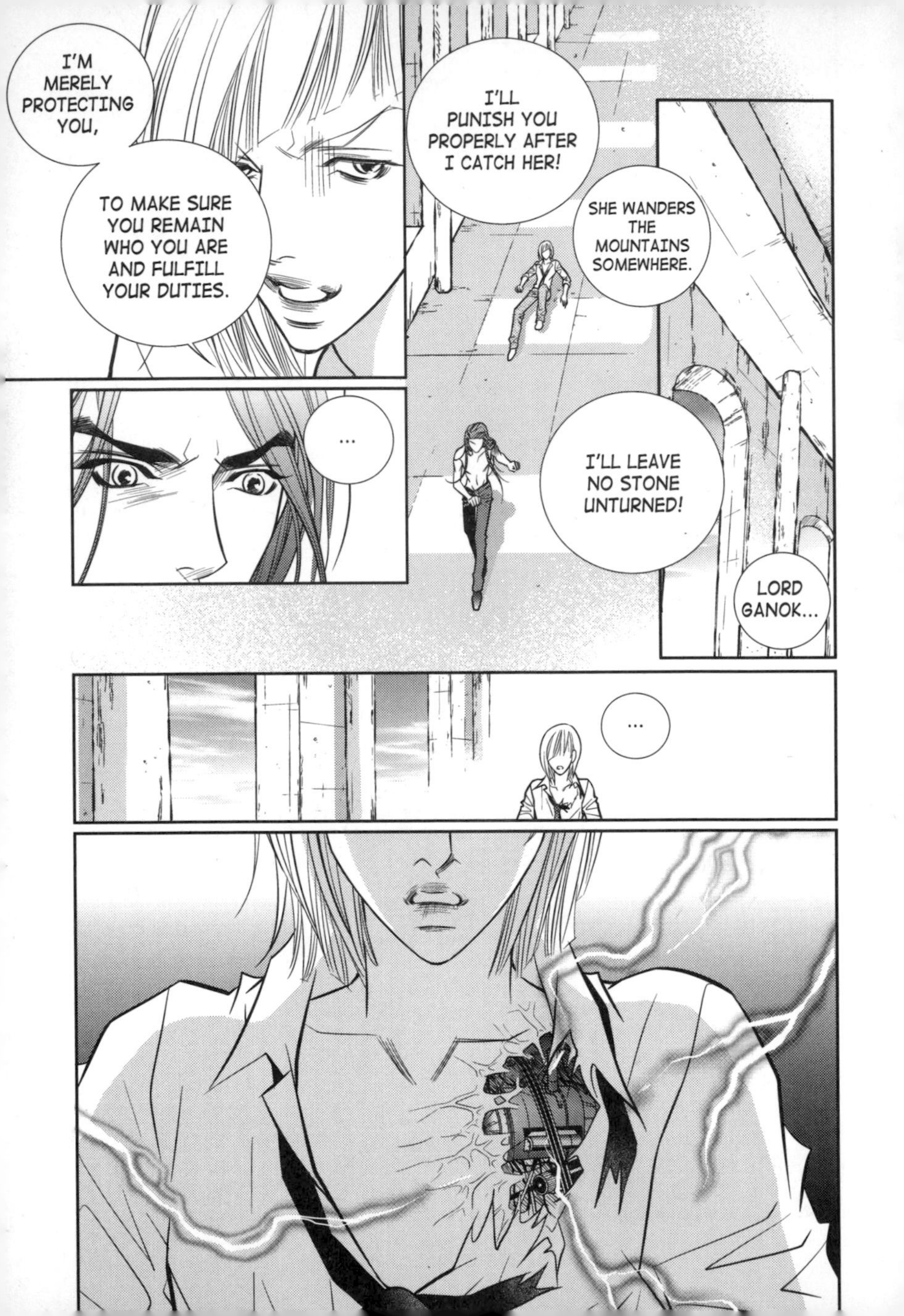
I'M MERELY PROTECTING YOU,
TO MAKE SURE YOU REMAIN WHO YOU ARE AND FULFILL YOUR DUTIES.
I'LL PUNISH YOU PROPERLY AFTER I CATCH HER!
SHE WANDERS THE MOUNTAINS SOMEWHERE.
...
I'LL LEAVE NO STONE UNTURNED!
LORD GANOK...
...

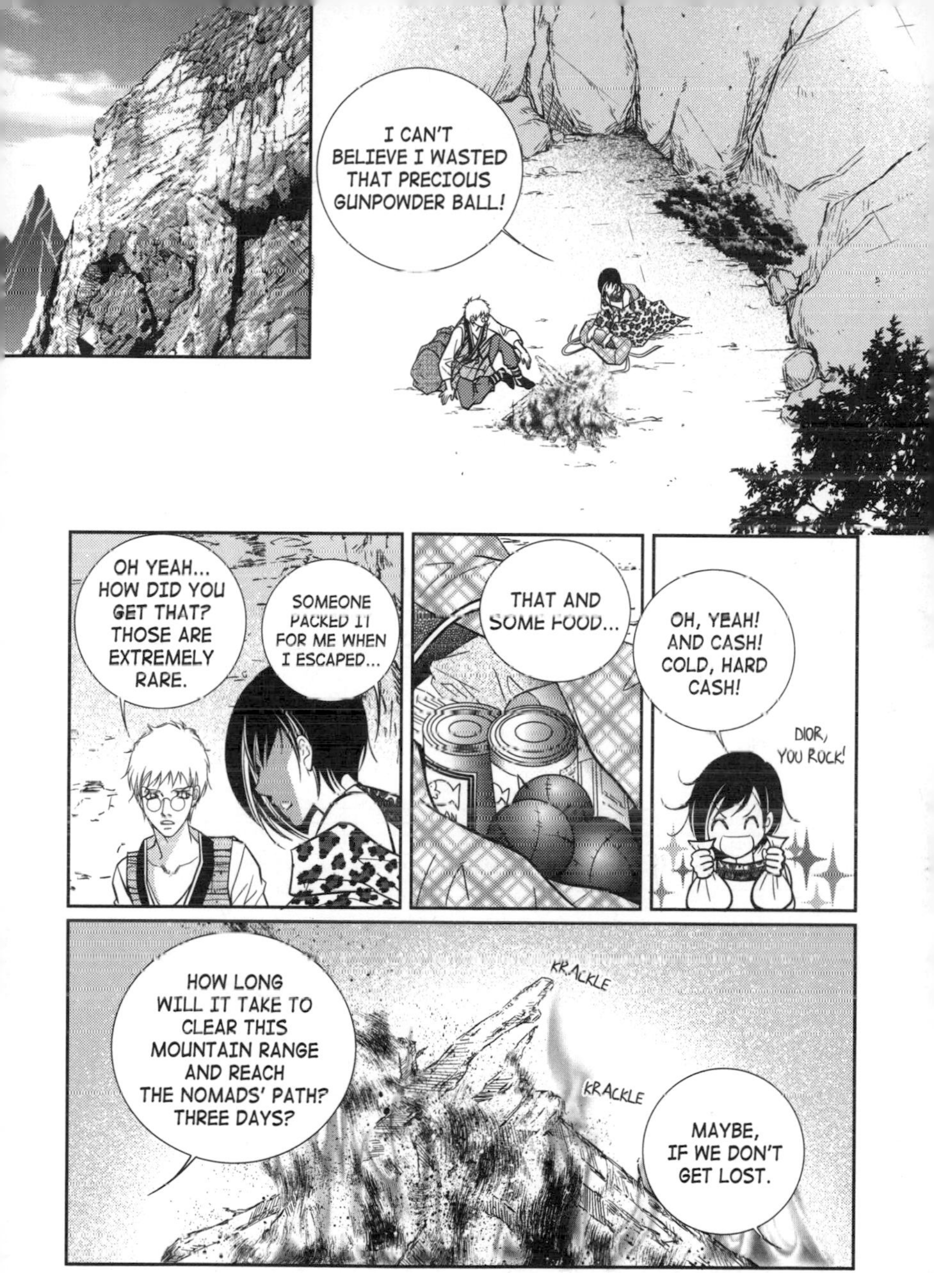
I CAN'T BELIEVE I WASTED THAT PRECIOUS GUNPOWDER BALL!
OH YEAH... HOW DID YOU GET THAT? THOSE ARE EXTREMELY RARE.
SOMEONE PACKED IT FOR ME WHEN I ESCAPED...
THAT AND SOME FOOD...
OH, YEAH! AND CASH! COLD, HARD CASH!
DIOR, YOU ROCK!
HOW LONG WILL IT TAKE TO CLEAR THIS MOUNTAIN RANGE AND REACH THE NOMADS' PATH? THREE DAYS?
KRACKLE
KRACKLE
MAYBE, IF WE DON'T GET LOST.

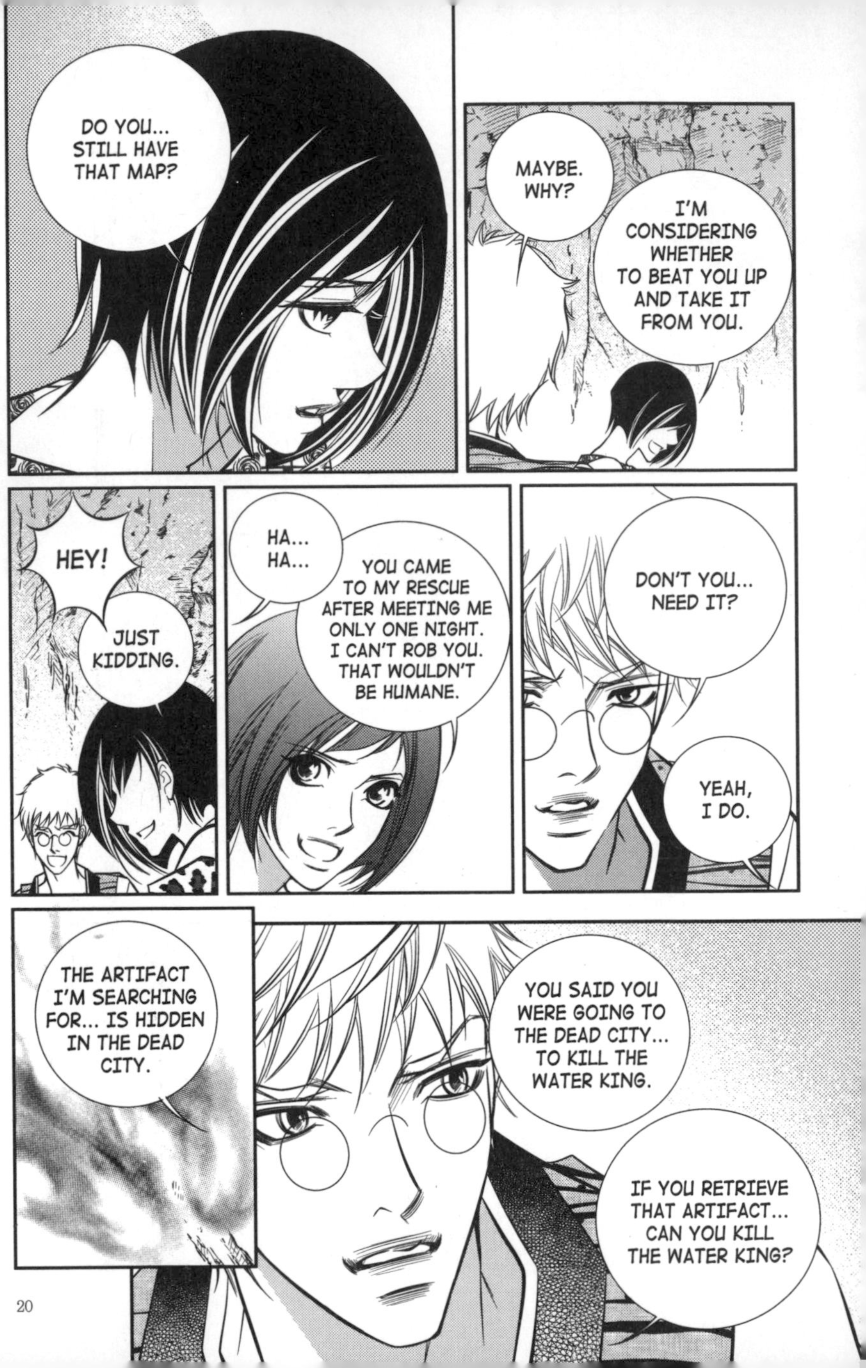
DO YOU... STILL HAVE THAT MAP?
MAYBE. WHY?
I'M CONSIDERING WHETHER TO BEAT YOU UP AND TAKE IT FROM YOU.
HEY!
JUST KIDDING.
HA... HA...
YOU CAME TO MY RESCUE AFTER MEETING ME ONLY ONE NIGHT. I CAN'T ROB YOU. THAT WOULDN'T BE HUMANE.
DON'T YOU... NEED IT?
YEAH, I DO.
THE ARTIFACT I'M SEARCHING FOR... IS HIDDEN IN THE DEAD CITY.
YOU SAID YOU WERE GOING TO THE DEAD CITY... TO KILL THE WATER KING.
IF YOU RETRIEVE THAT ARTIFACT... CAN YOU KILL THE WATER KING?

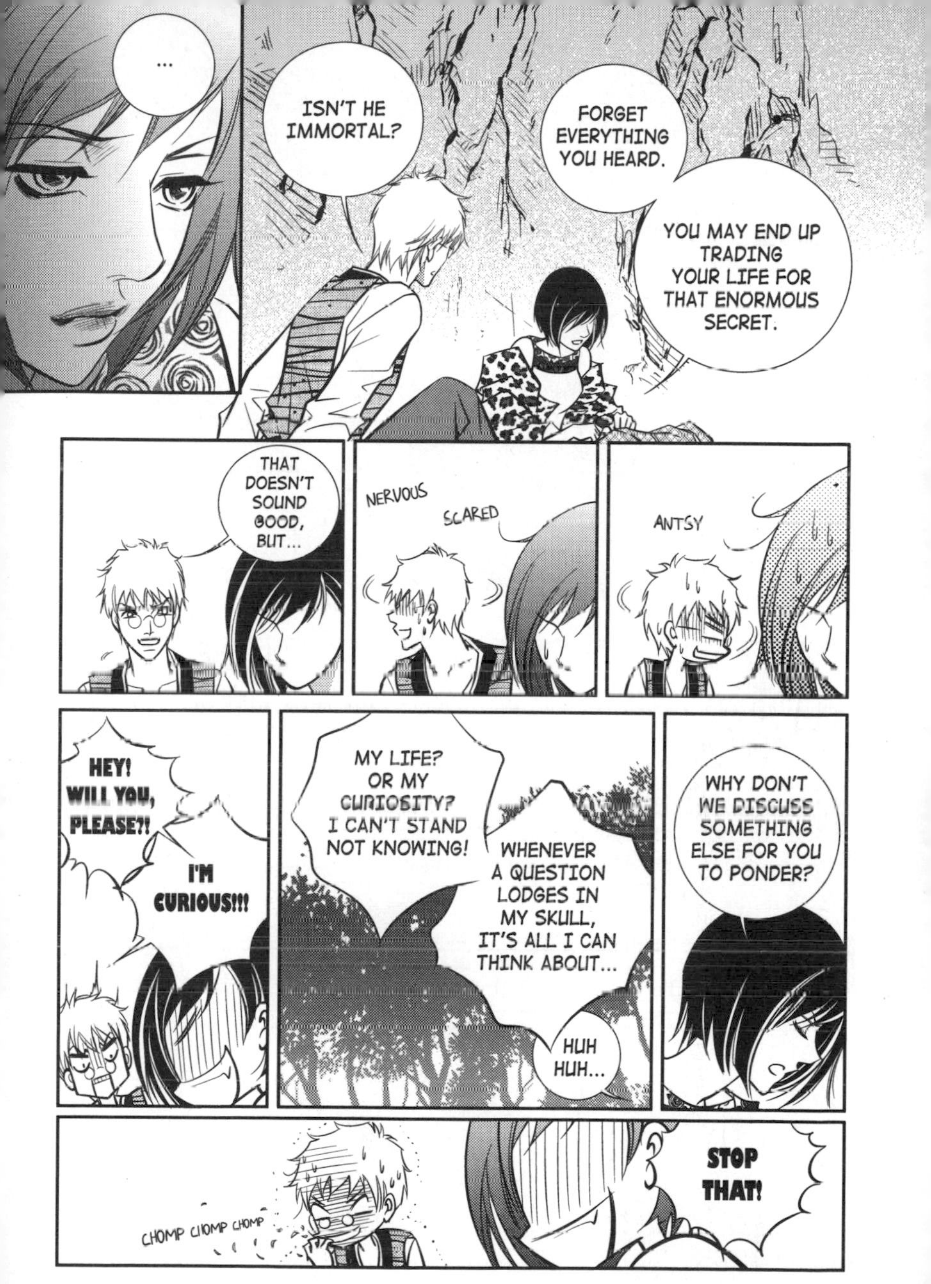
...
ISN'T HE IMMORTAL?
FORGET EVERYTHING YOU HEARD.
YOU MAY END UP TRADING YOUR LIFE FOR THAT ENORMOUS SECRET.
THAT DOESN'T SOUND GOOD, BUT...
NERVOUS
SCARED
ANTSY
HEY! WILL YOU, PLEASE?!
I'M CURIOUS!!!
MY LIFE? OR MY CURIOSITY? I CAN'T STAND NOT KNOWING!
WHENEVER A QUESTION LODGES IN MY SKULL, IT'S ALL I CAN THINK ABOUT...
HUH HUH...
WHY DON'T WE DISCUSS SOMETHING ELSE FOR YOU TO PONDER?
CHOMP CHOMP CHOMP
STOP THAT!

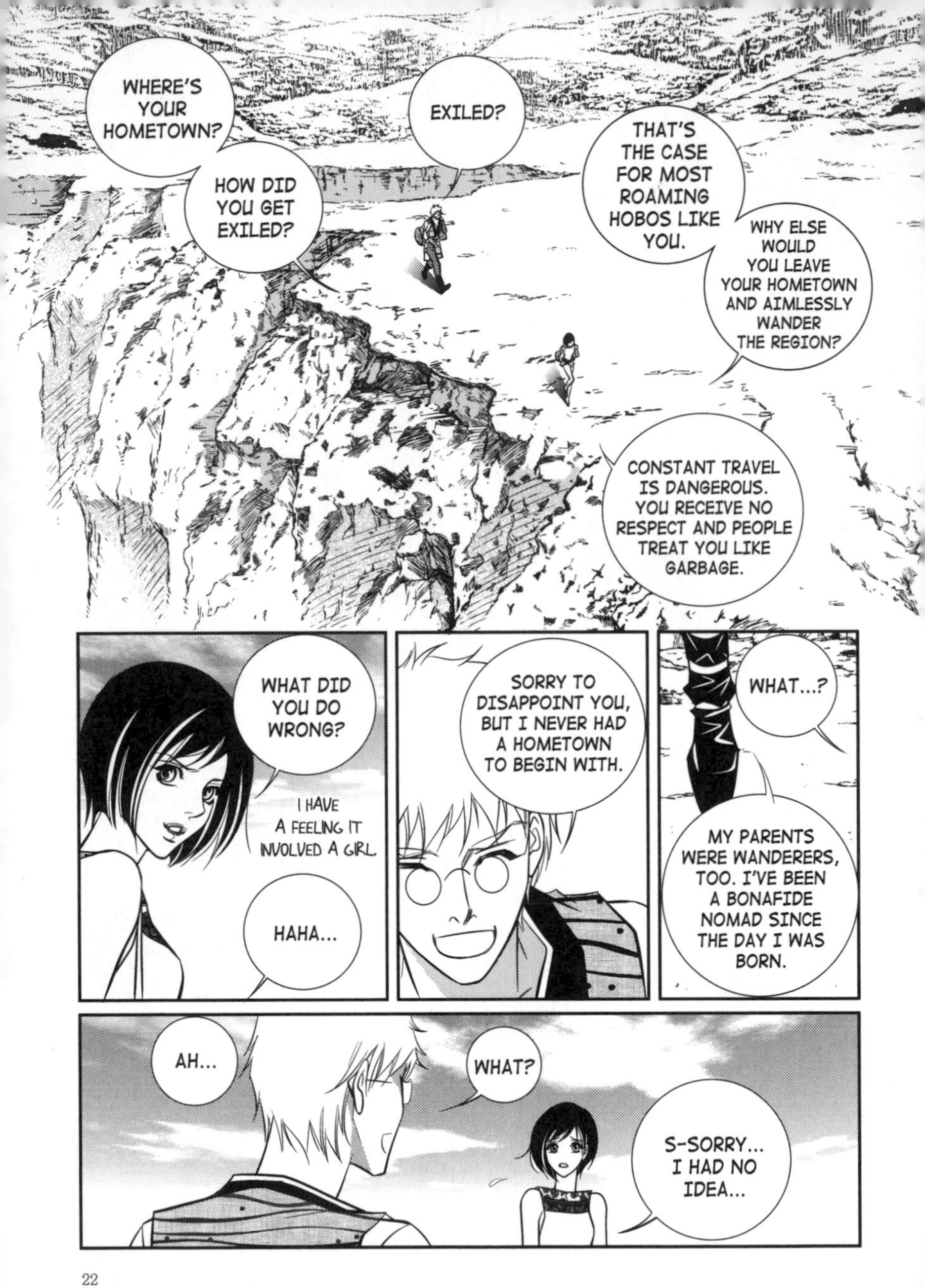
WHERE'S YOUR HOMETOWN?
HOW DID YOU GET EXILED?
EXILED?
THAT'S THE CASE FOR MOST ROAMING HOBOS LIKE YOU.
WHY ELSE WOULD YOU LEAVE YOUR HOMETOWN AND AIMLESSLY WANDER THE REGION?
CONSTANT TRAVEL IS DANGEROUS. YOU RECEIVE NO RESPECT AND PEOPLE TREAT YOU LIKE GARBAGE.
WHAT DID YOU DO WRONG?
I HAVE A FEELING IT INVOLVED A GIRL.
HAHA...
SORRY TO DISAPPOINT YOU, BUT I NEVER HAD A HOMETOWN TO BEGIN WITH.
WHAT...?
MY PARENTS WERE WANDERERS, TOO. I'VE BEEN A BONAFIDE NOMAD SINCE THE DAY I WAS BORN.
AH...
WHAT?
S-SORRY... I HAD NO IDEA...

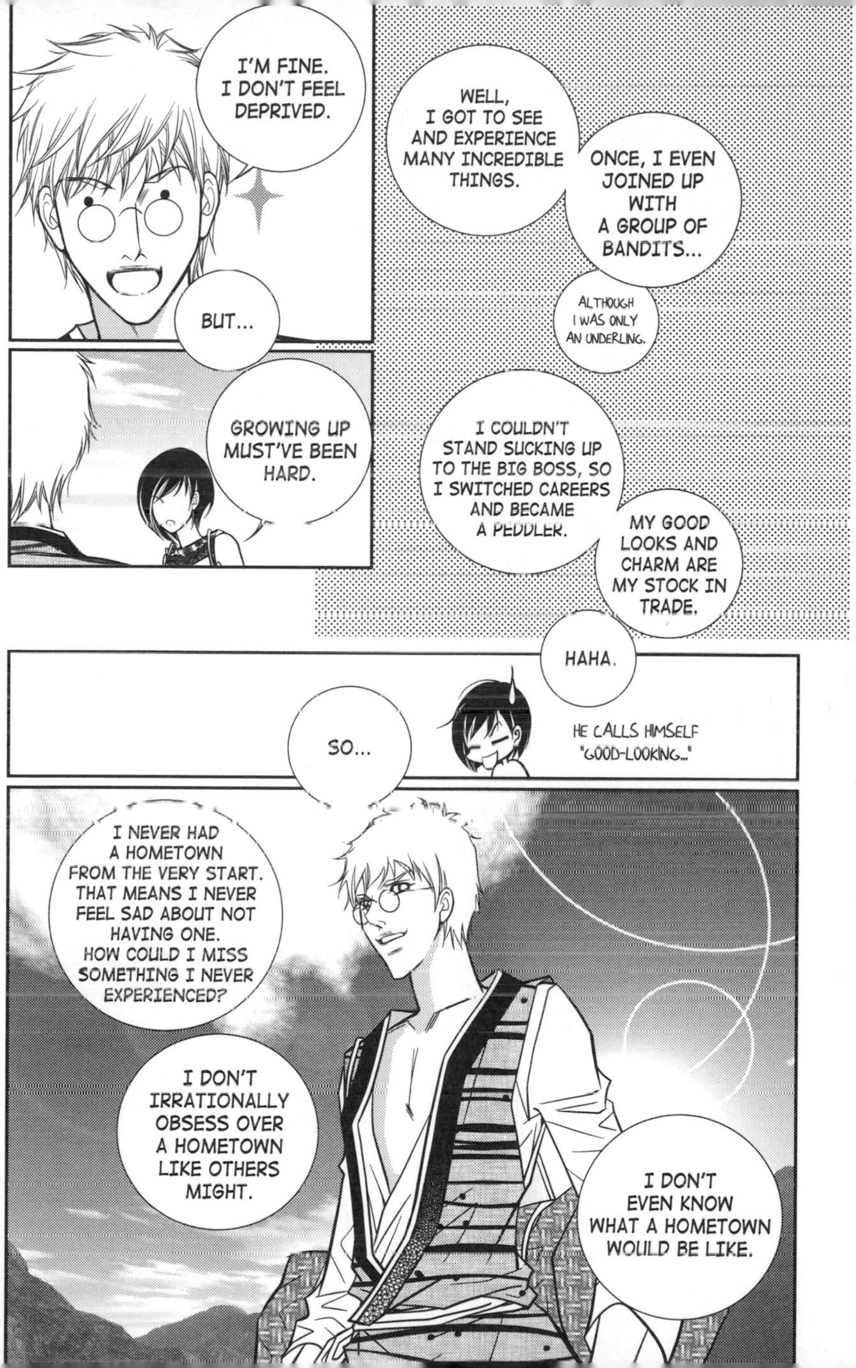

I'M FINE. I DON'T FEEL DEPRIVED.
BUT...
GROWING UP MUST'VE BEEN HARD.
WELL, I GOT TO SEE AND EXPERIENCE MANY INCREDIBLE THINGS.
ONCE, I EVEN JOINED UP WITH A GROUP OF BANDITS...
ALTHOUGH I WAS ONLY AN UNDERLING.
I COULDN'T STAND SUCKING UP TO THE BIG BOSS, SO I SWITCHED CAREERS AND BECAME A PEDDLER.
MY GOOD LOOKS AND CHARM ARE MY STOCK IN TRADE.
HAHA.
SO...
HE CALLS HIMSELF "GOOD-LOOKING..."
I NEVER HAD A HOMETOWN FROM THE VERY START. THAT MEANS I NEVER FEEL SAD ABOUT NOT HAVING ONE. HOW COULD I MISS SOMETHING I NEVER EXPERIENCED?
I DON'T IRRATIONALLY OBSESS OVER A HOMETOWN LIKE OTHERS MIGHT.
I DON'T EVEN KNOW WHAT A HOMETOWN WOULD BE LIKE.

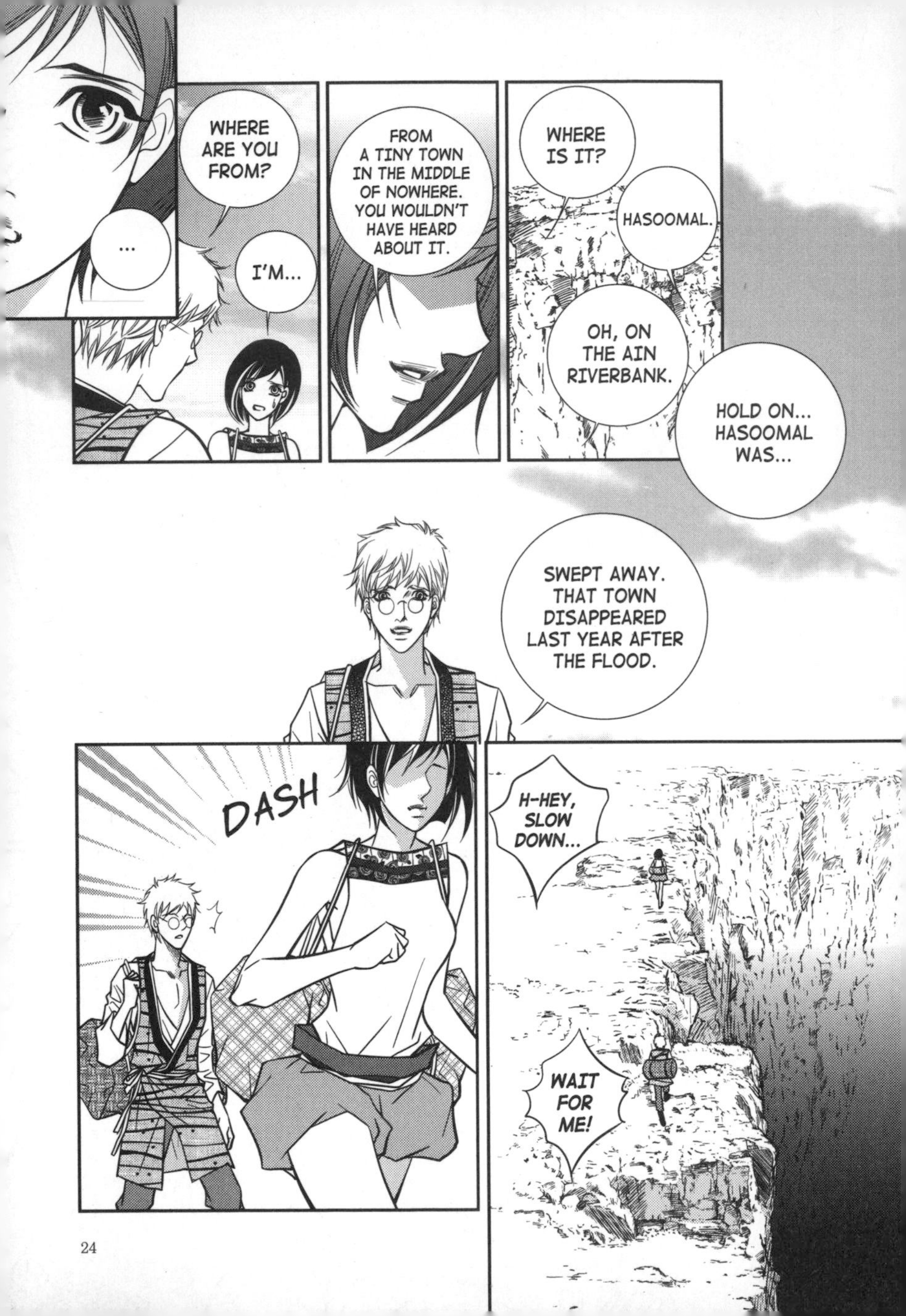

WHERE ARE YOU FROM?
...
I'M...
FROM A TINY TOWN IN THE MIDDLE OF NOWHERE. YOU WOULDN'T HAVE HEARD ABOUT IT.
WHERE IS IT?
HASOOMAL.
OH, ON THE AIN RIVERBANK.
HOLD ON... HASOOMAL WAS...
SWEPT AWAY. THAT TOWN DISAPPEARED LAST YEAR AFTER THE FLOOD.
DASH
H-HEY, SLOW DOWN...
WAIT FOR ME!

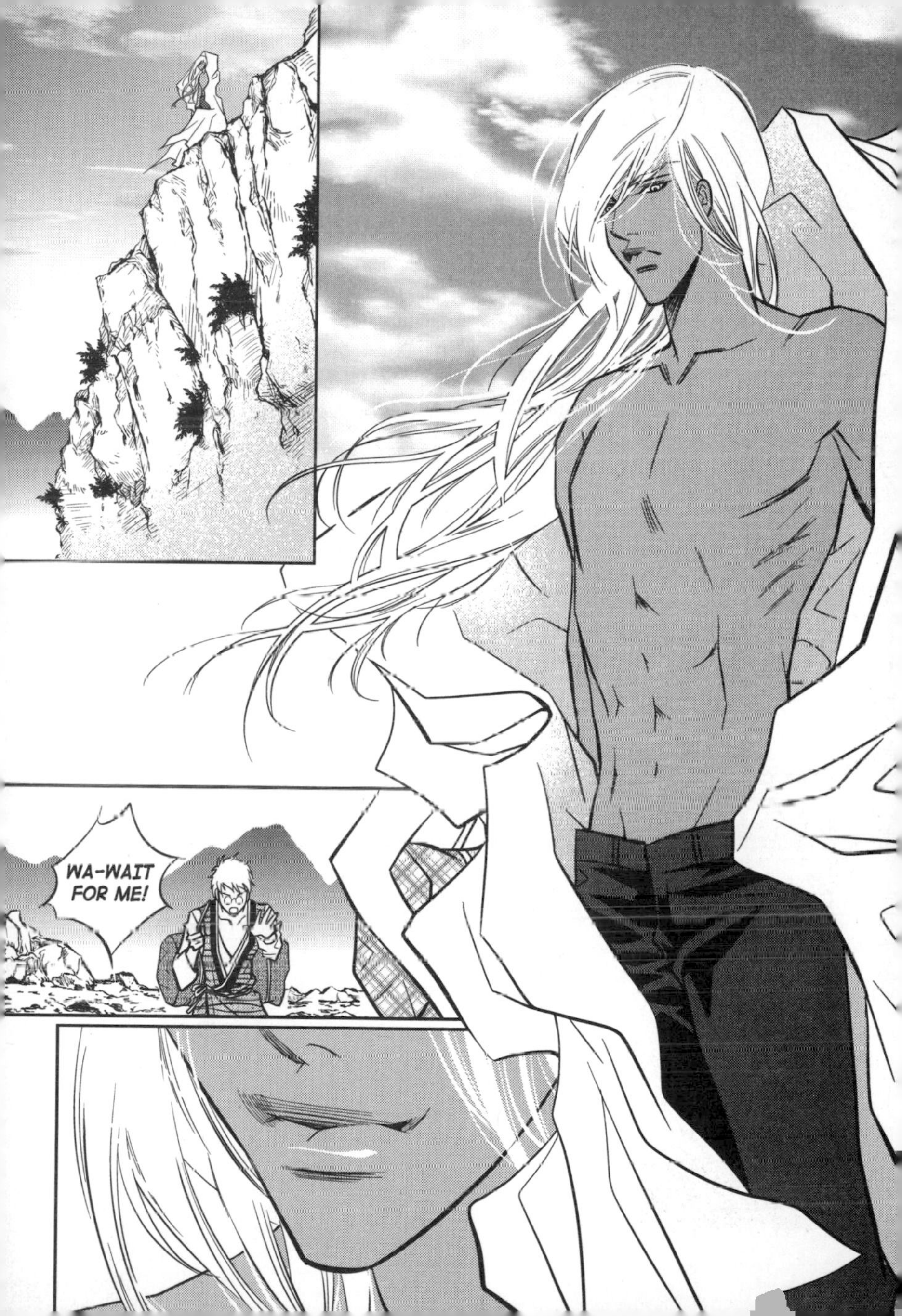
WA-WAIT FOR ME!

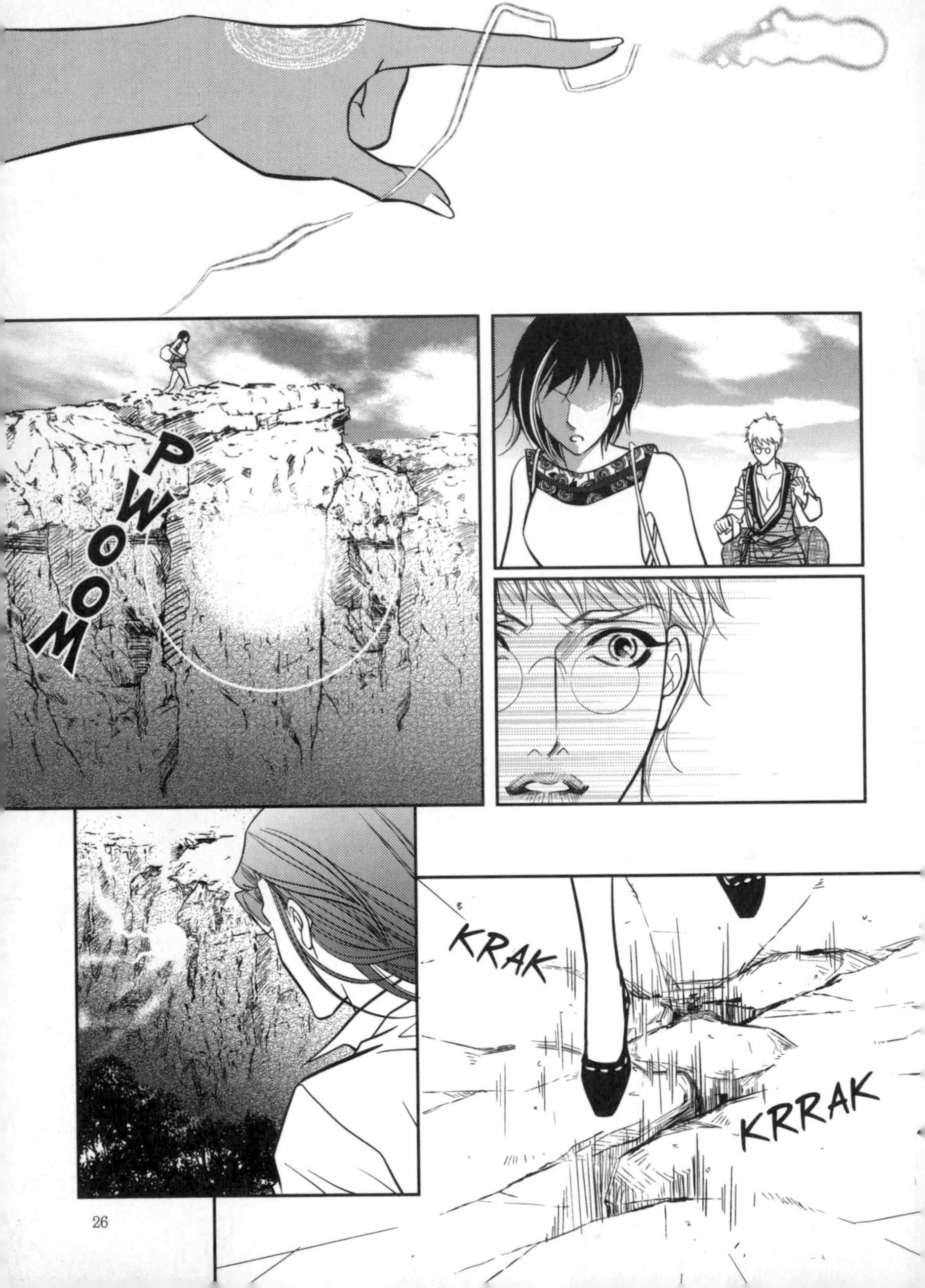
PWOOOM
KRAK
KRRAK

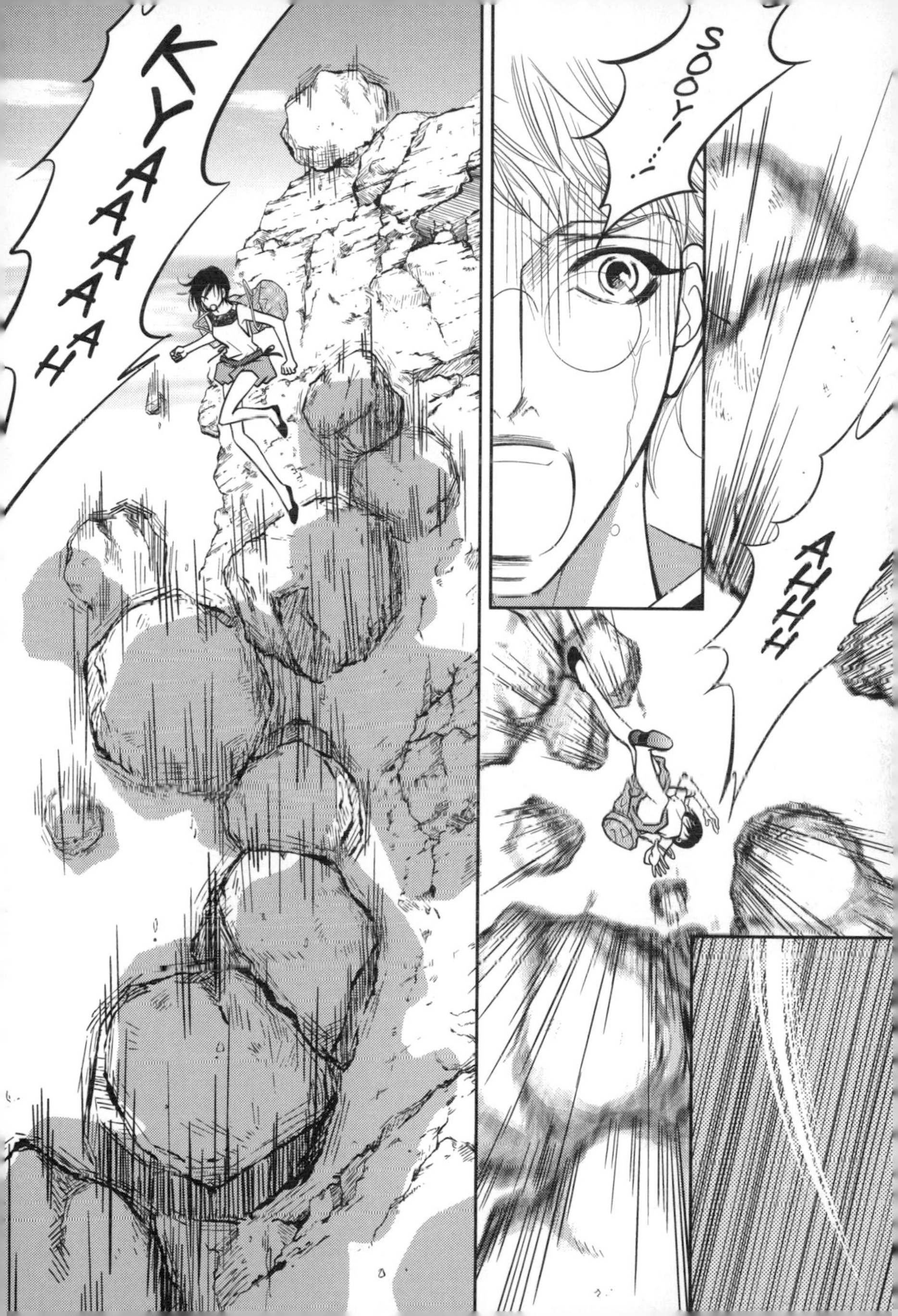
KYAAAAAH
SOOY—...!
AHHH

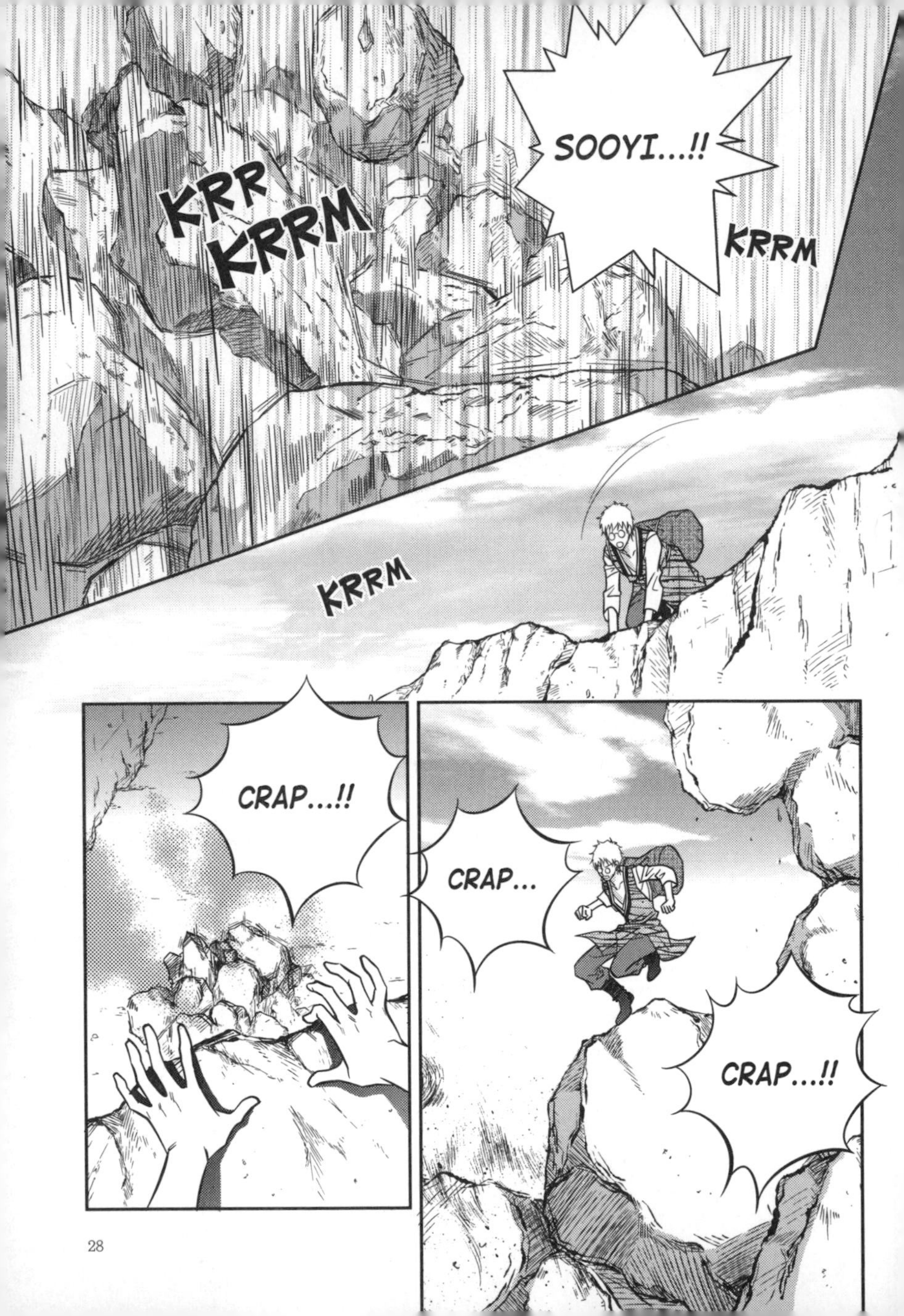
KRR KRRM
SOOYI...!!
KRRM
KRRM
CRAP...!!
CRAP...
CRAP...!!

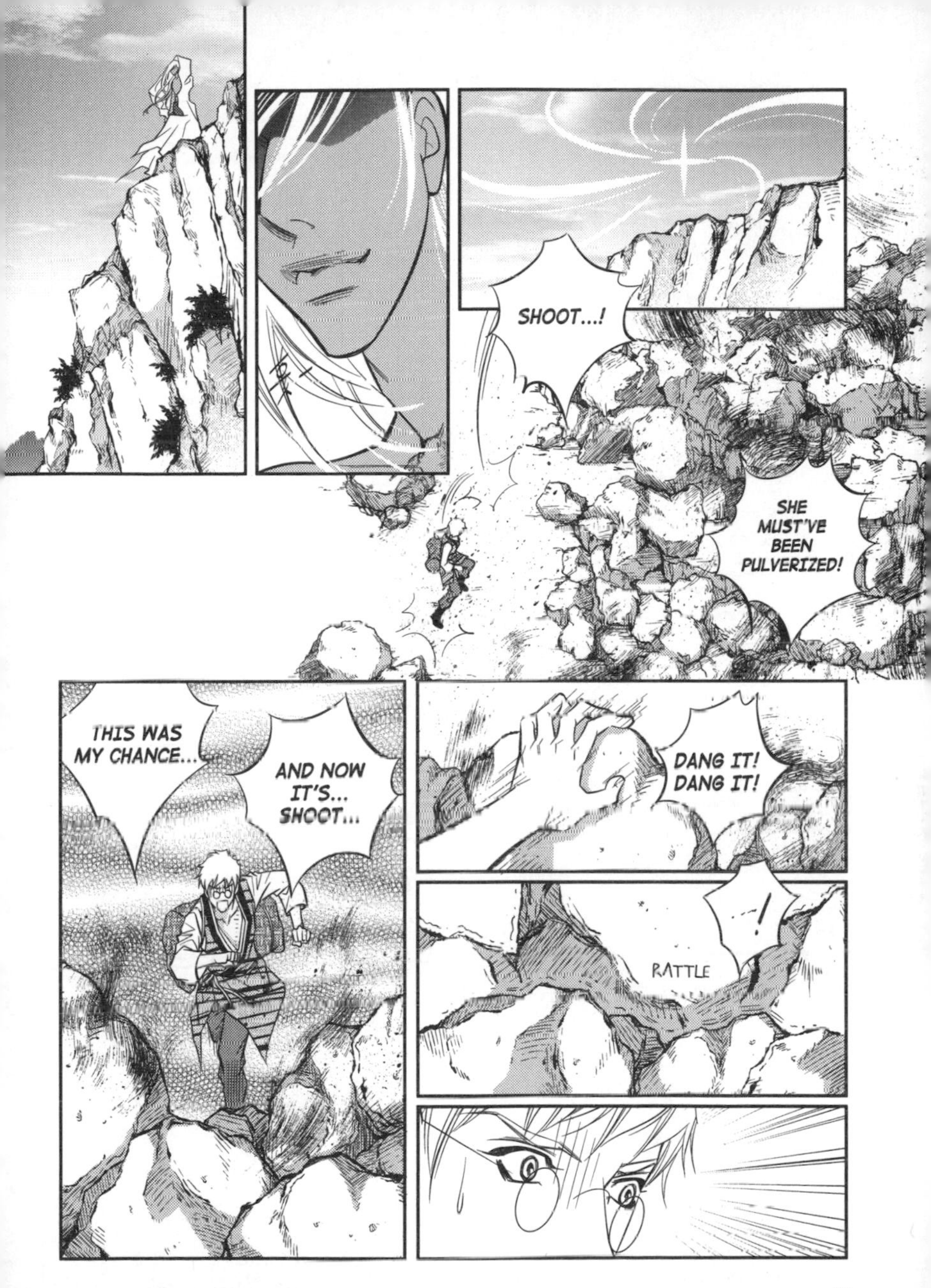
SHOOT...!
SHE MUST'VE BEEN PULVERIZED!
THIS WAS MY CHANCE...
AND NOW IT'S... SHOOT...
DANG IT! DANG IT!
!
RATTLE

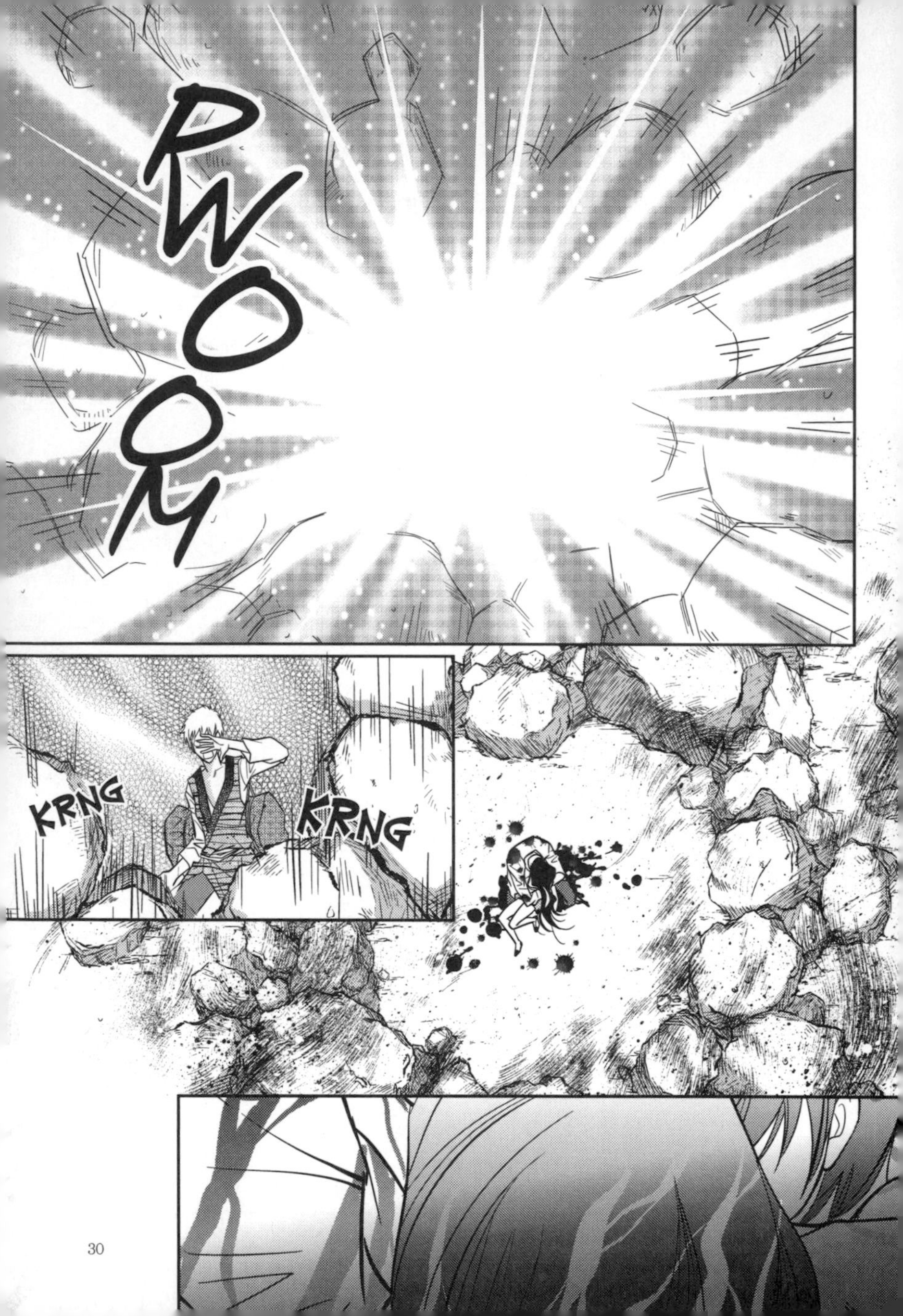
RWOOM
KRNG
KRNG

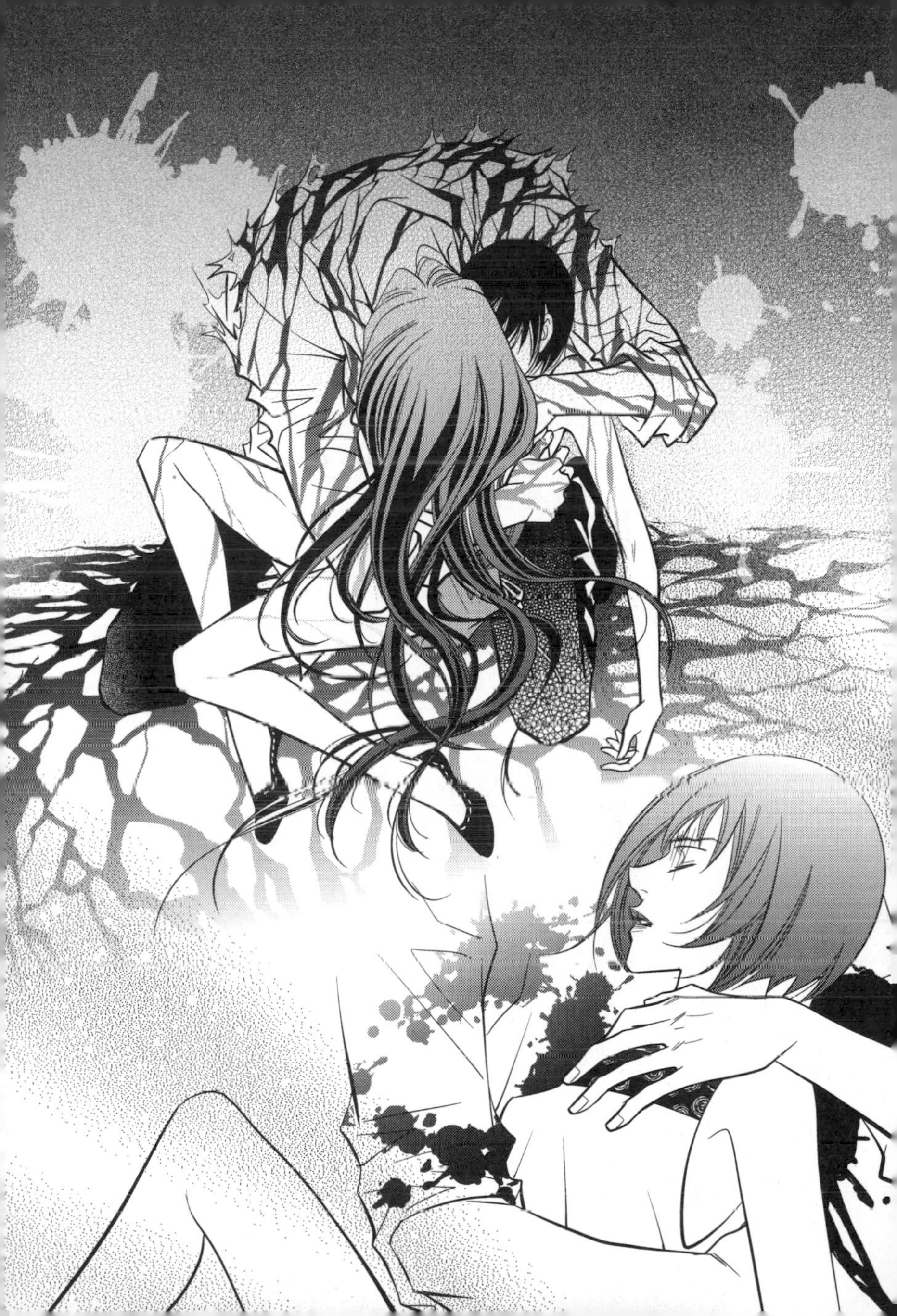

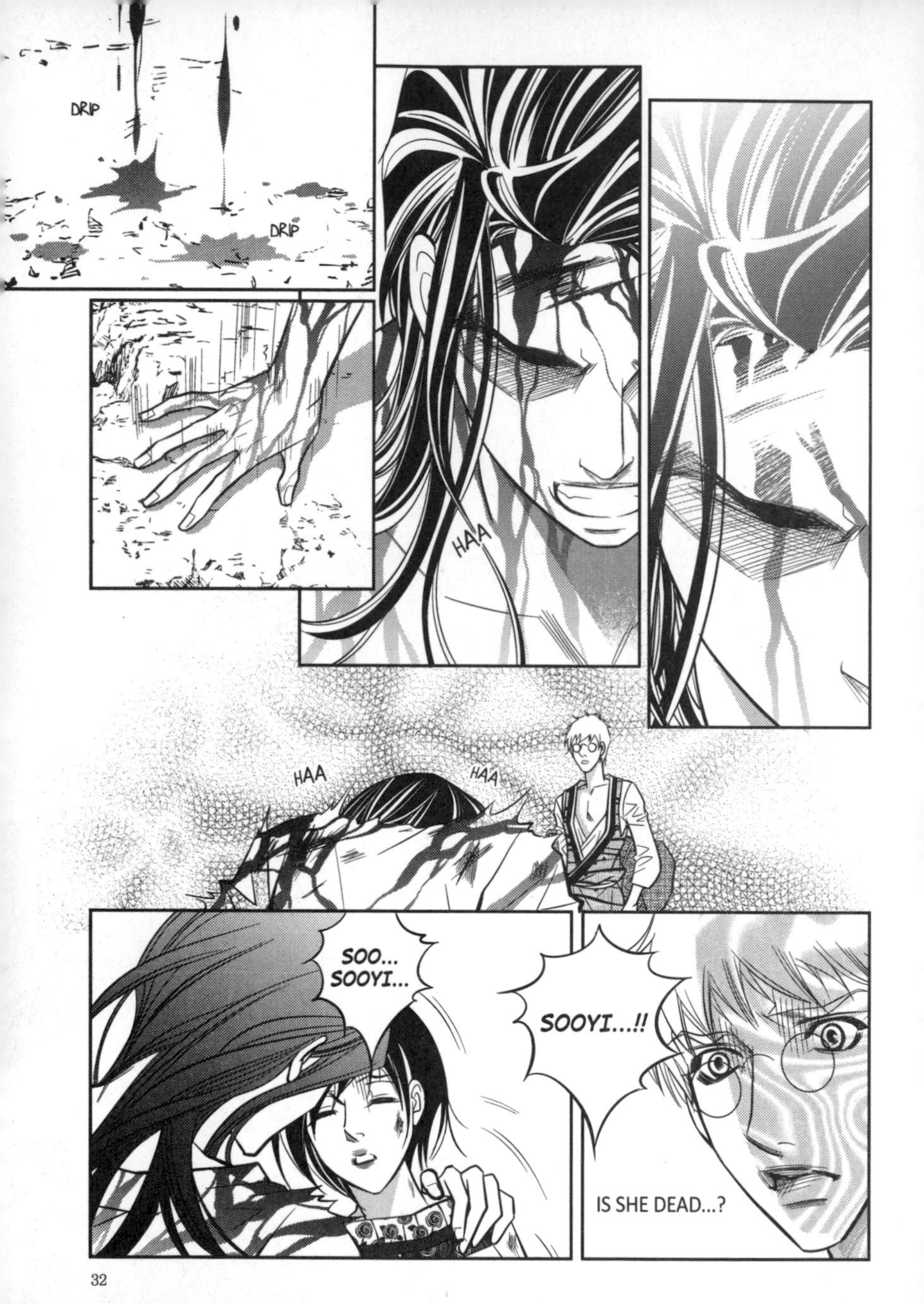
DRIP
DRIP
HAA
HAA
HAA
SOO... SOOYI...
SOOYI...!!
IS SHE DEAD...?

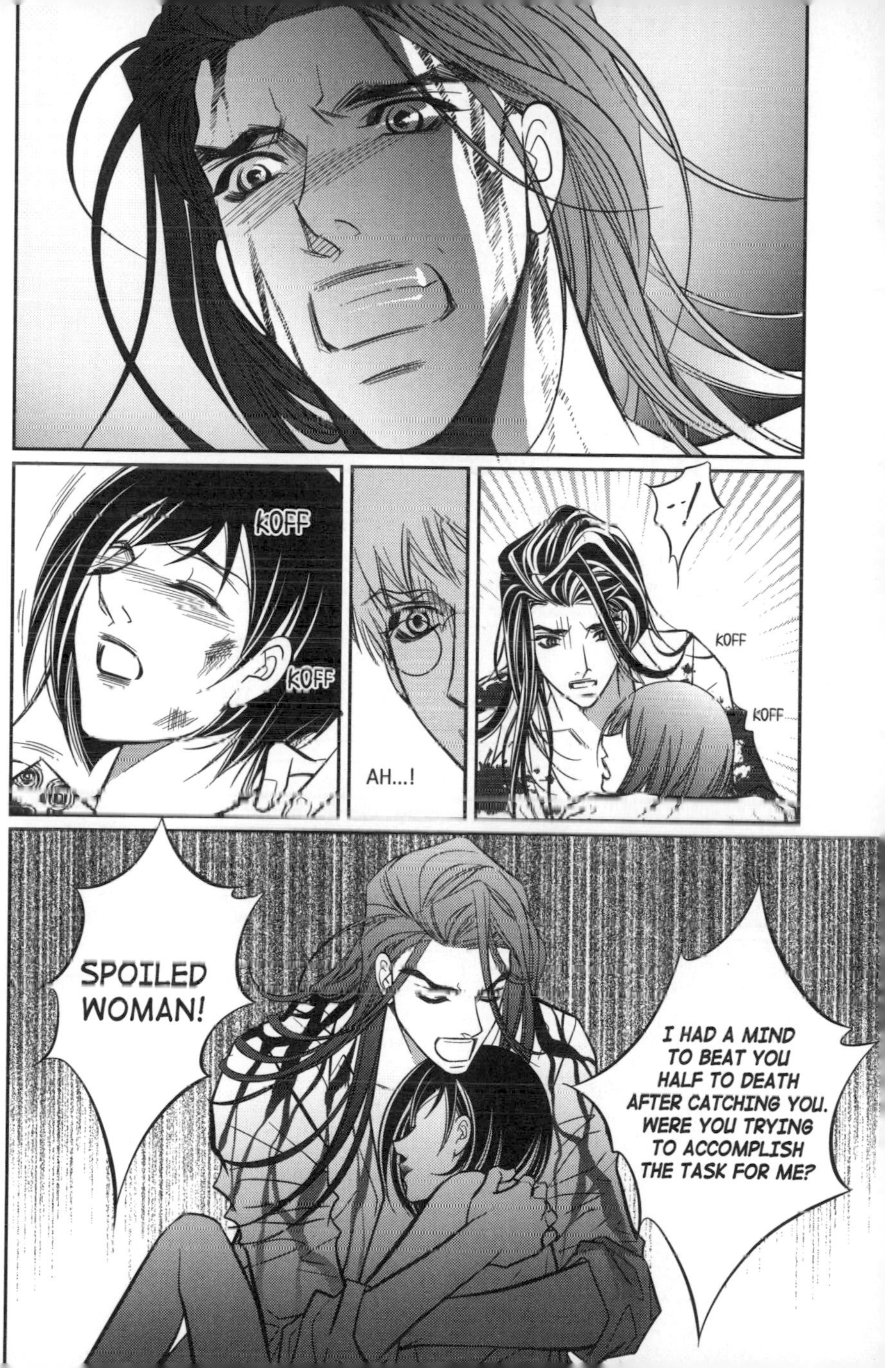
KOFF
KOFF
AH...!
--!
KOFF
KOFF...
SPOILED WOMAN!
I HAD A MIND TO BEAT YOU HALF TO DEATH AFTER CATCHING YOU. WERE YOU TRYING TO ACCOMPLISH THE TASK FOR ME?

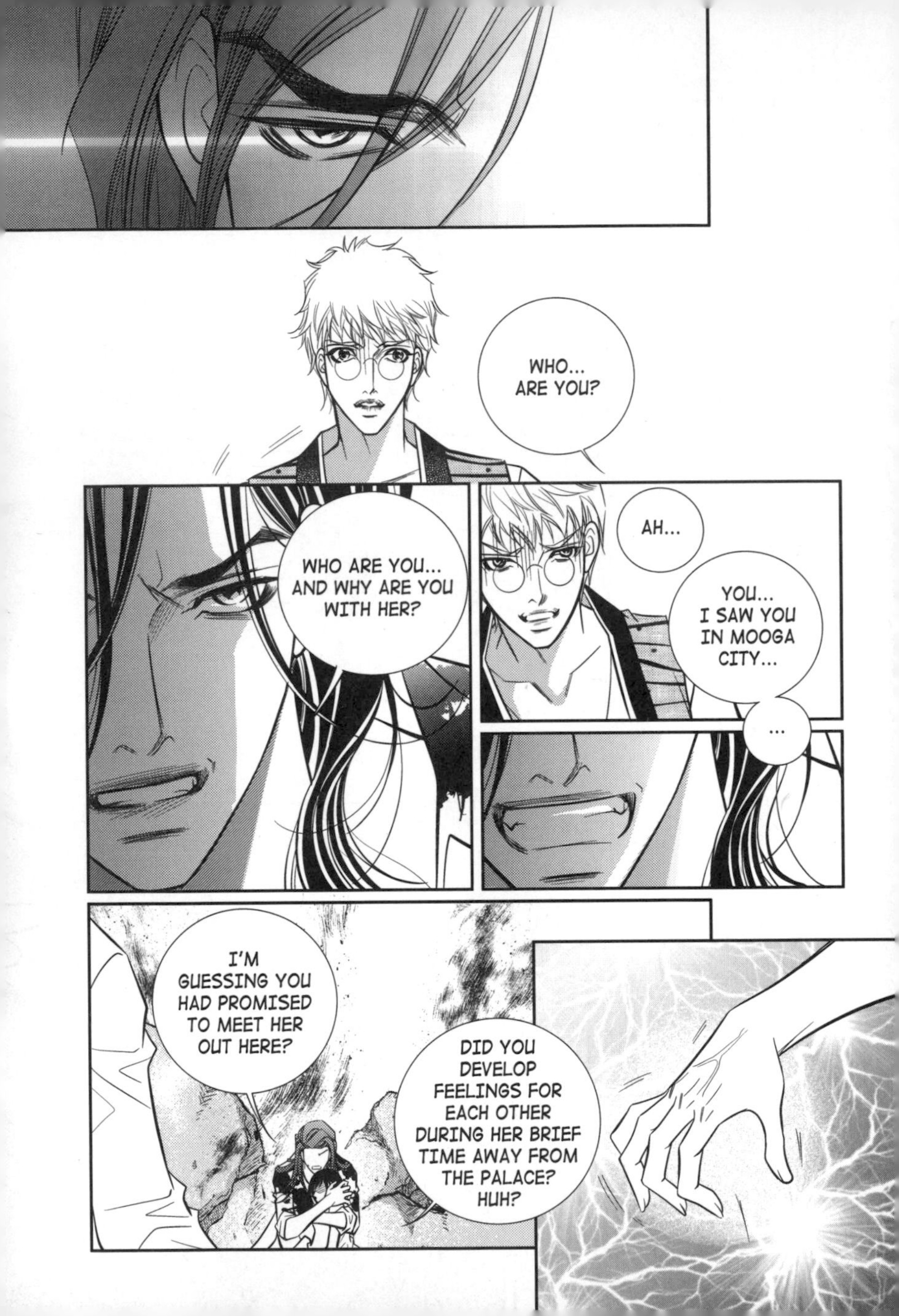
WHO... ARE YOU?
WHO ARE YOU... AND WHY ARE YOU WITH HER?
AH...
YOU... I SAW YOU IN MOOGA CITY...
...
I'M GUESSING YOU HAD PROMISED TO MEET HER OUT HERE?
DID YOU DEVELOP FEELINGS FOR EACH OTHER DURING HER BRIEF TIME AWAY FROM THE PALACE? HUH?

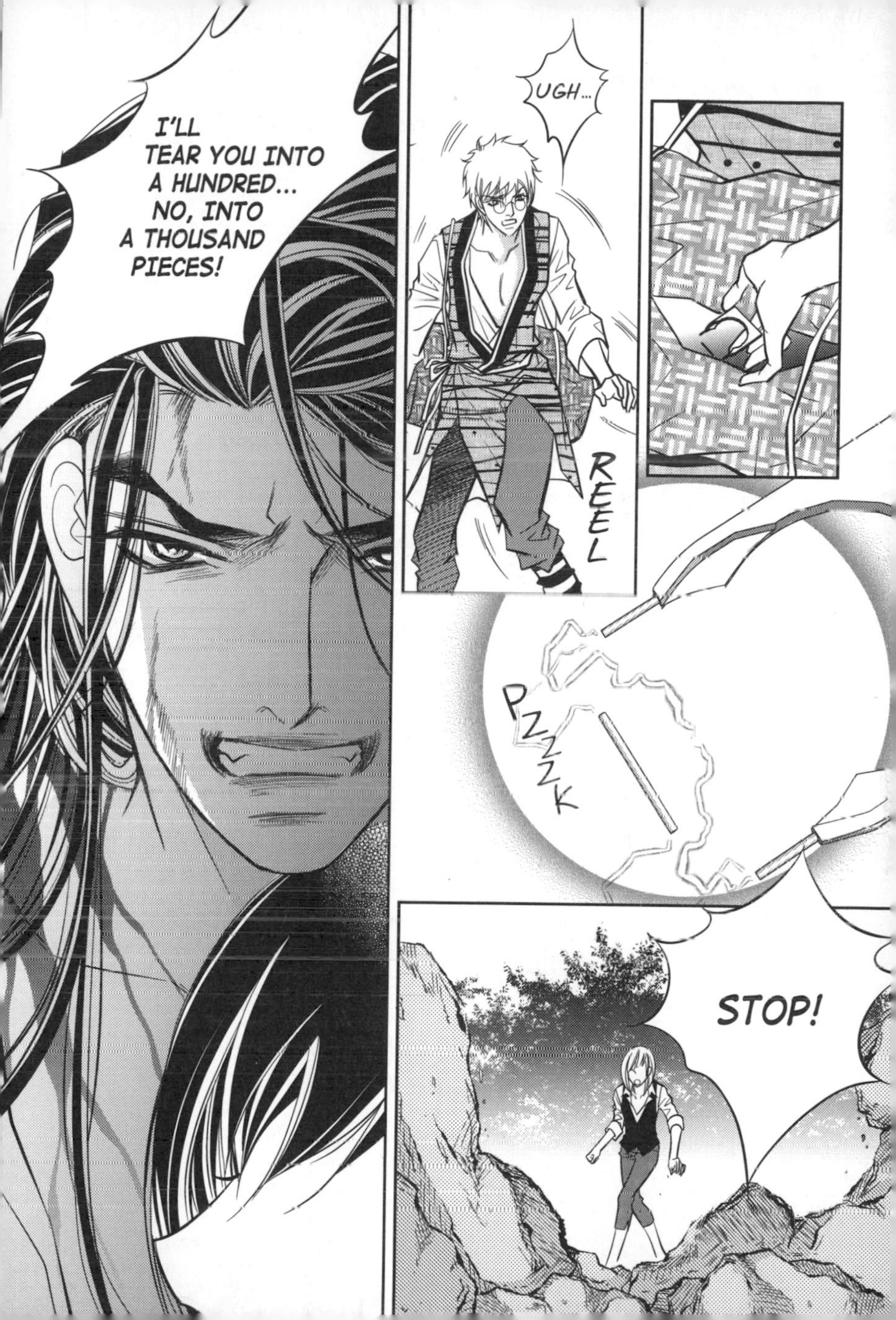
I'LL TEAR YOU INTO A HUNDRED... NO, INTO A THOUSAND PIECES!
UGH...
REEEL
PZZZK
STOP!

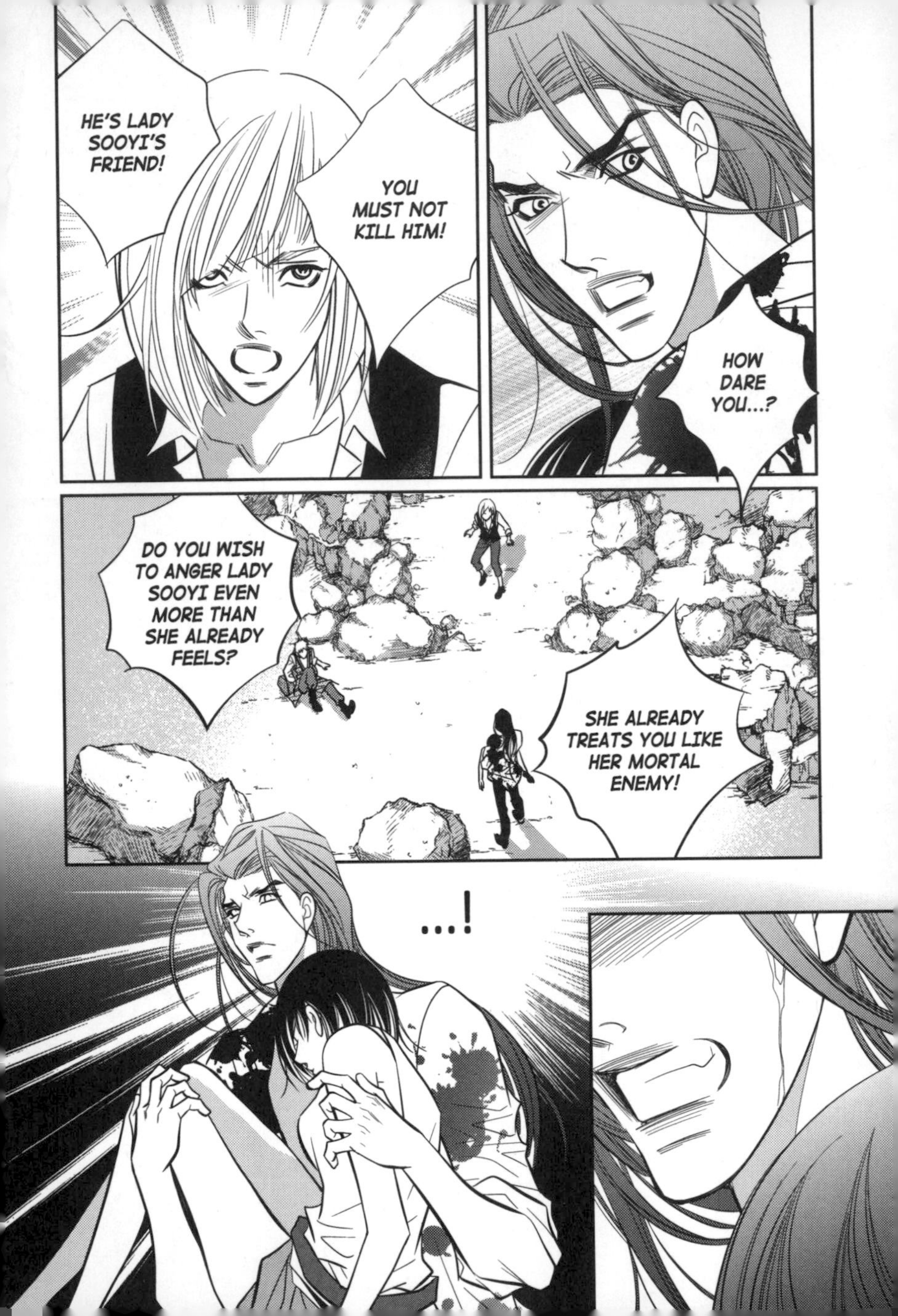
HE'S LADY SOOYI'S FRIEND!
YOU MUST NOT KILL HIM!
HOW DARE YOU...?
DO YOU WISH TO ANGER LADY SOOYI EVEN MORE THAN SHE ALREADY FEELS?
SHE ALREADY TREATS YOU LIKE HER MORTAL ENEMY!
...!

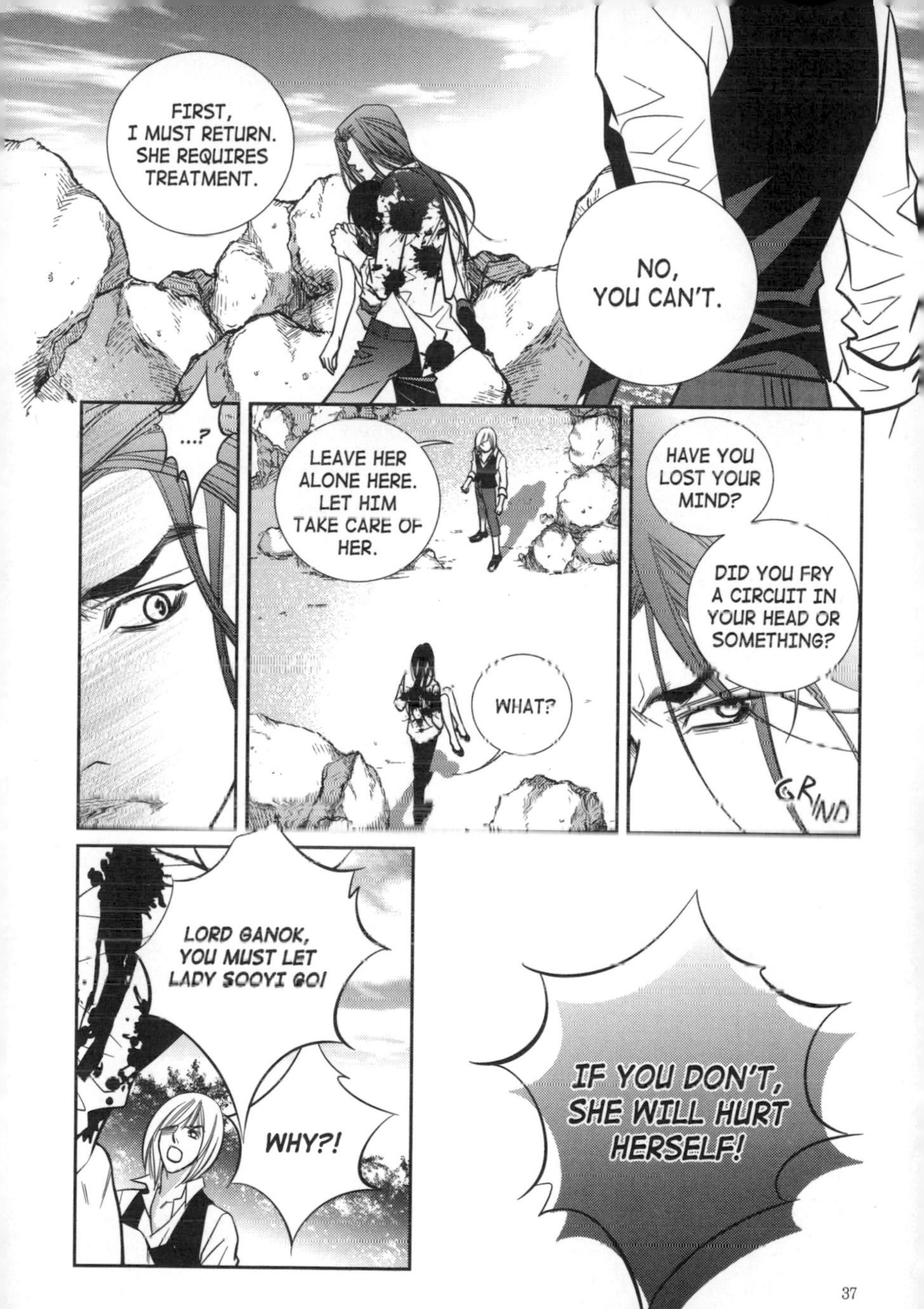
FIRST, I MUST RETURN. SHE REQUIRES TREATMENT.
NO, YOU CAN'T.
...?
LEAVE HER ALONE HERE. LET HIM TAKE CARE OF HER.
WHAT?
HAVE YOU LOST YOUR MIND?
DID YOU FRY A CIRCUIT IN YOUR HEAD OR SOMETHING?
GRIND
LORD GANOK, YOU MUST LET LADY SOOYI GO!
WHY?!
IF YOU DON'T, SHE WILL HURT HERSELF!

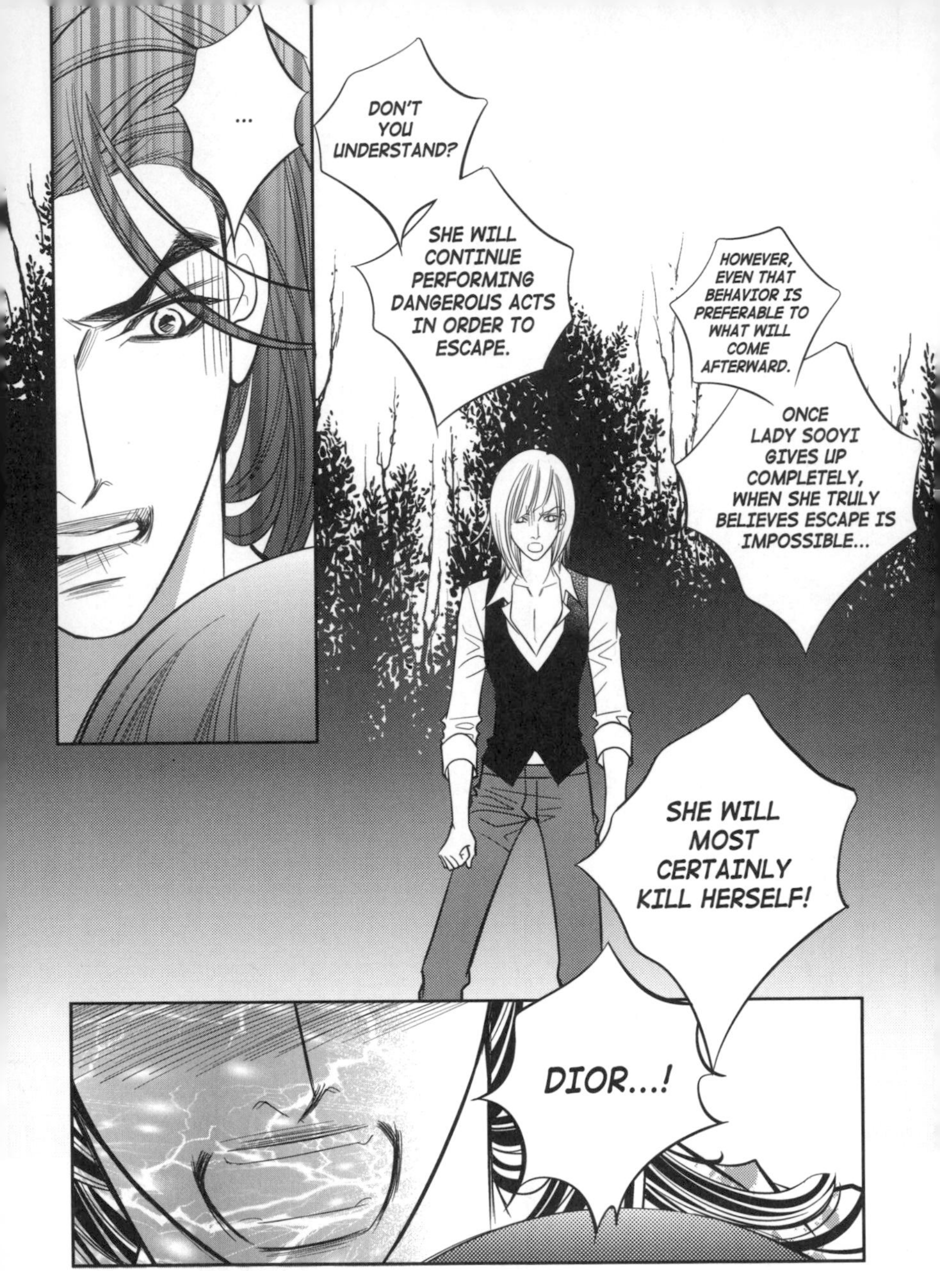
...
DON'T YOU UNDERSTAND?
SHE WILL CONTINUE PERFORMING DANGEROUS ACTS IN ORDER TO ESCAPE.
HOWEVER, EVEN THAT BEHAVIOR IS PREFERABLE TO WHAT WILL COME AFTERWARD.
ONCE LADY SOOYI GIVES UP COMPLETELY, WHEN SHE TRULY BELIEVES ESCAPE IS IMPOSSIBLE...
SHE WILL MOST CERTAINLY KILL HERSELF!
DIOR...!

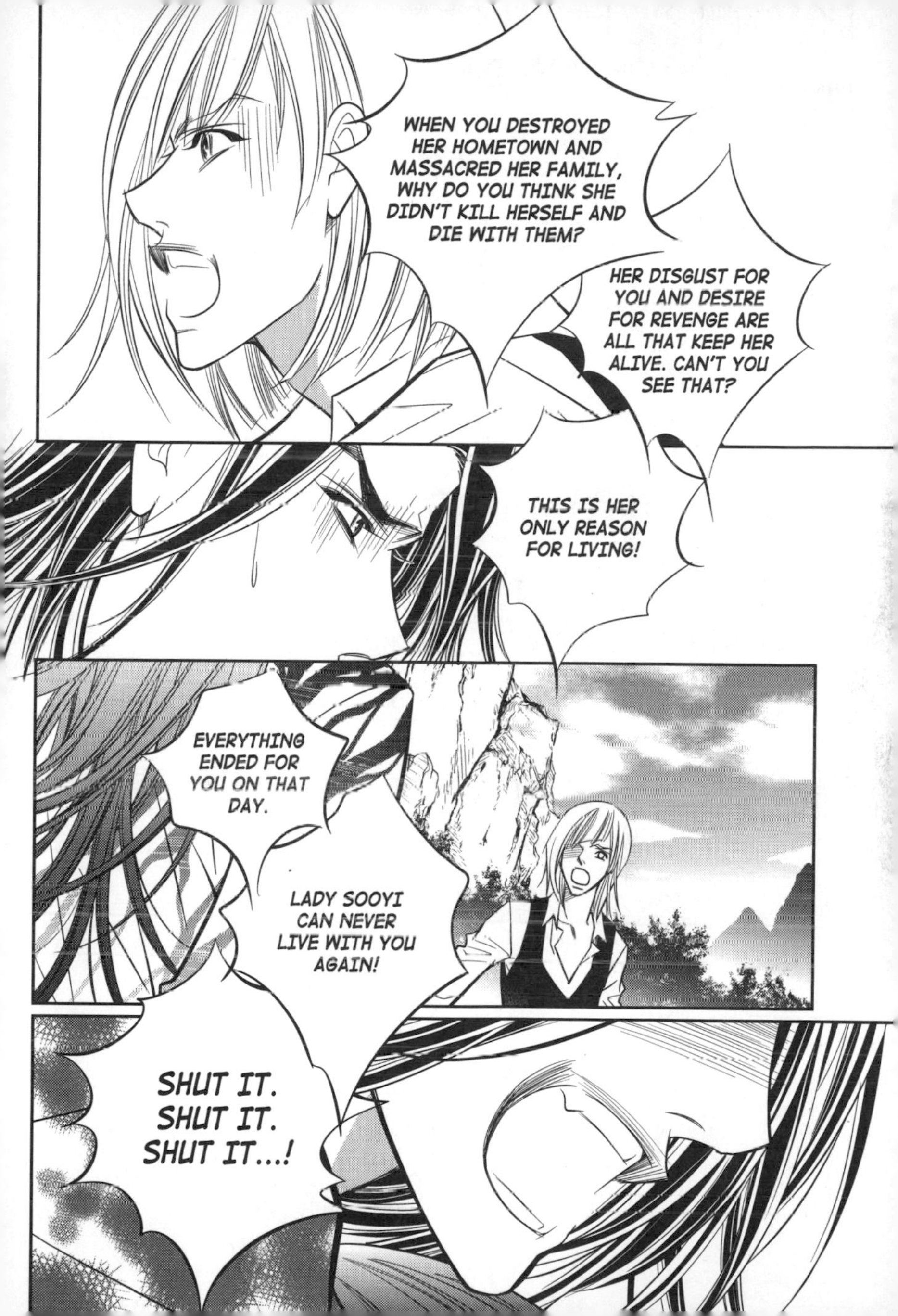
WHEN YOU DESTROYED HER HOMETOWN AND MASSACRED HER FAMILY, WHY DO YOU THINK SHE DIDN'T KILL HERSELF AND DIE WITH THEM?
HER DISGUST FOR YOU AND DESIRE FOR REVENGE ARE ALL THAT KEEP HER ALIVE. CAN'T YOU SEE THAT?
THIS IS HER ONLY REASON FOR LIVING!
EVERYTHING ENDED FOR YOU ON THAT DAY.
LADY SOOYI CAN NEVER LIVE WITH YOU AGAIN!
SHUT IT. SHUT IT. SHUT IT...!

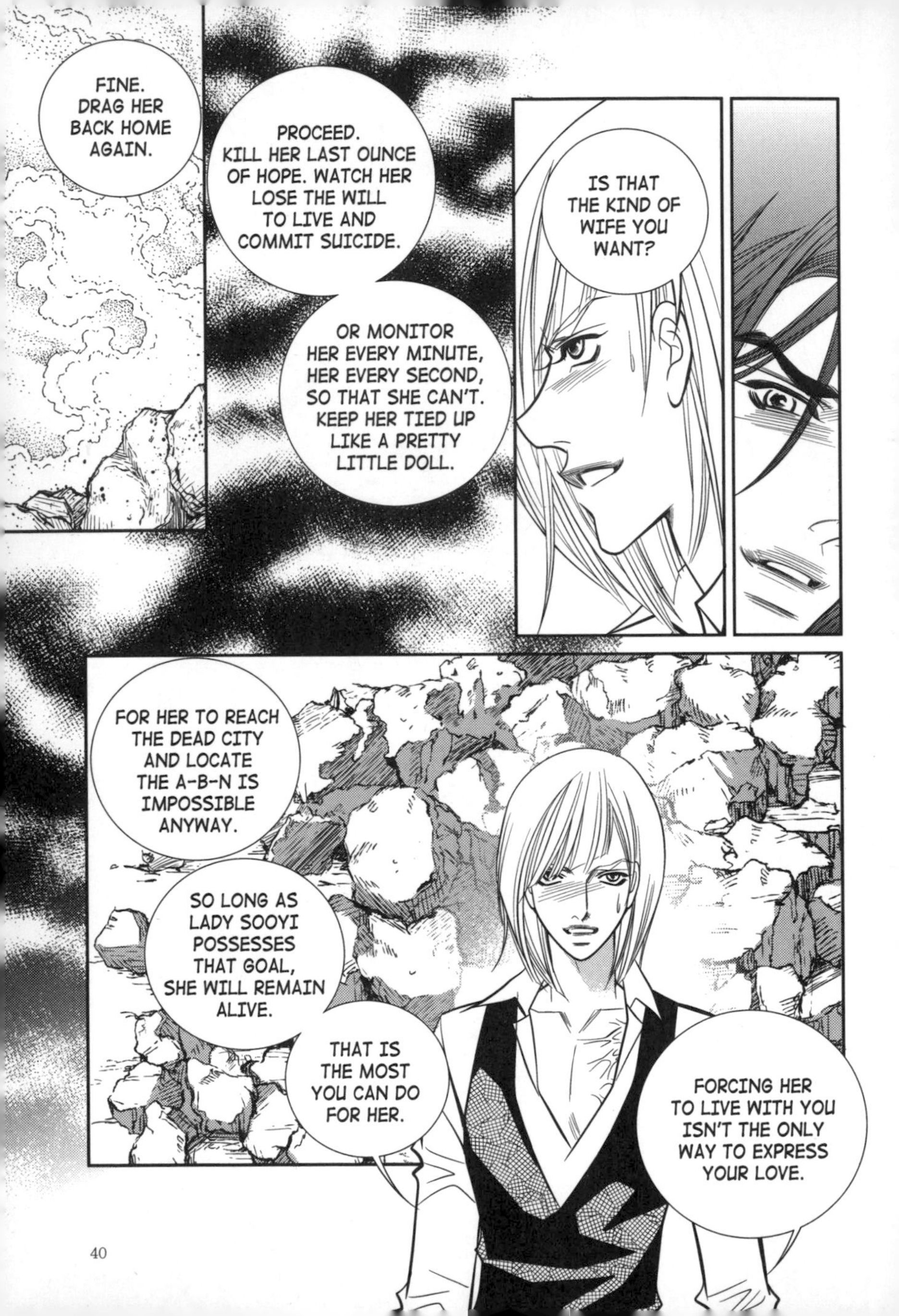
FINE. DRAG HER BACK HOME AGAIN.
PROCEED. KILL HER LAST OUNCE OF HOPE. WATCH HER LOSE THE WILL TO LIVE AND COMMIT SUICIDE.
OR MONITOR HER EVERY MINUTE, HER EVERY SECOND, SO THAT SHE CAN'T. KEEP HER TIED UP LIKE A PRETTY LITTLE DOLL.
IS THAT THE KIND OF WIFE YOU WANT?
FOR HER TO REACH THE DEAD CITY AND LOCATE THE A-B-N IS IMPOSSIBLE ANYWAY.
SO LONG AS LADY SOOYI POSSESSES THAT GOAL, SHE WILL REMAIN ALIVE.
THAT IS THE MOST YOU CAN DO FOR HER.
FORCING HER TO LIVE WITH YOU ISN'T THE ONLY WAY TO EXPRESS YOUR LOVE.

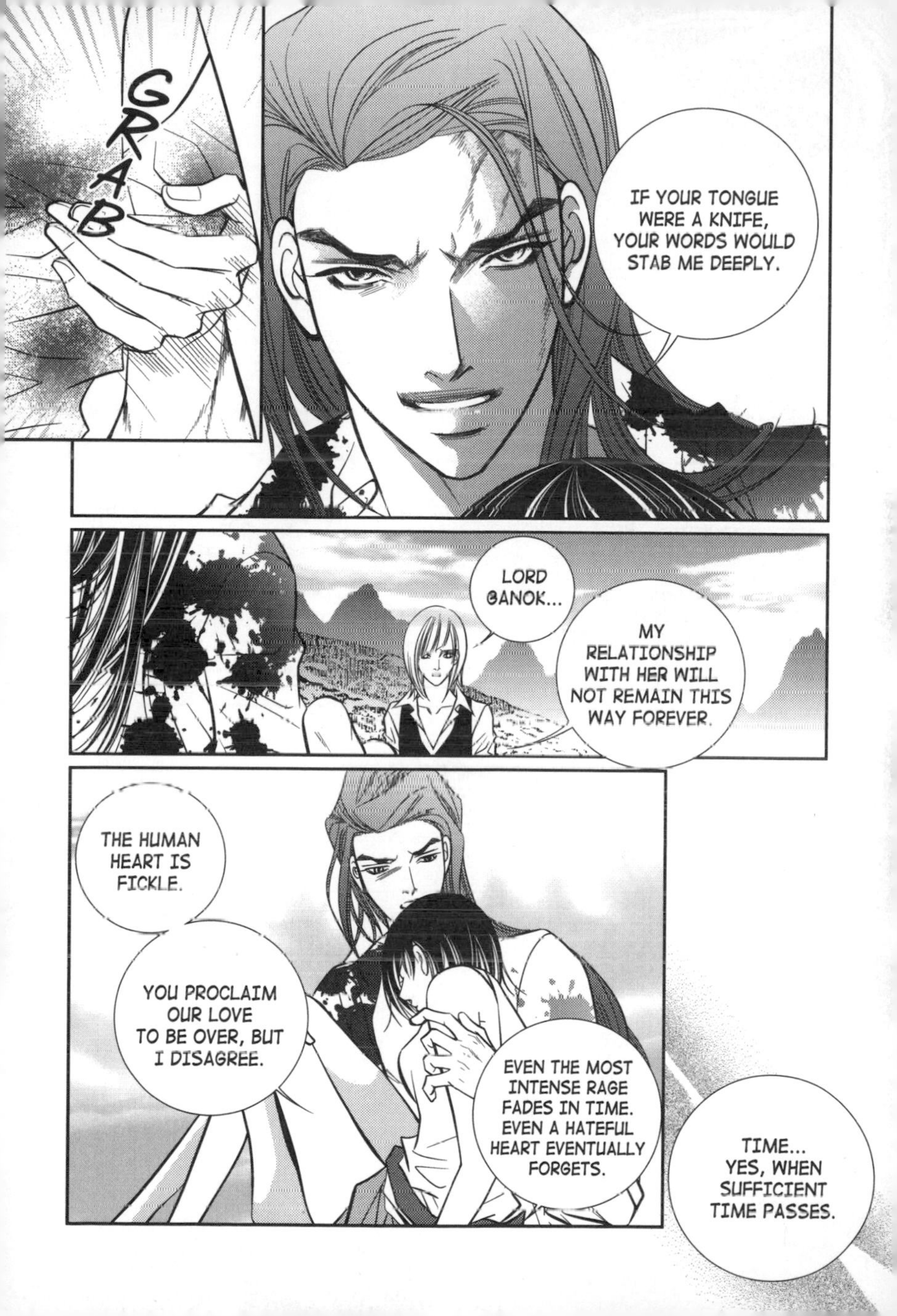
GRAB
IF YOUR TONGUE WERE A KNIFE, YOUR WORDS WOULD STAB ME DEEPLY.
LORD GANOK...
MY RELATIONSHIP WITH HER WILL NOT REMAIN THIS WAY FOREVER.
THE HUMAN HEART IS FICKLE.
YOU PROCLAIM OUR LOVE TO BE OVER, BUT I DISAGREE.
EVEN THE MOST INTENSE RAGE FADES IN TIME. EVEN A HATEFUL HEART EVENTUALLY FORGETS.
TIME... YES, WHEN SUFFICIENT TIME PASSES.

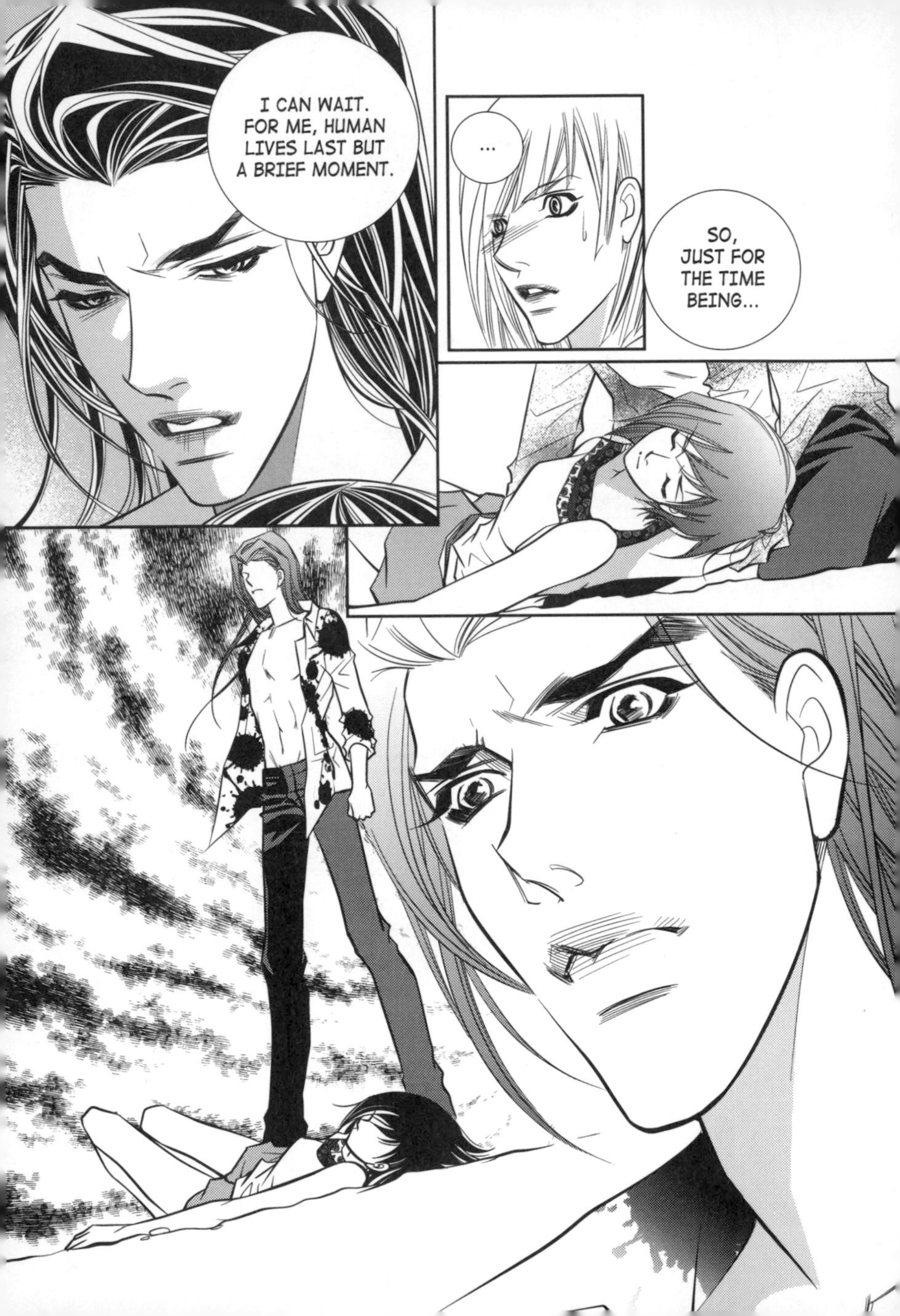
I CAN WAIT. FOR ME, HUMAN LIVES LAST BUT A BRIEF MOMENT.
...
SO, JUST FOR THE TIME BEING...

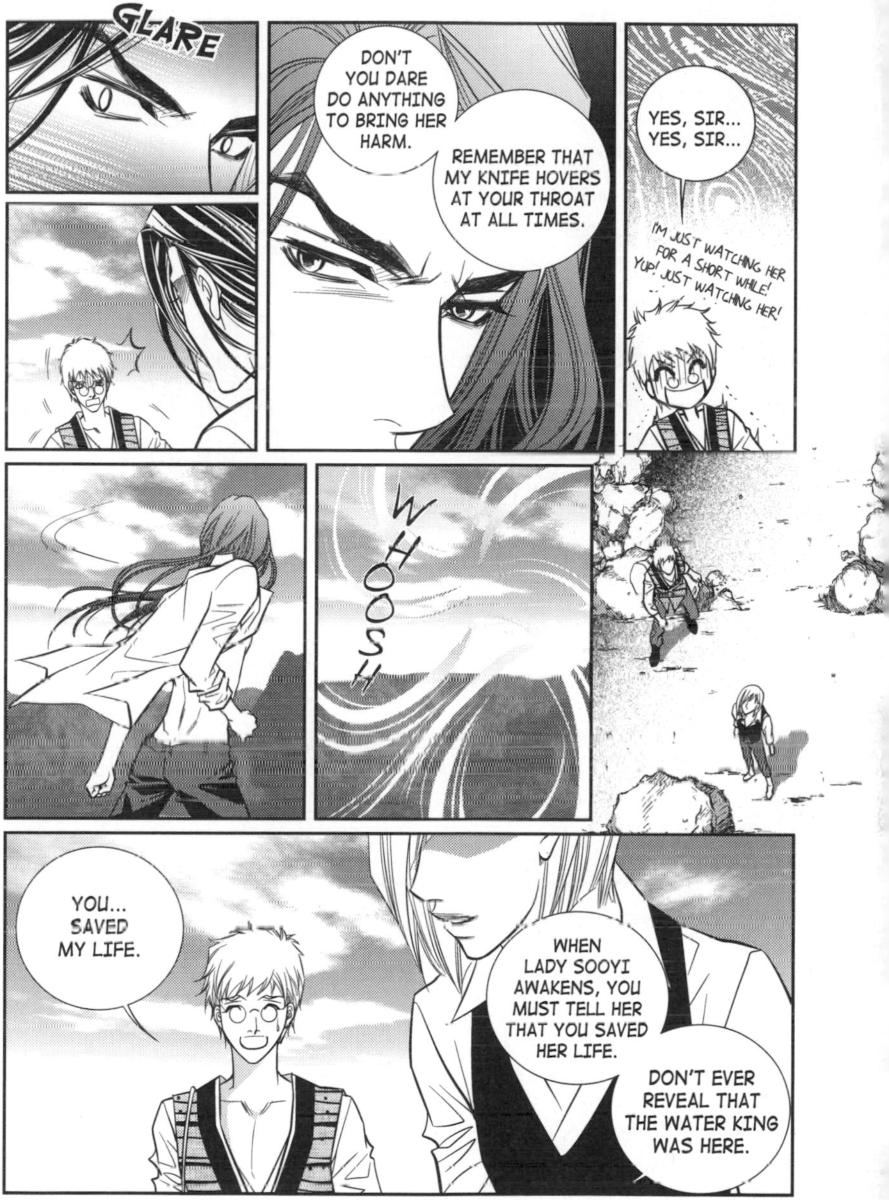
GLARE
DON'T YOU DARE DO ANYTHING TO BRING HER HARM.
REMEMBER THAT MY KNIFE HOVERS AT YOUR THROAT AT ALL TIMES.
YES, SIR... YES, SIR...
I'M JUST WATCHING HER FOR A SHORT WHILE! YUP! JUST WATCHING HER!
WHOOSH
YOU... SAVED MY LIFE.
WHEN LADY SOOYI AWAKENS, YOU MUST TELL HER THAT YOU SAVED HER LIFE.
DON'T EVER REVEAL THAT THE WATER KING WAS HERE.

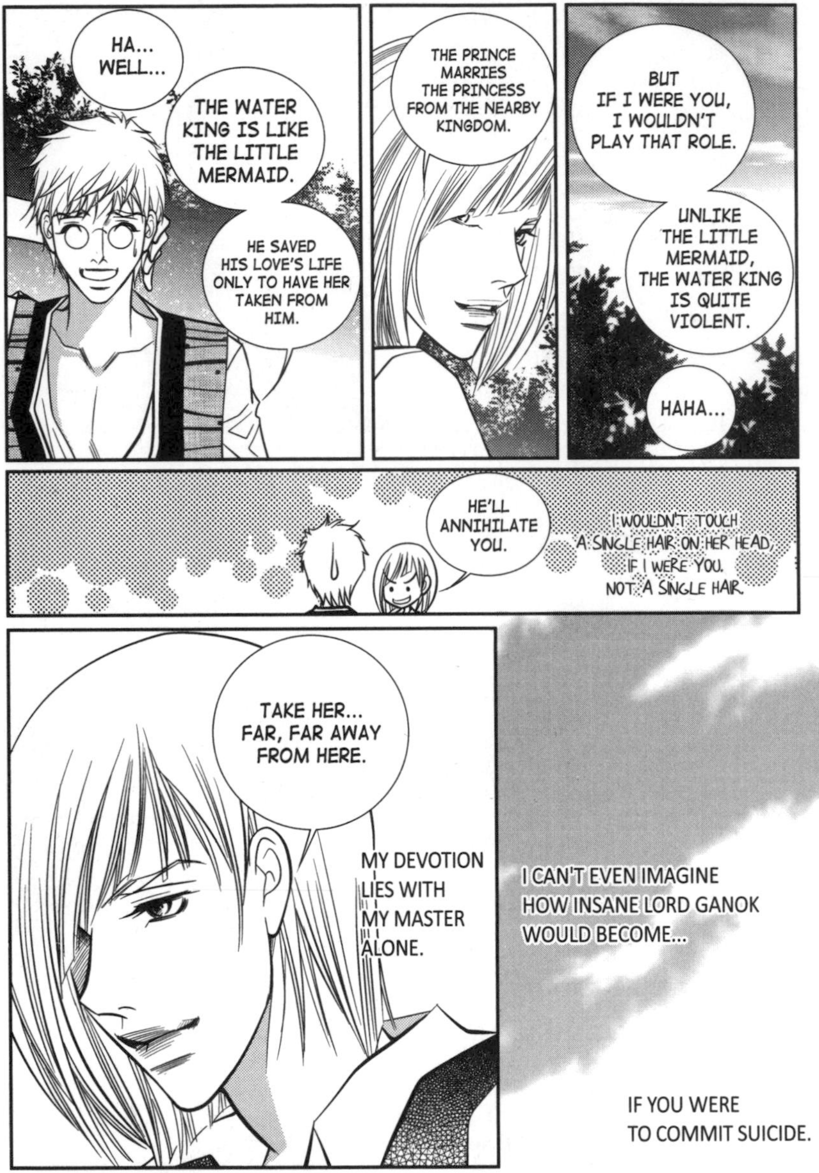
HA... WELL...
THE WATER KING IS LIKE THE LITTLE MERMAID.
HE SAVED HIS LOVE'S LIFE ONLY TO HAVE HER TAKEN FROM HIM.
THE PRINCE MARRIES THE PRINCESS FROM THE NEARBY KINGDOM.
BUT IF I WERE YOU, I WOULDN'T PLAY THAT ROLE.
UNLIKE THE LITTLE MERMAID, THE WATER KING IS QUITE VIOLENT.
HAHA...
HE'LL ANNIHILATE YOU.
I WOULDN'T TOUCH A SINGLE HAIR ON HER HEAD, IF I WERE YOU. NOT A SINGLE HAIR.
TAKE HER... FAR, FAR AWAY FROM HERE.
MY DEVOTION LIES WITH MY MASTER ALONE.
I CAN'T EVEN IMAGINE HOW INSANE LORD GANOK WOULD BECOME...
IF YOU WERE TO COMMIT SUICIDE.

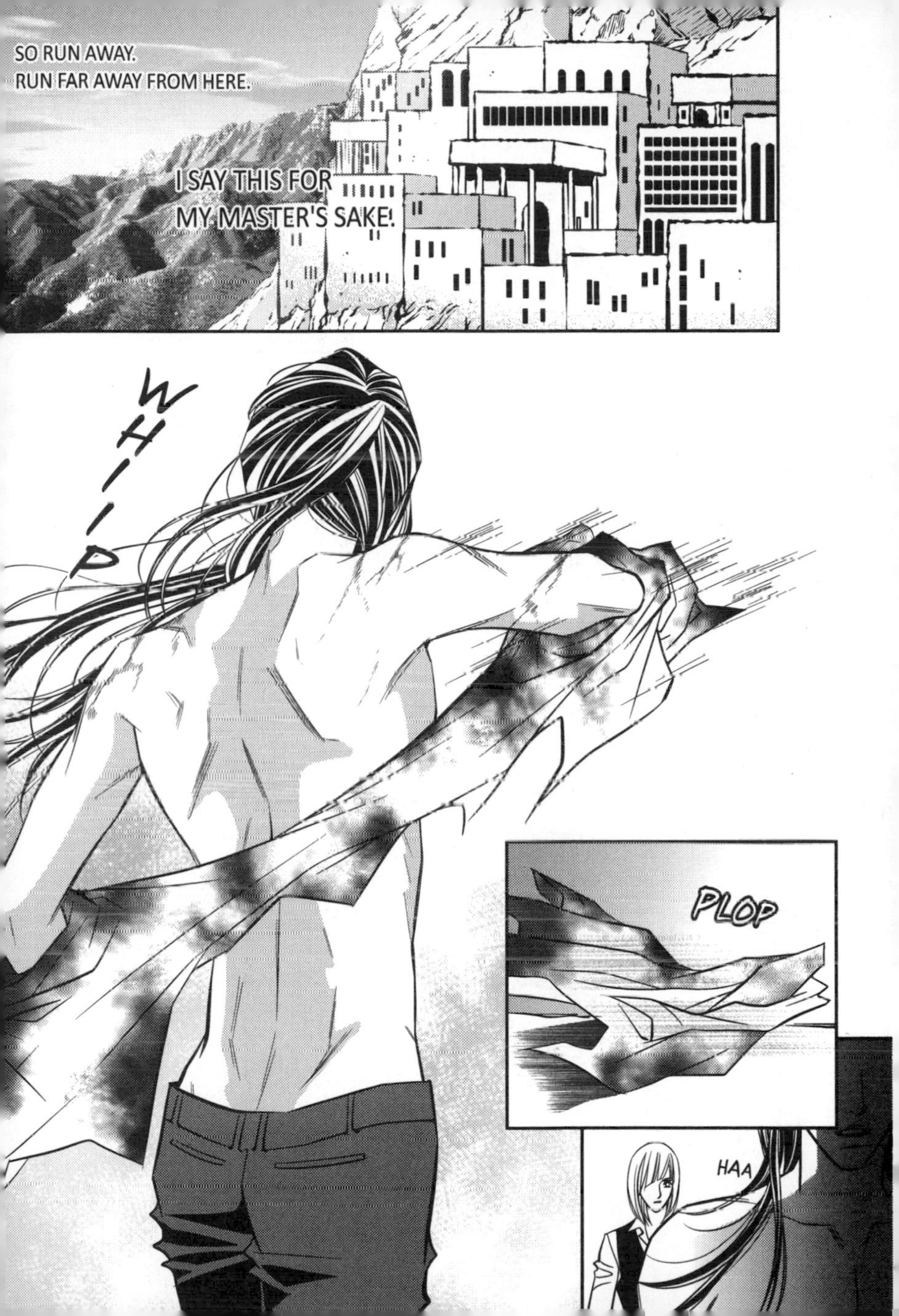
SO RUN AWAY.
RUN FAR AWAY FROM HERE.
I SAY THIS FOR MY MASTER'S SAKE!
WHIIP
PLOP
HAA

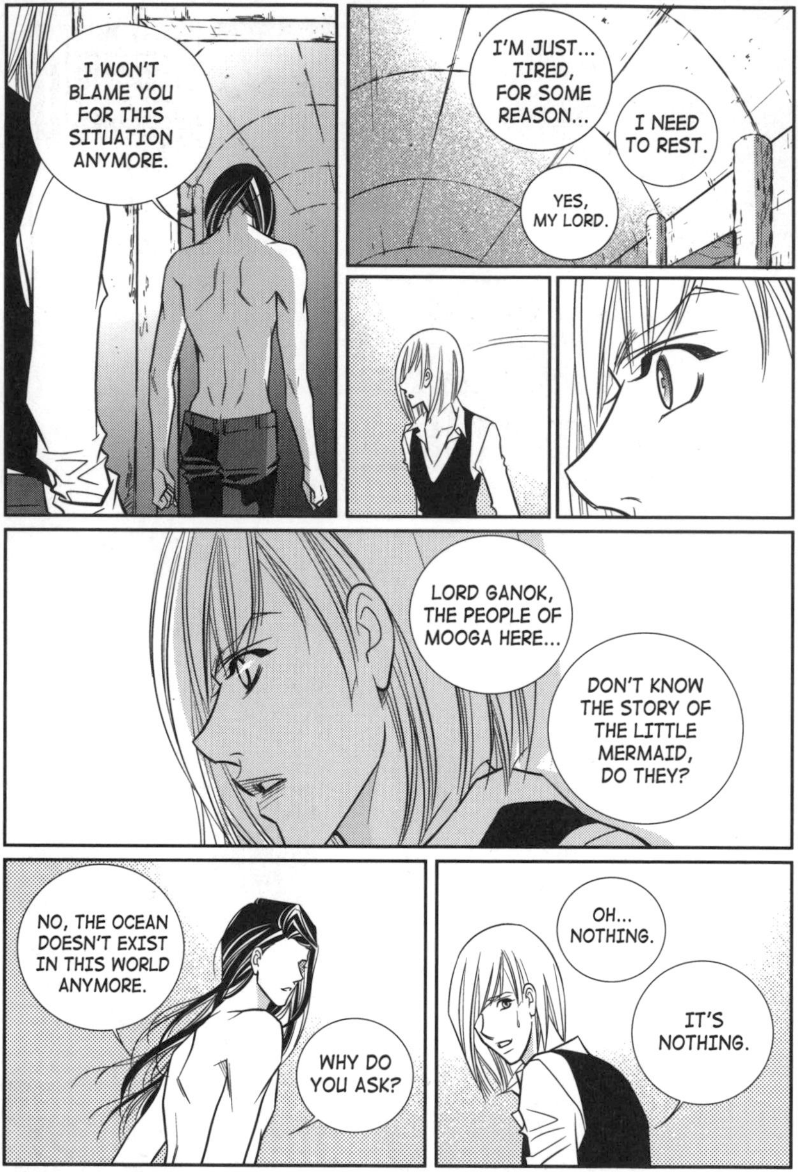
I WON'T BLAME YOU FOR THIS SITUATION ANYMORE.
I'M JUST... TIRED, FOR SOME REASON...
I NEED TO REST.
YES, MY LORD.
LORD GANOK, THE PEOPLE OF MOOGA HERE...
DON'T KNOW THE STORY OF THE LITTLE MERMAID, DO THEY?
NO, THE OCEAN DOESN'T EXIST IN THIS WORLD ANYMORE.
WHY DO YOU ASK?
OH... NOTHING.
IT'S NOTHING.

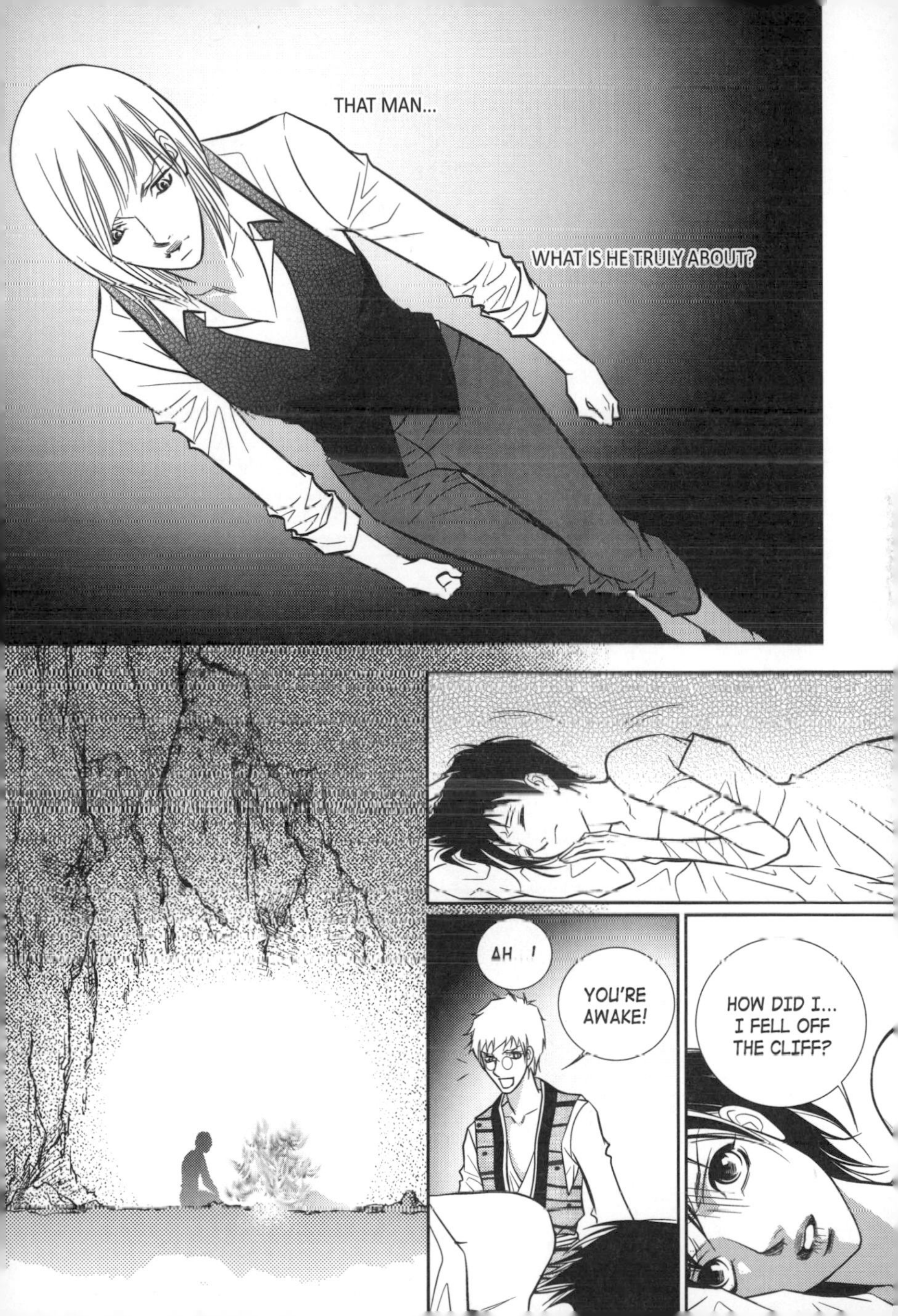
THAT MAN...
WHAT IS HE TRULY ABOUT?
AH...!
YOU'RE AWAKE!
HOW DID I... I FELL OFF THE CLIFF?

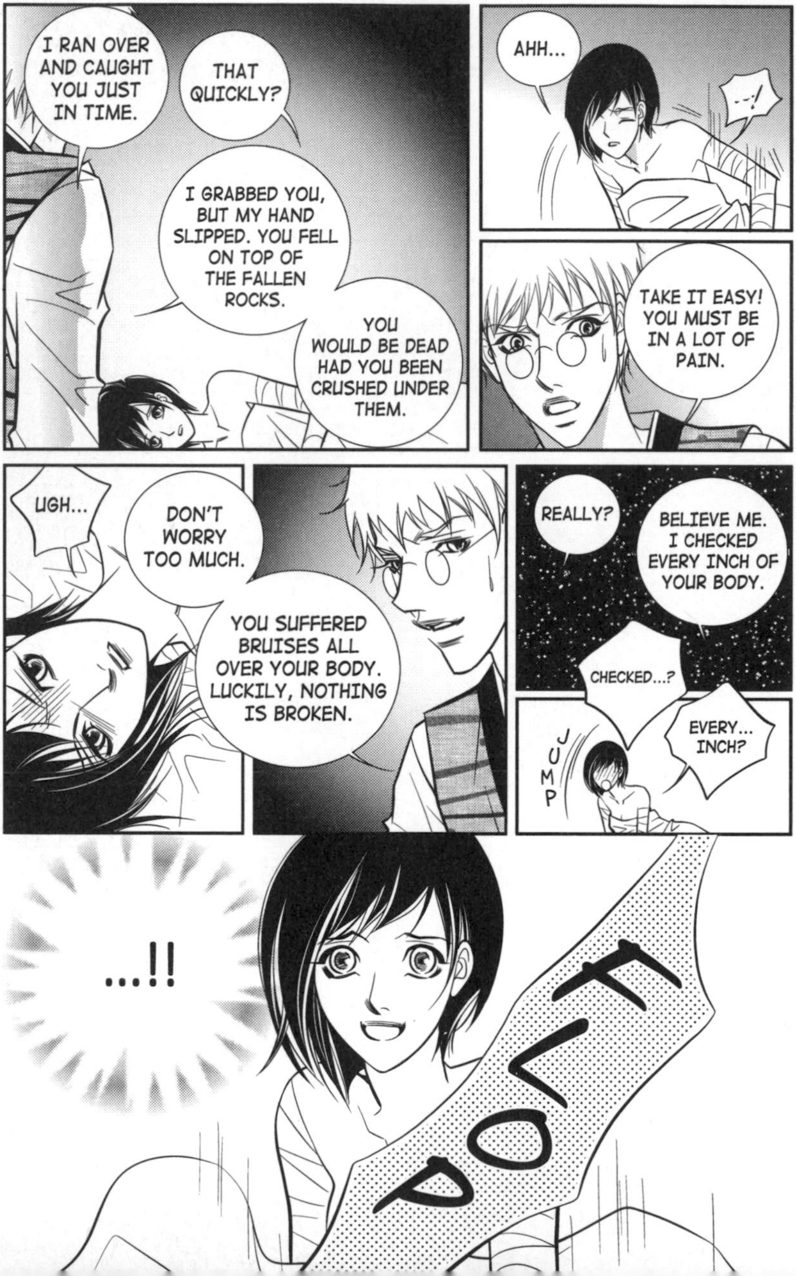
I RAN OVER AND CAUGHT YOU JUST IN TIME.
THAT QUICKLY?
I GRABBED YOU, BUT MY HAND SLIPPED. YOU FELL ON TOP OF THE FALLEN ROCKS.
YOU WOULD BE DEAD HAD YOU BEEN CRUSHED UNDER THEM.
AHH...
TAKE IT EASY! YOU MUST BE IN A LOT OF PAIN.
UGH...
DON'T WORRY TOO MUCH.
YOU SUFFERED BRUISES ALL OVER YOUR BODY. LUCKILY, NOTHING IS BROKEN.
REALLY?
BELIEVE ME. I CHECKED EVERY INCH OF YOUR BODY.
CHECKED...?
JUMP
EVERY... INCH?
...!!
FLOP

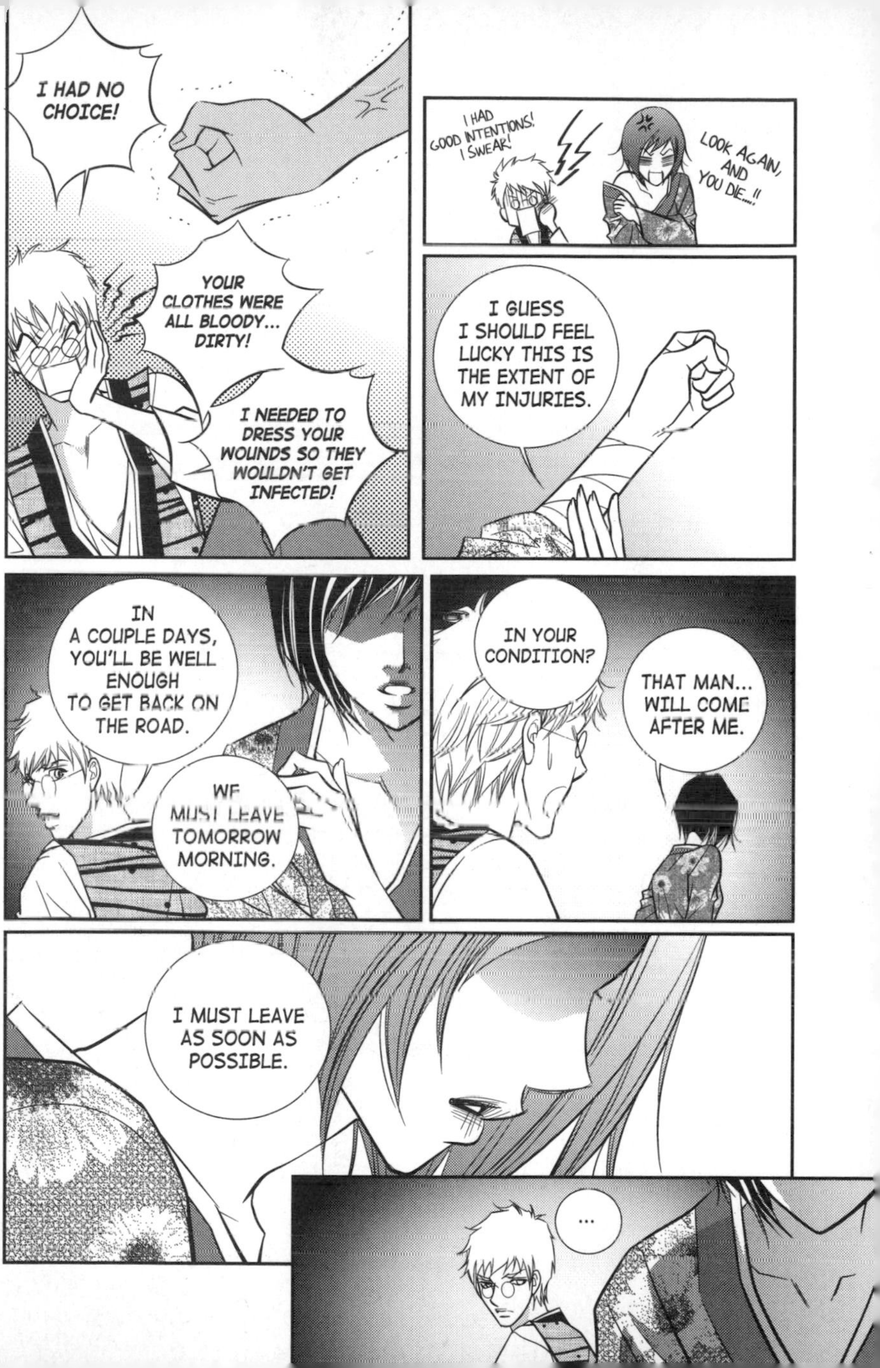
I HAD NO CHOICE!
YOUR CLOTHES WERE ALL BLOODY... DIRTY!
I NEEDED TO DRESS YOUR WOUNDS SO THEY WOULDN'T GET INFECTED!
I HAD GOOD INTENTIONS! I SWEAR!
LOOK AGAIN, AND YOU DIE...!!
I GUESS I SHOULD FEEL LUCKY THIS IS THE EXTENT OF MY INJURIES.
IN A COUPLE DAYS, YOU'LL BE WELL ENOUGH TO GET BACK ON THE ROAD.
WE MUST LEAVE TOMORROW MORNING.
IN YOUR CONDITION?
THAT MAN... WILL COME AFTER ME.
I MUST LEAVE AS SOON AS POSSIBLE.
...

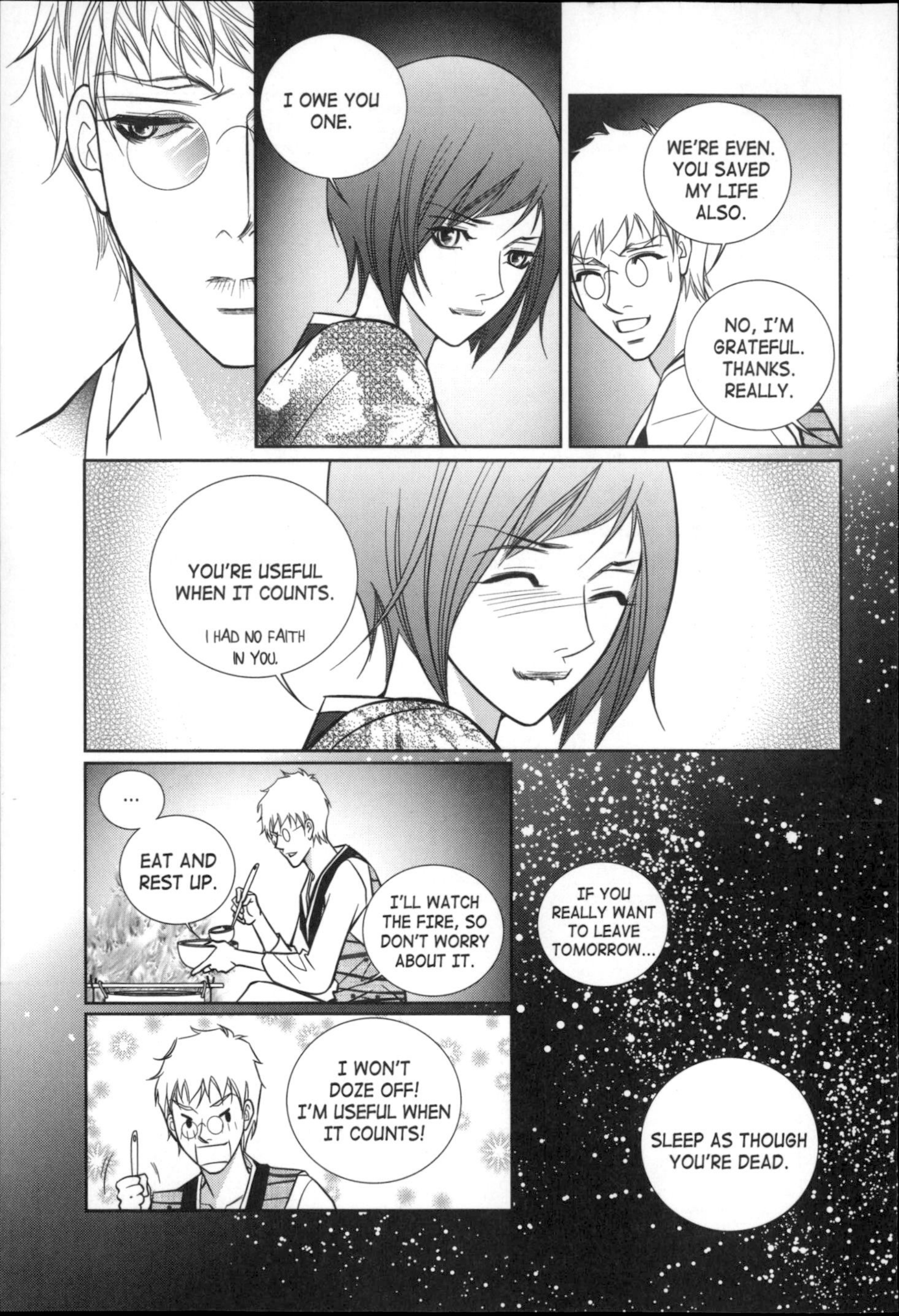
I OWE YOU ONE.
WE'RE EVEN. YOU SAVED MY LIFE ALSO.
NO, I'M GRATEFUL. THANKS. REALLY.
YOU'RE USEFUL WHEN IT COUNTS.
I HAD NO FAITH IN YOU.
...
EAT AND REST UP.
I'LL WATCH THE FIRE, SO DON'T WORRY ABOUT IT.
IF YOU REALLY WANT TO LEAVE TOMORROW...
I WON'T DOZE OFF! I'M USEFUL WHEN IT COUNTS!
SLEEP AS THOUGH YOU'RE DEAD.

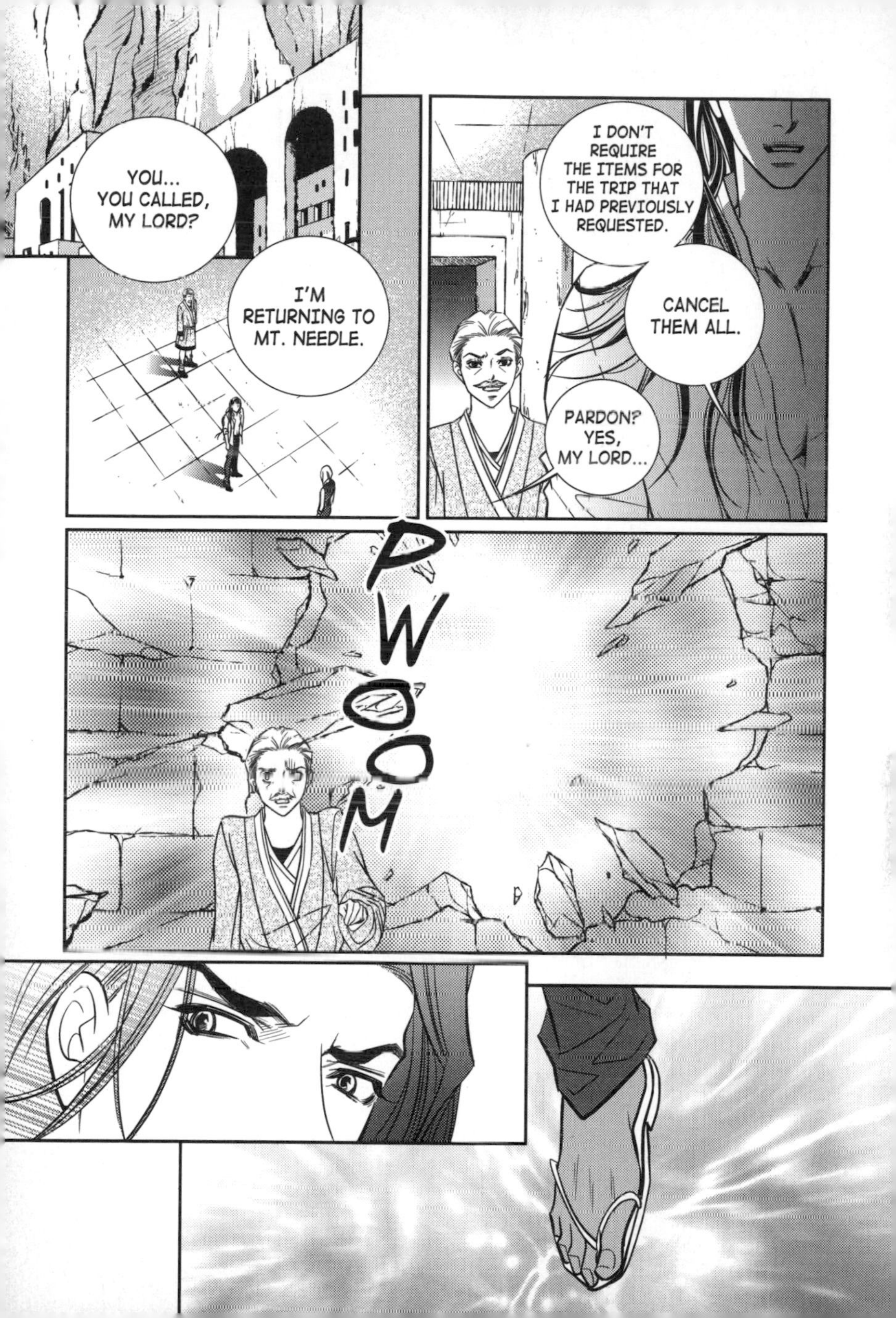
YOU... YOU CALLED, MY LORD?
I'M RETURNING TO MT. NEEDLE.
I DON'T REQUIRE THE ITEMS FOR THE TRIP THAT I HAD PREVIOUSLY REQUESTED.
CANCEL THEM ALL.
PARDON? YES, MY LORD...
PWOOM

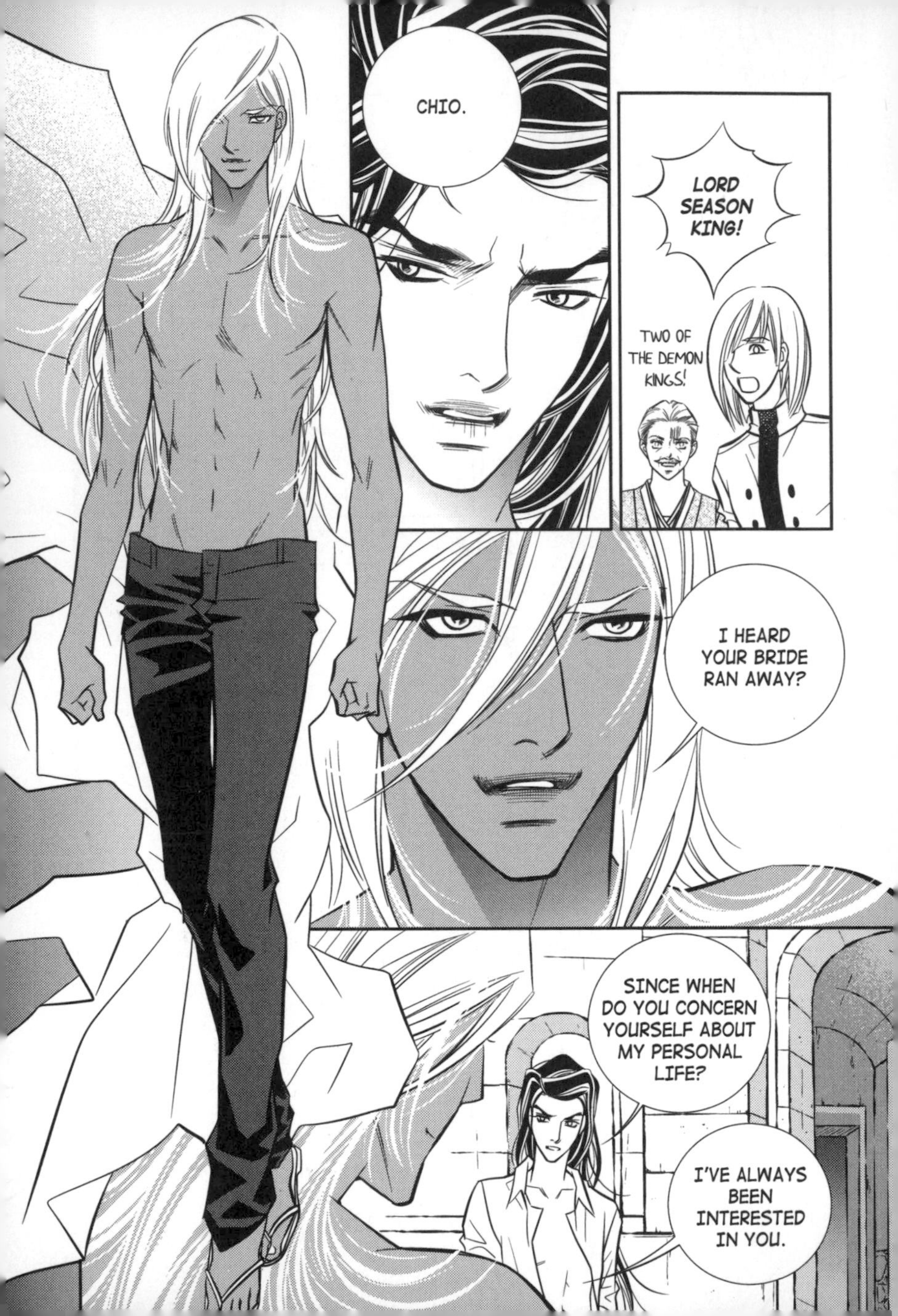
CHIO.
LORD SEASON KING!
TWO OF THE DEMON KINGS!
I HEARD YOUR BRIDE RAN AWAY?
SINCE WHEN DO YOU CONCERN YOURSELF ABOUT MY PERSONAL LIFE?
I'VE ALWAYS BEEN INTERESTED IN YOU.

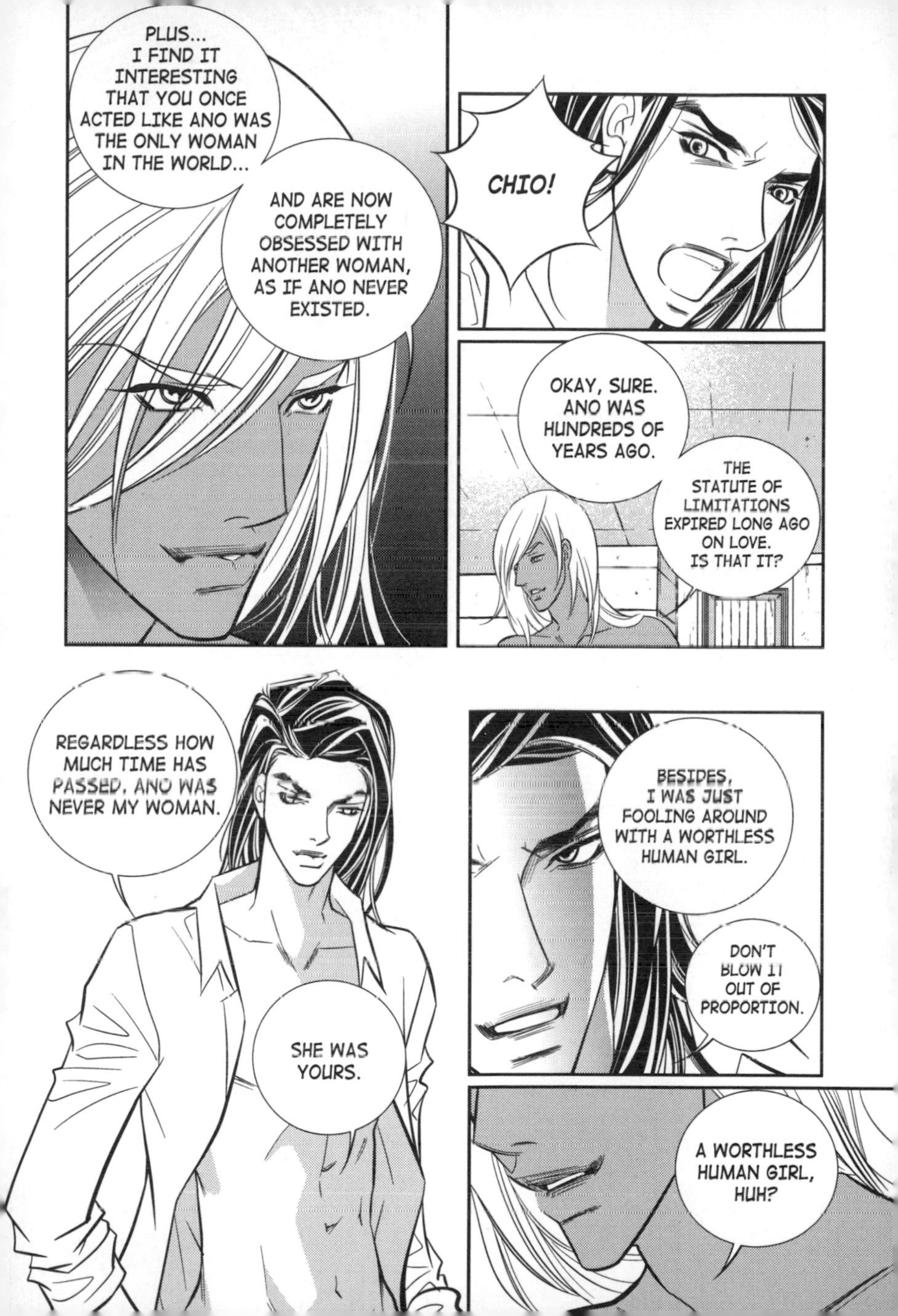
PLUS... I FIND IT INTERESTING THAT YOU ONCE ACTED LIKE ANO WAS THE ONLY WOMAN IN THE WORLD...
AND ARE NOW COMPLETELY OBSESSED WITH ANOTHER WOMAN, AS IF ANO NEVER EXISTED.
CHIO!
OKAY, SURE. ANO WAS HUNDREDS OF YEARS AGO.
THE STATUTE OF LIMITATIONS EXPIRED LONG AGO ON LOVE. IS THAT IT?
REGARDLESS HOW MUCH TIME HAS PASSED, ANO WAS NEVER MY WOMAN.
SHE WAS YOURS.
BESIDES, I WAS JUST FOOLING AROUND WITH A WORTHLESS HUMAN GIRL.
DON'T BLOW IT OUT OF PROPORTION.
A WORTHLESS HUMAN GIRL, HUH?

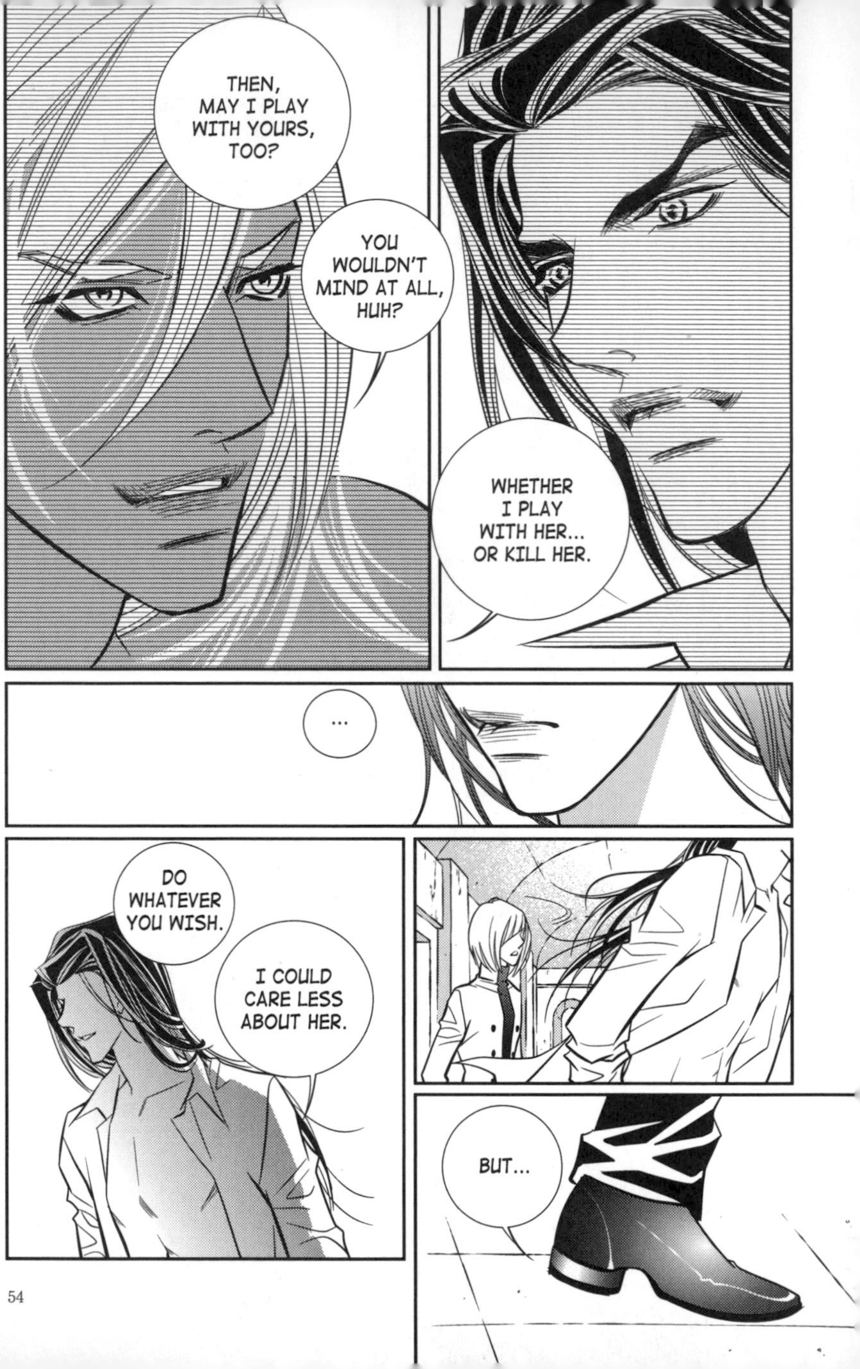
THEN, MAY I PLAY WITH YOURS, TOO?
YOU WOULDN'T MIND AT ALL, HUH?
WHETHER I PLAY WITH HER... OR KILL HER.
...
DO WHATEVER YOU WISH.
I COULD CARE LESS ABOUT HER.
BUT...

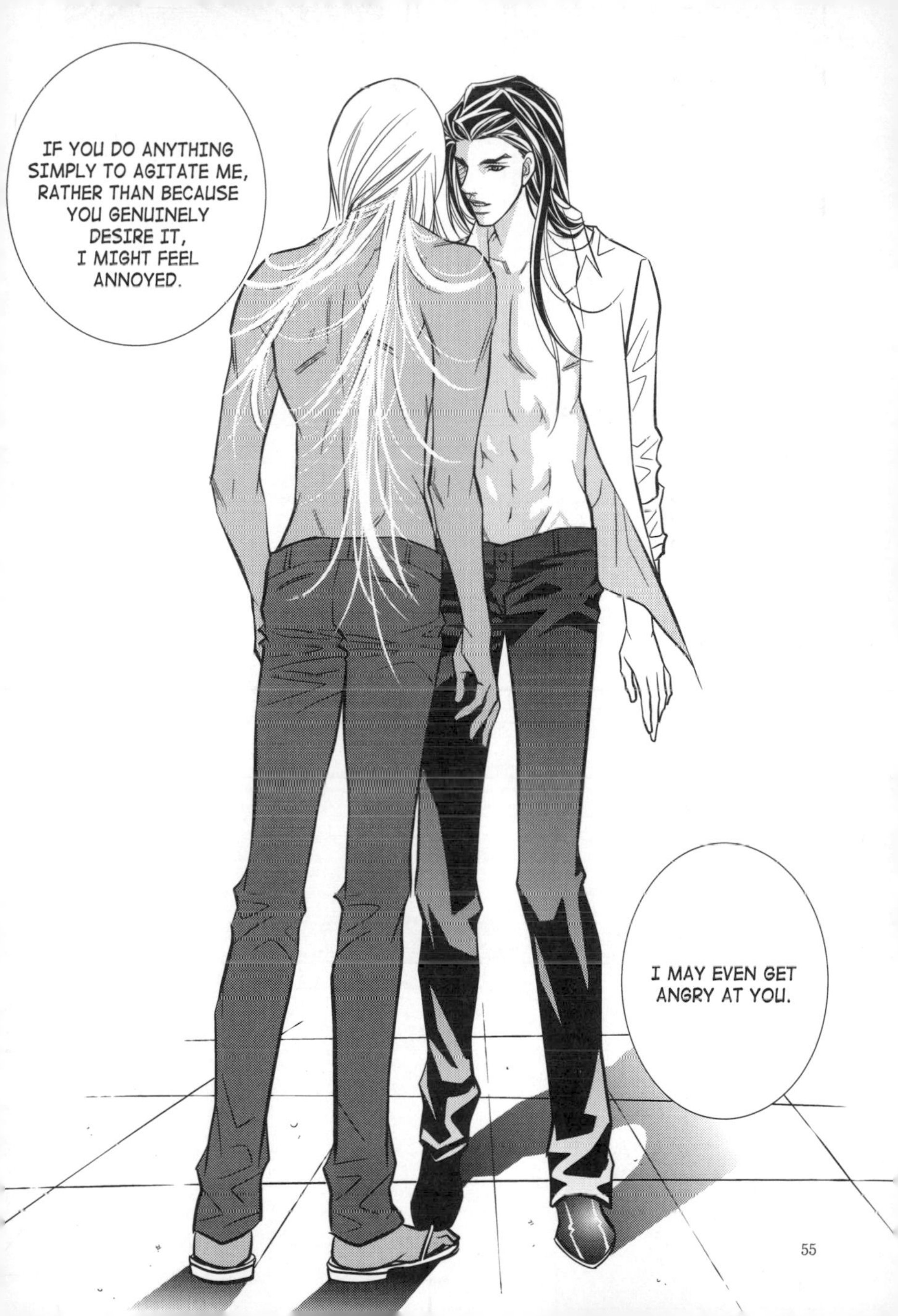
IF YOU DO ANYTHING SIMPLY TO AGITATE ME, RATHER THAN BECAUSE YOU GENUINELY DESIRE IT, I MIGHT FEEL ANNOYED.
I MAY EVEN GET ANGRY AT YOU.

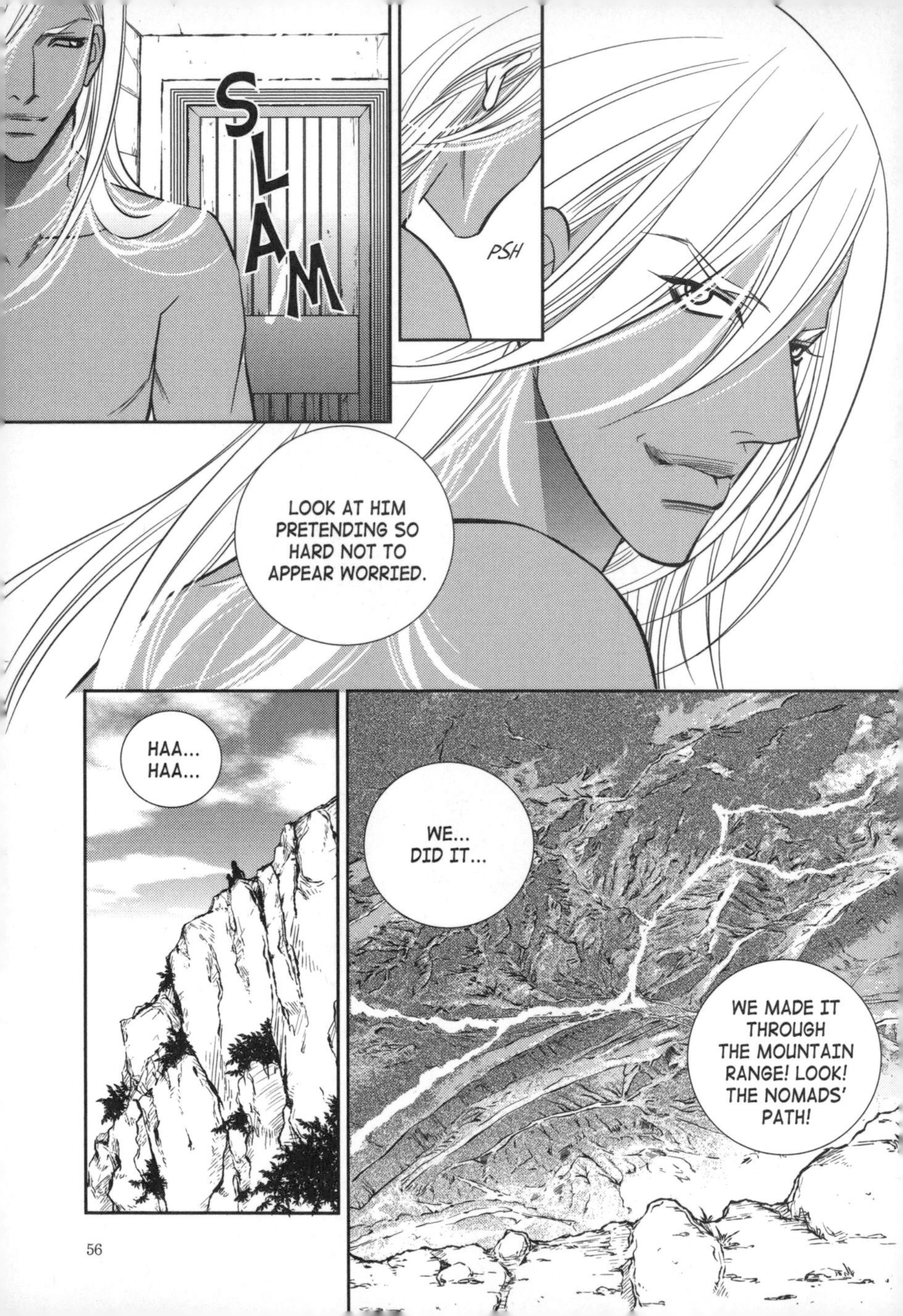
SLAM
PSH
LOOK AT HIM PRETENDING SO HARD NOT TO APPEAR WORRIED.
HAA... HAA...
WE... DID IT...
WE MADE IT THROUGH THE MOUNTAIN RANGE! LOOK! THE NOMADS' PATH!

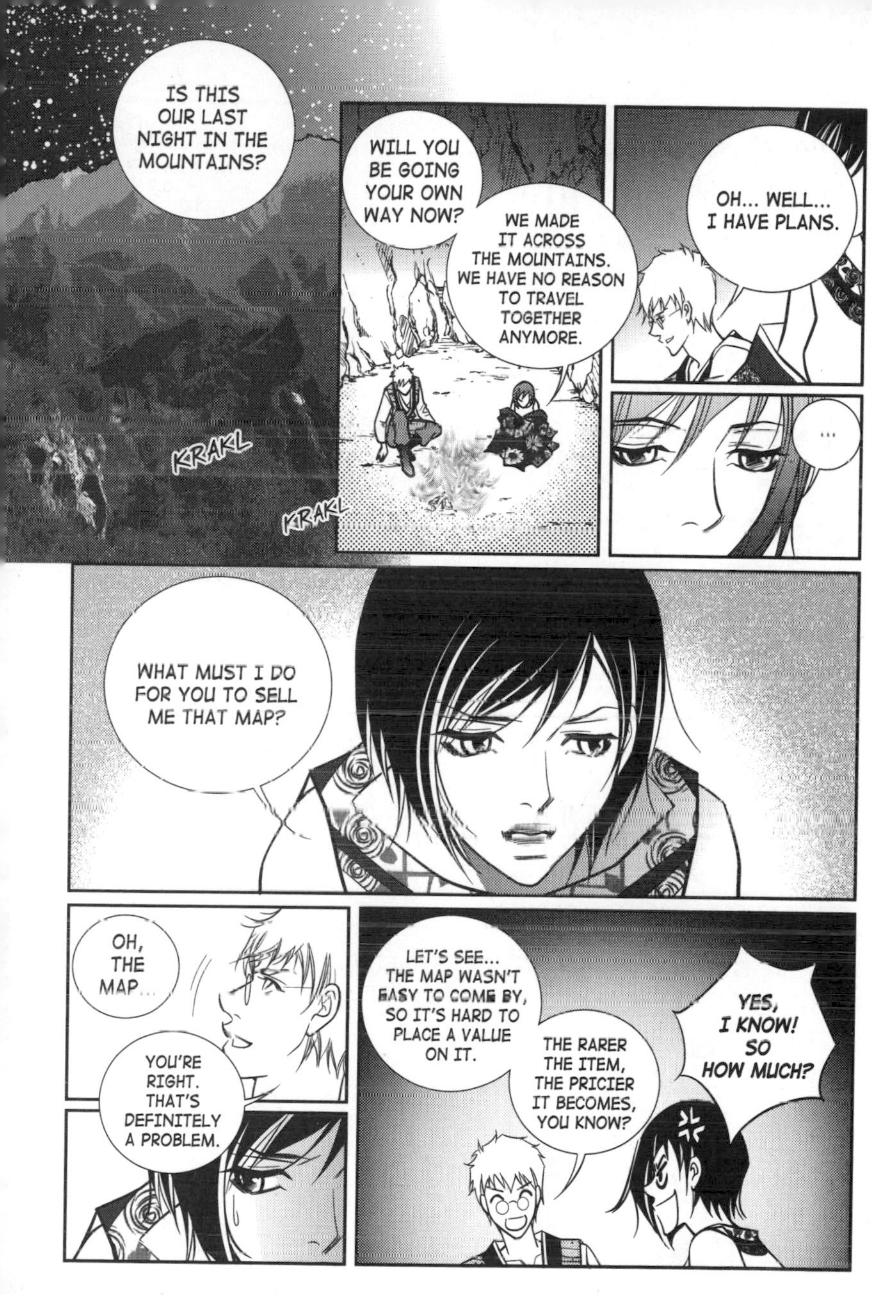
IS THIS OUR LAST NIGHT IN THE MOUNTAINS?
KRAKL
KRAKL
WILL YOU BE GOING YOUR OWN WAY NOW?
WE MADE IT ACROSS THE MOUNTAINS. WE HAVE NO REASON TO TRAVEL TOGETHER ANYMORE.
OH... WELL... I HAVE PLANS.
...
WHAT MUST I DO FOR YOU TO SELL ME THAT MAP?
OH, THE MAP...
YOU'RE RIGHT. THAT'S DEFINITELY A PROBLEM.
LET'S SEE... THE MAP WASN'T EASY TO COME BY, SO IT'S HARD TO PLACE A VALUE ON IT.
THE RARER THE ITEM, THE PRICIER IT BECOMES, YOU KNOW?
YES, I KNOW! SO HOW MUCH?

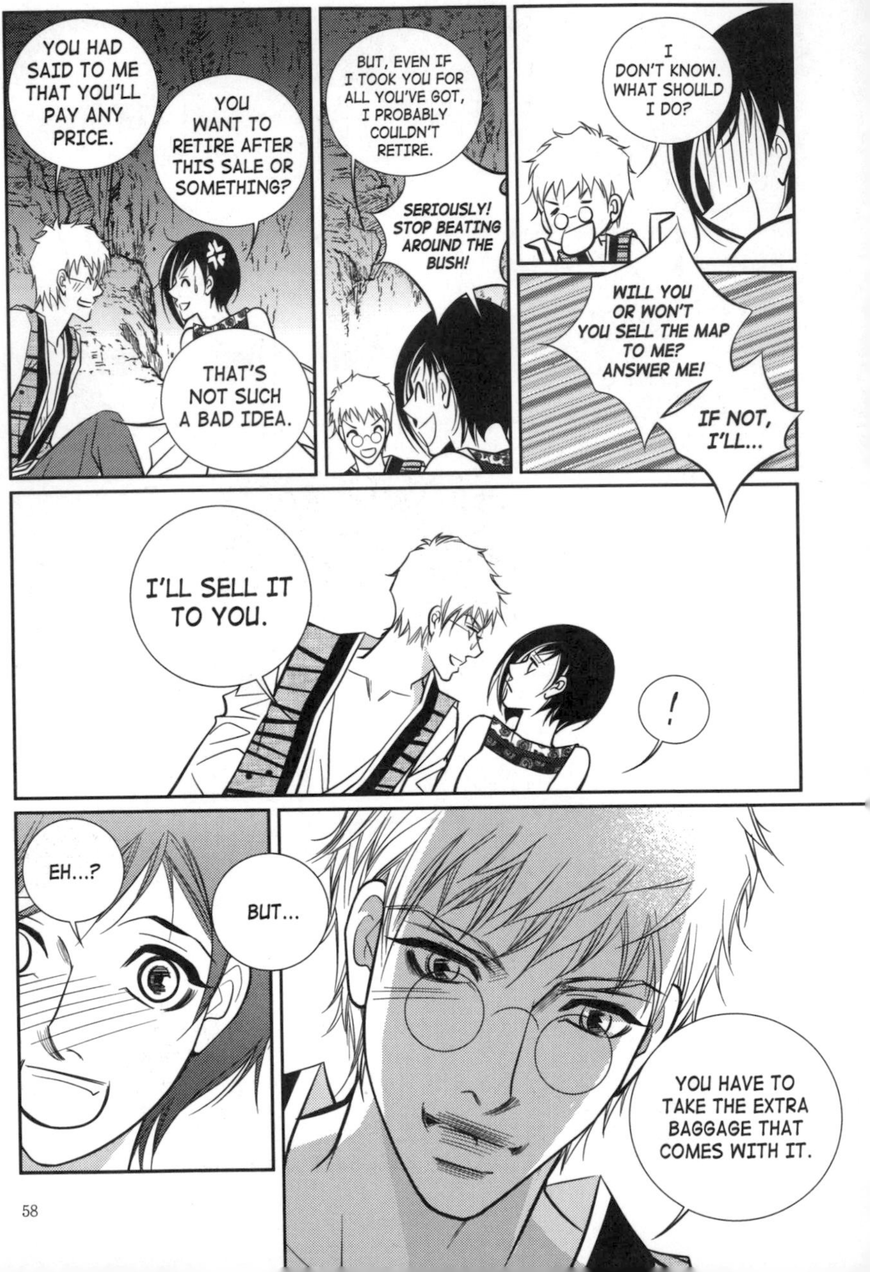
YOU HAD SAID TO ME THAT YOU'LL PAY ANY PRICE.
YOU WANT TO RETIRE AFTER THIS SALE OR SOMETHING?
THAT'S NOT SUCH A BAD IDEA.
BUT, EVEN IF I TOOK YOU FOR ALL YOU'VE GOT, I PROBABLY COULDN'T RETIRE.
SERIOUSLY! STOP BEATING AROUND THE BUSH!
I DON'T KNOW. WHAT SHOULD I DO?
WILL YOU OR WON'T YOU SELL THE MAP TO ME? ANSWER ME!
IF NOT, I'LL...
I'LL SELL IT TO YOU.
!
EH...?
BUT...
YOU HAVE TO TAKE THE EXTRA BAGGAGE THAT COMES WITH IT.

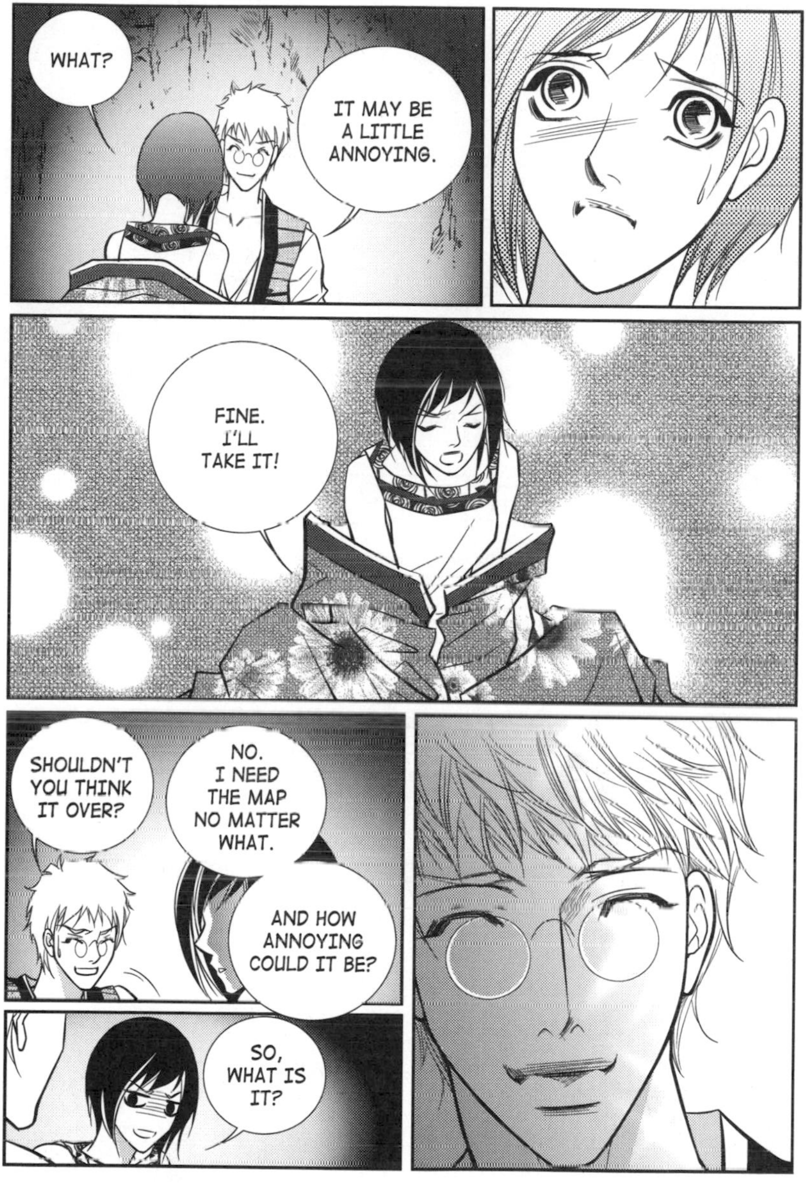
WHAT?
IT MAY BE A LITTLE ANNOYING.
FINE. I'LL TAKE IT!
SHOULDN'T YOU THINK IT OVER?
NO. I NEED THE MAP NO MATTER WHAT.
AND HOW ANNOYING COULD IT BE?
SO, WHAT IS IT?

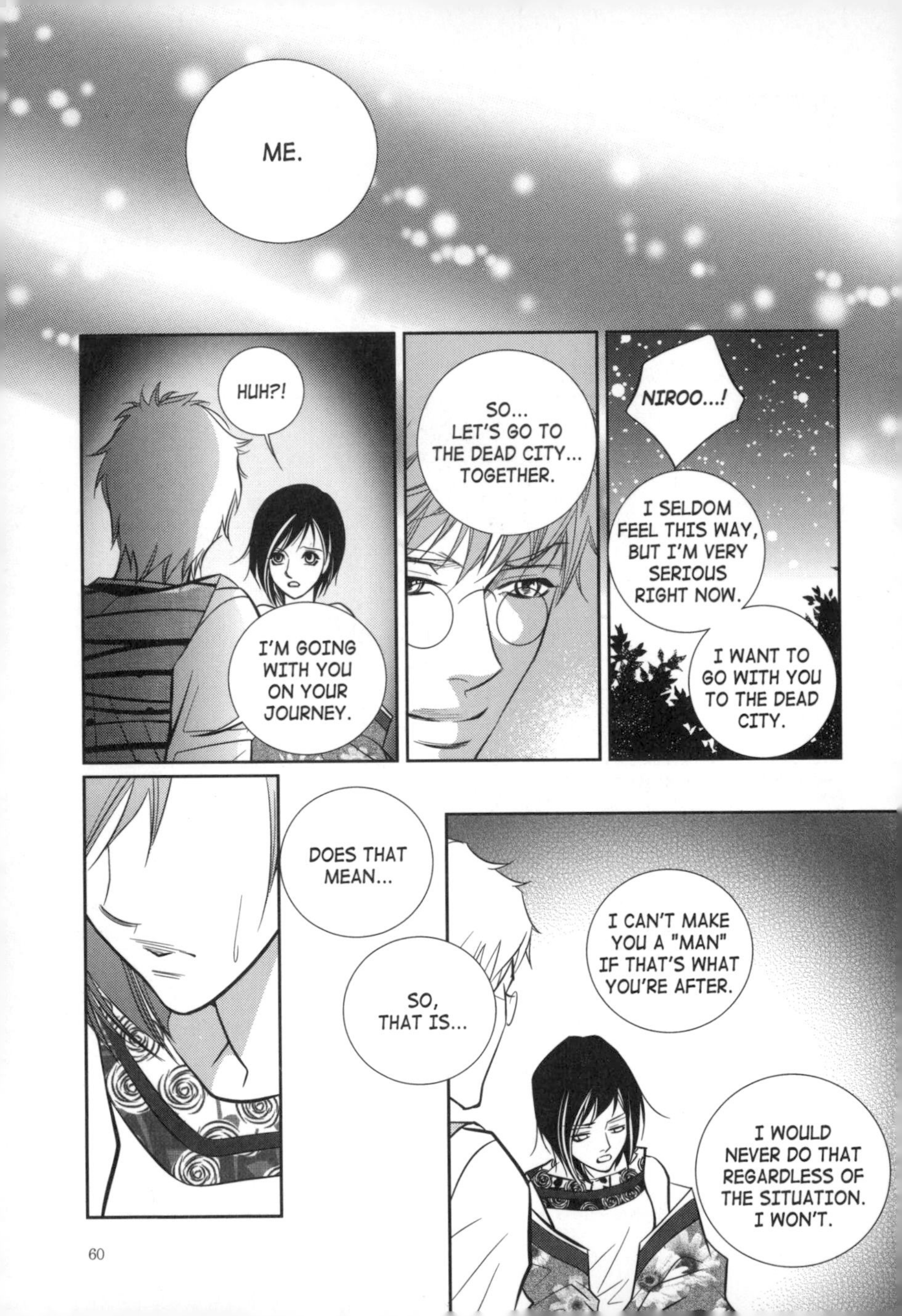
ME.
HUH?!
I'M GOING WITH YOU ON YOUR JOURNEY.
SO... LET'S GO TO THE DEAD CITY... TOGETHER.
NIROO...!
I SELDOM FEEL THIS WAY, BUT I'M VERY SERIOUS RIGHT NOW.
I WANT TO GO WITH YOU TO THE DEAD CITY.
DOES THAT MEAN...
SO, THAT IS...
I CAN'T MAKE YOU A "MAN" IF THAT'S WHAT YOU'RE AFTER.
I WOULD NEVER DO THAT REGARDLESS OF THE SITUATION. I WON'T.

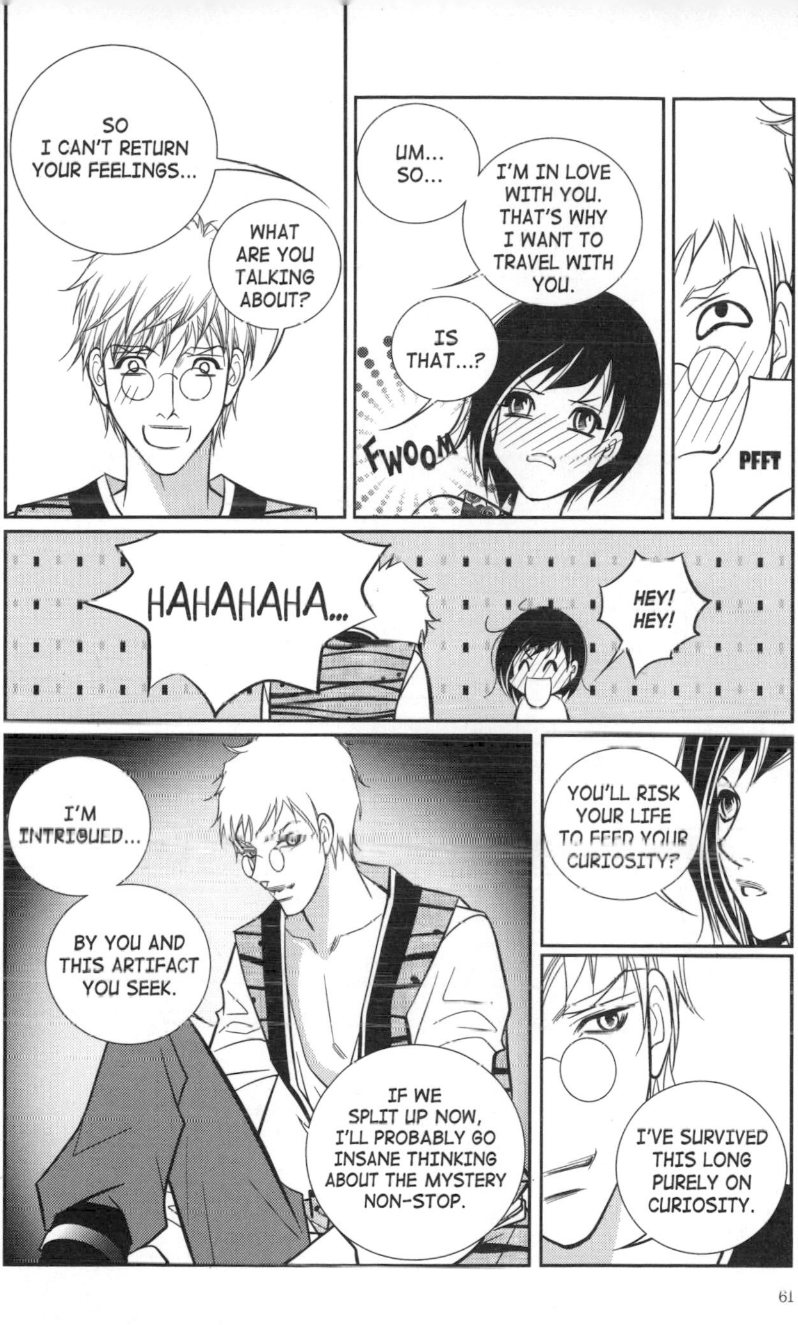
SO
I CAN'T RETURN
YOUR FEELINGS...
WHAT
ARE YOU
TALKING
ABOUT?
UM...
SO...
I'M IN LOVE
WITH YOU.
THAT'S WHY
I WANT TO
TRAVEL WITH
YOU.
IS
THAT...?
FWOOM
PFFT
HAHAHAHA...
HEY!
HEY!
I'M
INTRIGUED...
BY YOU AND
THIS ARTIFACT
YOU SEEK.
IF WE
SPLIT UP NOW,
I'LL PROBABLY GO
INSANE THINKING
ABOUT THE MYSTERY
NON-STOP.
YOU'LL RISK
YOUR LIFE
TO FEED YOUR
CURIOSITY?
I'VE SURVIVED
THIS LONG
PURELY ON
CURIOSITY.

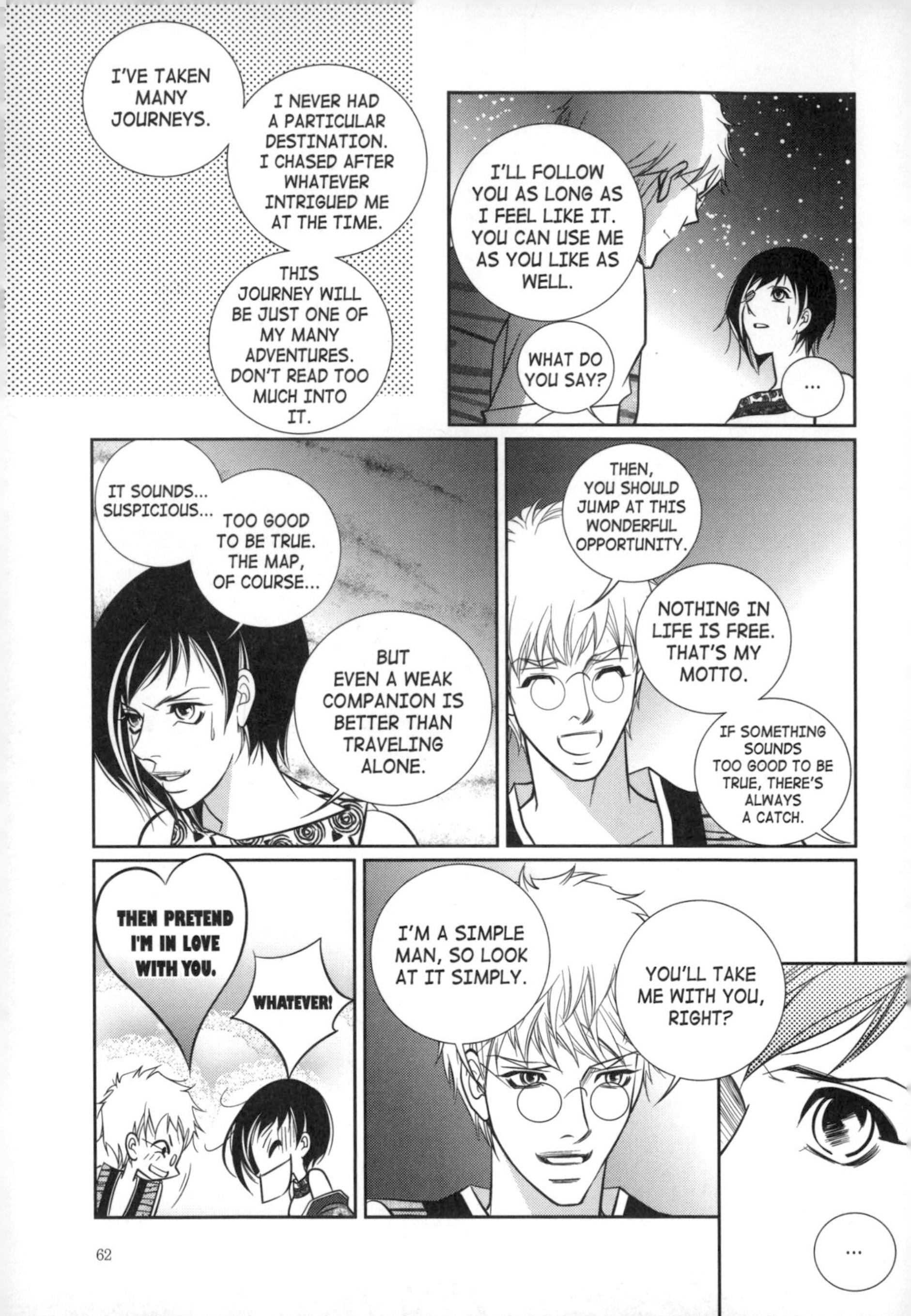
I'VE TAKEN MANY JOURNEYS.
I NEVER HAD A PARTICULAR DESTINATION. I CHASED AFTER WHATEVER INTRIGUED ME AT THE TIME.
THIS JOURNEY WILL BE JUST ONE OF MY MANY ADVENTURES. DON'T READ TOO MUCH INTO IT.
I'LL FOLLOW YOU AS LONG AS I FEEL LIKE IT. YOU CAN USE ME AS YOU LIKE AS WELL.
WHAT DO YOU SAY?
...
IT SOUNDS... SUSPICIOUS...
TOO GOOD TO BE TRUE. THE MAP, OF COURSE...
BUT EVEN A WEAK COMPANION IS BETTER THAN TRAVELING ALONE.
THEN, YOU SHOULD JUMP AT THIS WONDERFUL OPPORTUNITY.
NOTHING IN LIFE IS FREE. THAT'S MY MOTTO.
IF SOMETHING SOUNDS TOO GOOD TO BE TRUE, THERE'S ALWAYS A CATCH.
THEN PRETEND I'M IN LOVE WITH YOU.
WHATEVER!
I'M A SIMPLE MAN, SO LOOK AT IT SIMPLY.
YOU'LL TAKE ME WITH YOU, RIGHT?
...

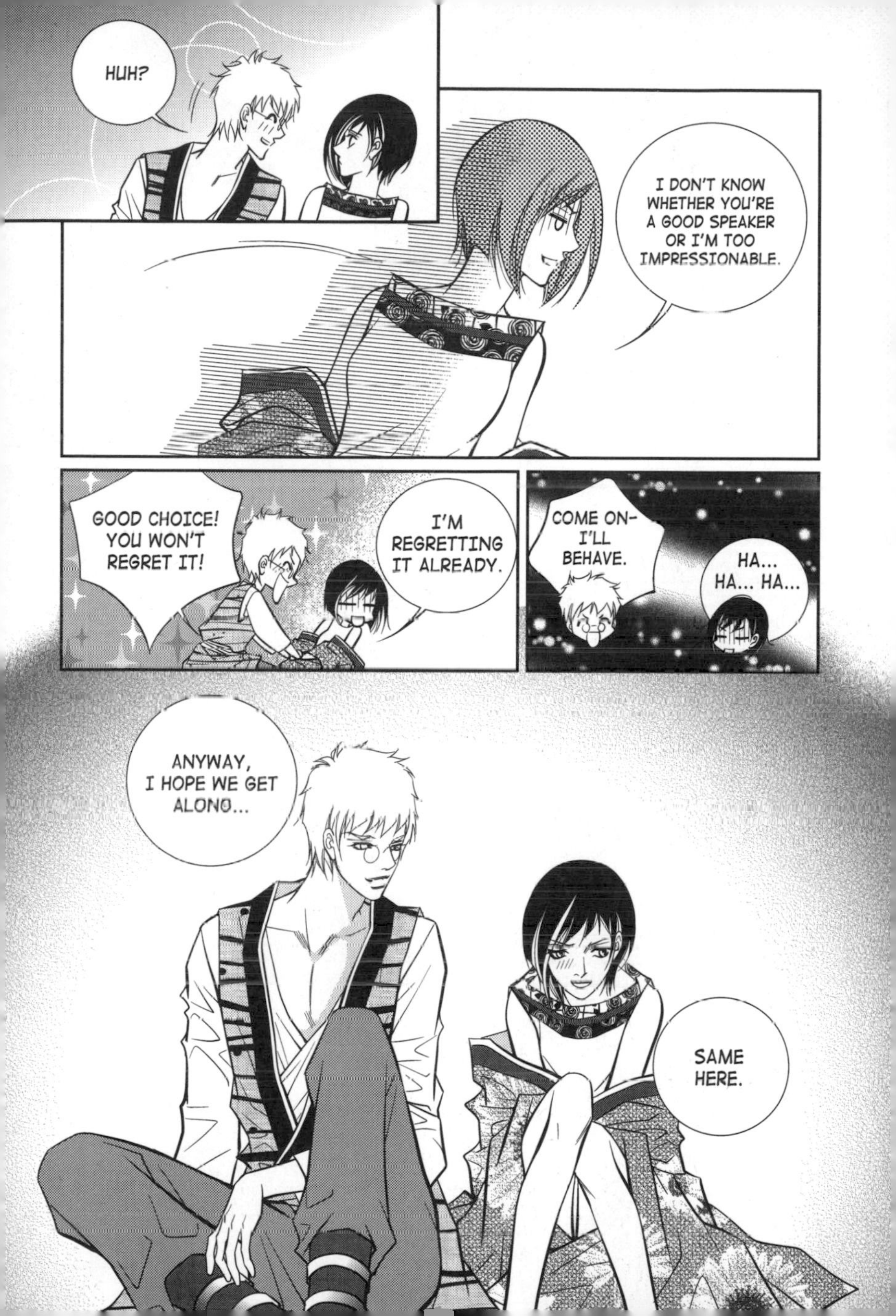
HUH?
I DON'T KNOW WHETHER YOU'RE A GOOD SPEAKER OR I'M TOO IMPRESSIONABLE.
GOOD CHOICE! YOU WON'T REGRET IT!
I'M REGRETTING IT ALREADY.
COME ON– I'LL BEHAVE.
HA... HA... HA...
ANYWAY, I HOPE WE GET ALONG...
SAME HERE.

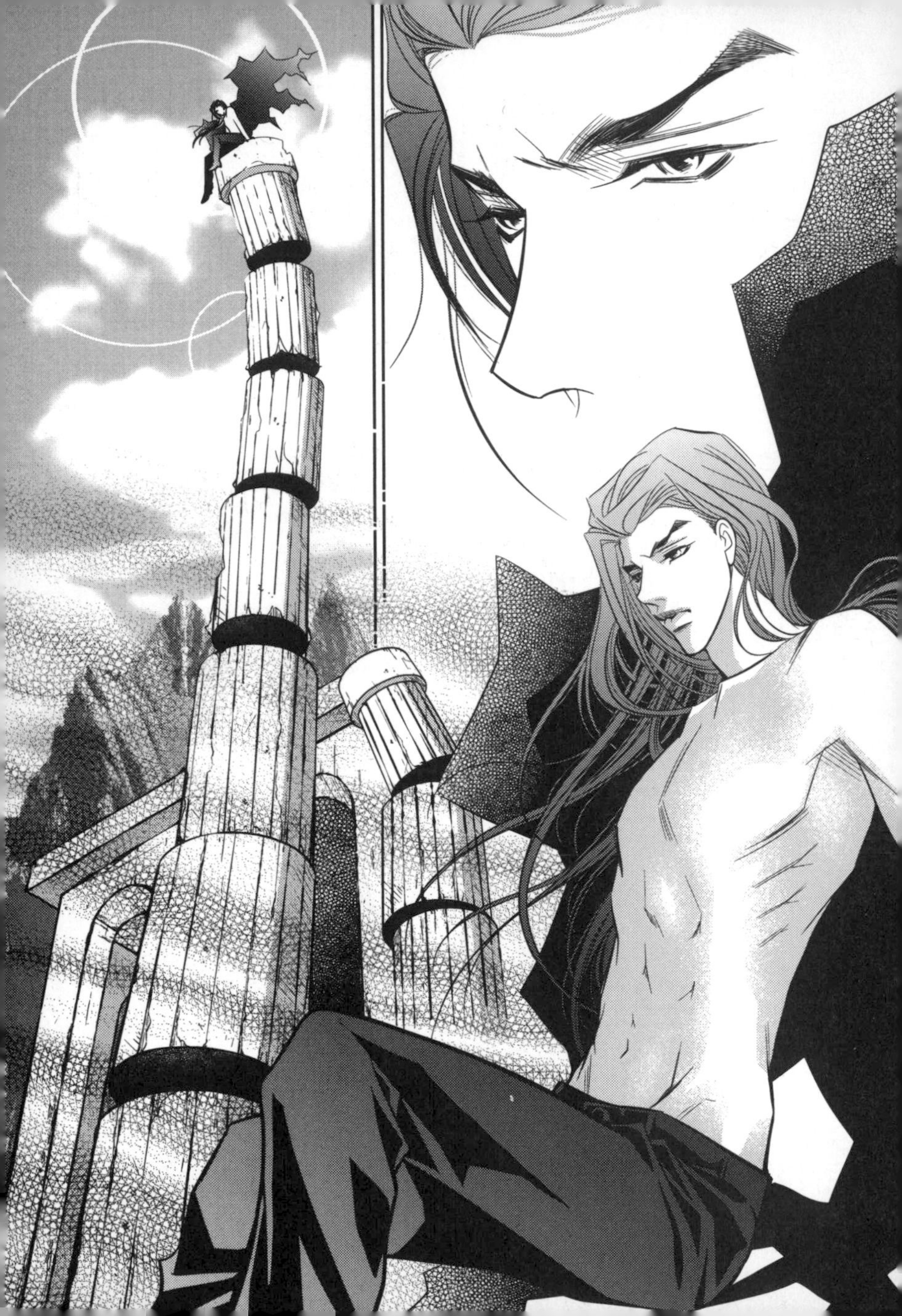

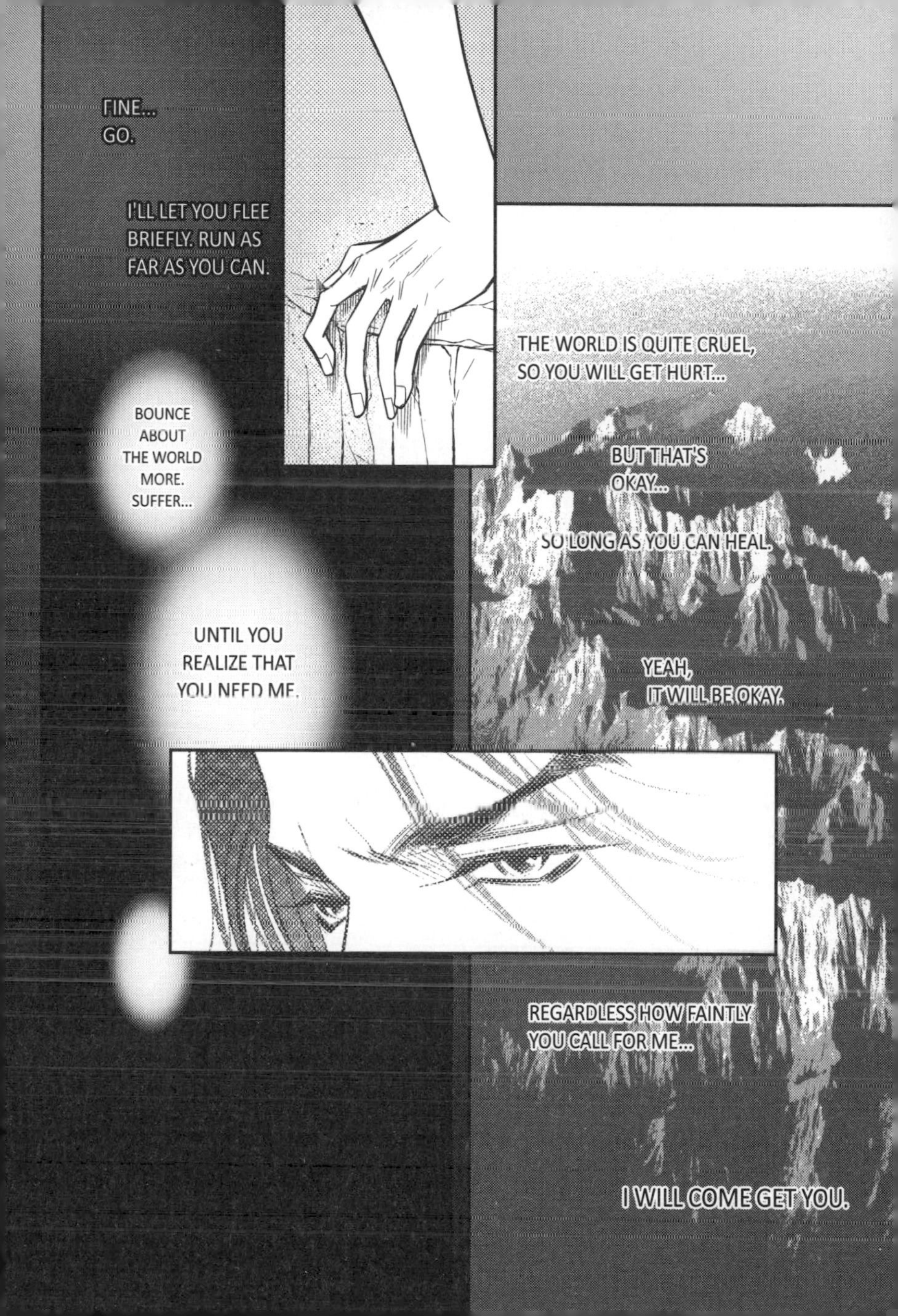
FINE... GO.
I'LL LET YOU FLEE BRIEFLY. RUN AS FAR AS YOU CAN.
BOUNCE ABOUT THE WORLD MORE. SUFFER...
UNTIL YOU REALIZE THAT YOU NEED ME.
THE WORLD IS QUITE CRUEL, SO YOU WILL GET HURT...
BUT THAT'S OKAY...
SO LONG AS YOU CAN HEAL.
YEAH, IT WILL BE OKAY.
REGARDLESS HOW FAINTLY YOU CALL FOR ME...
I WILL COME GET YOU.

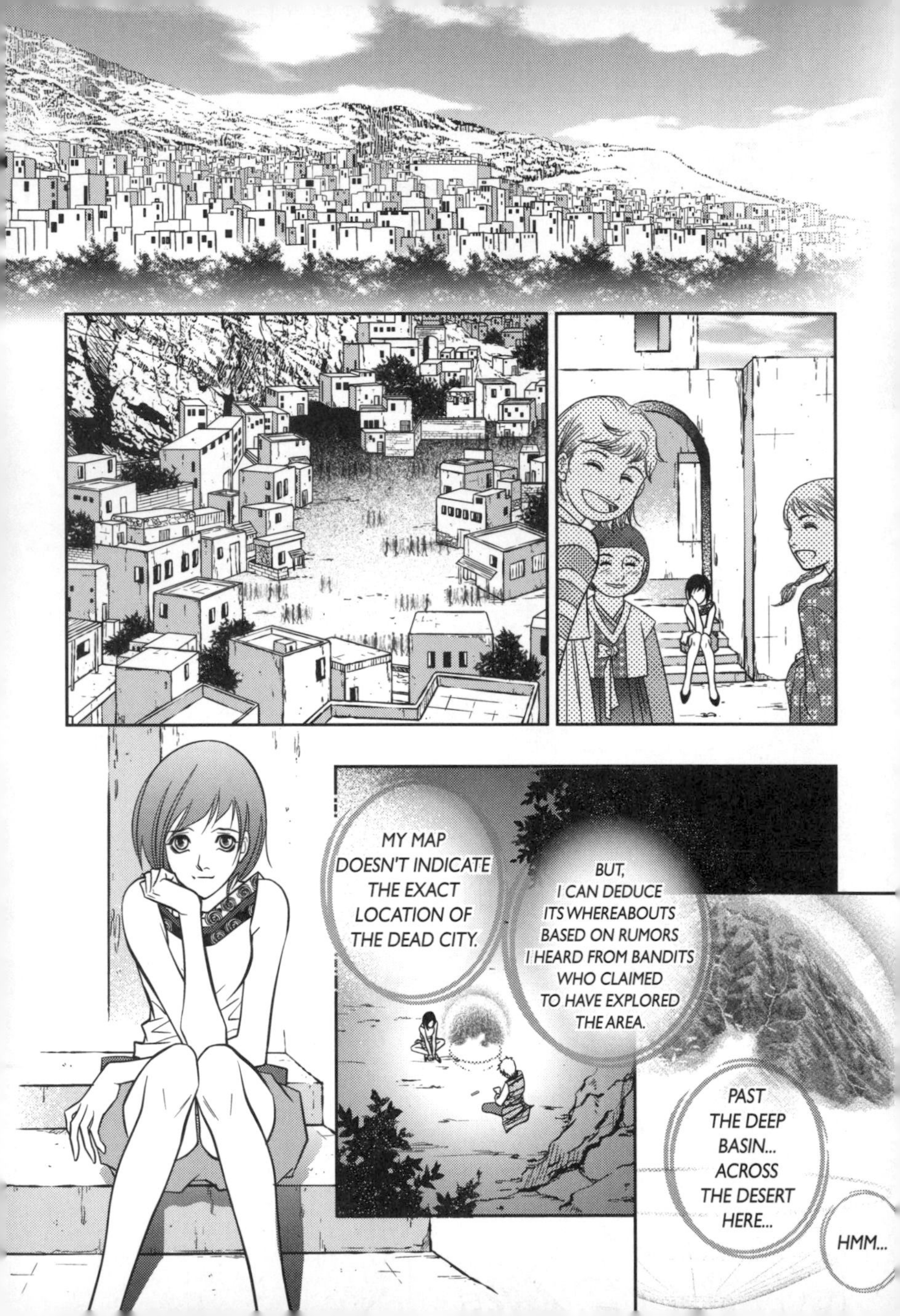
MY MAP DOESN'T INDICATE THE EXACT LOCATION OF THE DEAD CITY.
BUT, I CAN DEDUCE ITS WHEREABOUTS BASED ON RUMORS I HEARD FROM BANDITS WHO CLAIMED TO HAVE EXPLORED THE AREA.
PAST THE DEEP BASIN... ACROSS THE DESERT HERE...
HMM...

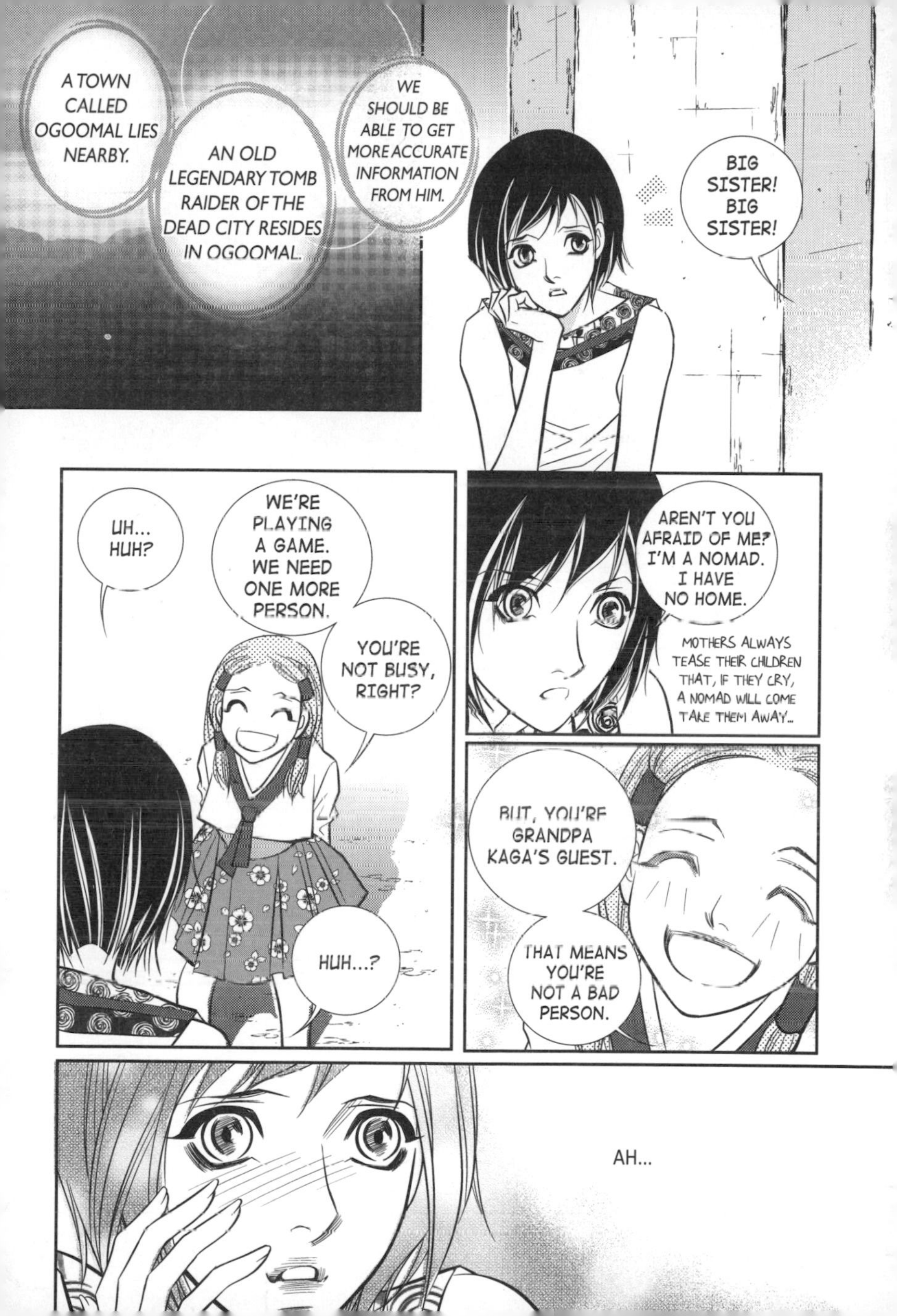
A TOWN CALLED OGOOMAL LIES NEARBY.
AN OLD LEGENDARY TOMB RAIDER OF THE DEAD CITY RESIDES IN OGOOMAL.
WE SHOULD BE ABLE TO GET MORE ACCURATE INFORMATION FROM HIM.
BIG SISTER! BIG SISTER!
UH... HUH?
WE'RE PLAYING A GAME. WE NEED ONE MORE PERSON.
YOU'RE NOT BUSY, RIGHT?
HUH...?
AREN'T YOU AFRAID OF ME? I'M A NOMAD. I HAVE NO HOME.
MOTHERS ALWAYS TEASE THEIR CHILDREN THAT, IF THEY CRY, A NOMAD WILL COME TAKE THEM AWAY...
BUT, YOU'RE GRANDPA KAGA'S GUEST.
THAT MEANS YOU'RE NOT A BAD PERSON.
AH...

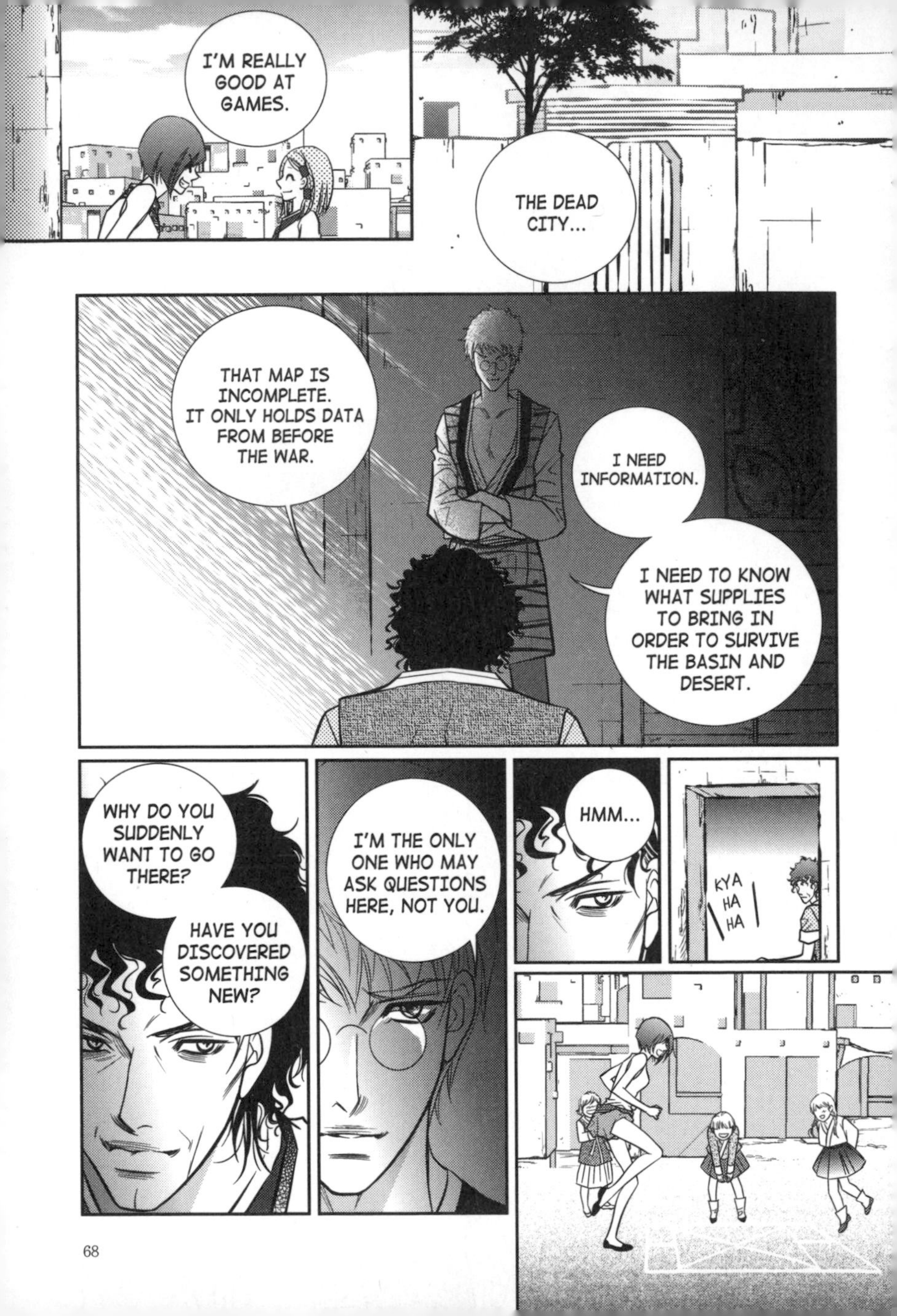
I'M REALLY GOOD AT GAMES.
THE DEAD CITY...
THAT MAP IS INCOMPLETE. IT ONLY HOLDS DATA FROM BEFORE THE WAR.
I NEED INFORMATION.
I NEED TO KNOW WHAT SUPPLIES TO BRING IN ORDER TO SURVIVE THE BASIN AND DESERT.
WHY DO YOU SUDDENLY WANT TO GO THERE?
HAVE YOU DISCOVERED SOMETHING NEW?
I'M THE ONLY ONE WHO MAY ASK QUESTIONS HERE, NOT YOU.
HMM...
KYA HA HA

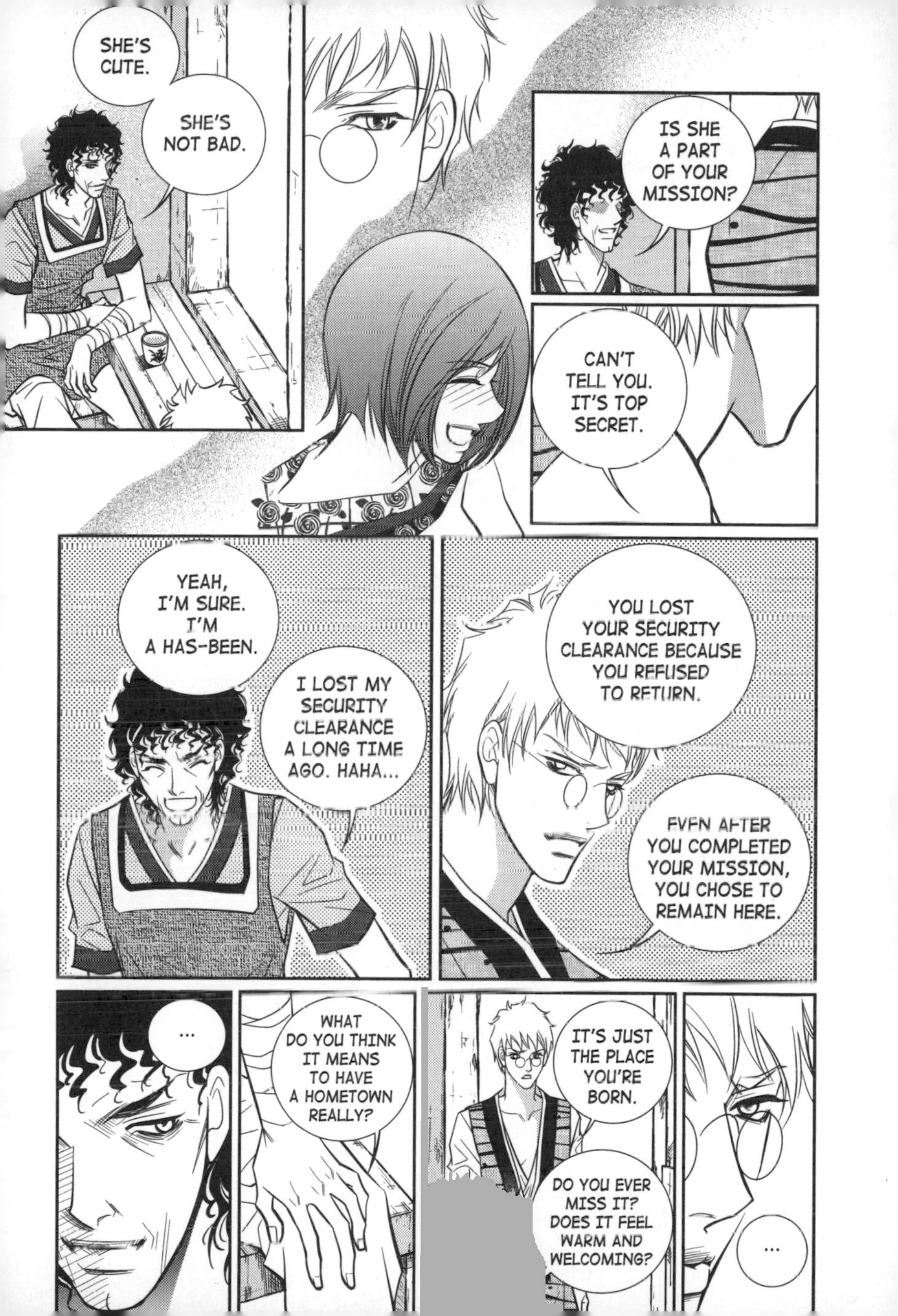
SHE'S CUTE.
SHE'S NOT BAD.
IS SHE A PART OF YOUR MISSION?
CAN'T TELL YOU. IT'S TOP SECRET.
YEAH, I'M SURE. I'M A HAS-BEEN.
I LOST MY SECURITY CLEARANCE A LONG TIME AGO. HAHA...
YOU LOST YOUR SECURITY CLEARANCE BECAUSE YOU REFUSED TO RETURN.
EVEN AFTER YOU COMPLETED YOUR MISSION, YOU CHOSE TO REMAIN HERE.
...
WHAT DO YOU THINK IT MEANS TO HAVE A HOMETOWN REALLY?
IT'S JUST THE PLACE YOU'RE BORN.
DO YOU EVER MISS IT? DOES IT FEEL WARM AND WELCOMING?
...

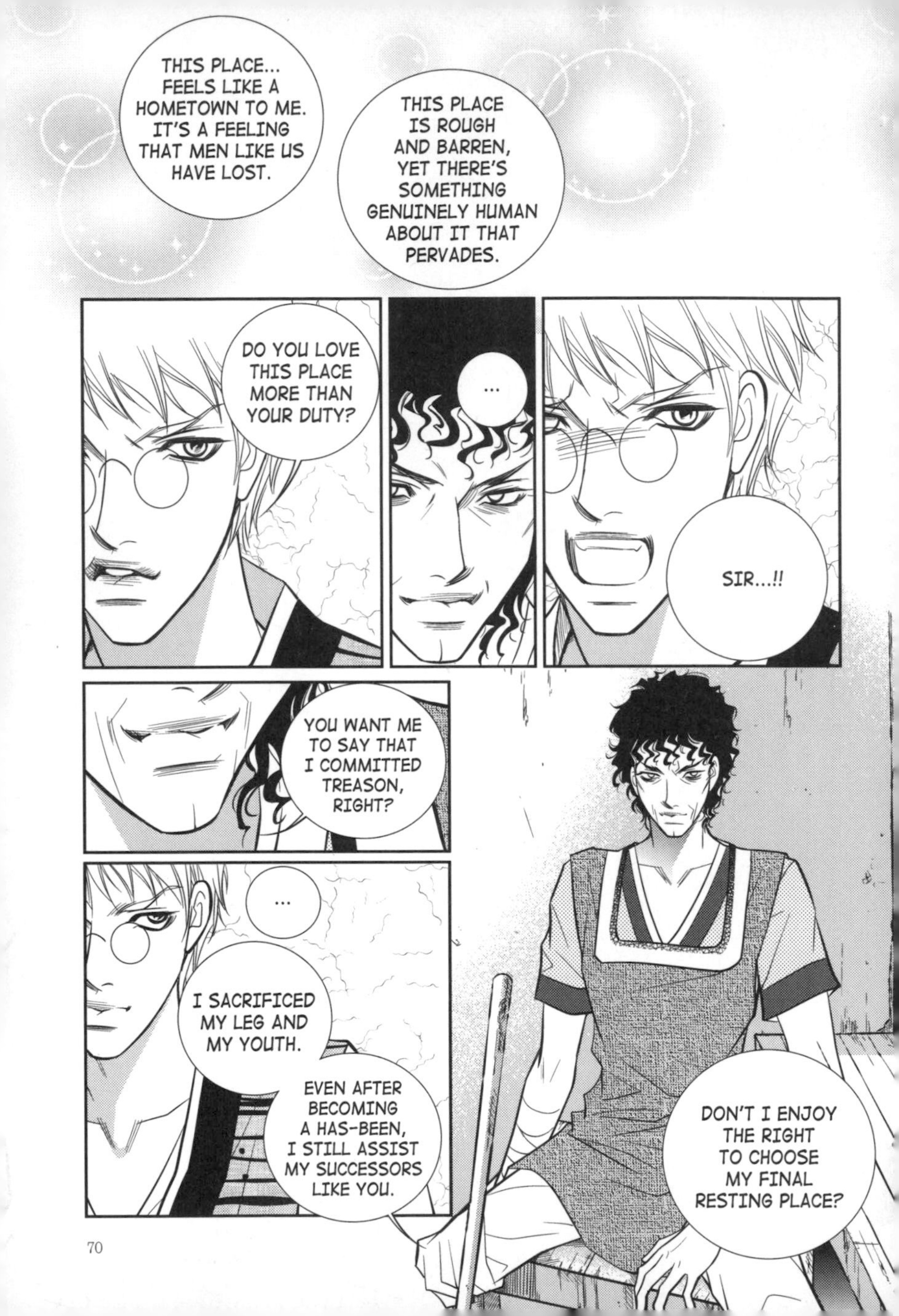
THIS PLACE... FEELS LIKE A HOMETOWN TO ME. IT'S A FEELING THAT MEN LIKE US HAVE LOST.
THIS PLACE IS ROUGH AND BARREN, YET THERE'S SOMETHING GENUINELY HUMAN ABOUT IT THAT PERVADES.
DO YOU LOVE THIS PLACE MORE THAN YOUR DUTY?
...
SIR...!!
YOU WANT ME TO SAY THAT I COMMITTED TREASON, RIGHT?
...
I SACRIFICED MY LEG AND MY YOUTH.
EVEN AFTER BECOMING A HAS-BEEN, I STILL ASSIST MY SUCCESSORS LIKE YOU.
DON'T I ENJOY THE RIGHT TO CHOOSE MY FINAL RESTING PLACE?

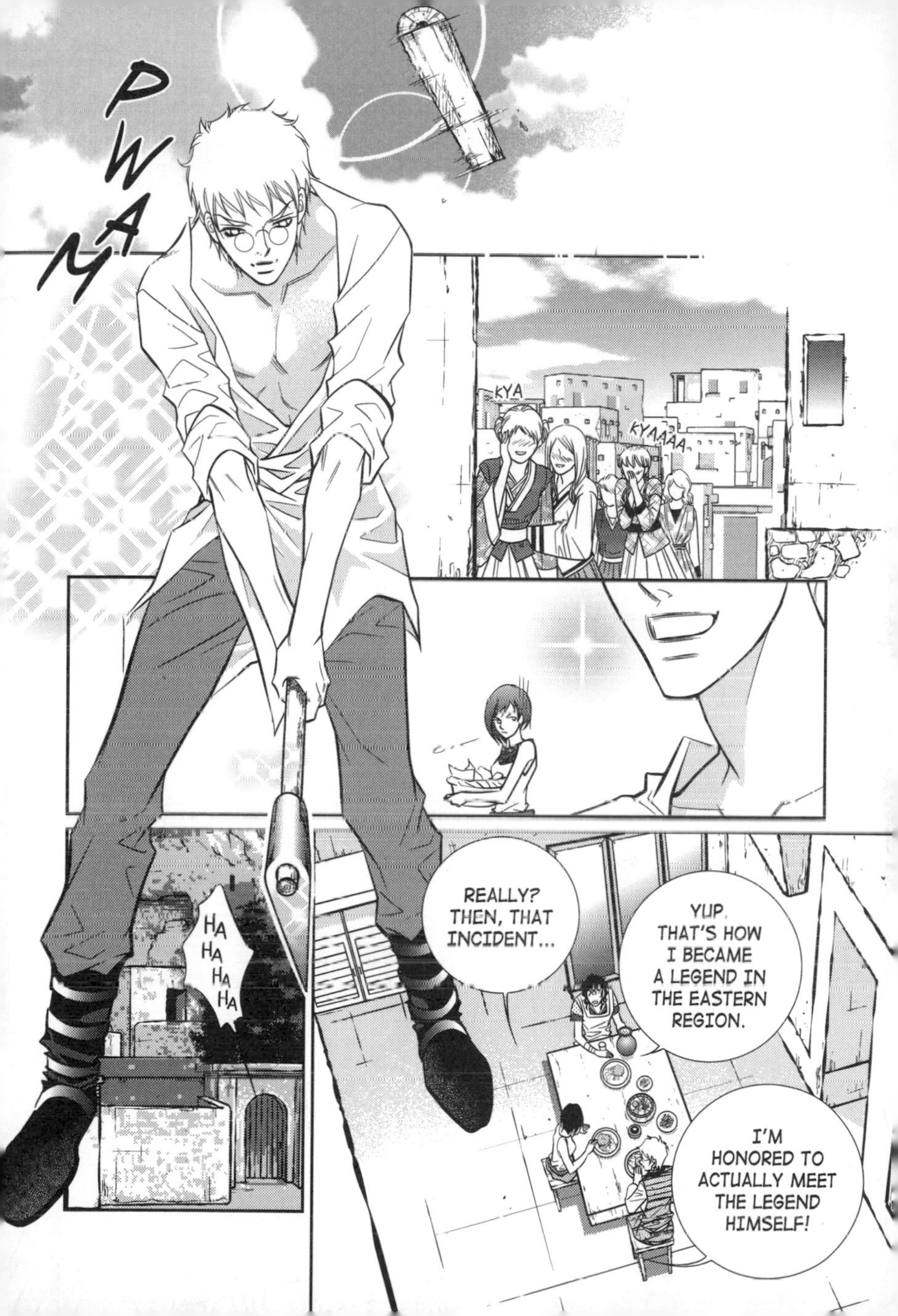
PWAM
KYA
KYAAAA
HA HA HA HA
REALLY? THEN, THAT INCIDENT...
YUP. THAT'S HOW I BECAME A LEGEND IN THE EASTERN REGION.
I'M HONORED TO ACTUALLY MEET THE LEGEND HIMSELF!

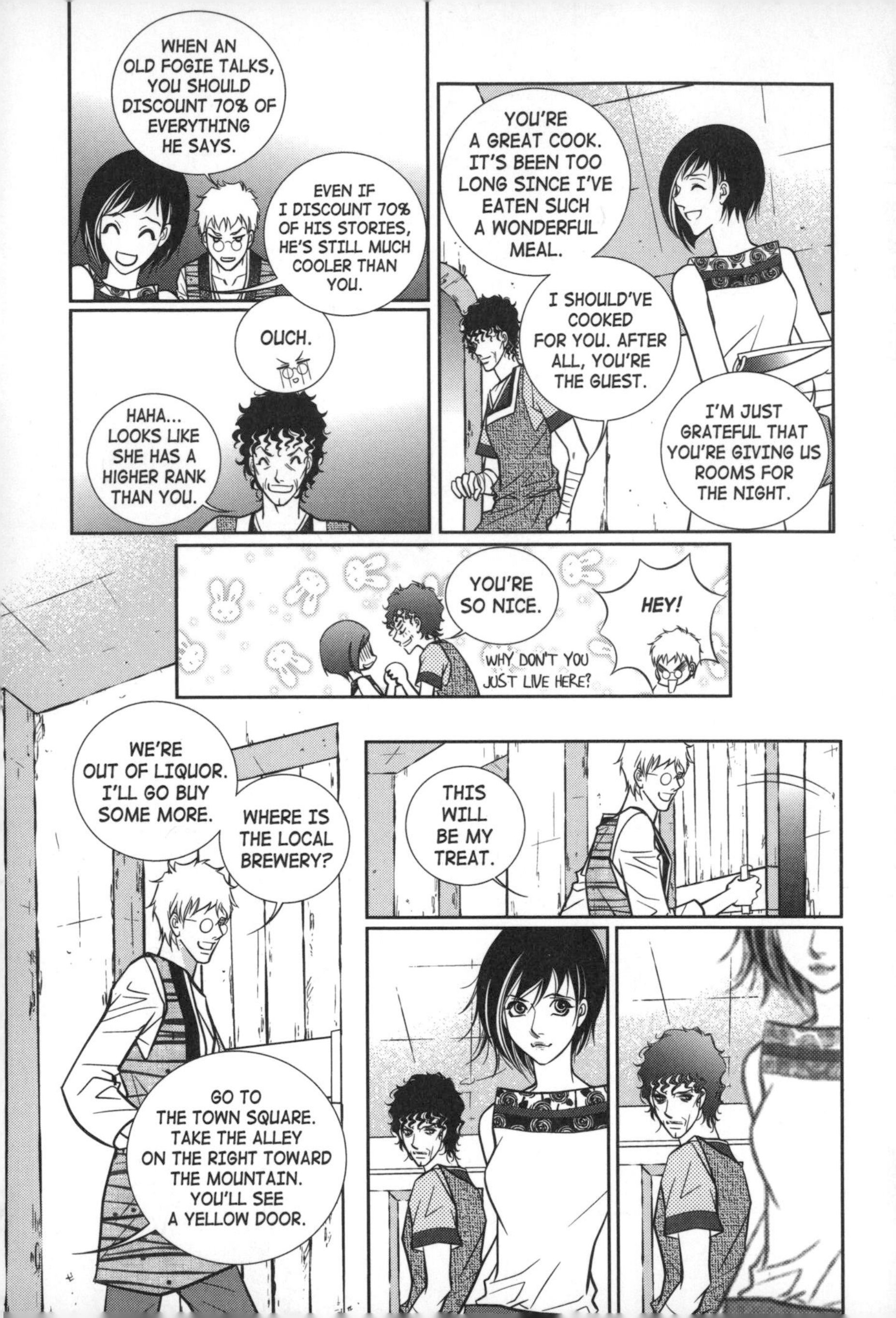
WHEN AN OLD FOGIE TALKS, YOU SHOULD DISCOUNT 70% OF EVERYTHING HE SAYS.
EVEN IF I DISCOUNT 70% OF HIS STORIES, HE'S STILL MUCH COOLER THAN YOU.
OUCH.
HAHA... LOOKS LIKE SHE HAS A HIGHER RANK THAN YOU.
YOU'RE A GREAT COOK. IT'S BEEN TOO LONG SINCE I'VE EATEN SUCH A WONDERFUL MEAL.
I SHOULD'VE COOKED FOR YOU. AFTER ALL, YOU'RE THE GUEST.
I'M JUST GRATEFUL THAT YOU'RE GIVING US ROOMS FOR THE NIGHT.
YOU'RE SO NICE.
HEY!
WHY DON'T YOU JUST LIVE HERE?
WE'RE OUT OF LIQUOR. I'LL GO BUY SOME MORE.
WHERE IS THE LOCAL BREWERY?
GO TO THE TOWN SQUARE. TAKE THE ALLEY ON THE RIGHT TOWARD THE MOUNTAIN. YOU'LL SEE A YELLOW DOOR.
THIS WILL BE MY TREAT.

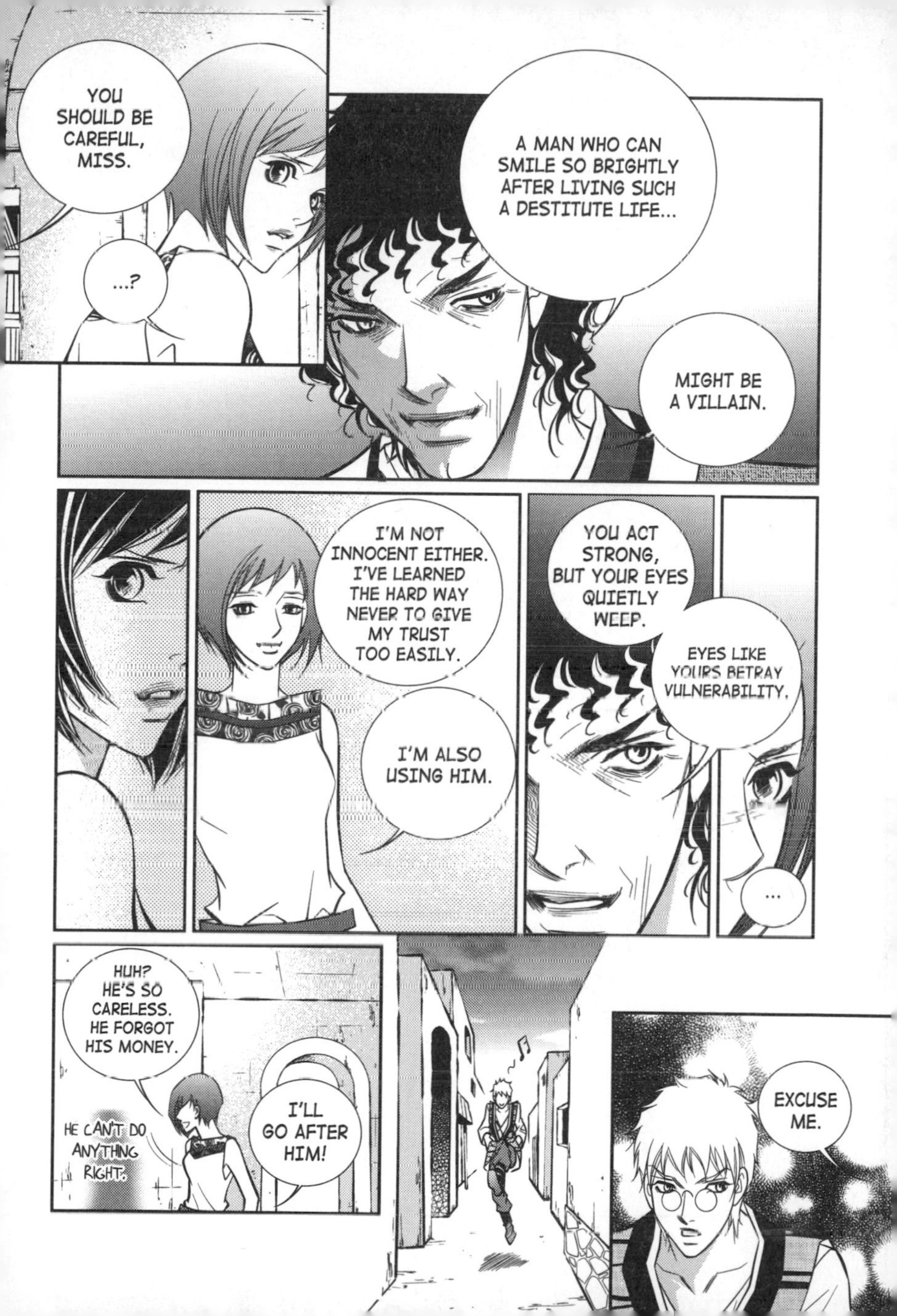
YOU SHOULD BE CAREFUL, MISS.
...?
A MAN WHO CAN SMILE SO BRIGHTLY AFTER LIVING SUCH A DESTITUTE LIFE...
MIGHT BE A VILLAIN.
I'M NOT INNOCENT EITHER. I'VE LEARNED THE HARD WAY NEVER TO GIVE MY TRUST TOO EASILY.
I'M ALSO USING HIM.
YOU ACT STRONG, BUT YOUR EYES QUIETLY WEEP.
EYES LIKE YOURS BETRAY VULNERABILITY.
...
HUH? HE'S SO CARELESS. HE FORGOT HIS MONEY.
HE CAN'T DO ANYTHING RIGHT.
I'LL GO AFTER HIM!
EXCUSE ME.

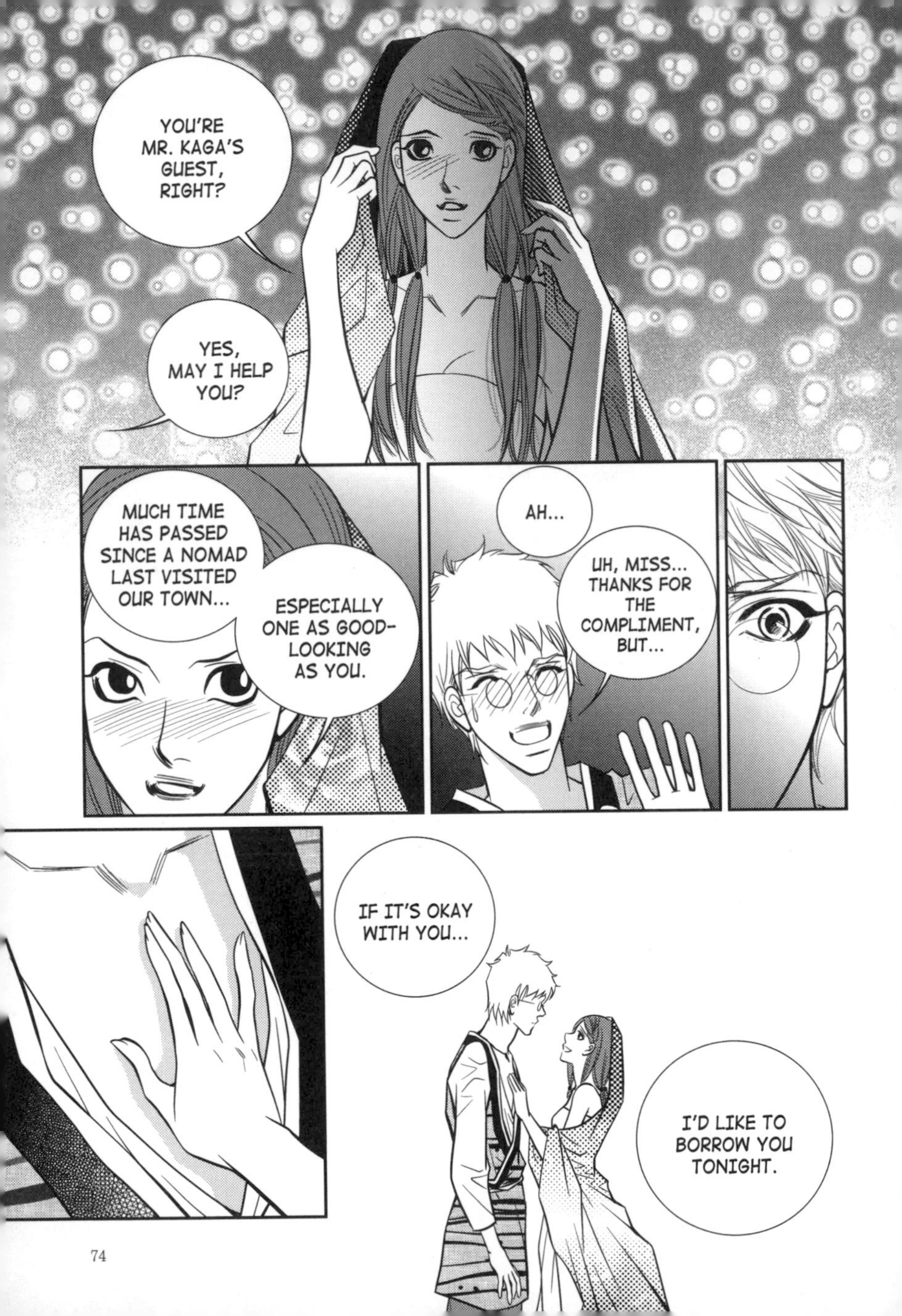
YOU'RE MR. KAGA'S GUEST, RIGHT?
YES, MAY I HELP YOU?
MUCH TIME HAS PASSED SINCE A NOMAD LAST VISITED OUR TOWN...
ESPECIALLY ONE AS GOOD-LOOKING AS YOU.
AH...
UH, MISS... THANKS FOR THE COMPLIMENT, BUT...
IF IT'S OKAY WITH YOU...
I'D LIKE TO BORROW YOU TONIGHT.

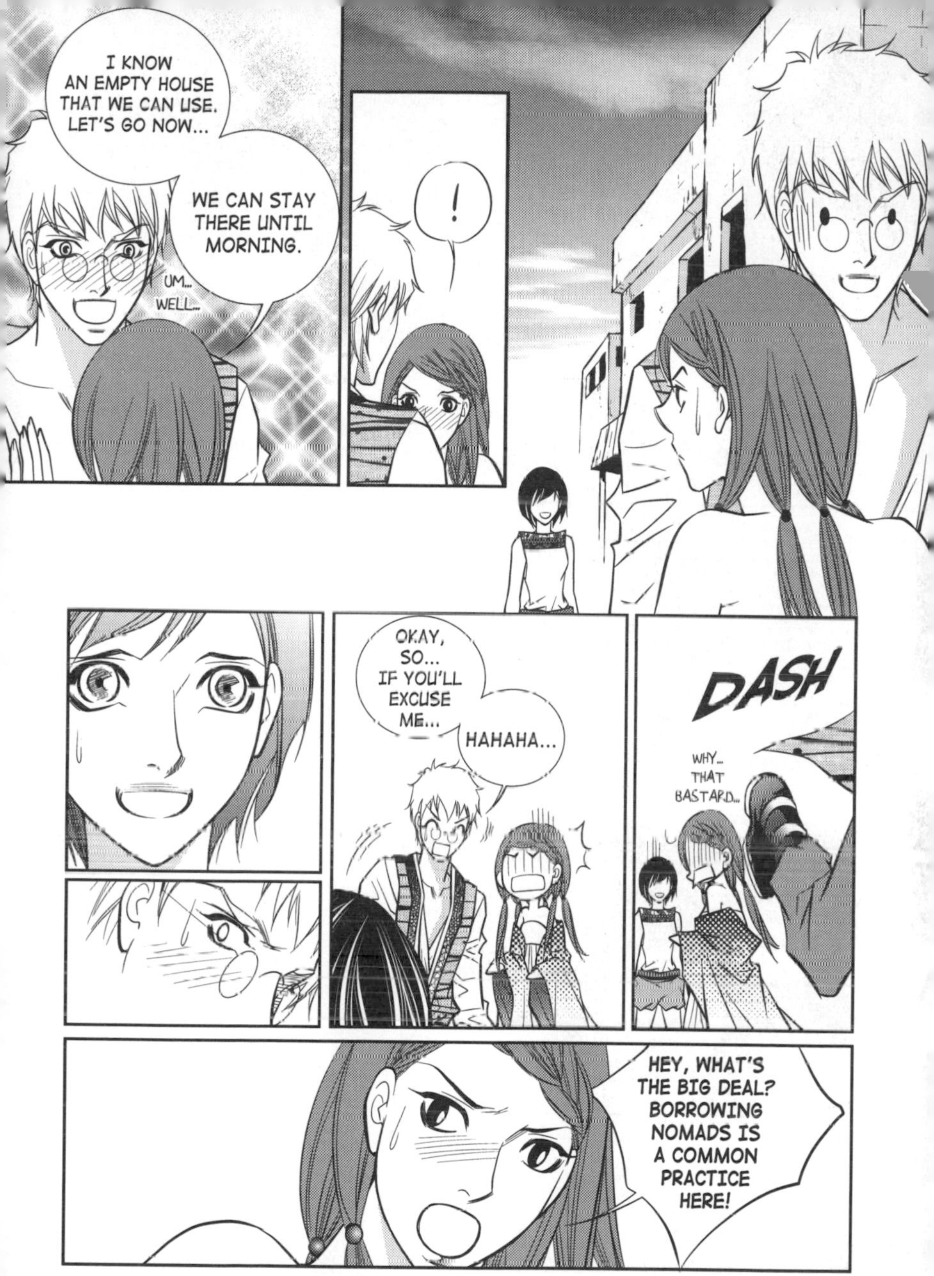

I KNOW AN EMPTY HOUSE THAT WE CAN USE. LET'S GO NOW...
WE CAN STAY THERE UNTIL MORNING.
UM... WELL...
!
OKAY, SO... IF YOU'LL EXCUSE ME...
HAHAHA...
DASH
WHY... THAT BASTARD...
HEY, WHAT'S THE BIG DEAL? BORROWING NOMADS IS A COMMON PRACTICE HERE!

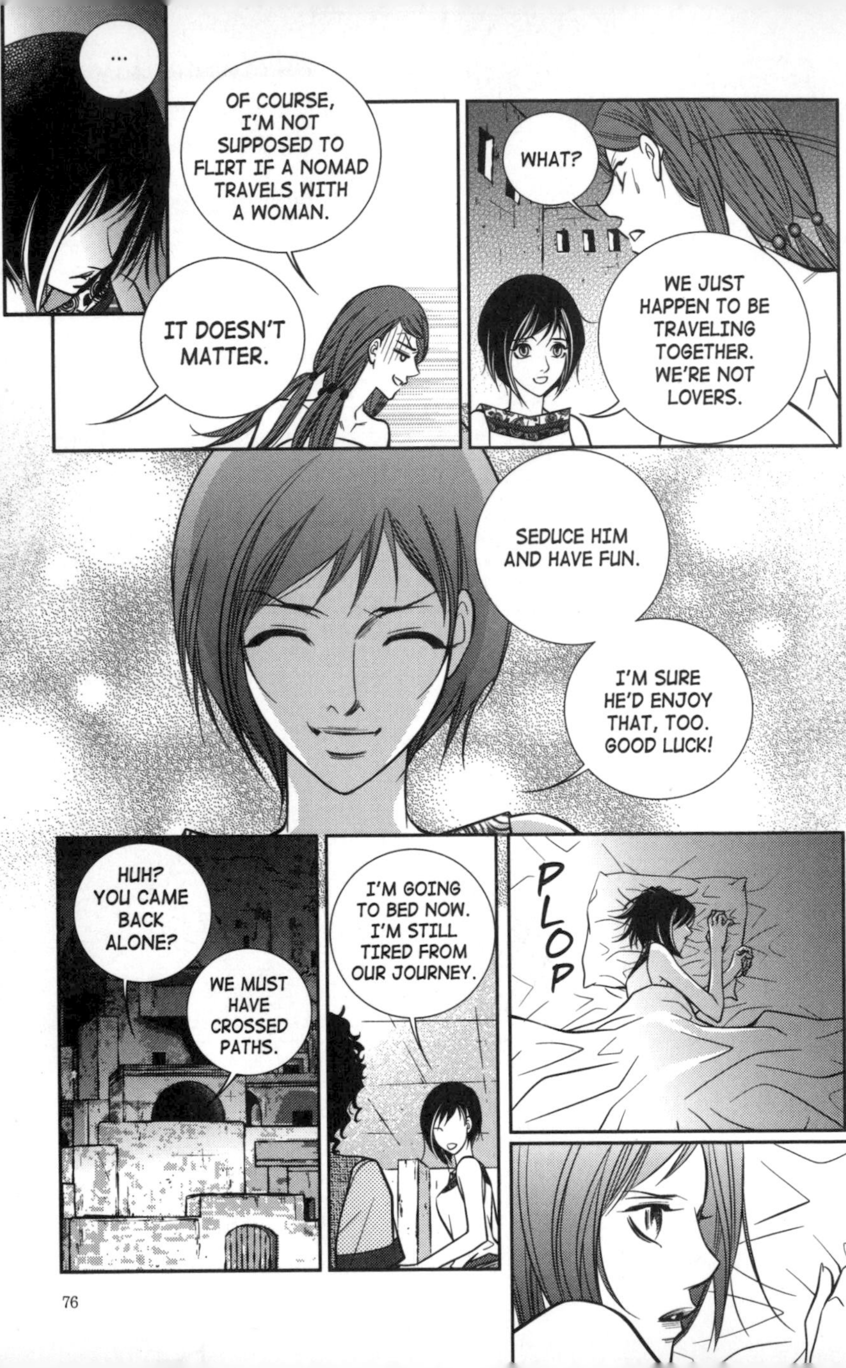
...
OF COURSE, I'M NOT SUPPOSED TO FLIRT IF A NOMAD TRAVELS WITH A WOMAN.
IT DOESN'T MATTER.
WHAT?
WE JUST HAPPEN TO BE TRAVELING TOGETHER. WE'RE NOT LOVERS.
SEDUCE HIM AND HAVE FUN.
I'M SURE HE'D ENJOY THAT, TOO. GOOD LUCK!
HUH? YOU CAME BACK ALONE?
WE MUST HAVE CROSSED PATHS.
I'M GOING TO BED NOW. I'M STILL TIRED FROM OUR JOURNEY.
PLOP

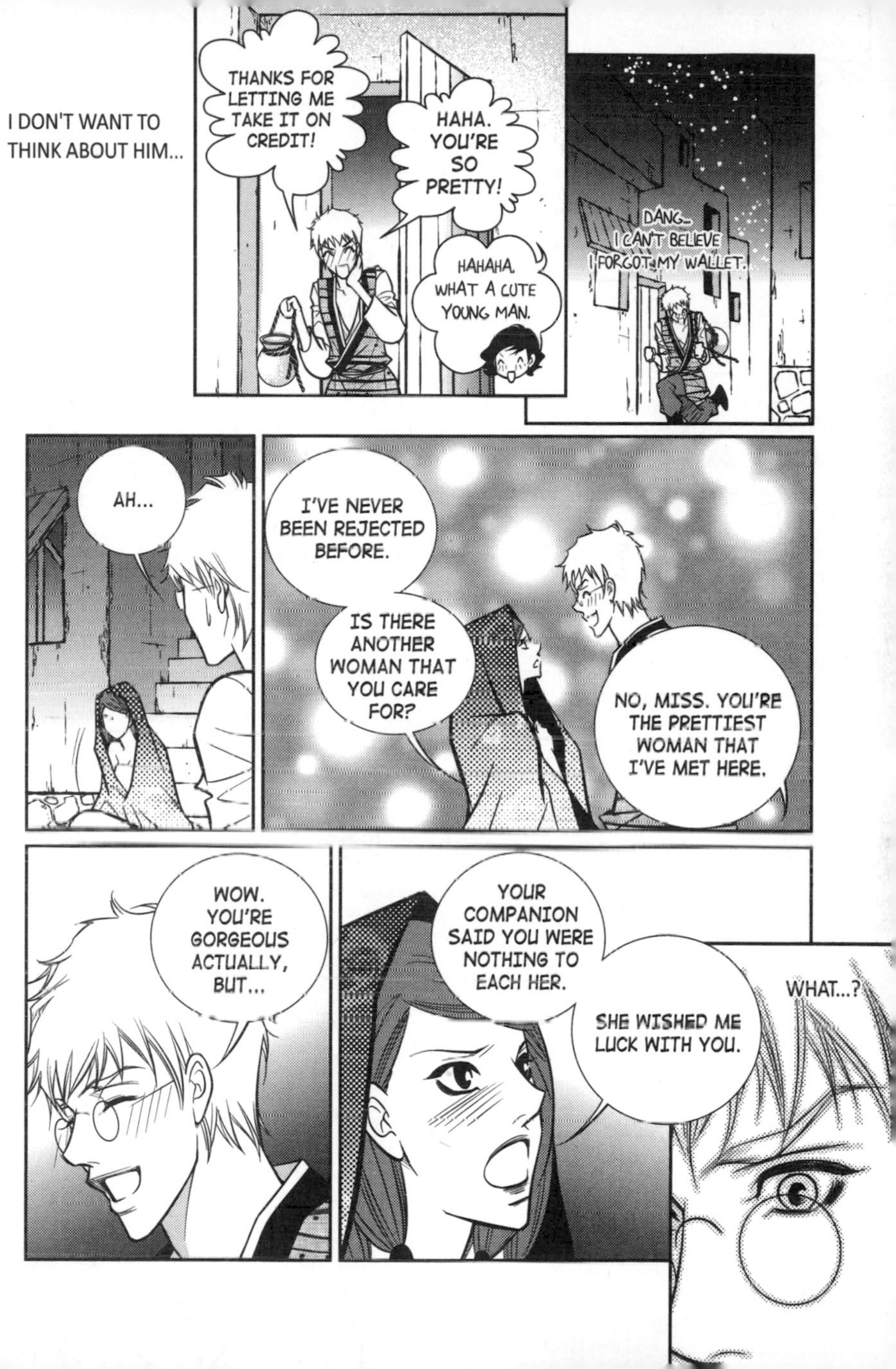
I DON'T WANT TO THINK ABOUT HIM...
THANKS FOR LETTING ME TAKE IT ON CREDIT!
HAHA. YOU'RE SO PRETTY!
HAHAHA. WHAT A CUTE YOUNG MAN.
DANG... I CAN'T BELIEVE I FORGOT MY WALLET.
AH...
I'VE NEVER BEEN REJECTED BEFORE.
IS THERE ANOTHER WOMAN THAT YOU CARE FOR?
NO, MISS. YOU'RE THE PRETTIEST WOMAN THAT I'VE MET HERE.
WOW. YOU'RE GORGEOUS ACTUALLY, BUT...
YOUR COMPANION SAID YOU WERE NOTHING TO EACH HER.
SHE WISHED ME LUCK WITH YOU.
WHAT...?

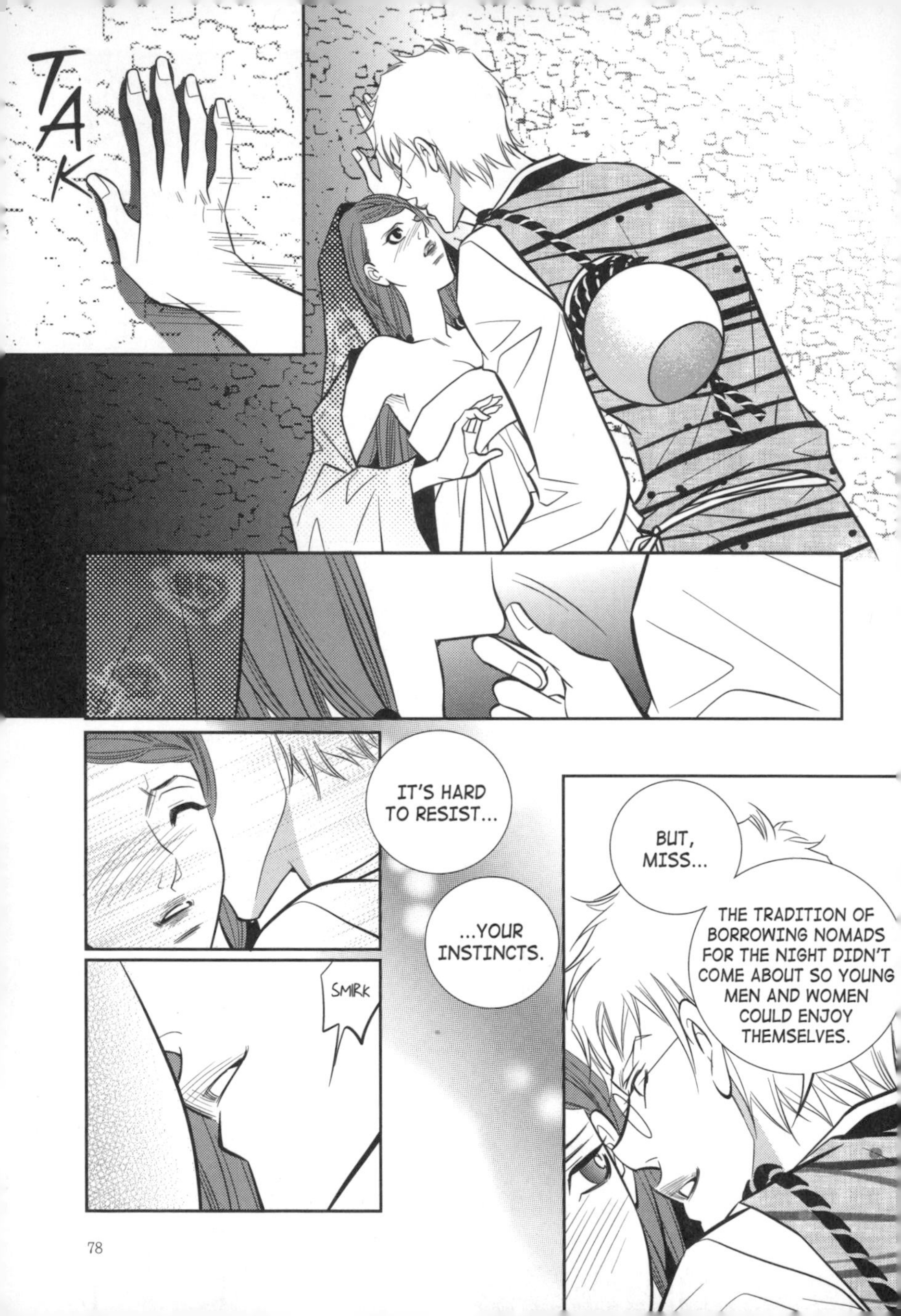
TAK
IT'S HARD TO RESIST...
...YOUR INSTINCTS.
SMIRK
BUT, MISS...
THE TRADITION OF BORROWING NOMADS FOR THE NIGHT DIDN'T COME ABOUT SO YOUNG MEN AND WOMEN COULD ENJOY THEMSELVES.

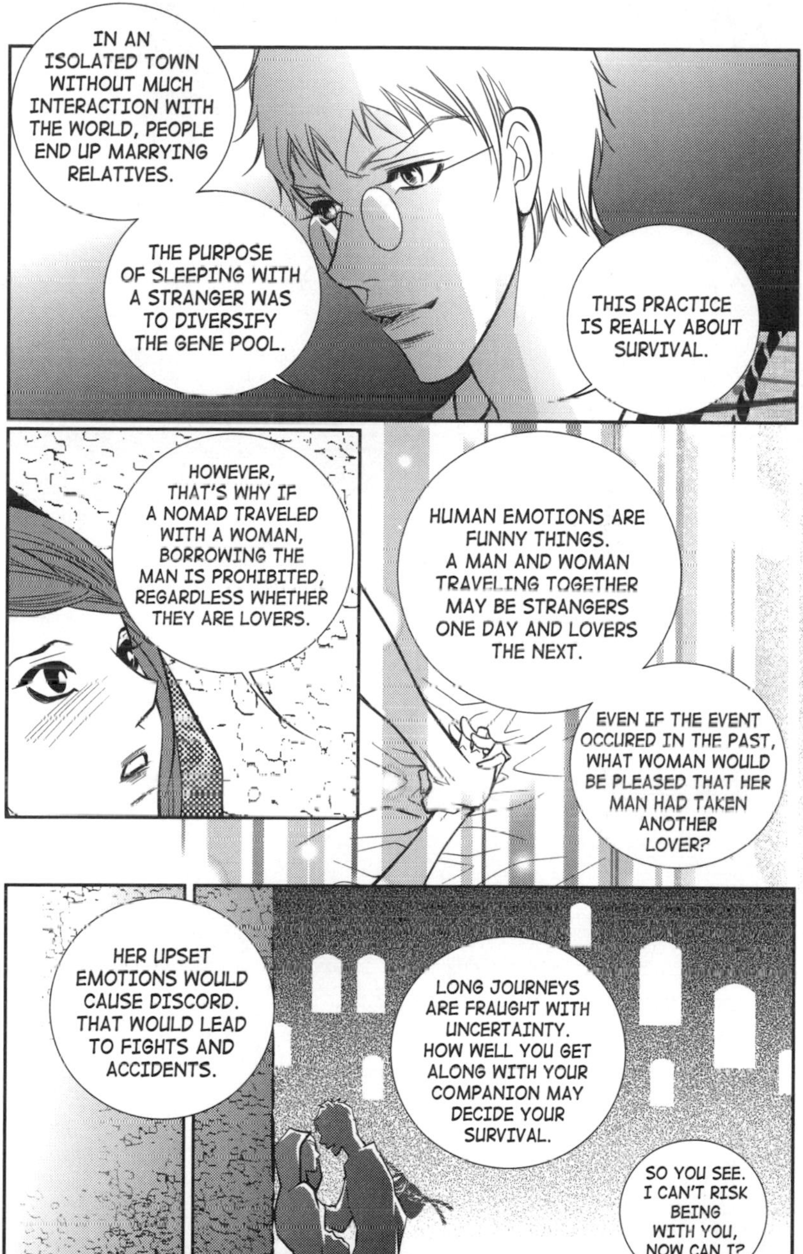
IN AN ISOLATED TOWN WITHOUT MUCH INTERACTION WITH THE WORLD, PEOPLE END UP MARRYING RELATIVES.
THE PURPOSE OF SLEEPING WITH A STRANGER WAS TO DIVERSIFY THE GENE POOL.
THIS PRACTICE IS REALLY ABOUT SURVIVAL.
HOWEVER, THAT'S WHY IF A NOMAD TRAVELED WITH A WOMAN, BORROWING THE MAN IS PROHIBITED, REGARDLESS WHETHER THEY ARE LOVERS.
HUMAN EMOTIONS ARE FUNNY THINGS. A MAN AND WOMAN TRAVELING TOGETHER MAY BE STRANGERS ONE DAY AND LOVERS THE NEXT.
EVEN IF THE EVENT OCCURED IN THE PAST, WHAT WOMAN WOULD BE PLEASED THAT HER MAN HAD TAKEN ANOTHER LOVER?
HER UPSET EMOTIONS WOULD CAUSE DISCORD. THAT WOULD LEAD TO FIGHTS AND ACCIDENTS.
LONG JOURNEYS ARE FRAUGHT WITH UNCERTAINTY. HOW WELL YOU GET ALONG WITH YOUR COMPANION MAY DECIDE YOUR SURVIVAL.
SO YOU SEE. I CAN'T RISK BEING WITH YOU, NOW CAN I?

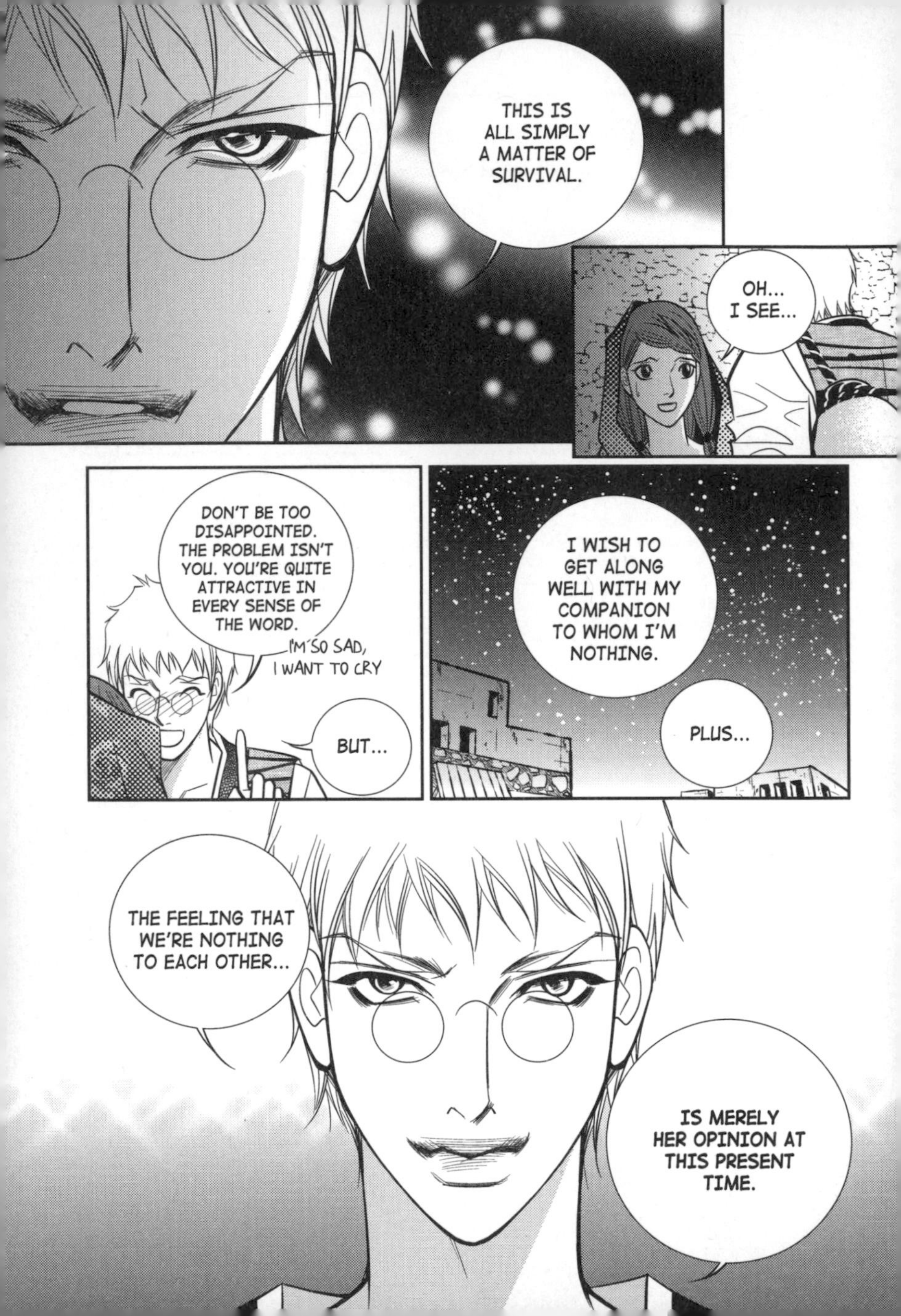
THIS IS ALL SIMPLY A MATTER OF SURVIVAL.
OH... I SEE...
DON'T BE TOO DISAPPOINTED. THE PROBLEM ISN'T YOU. YOU'RE QUITE ATTRACTIVE IN EVERY SENSE OF THE WORD.
I'M SO SAD, I WANT TO CRY
BUT...
I WISH TO GET ALONG WELL WITH MY COMPANION TO WHOM I'M NOTHING.
PLUS...
THE FEELING THAT WE'RE NOTHING TO EACH OTHER...
IS MERELY HER OPINION AT THIS PRESENT TIME.

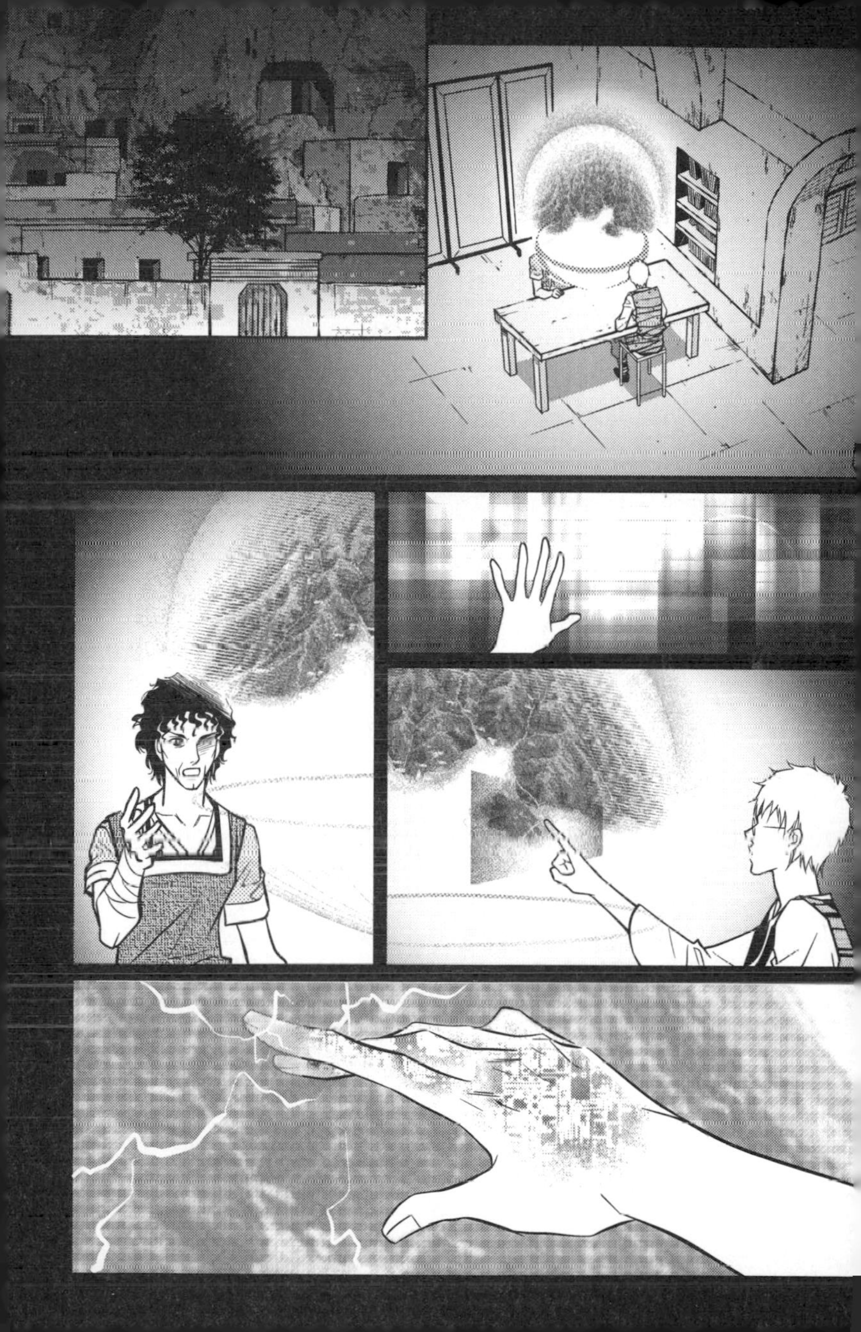

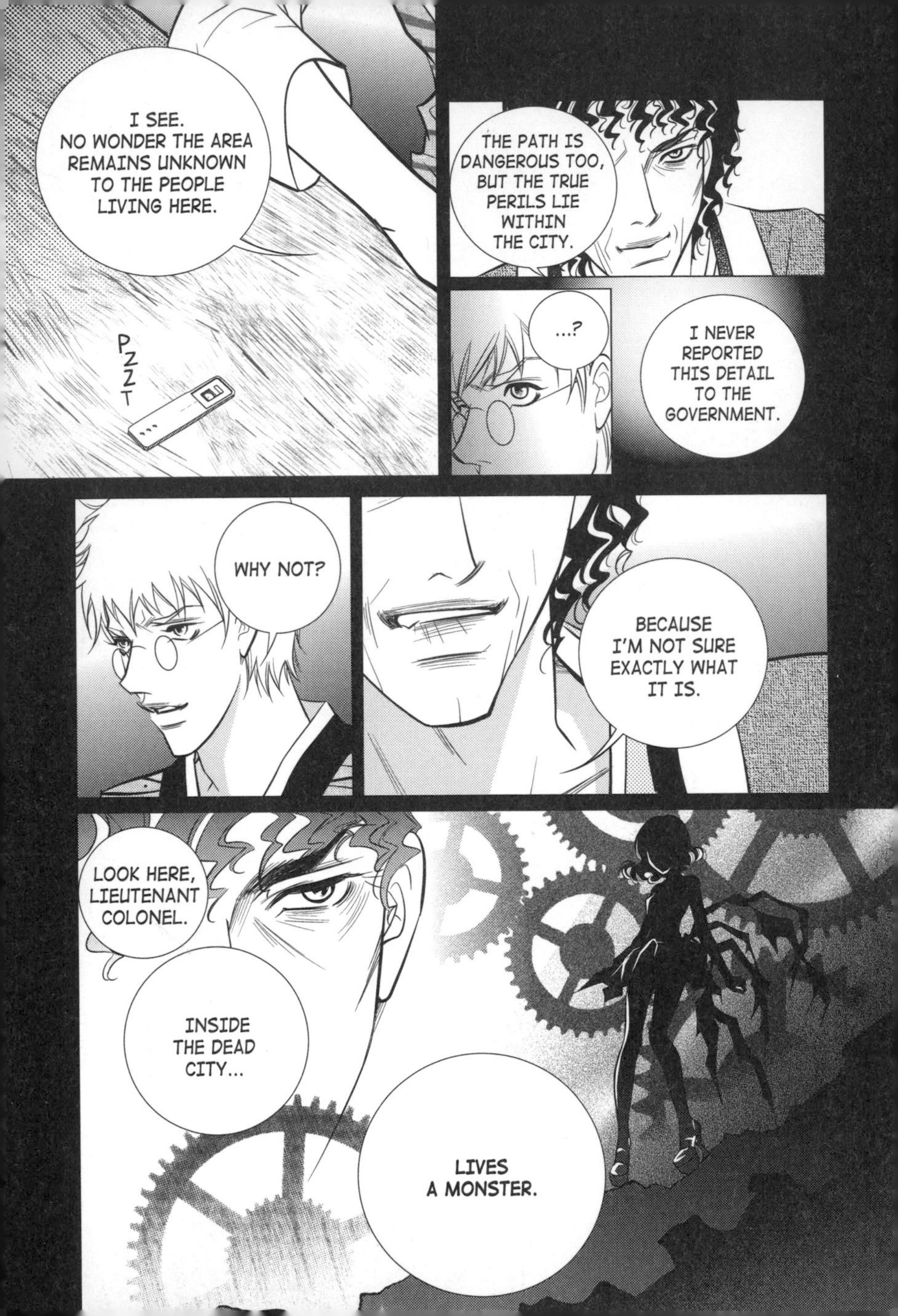
I SEE. NO WONDER THE AREA REMAINS UNKNOWN TO THE PEOPLE LIVING HERE.
PZZT
THE PATH IS DANGEROUS TOO, BUT THE TRUE PERILS LIE WITHIN THE CITY.
...?
I NEVER REPORTED THIS DETAIL TO THE GOVERNMENT.
WHY NOT?
BECAUSE I'M NOT SURE EXACTLY WHAT IT IS.
LOOK HERE, LIEUTENANT COLONEL.
INSIDE THE DEAD CITY...
LIVES A MONSTER.

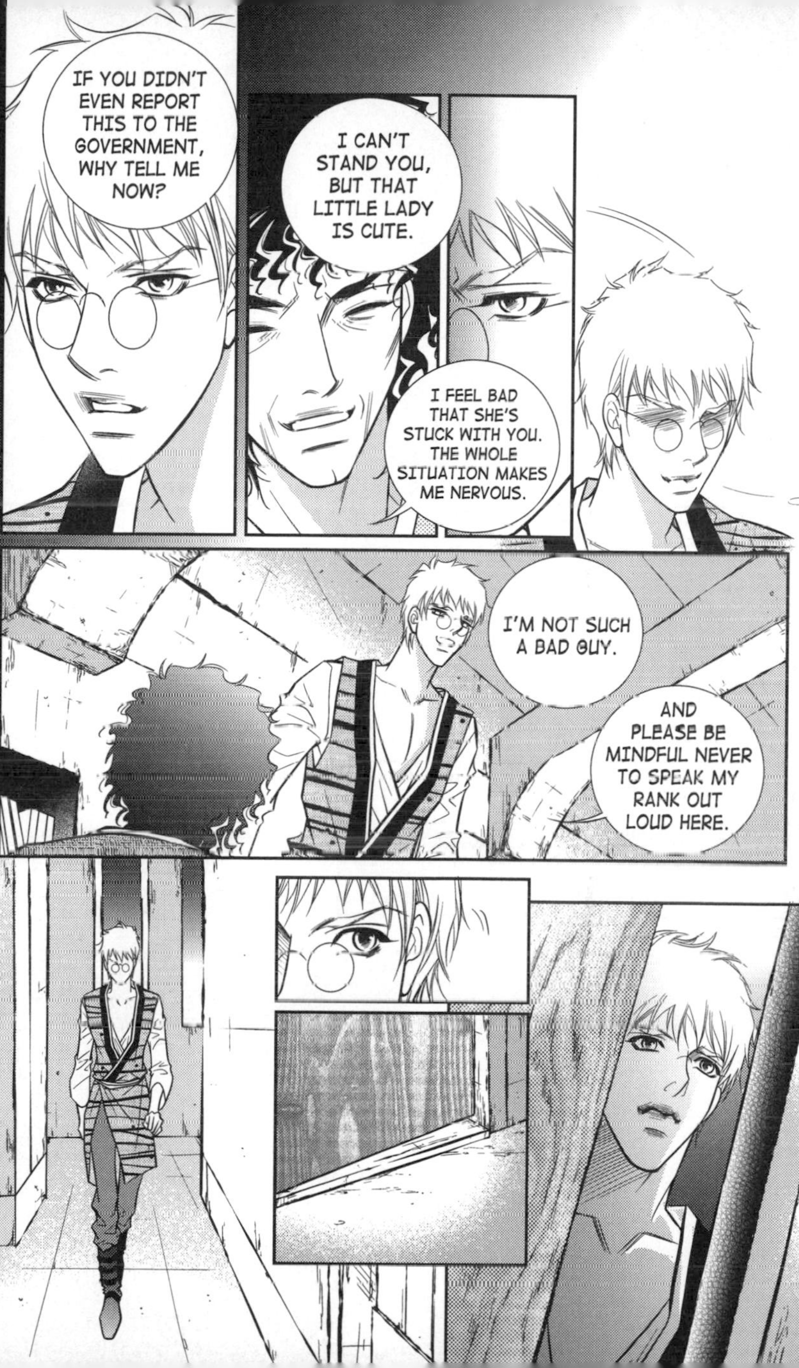
IF YOU DIDN'T EVEN REPORT THIS TO THE GOVERNMENT, WHY TELL ME NOW?
I CAN'T STAND YOU, BUT THAT LITTLE LADY IS CUTE.
I FEEL BAD THAT SHE'S STUCK WITH YOU. THE WHOLE SITUATION MAKES ME NERVOUS.
I'M NOT SUCH A BAD GUY.
AND PLEASE BE MINDFUL NEVER TO SPEAK MY RANK OUT LOUD HERE.

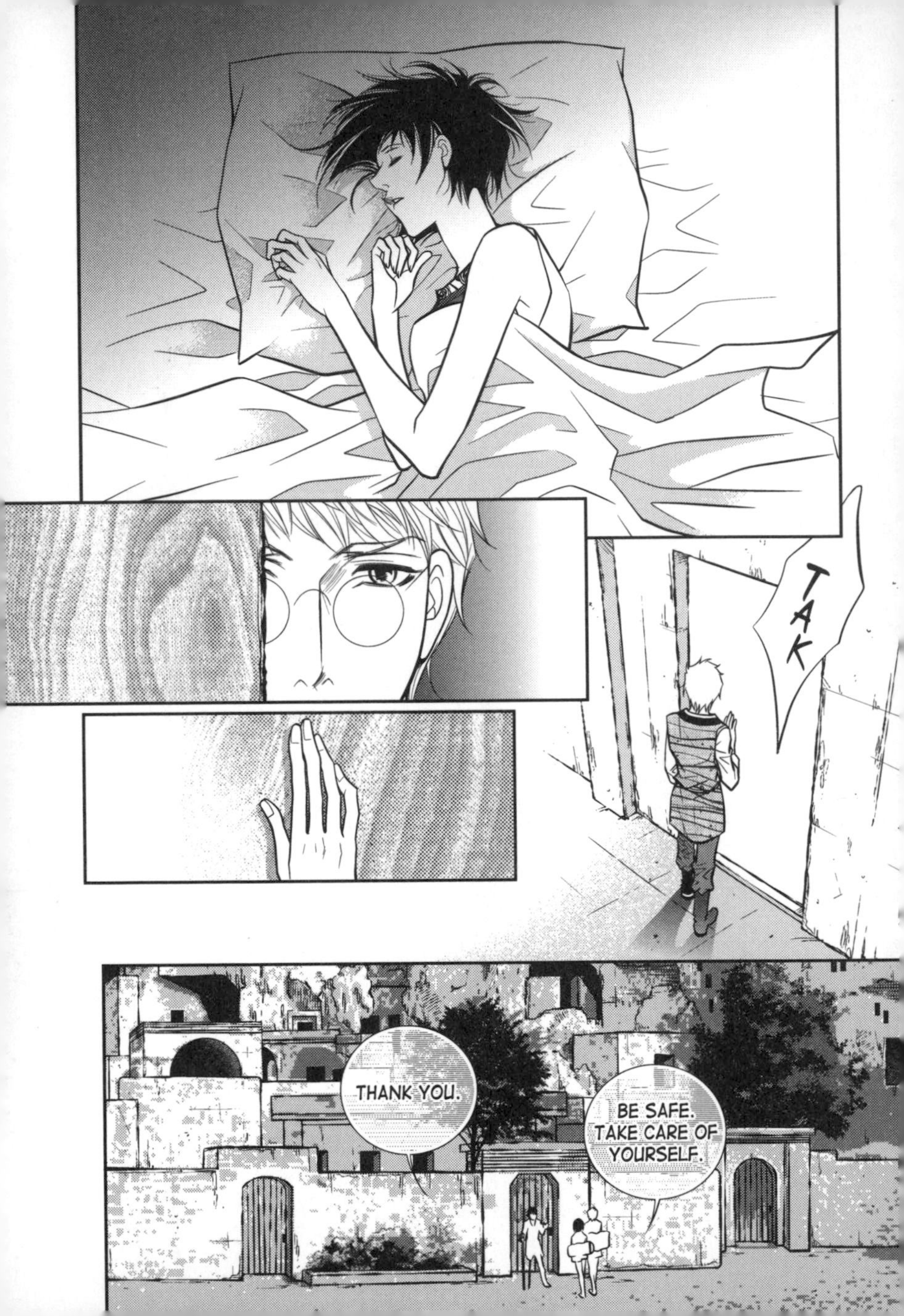
TAK
THANK YOU.
BE SAFE. TAKE CARE OF YOURSELF.

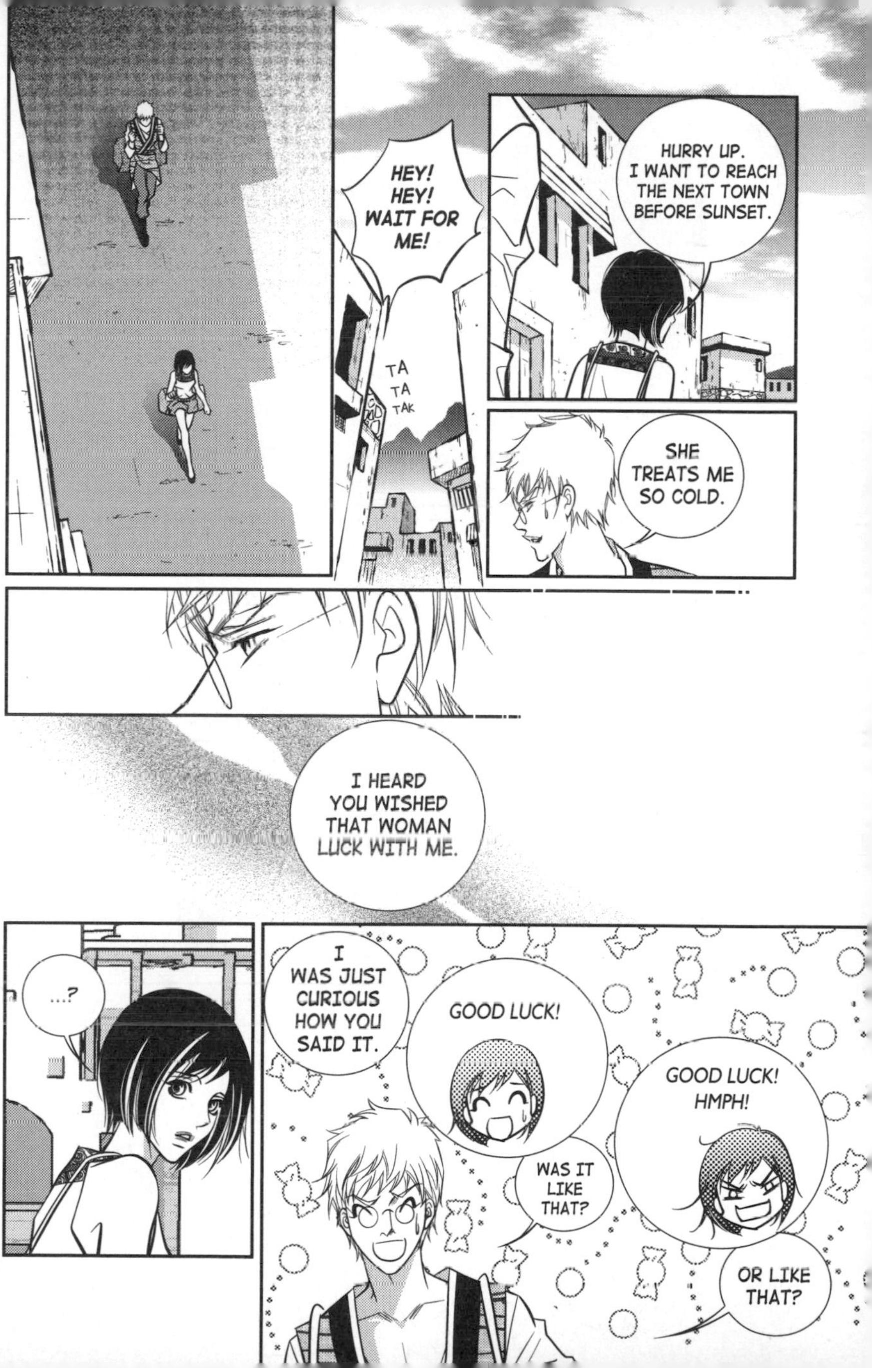
HEY! HEY! WAIT FOR ME!
TA TA TAK
HURRY UP. I WANT TO REACH THE NEXT TOWN BEFORE SUNSET.
SHE TREATS ME SO COLD.
I HEARD YOU WISHED THAT WOMAN LUCK WITH ME.
...?
I WAS JUST CURIOUS HOW YOU SAID IT.
GOOD LUCK!
WAS IT LIKE THAT?
GOOD LUCK! HMPH!
OR LIKE THAT?

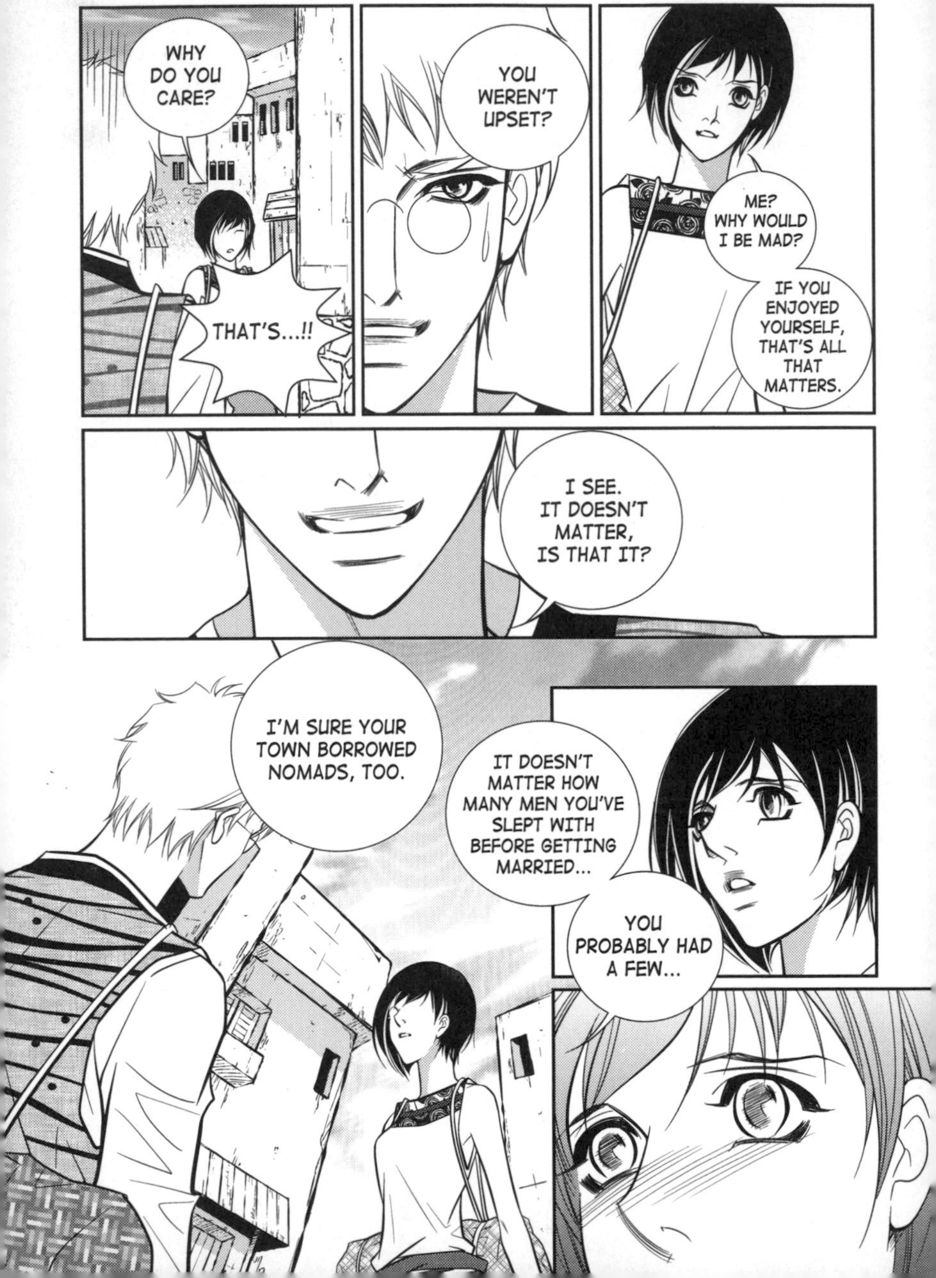
WHY DO YOU CARE?
THAT'S...!!
YOU WEREN'T UPSET?
ME? WHY WOULD I BE MAD?
IF YOU ENJOYED YOURSELF, THAT'S ALL THAT MATTERS.
I SEE. IT DOESN'T MATTER, IS THAT IT?
I'M SURE YOUR TOWN BORROWED NOMADS, TOO.
IT DOESN'T MATTER HOW MANY MEN YOU'VE SLEPT WITH BEFORE GETTING MARRIED...
YOU PROBABLY HAD A FEW...

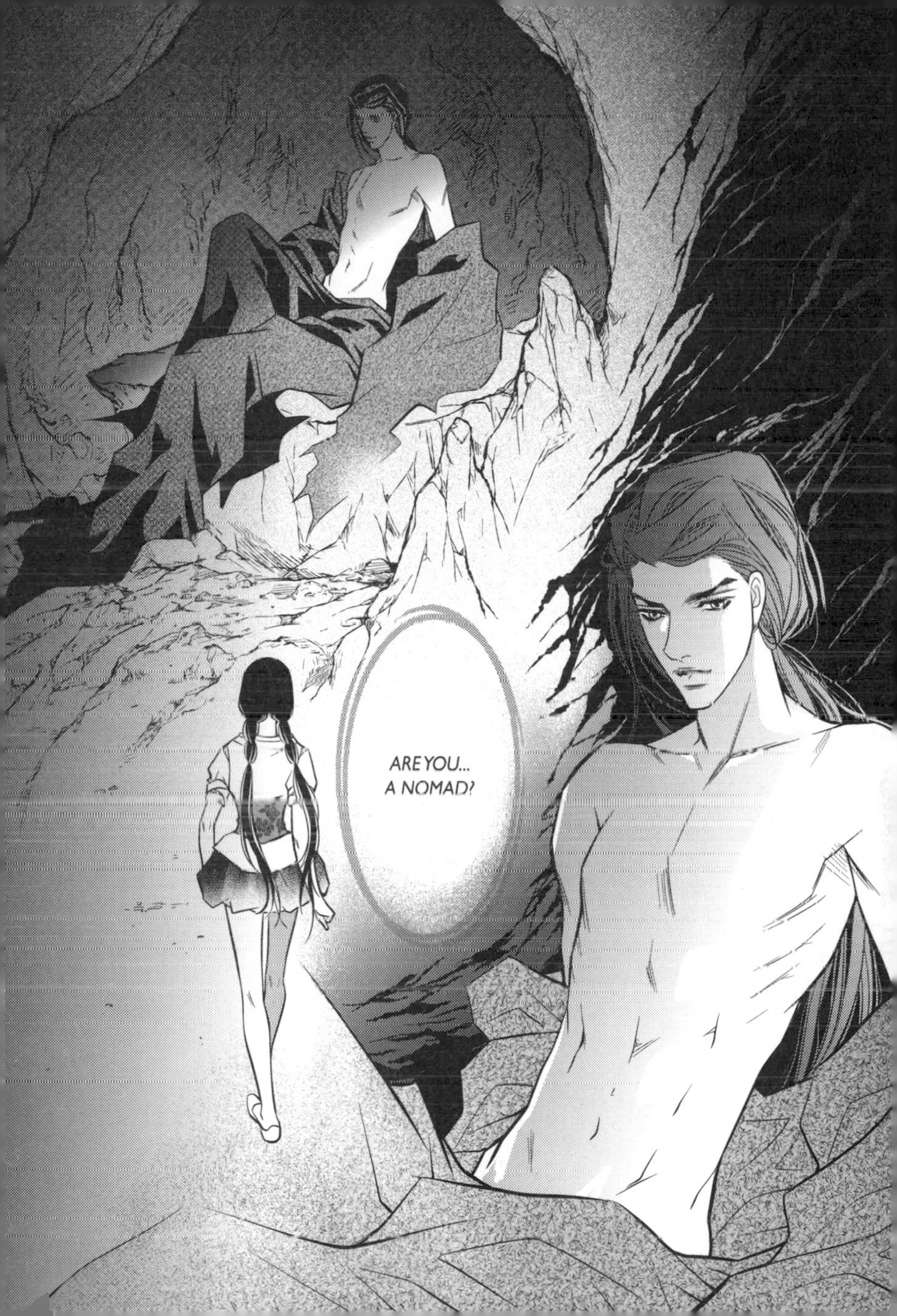
ARE YOU... A NOMAD?

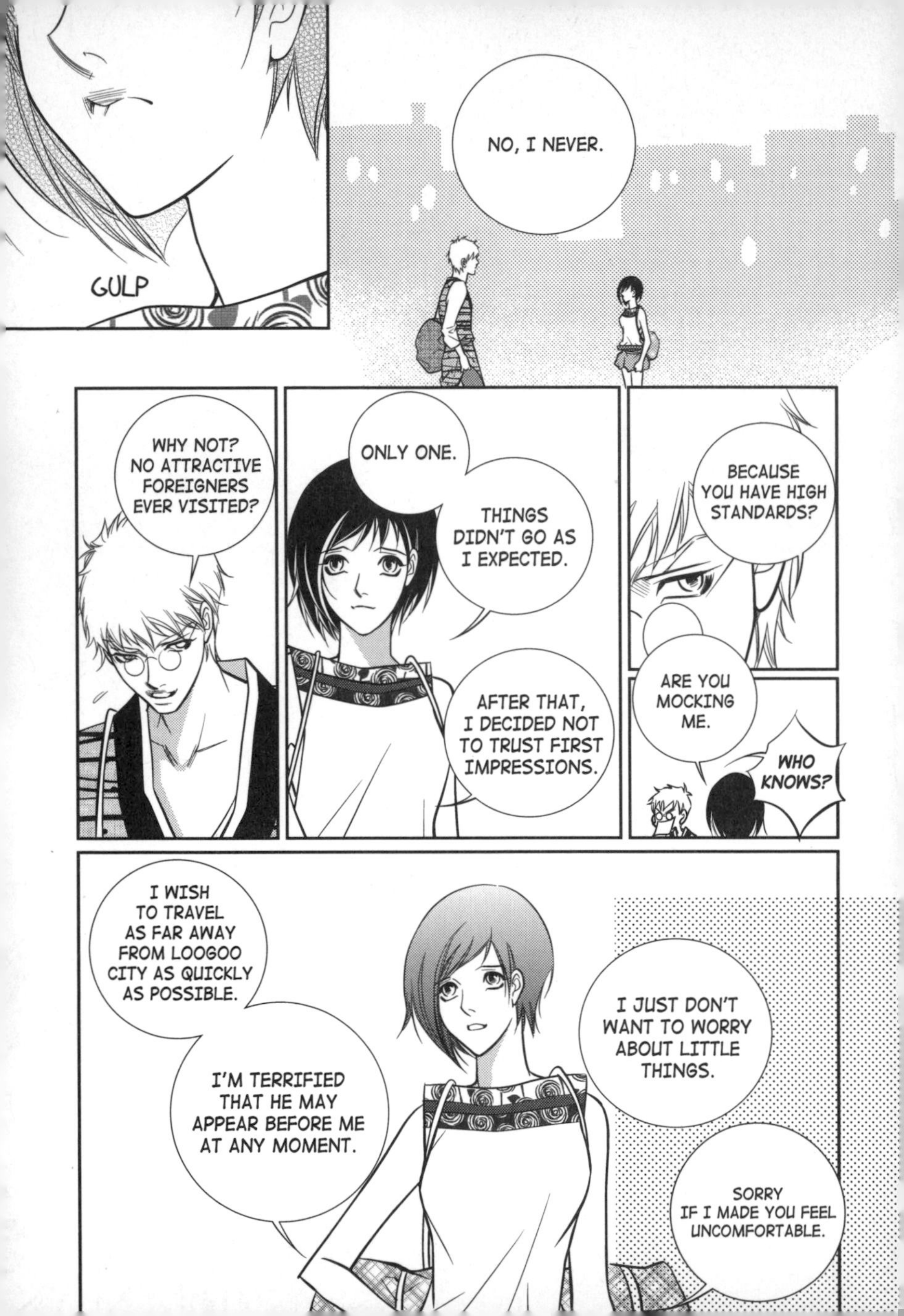
GULP
NO, I NEVER.
WHY NOT? NO ATTRACTIVE FOREIGNERS EVER VISITED?
ONLY ONE.
THINGS DIDN'T GO AS I EXPECTED.
AFTER THAT, I DECIDED NOT TO TRUST FIRST IMPRESSIONS.
BECAUSE YOU HAVE HIGH STANDARDS?
ARE YOU MOCKING ME.
WHO KNOWS?
I WISH TO TRAVEL AS FAR AWAY FROM LOOGOO CITY AS QUICKLY AS POSSIBLE.
I'M TERRIFIED THAT HE MAY APPEAR BEFORE ME AT ANY MOMENT.
I JUST DON'T WANT TO WORRY ABOUT LITTLE THINGS.
SORRY IF I MADE YOU FEEL UNCOMFORTABLE.

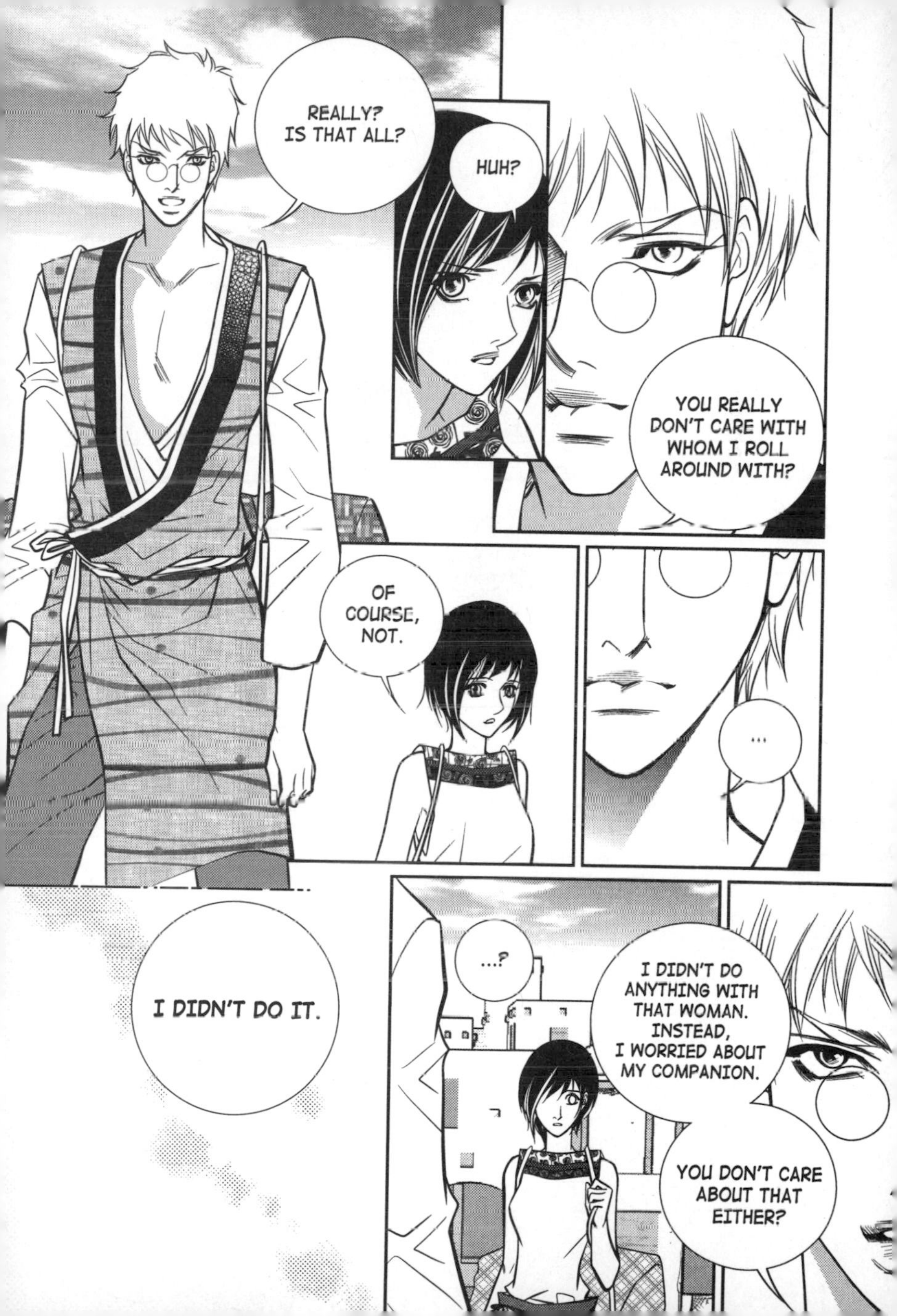
REALLY? IS THAT ALL?
HUH?
YOU REALLY DON'T CARE WITH WHOM I ROLL AROUND WITH?
OF COURSE, NOT.
...
I DIDN'T DO IT.
...?
I DIDN'T DO ANYTHING WITH THAT WOMAN. INSTEAD, I WORRIED ABOUT MY COMPANION.
YOU DON'T CARE ABOUT THAT EITHER?

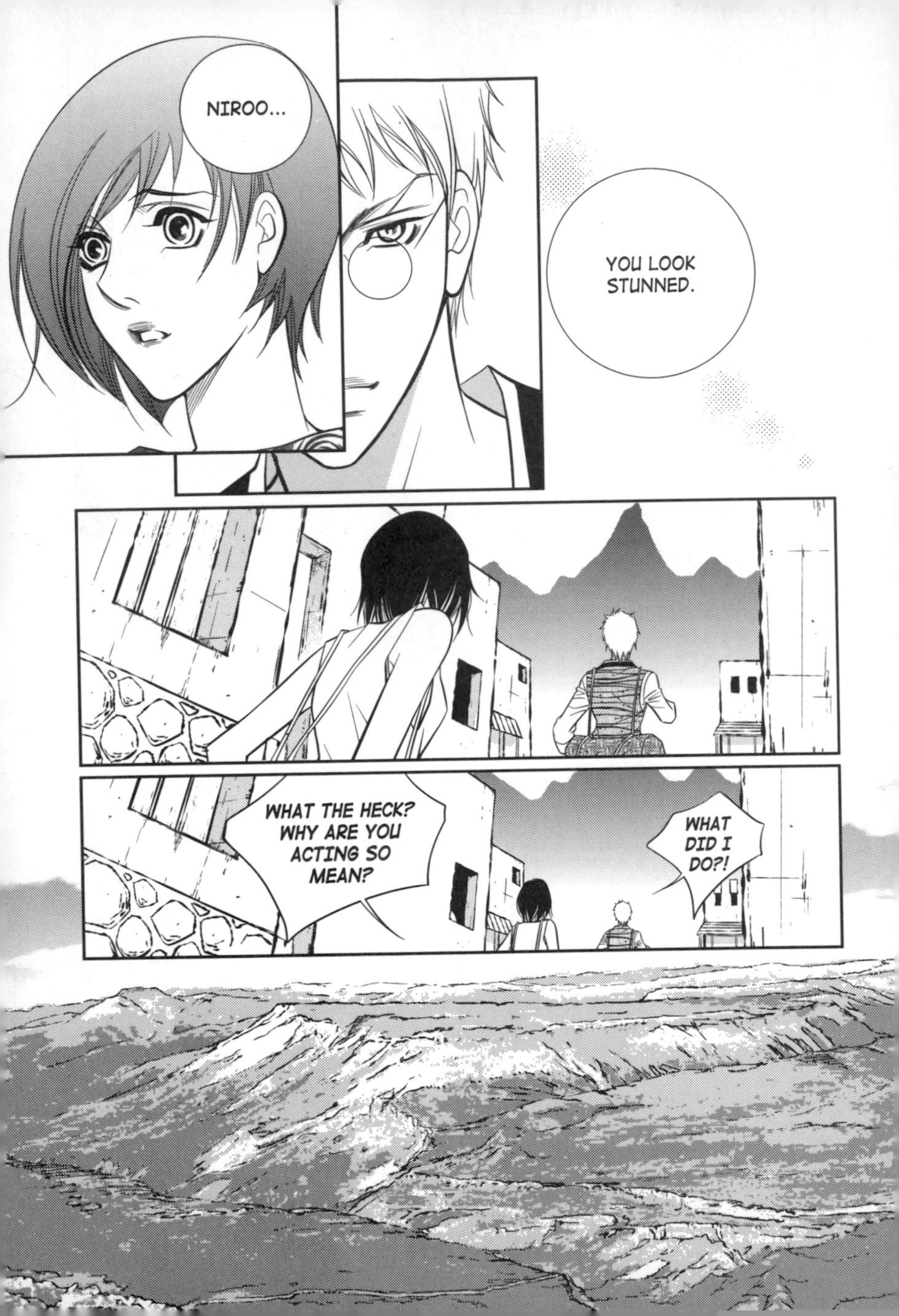
NIROO...
YOU LOOK STUNNED.
WHAT THE HECK? WHY ARE YOU ACTING SO MEAN?
WHAT DID I DO?!

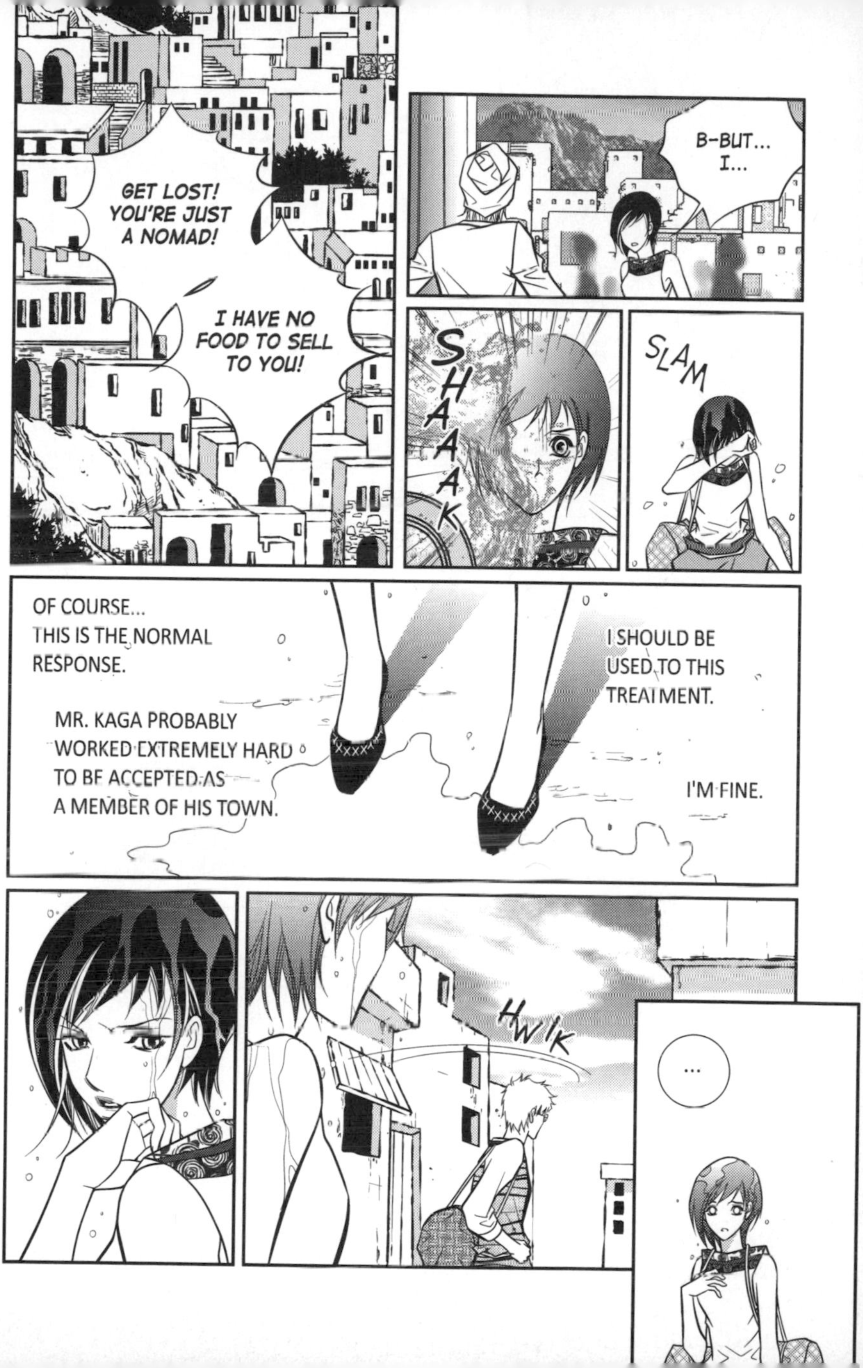
GET LOST! YOU'RE JUST A NOMAD!
I HAVE NO FOOD TO SELL TO YOU!
B-BUT... I...
SHAAAAK
SLAM
OF COURSE... THIS IS THE NORMAL RESPONSE.
MR. KAGA PROBABLY WORKED EXTREMELY HARD TO BE ACCEPTED AS A MEMBER OF HIS TOWN.
I SHOULD BE USED TO THIS TREATMENT.
I'M FINE.
HWIK
...

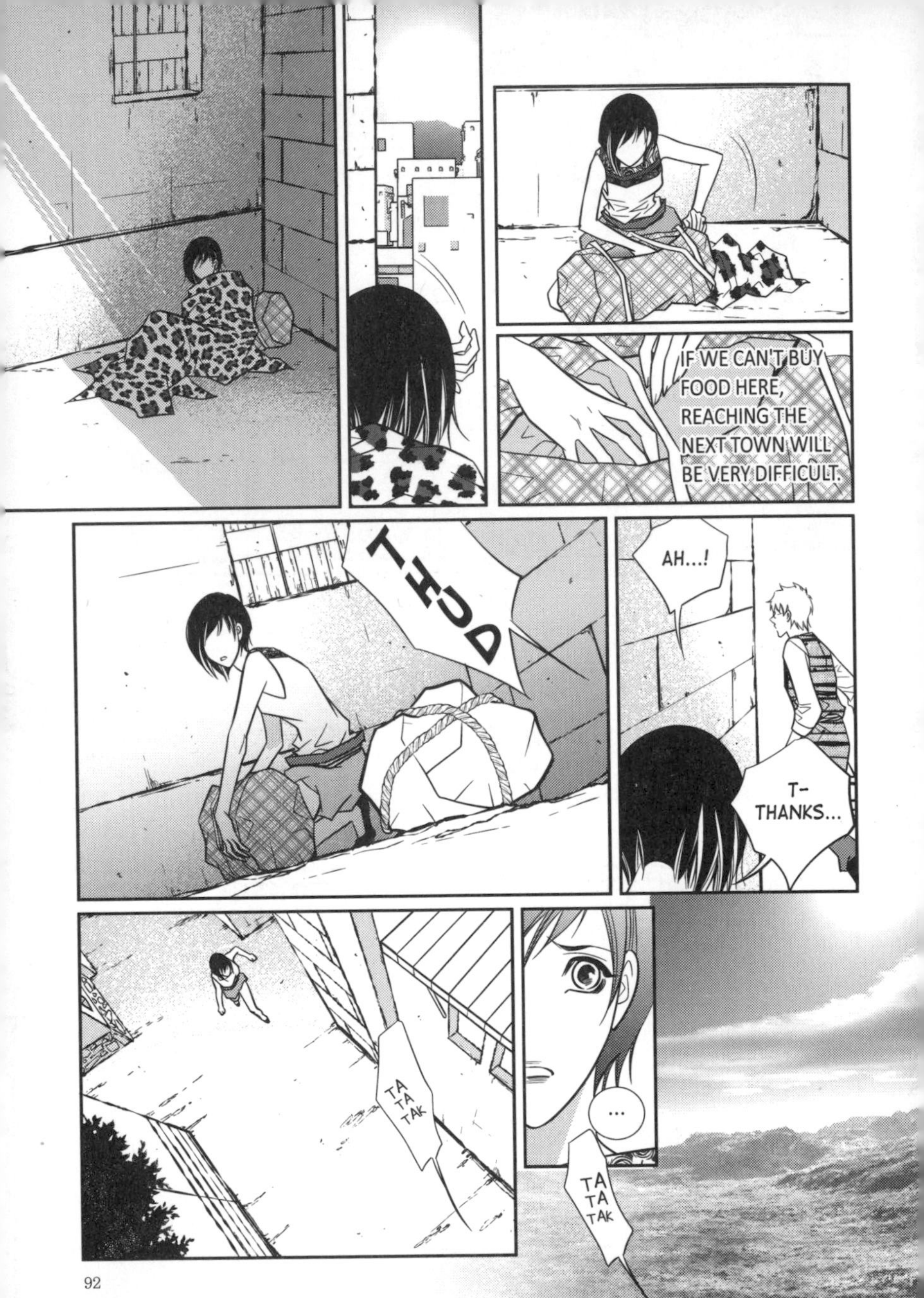
IF WE CAN'T BUY FOOD HERE, REACHING THE NEXT TOWN WILL BE VERY DIFFICULT.
THUD
AH...!
T-THANKS...
TA TA TAK
...
TA TA TAK

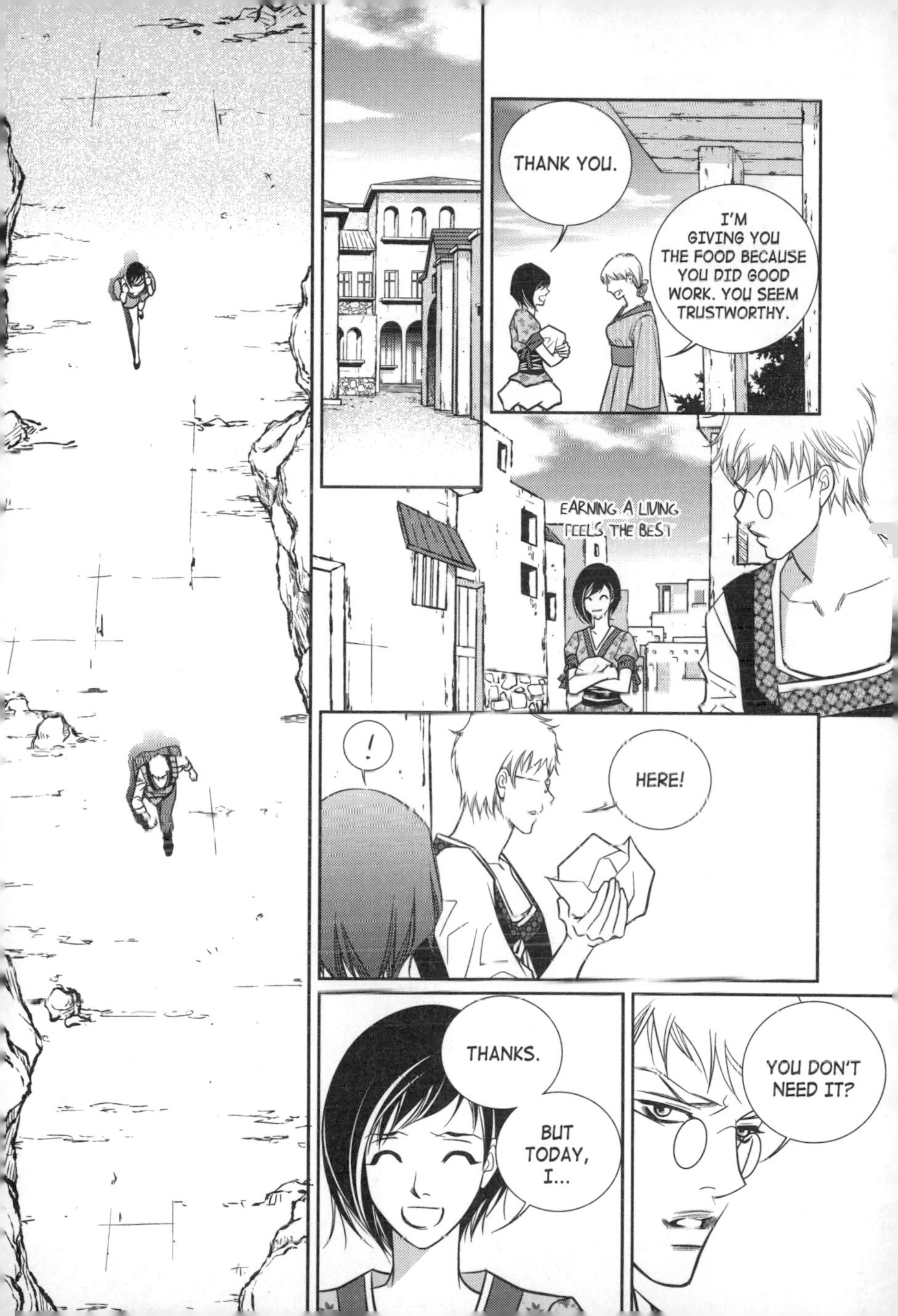
THANK YOU.
I'M GIVING YOU THE FOOD BECAUSE YOU DID GOOD WORK. YOU SEEM TRUSTWORTHY.
EARNING A LIVING FEELS THE BEST
!
HERE!
THANKS.
BUT TODAY, I...
YOU DON'T NEED IT?

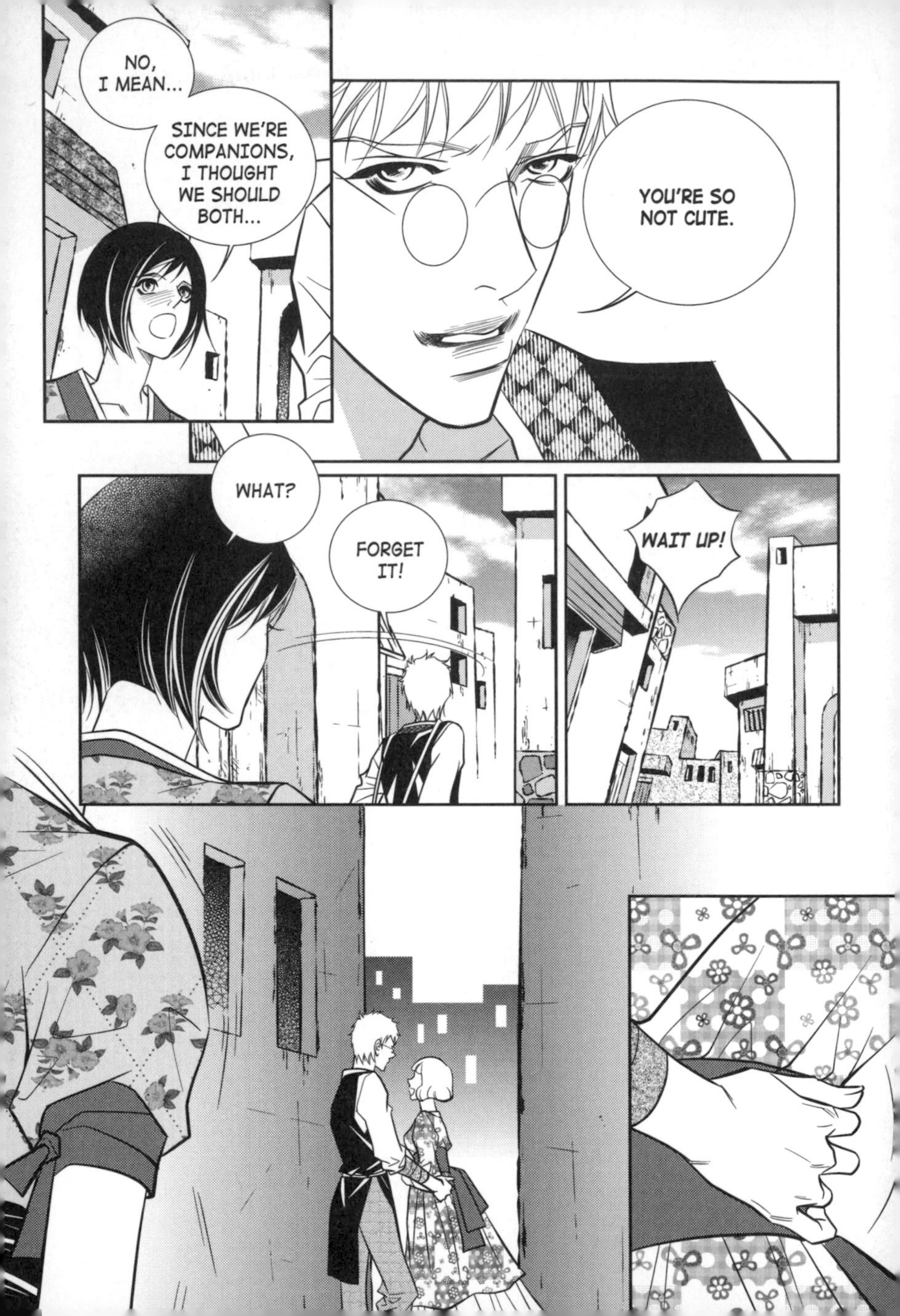
NO, I MEAN...
SINCE WE'RE COMPANIONS, I THOUGHT WE SHOULD BOTH...
YOU'RE SO NOT CUTE.
WHAT?
FORGET IT!
WAIT UP!

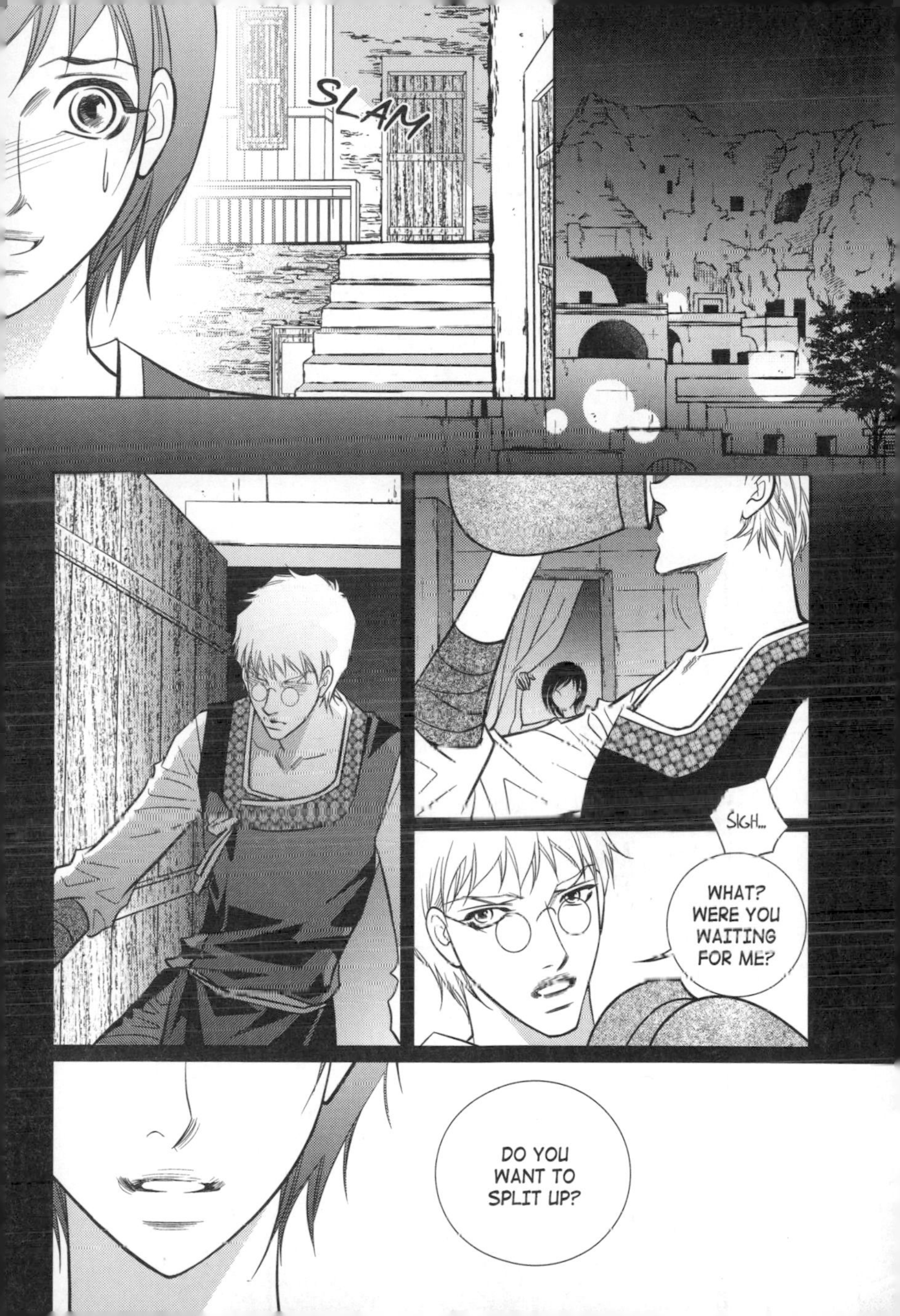
SLAM
SIGH...
WHAT? WERE YOU WAITING FOR ME?
DO YOU WANT TO SPLIT UP?

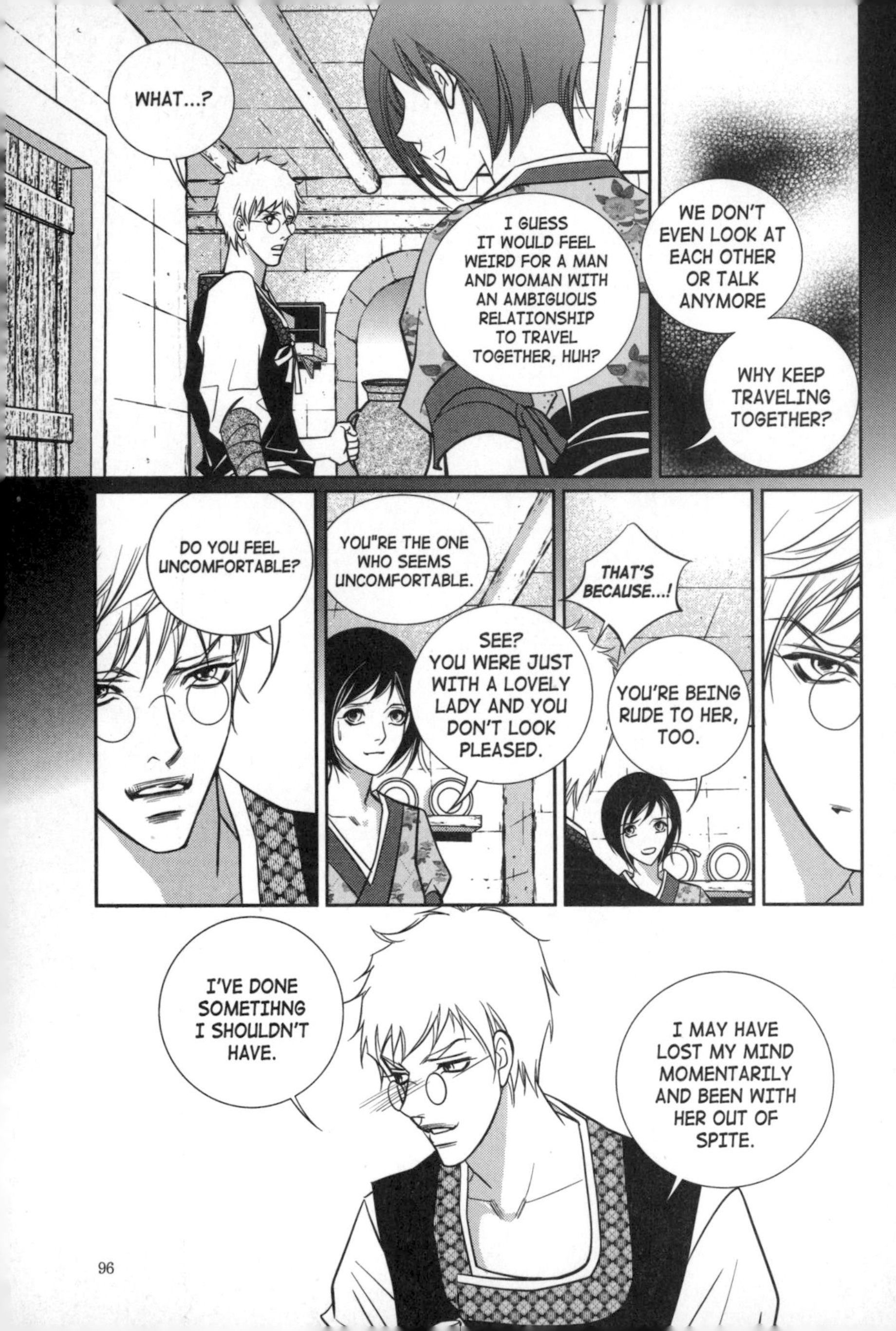
WHAT...?
I GUESS IT WOULD FEEL WEIRD FOR A MAN AND WOMAN WITH AN AMBIGUOUS RELATIONSHIP TO TRAVEL TOGETHER, HUH?
WE DON'T EVEN LOOK AT EACH OTHER OR TALK ANYMORE
WHY KEEP TRAVELING TOGETHER?
DO YOU FEEL UNCOMFORTABLE?
YOU"RE THE ONE WHO SEEMS UNCOMFORTABLE.
SEE? YOU WERE JUST WITH A LOVELY LADY AND YOU DON'T LOOK PLEASED.
THAT'S BECAUSE...!
YOU'RE BEING RUDE TO HER, TOO.
I'VE DONE SOMETIHNG I SHOULDN'T HAVE.
I MAY HAVE LOST MY MIND MOMENTARILY AND BEEN WITH HER OUT OF SPITE.

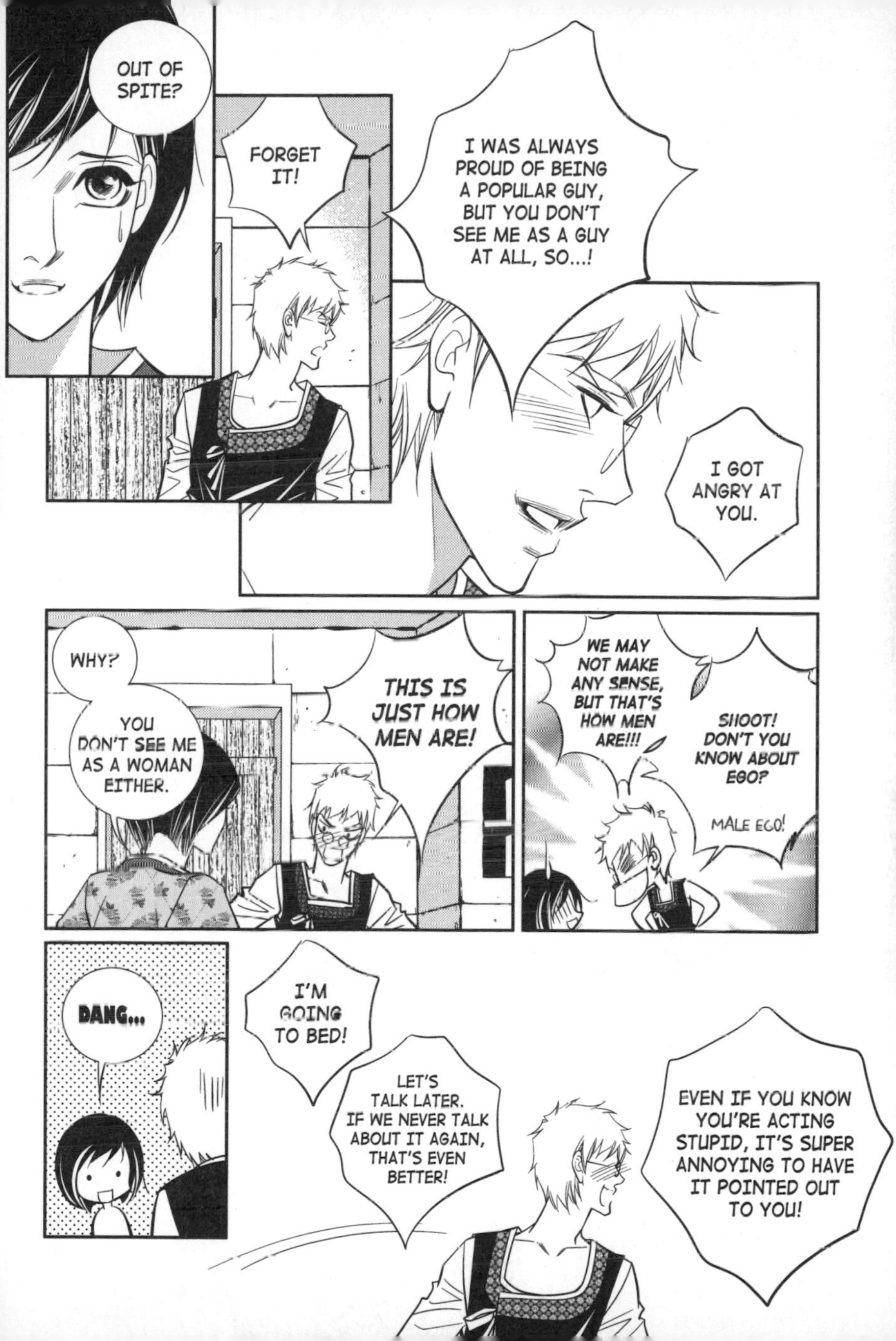
OUT OF SPITE?
FORGET IT!
I WAS ALWAYS PROUD OF BEING A POPULAR GUY, BUT YOU DON'T SEE ME AS A GUY AT ALL, SO...!
I GOT ANGRY AT YOU.
WHY?
YOU DON'T SEE ME AS A WOMAN EITHER.
THIS IS JUST HOW MEN ARE!
WE MAY NOT MAKE ANY SENSE, BUT THAT'S HOW MEN ARE!!!
SHOOT! DON'T YOU KNOW ABOUT EGO?
MALE EGO!
DANG...
I'M GOING TO BED!
LET'S TALK LATER. IF WE NEVER TALK ABOUT IT AGAIN, THAT'S EVEN BETTER!
EVEN IF YOU KNOW YOU'RE ACTING STUPID, IT'S SUPER ANNOYING TO HAVE IT POINTED OUT TO YOU!

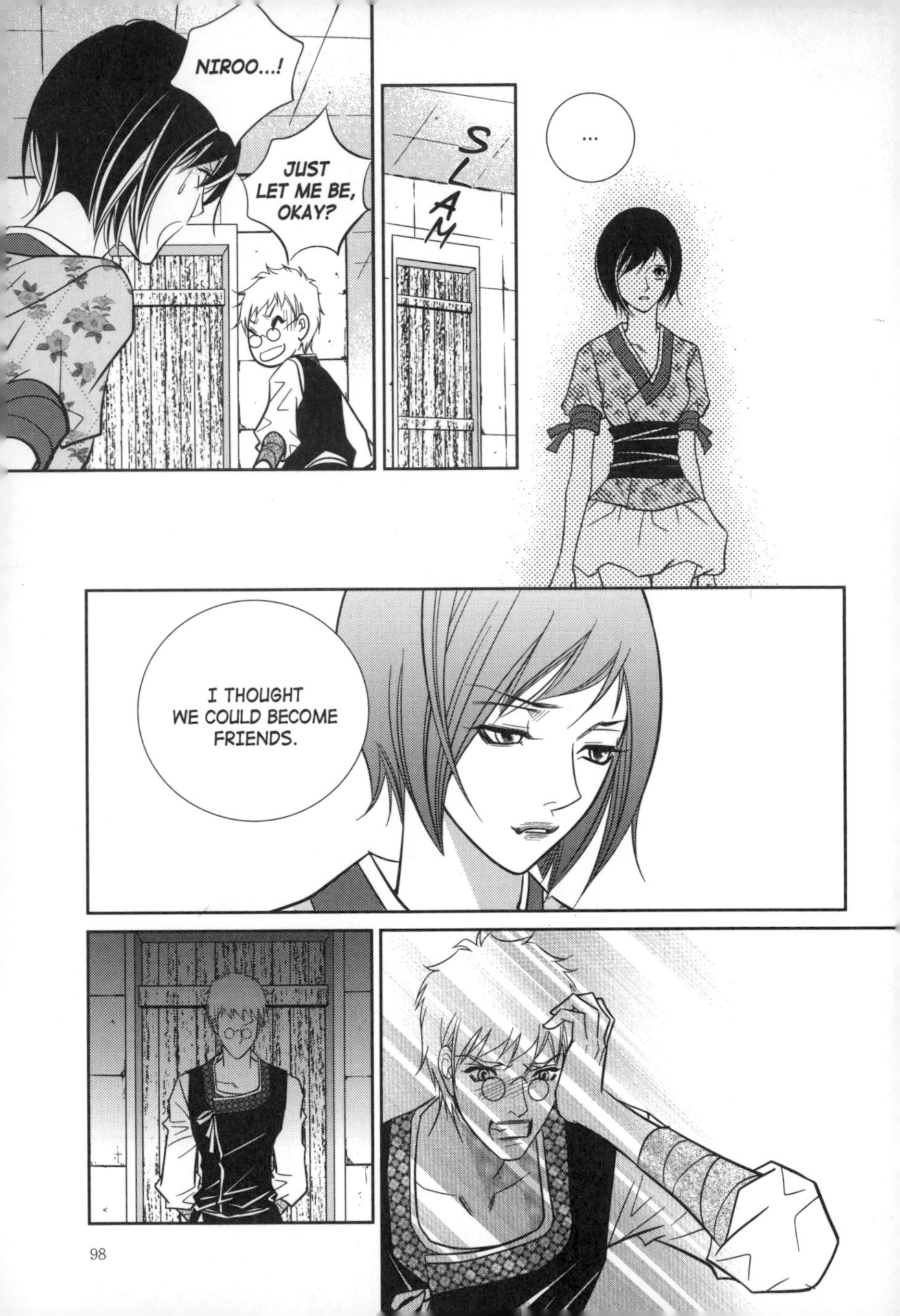
NIROO...!
JUST LET ME BE, OKAY?
SLAM
...
I THOUGHT WE COULD BECOME FRIENDS.

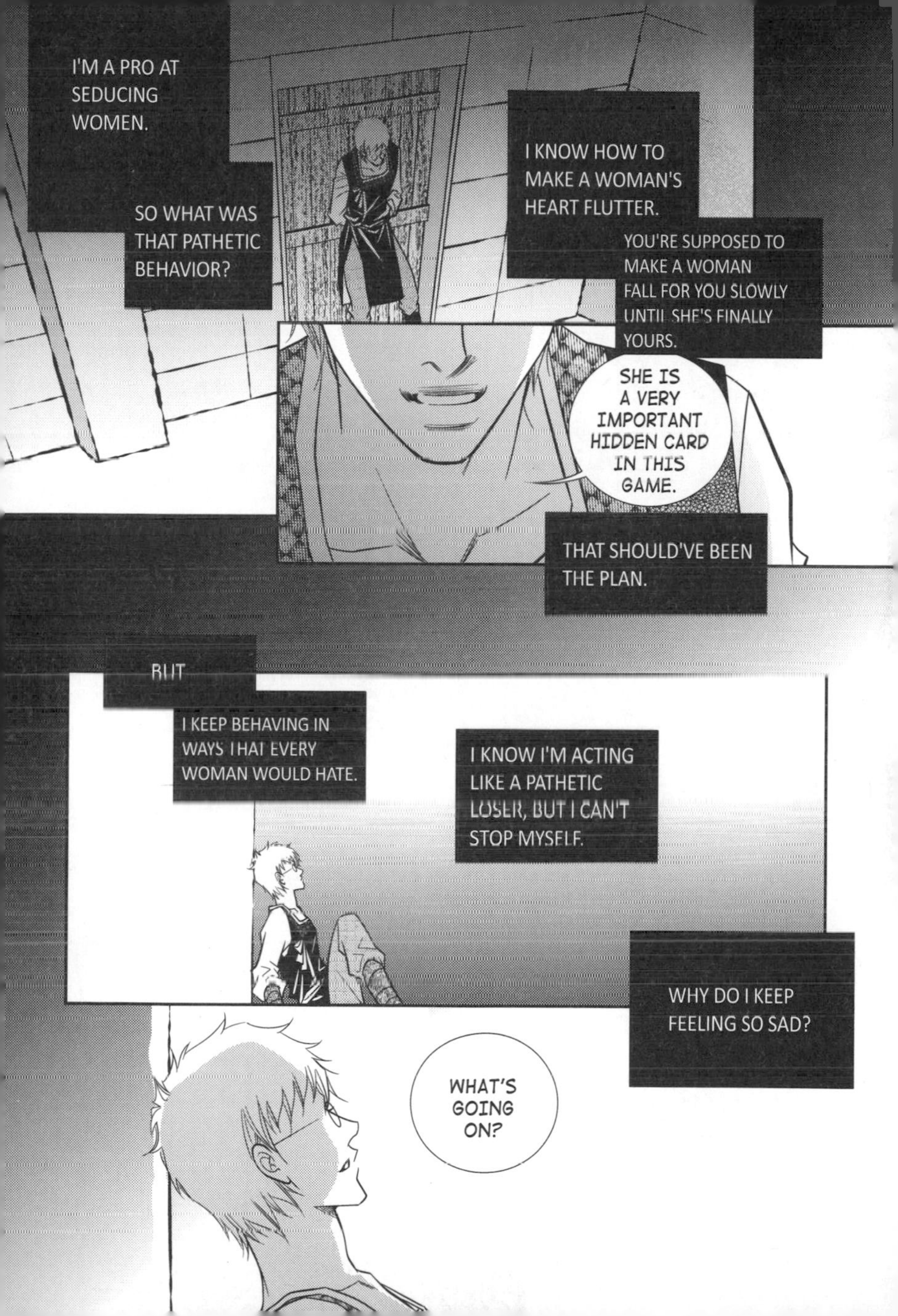
I'M A PRO AT SEDUCING WOMEN.
SO WHAT WAS THAT PATHETIC BEHAVIOR?
I KNOW HOW TO MAKE A WOMAN'S HEART FLUTTER.
YOU'RE SUPPOSED TO MAKE A WOMAN FALL FOR YOU SLOWLY UNTIL SHE'S FINALLY YOURS.
SHE IS A VERY IMPORTANT HIDDEN CARD IN THIS GAME.
THAT SHOULD'VE BEEN THE PLAN.
BUT
I KEEP BEHAVING IN WAYS THAT EVERY WOMAN WOULD HATE.
I KNOW I'M ACTING LIKE A PATHETIC LOSER, BUT I CAN'T STOP MYSELF.
WHY DO I KEEP FEELING SO SAD?
WHAT'S GOING ON?

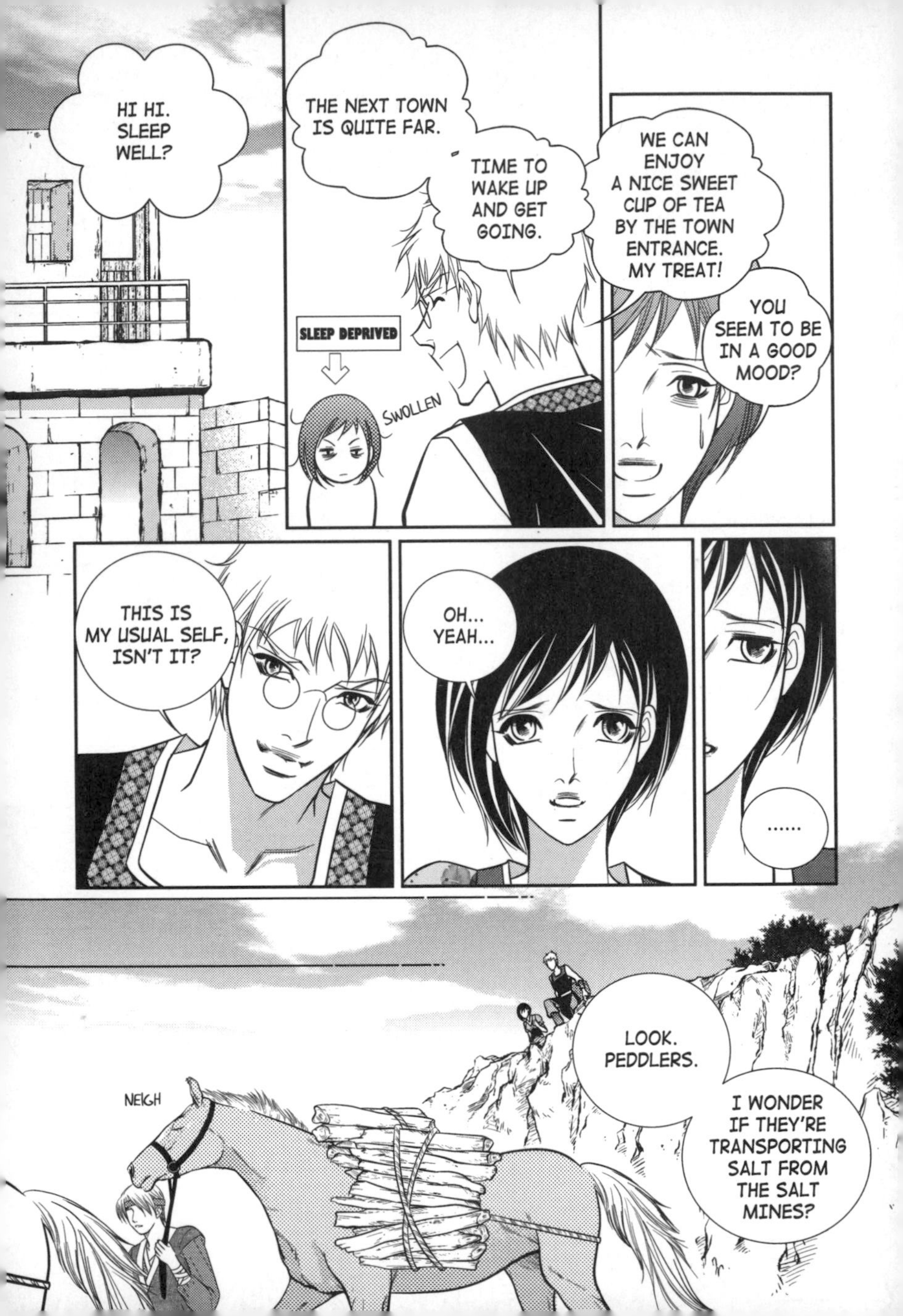
HI HI. SLEEP WELL?
THE NEXT TOWN IS QUITE FAR.
TIME TO WAKE UP AND GET GOING.
SLEEP DEPRIVED
SWOLLEN
WE CAN ENJOY A NICE SWEET CUP OF TEA BY THE TOWN ENTRANCE. MY TREAT!
YOU SEEM TO BE IN A GOOD MOOD?
THIS IS MY USUAL SELF, ISN'T IT?
OH... YEAH...
......
NEIGH
LOOK. PEDDLERS.
I WONDER IF THEY'RE TRANSPORTING SALT FROM THE SALT MINES?

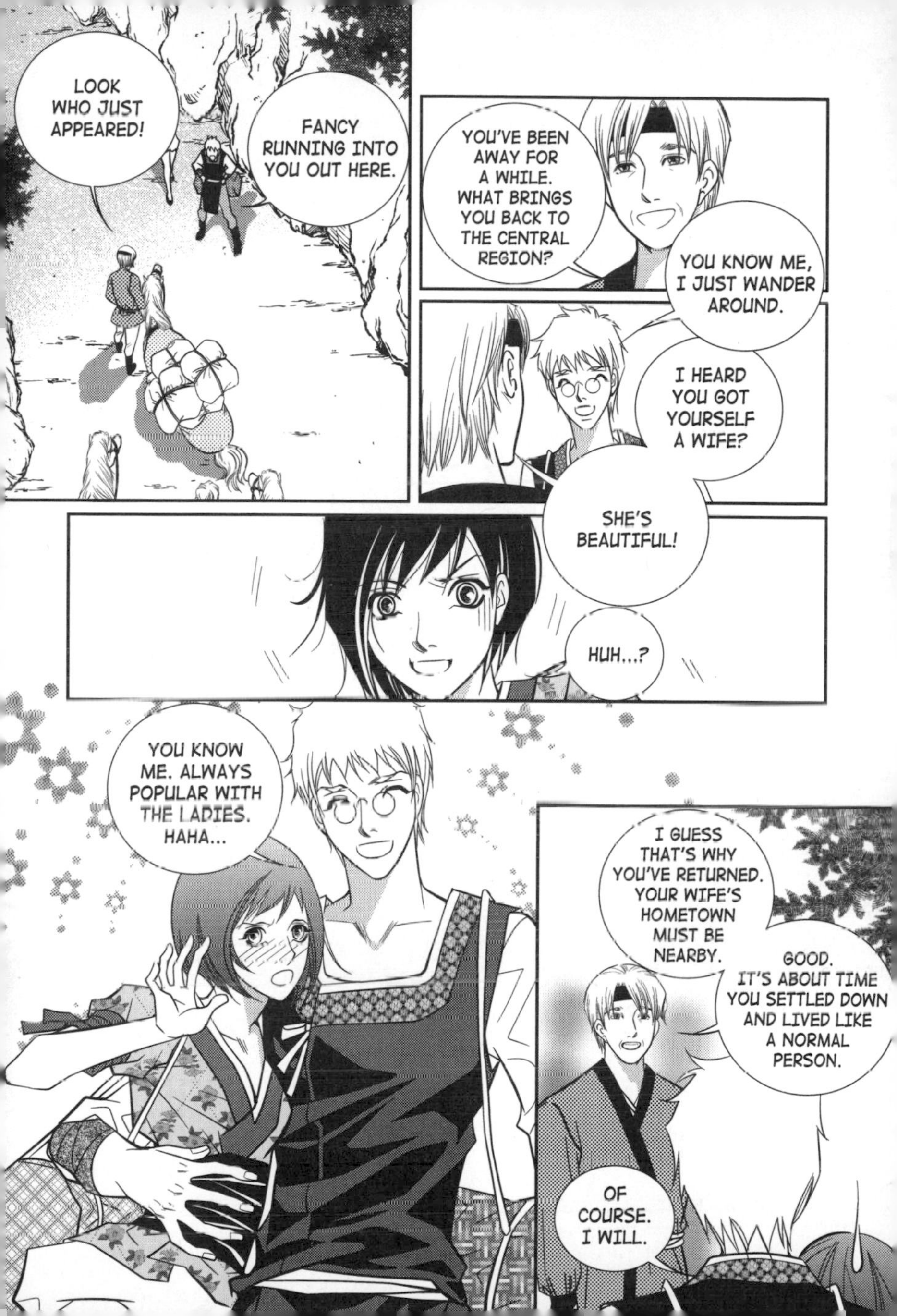
LOOK WHO JUST APPEARED!
FANCY RUNNING INTO YOU OUT HERE.
YOU'VE BEEN AWAY FOR A WHILE. WHAT BRINGS YOU BACK TO THE CENTRAL REGION?
YOU KNOW ME, I JUST WANDER AROUND.
I HEARD YOU GOT YOURSELF A WIFE?
SHE'S BEAUTIFUL!
HUH...?
YOU KNOW ME. ALWAYS POPULAR WITH THE LADIES. HAHA...
I GUESS THAT'S WHY YOU'VE RETURNED. YOUR WIFE'S HOMETOWN MUST BE NEARBY.
GOOD. IT'S ABOUT TIME YOU SETTLED DOWN AND LIVED LIKE A NORMAL PERSON.
OF COURSE. I WILL.

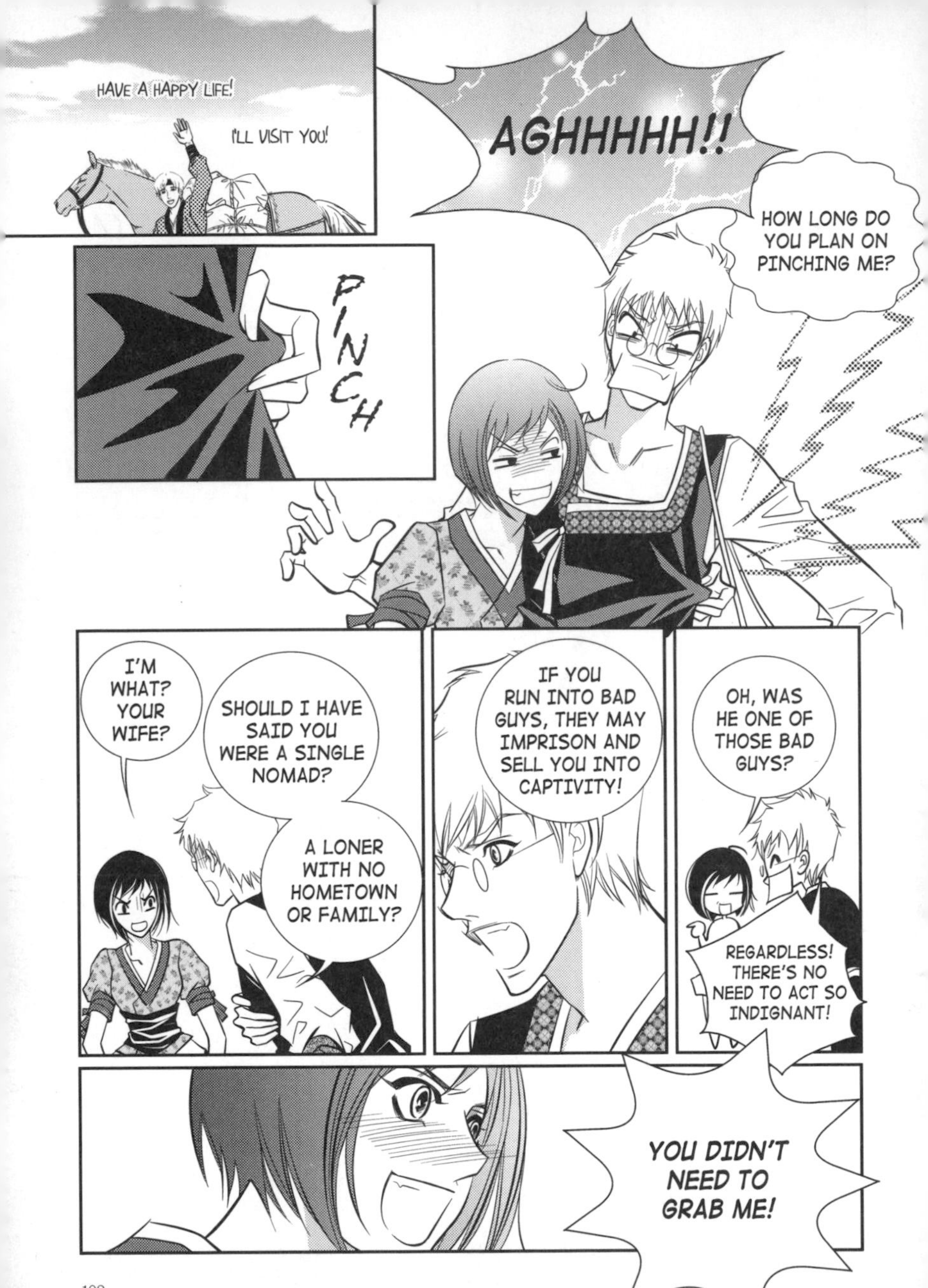
HAVE A HAPPY LIFE!
I'LL VISIT YOU!
AGHHHHH!!
PINCH
HOW LONG DO YOU PLAN ON PINCHING ME?
I'M WHAT? YOUR WIFE?
SHOULD I HAVE SAID YOU WERE A SINGLE NOMAD?
A LONER WITH NO HOMETOWN OR FAMILY?
IF YOU RUN INTO BAD GUYS, THEY MAY IMPRISON AND SELL YOU INTO CAPTIVITY!
OH, WAS HE ONE OF THOSE BAD GUYS?
REGARDLESS! THERE'S NO NEED TO ACT SO INDIGNANT!
YOU DIDN'T NEED TO GRAB ME!

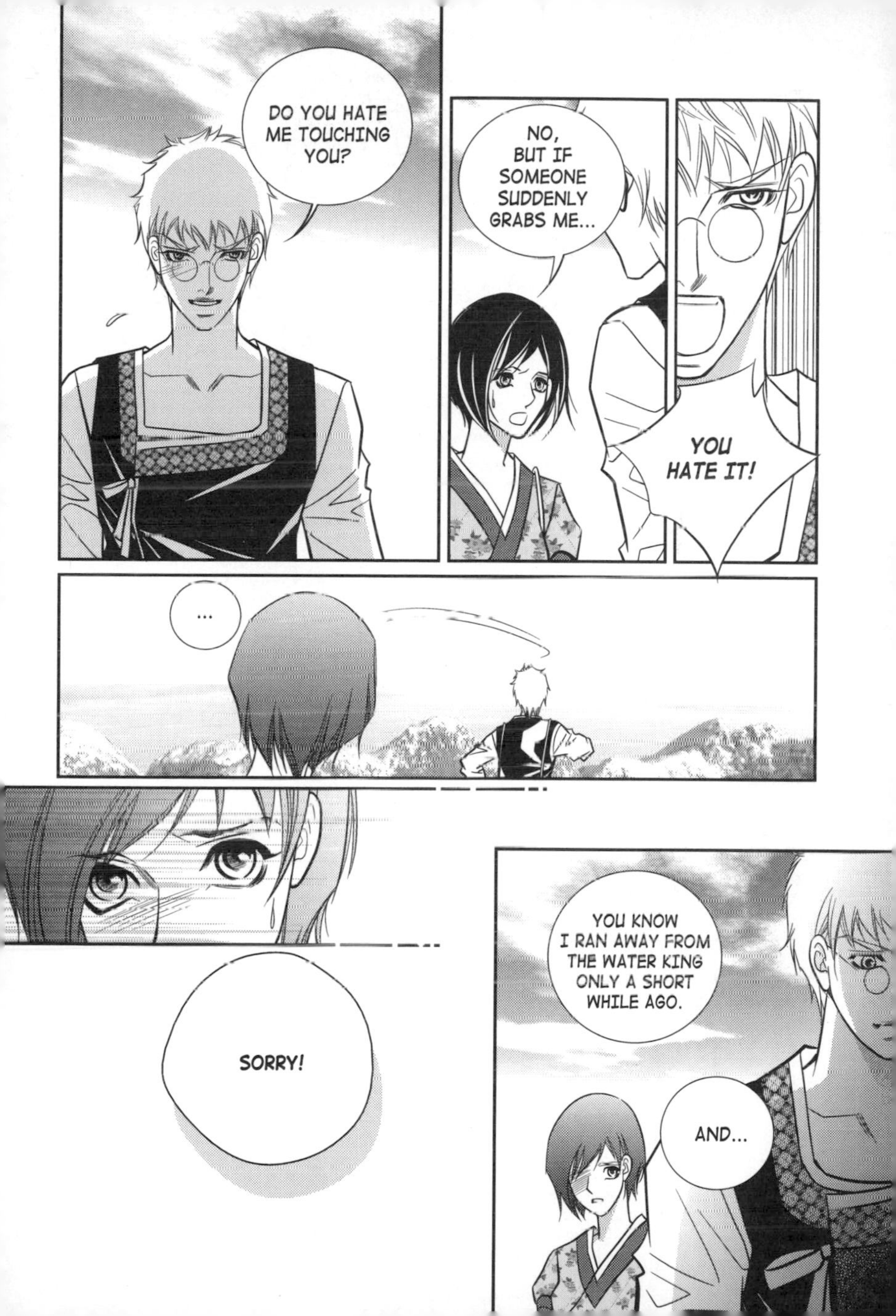
DO YOU HATE ME TOUCHING YOU?
NO, BUT IF SOMEONE SUDDENLY GRABS ME...
YOU HATE IT!
...
SORRY!
YOU KNOW I RAN AWAY FROM THE WATER KING ONLY A SHORT WHILE AGO.
AND...

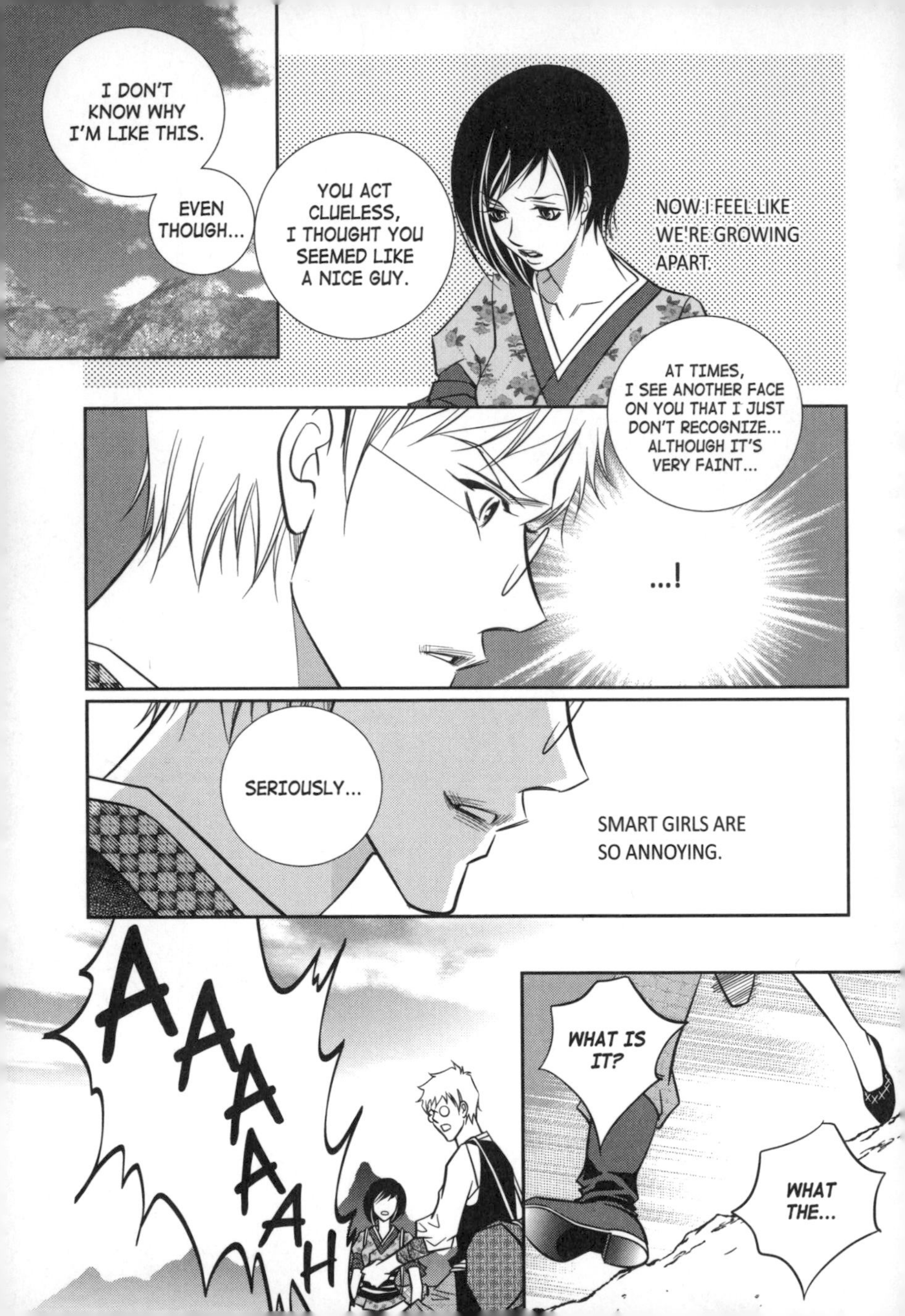
I DON'T KNOW WHY I'M LIKE THIS.
EVEN THOUGH...
YOU ACT CLUELESS, I THOUGHT YOU SEEMED LIKE A NICE GUY.
NOW I FEEL LIKE WE'RE GROWING APART.
AT TIMES, I SEE ANOTHER FACE ON YOU THAT I JUST DON'T RECOGNIZE... ALTHOUGH IT'S VERY FAINT...
...!
SERIOUSLY...
SMART GIRLS ARE SO ANNOYING.
AAAAAAAH
WHAT IS IT?
WHAT THE...

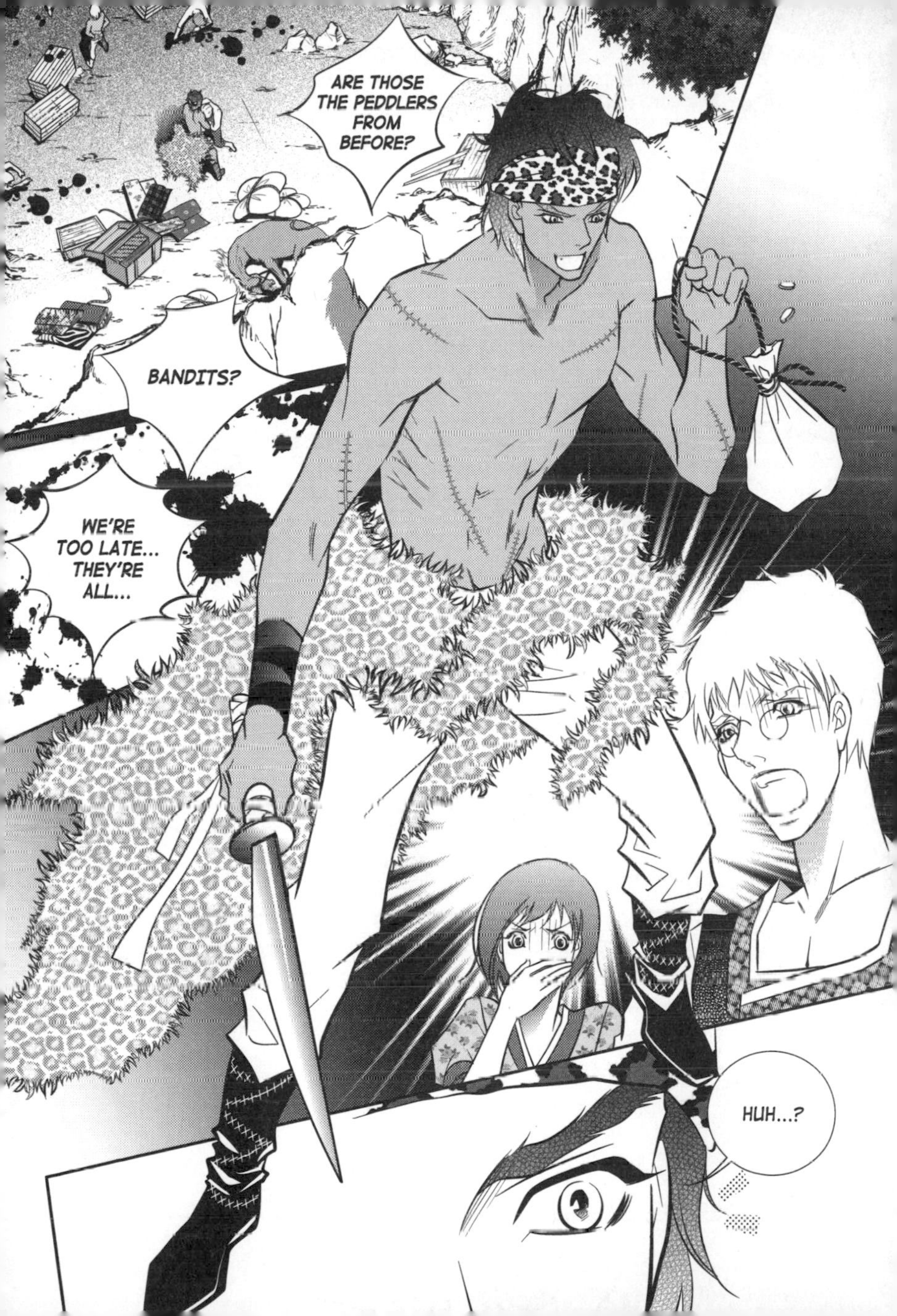
ARE THOSE THE PEDDLERS FROM BEFORE?
BANDITS?
WE'RE TOO LATE... THEY'RE ALL...
HUH...?

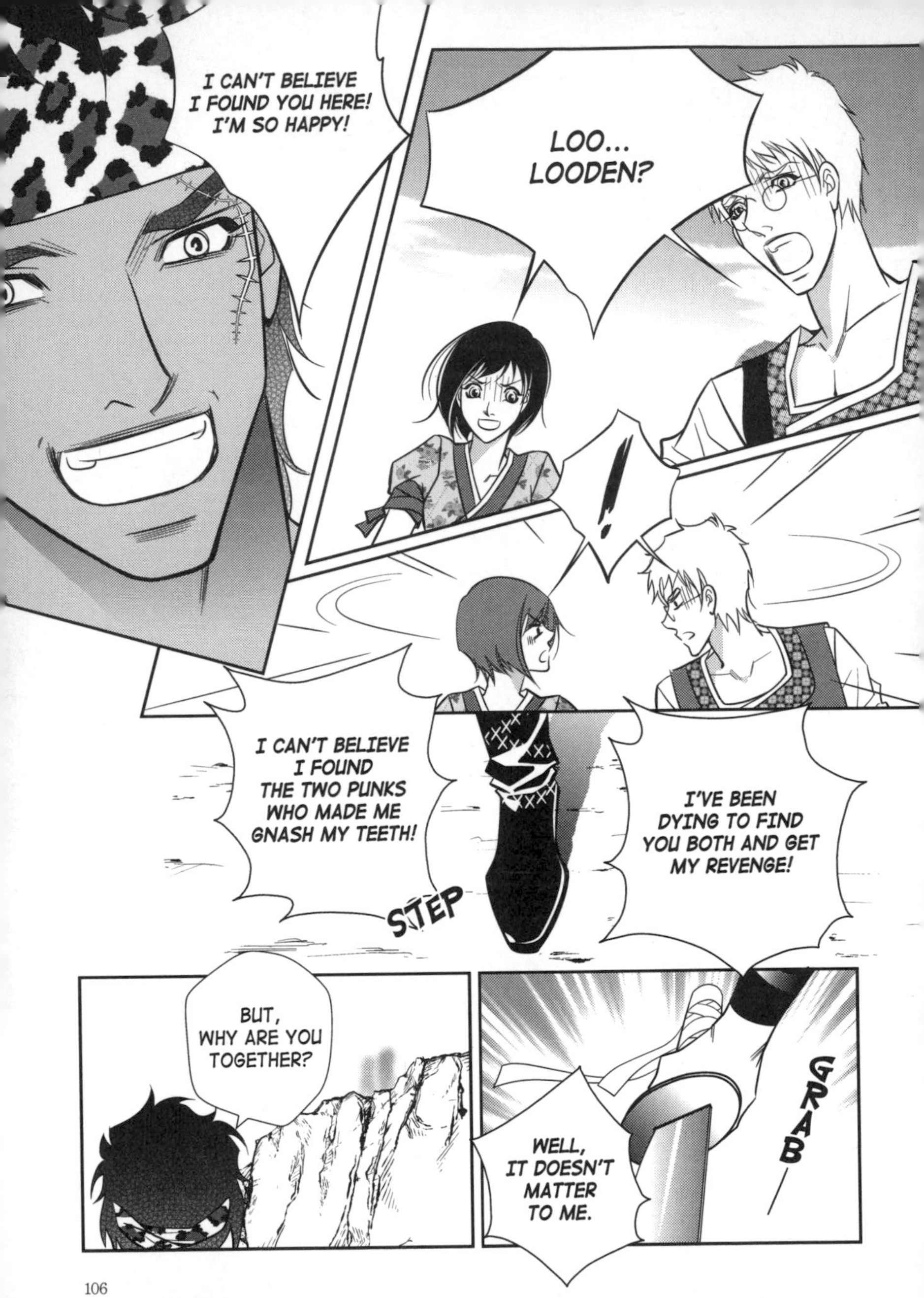
I CAN'T BELIEVE I FOUND YOU HERE! I'M SO HAPPY!
LOO... LOODEN?
!
I CAN'T BELIEVE I FOUND THE TWO PUNKS WHO MADE ME GNASH MY TEETH!
STEP
I'VE BEEN DYING TO FIND YOU BOTH AND GET MY REVENGE!
BUT, WHY ARE YOU TOGETHER?
GRAB
WELL, IT DOESN'T MATTER TO ME.

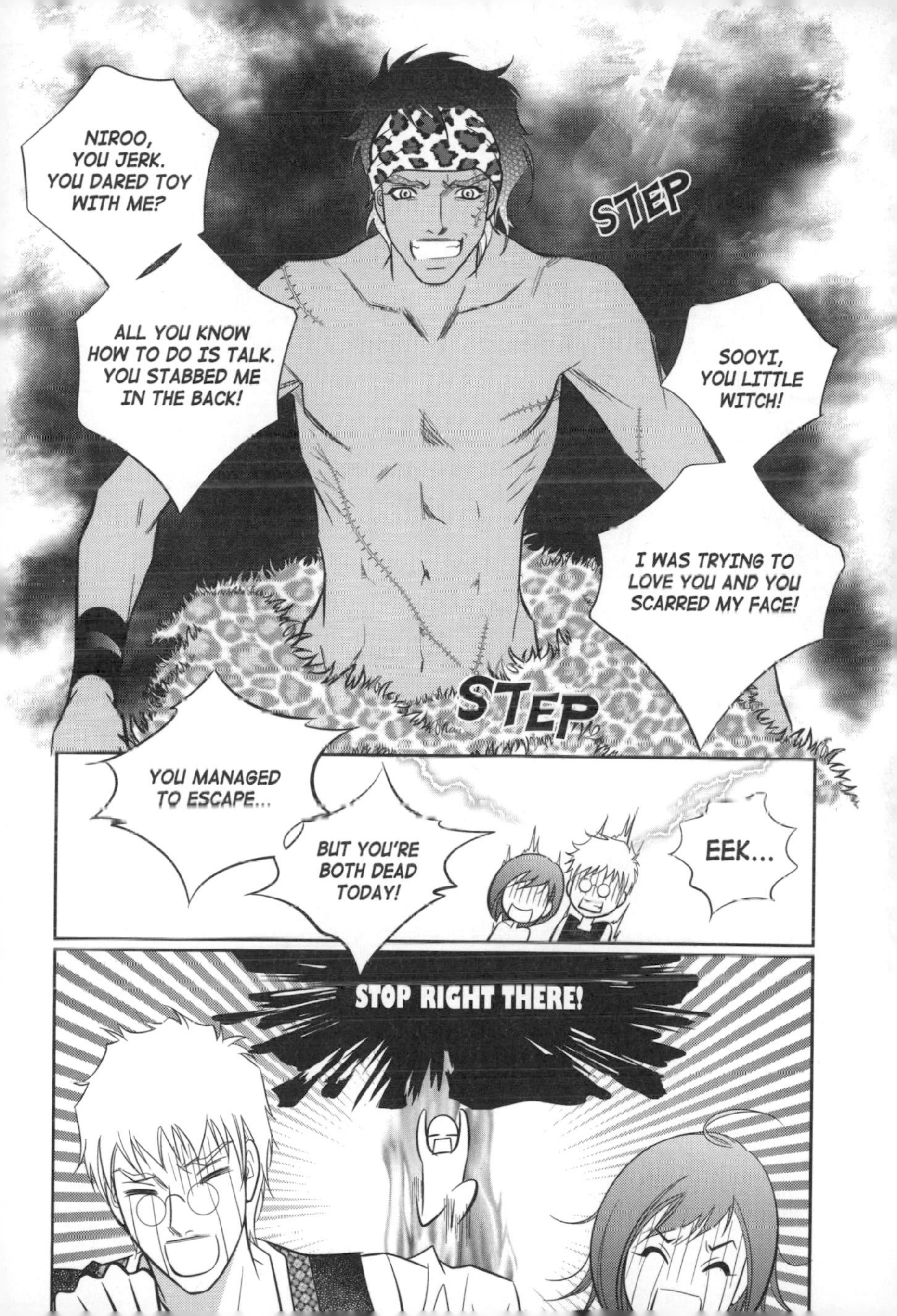
NIROO, YOU JERK. YOU DARED TOY WITH ME?
STEP
ALL YOU KNOW HOW TO DO IS TALK. YOU STABBED ME IN THE BACK!
SOOYI, YOU LITTLE WITCH!
I WAS TRYING TO LOVE YOU AND YOU SCARRED MY FACE!
STEP
YOU MANAGED TO ESCAPE...
BUT YOU'RE BOTH DEAD TODAY!
EEK...
STOP RIGHT THERE!

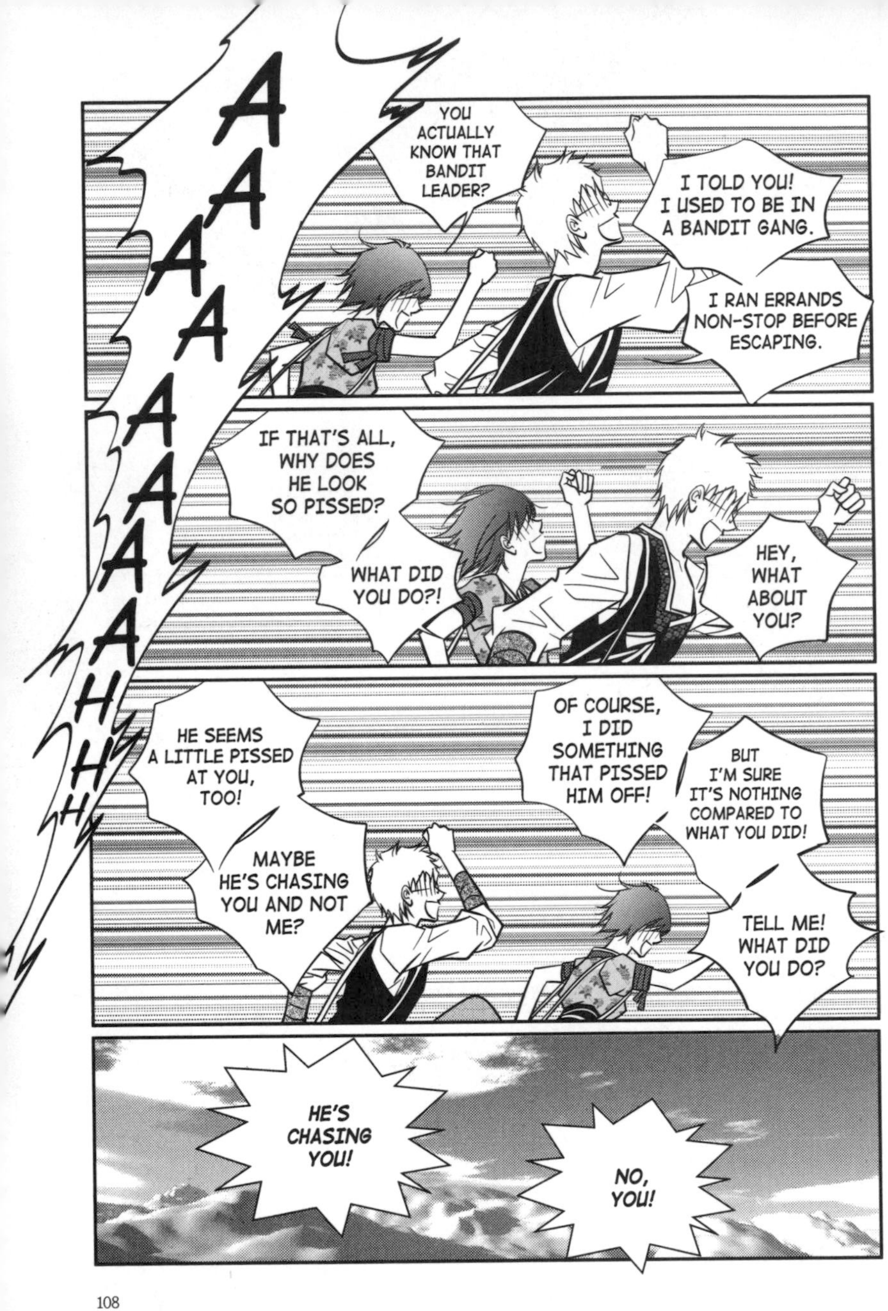
AAAAAAAAHHH
YOU ACTUALLY KNOW THAT BANDIT LEADER?
I TOLD YOU! I USED TO BE IN A BANDIT GANG.
I RAN ERRANDS NON-STOP BEFORE ESCAPING.
IF THAT'S ALL, WHY DOES HE LOOK SO PISSED?
WHAT DID YOU DO?!
HEY, WHAT ABOUT YOU?
HE SEEMS A LITTLE PISSED AT YOU, TOO!
MAYBE HE'S CHASING YOU AND NOT ME?
OF COURSE, I DID SOMETHING THAT PISSED HIM OFF!
BUT I'M SURE IT'S NOTHING COMPARED TO WHAT YOU DID!
TELL ME! WHAT DID YOU DO?
HE'S CHASING YOU!
NO, YOU!

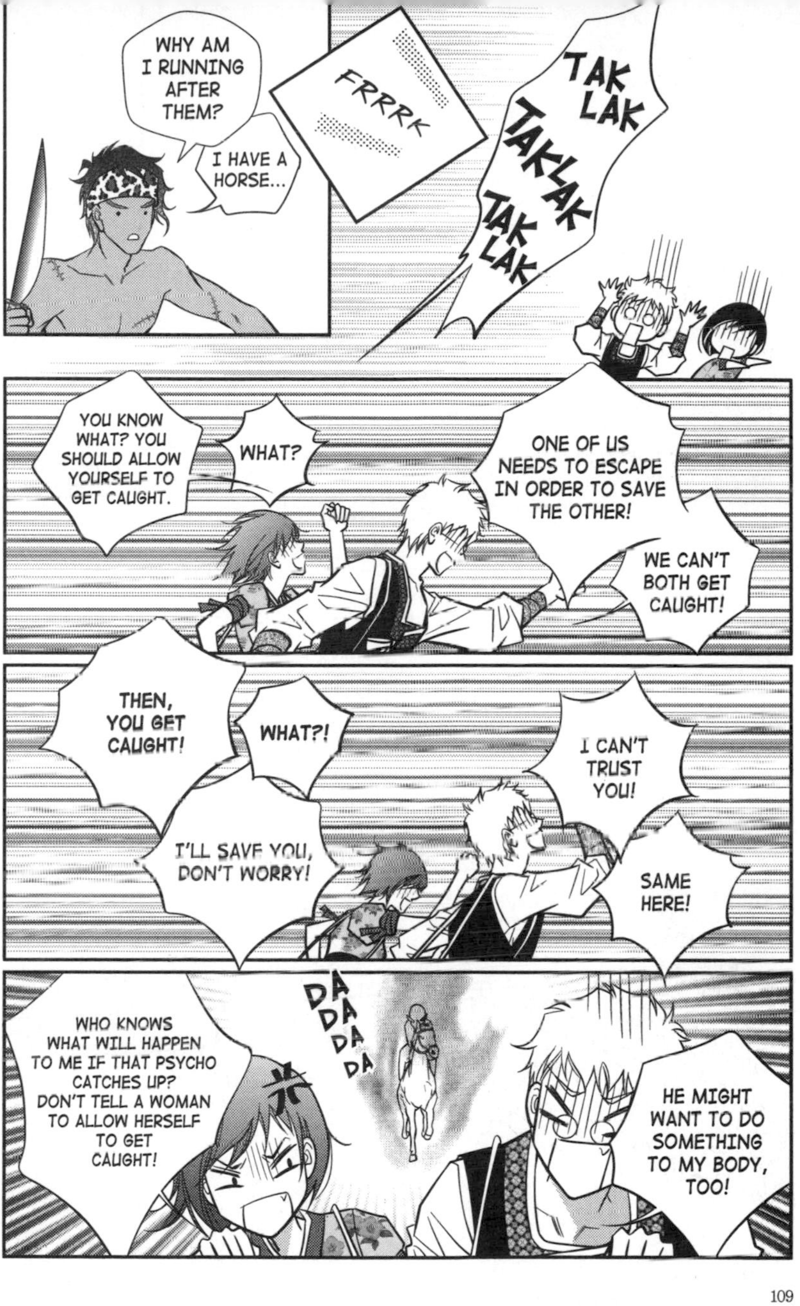
WHY AM I RUNNING AFTER THEM?
I HAVE A HORSE...
FRRRK
TAK LAK
TAK LAK
TAK LAK
YOU KNOW WHAT? YOU SHOULD ALLOW YOURSELF TO GET CAUGHT.
WHAT?
ONE OF US NEEDS TO ESCAPE IN ORDER TO SAVE THE OTHER!
WE CAN'T BOTH GET CAUGHT!
THEN, YOU GET CAUGHT!
WHAT?!
I CAN'T TRUST YOU!
I'LL SAVE YOU, DON'T WORRY!
SAME HERE!
WHO KNOWS WHAT WILL HAPPEN TO ME IF THAT PSYCHO CATCHES UP? DON'T TELL A WOMAN TO ALLOW HERSELF TO GET CAUGHT!
DA DA DA DA DA
HE MIGHT WANT TO DO SOMETHING TO MY BODY, TOO!

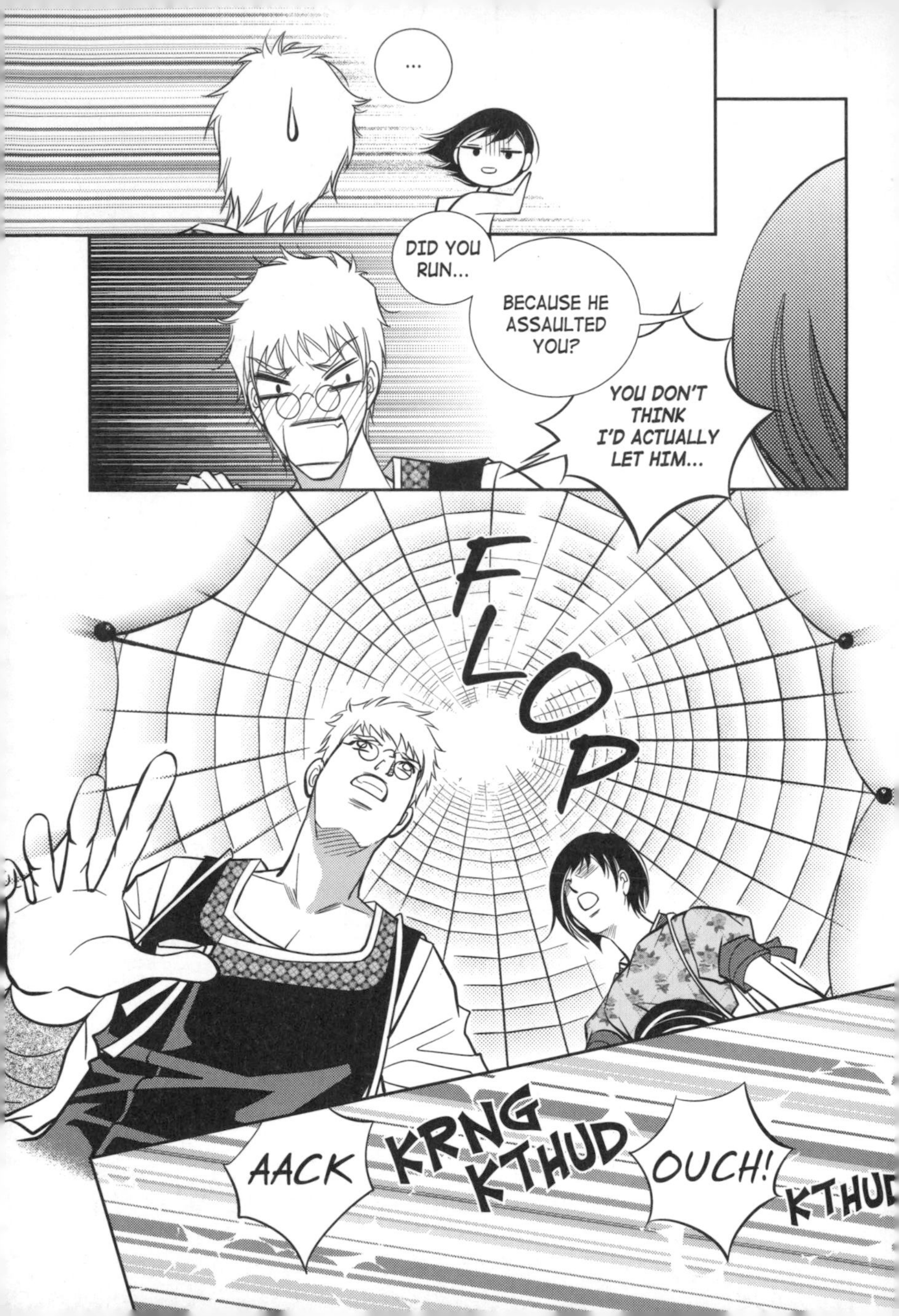
...
DID YOU RUN...
BECAUSE HE ASSAULTED YOU?
YOU DON'T THINK I'D ACTUALLY LET HIM...
FLOP
AACK
KRNG
KTHUD
OUCH!
KTHUD

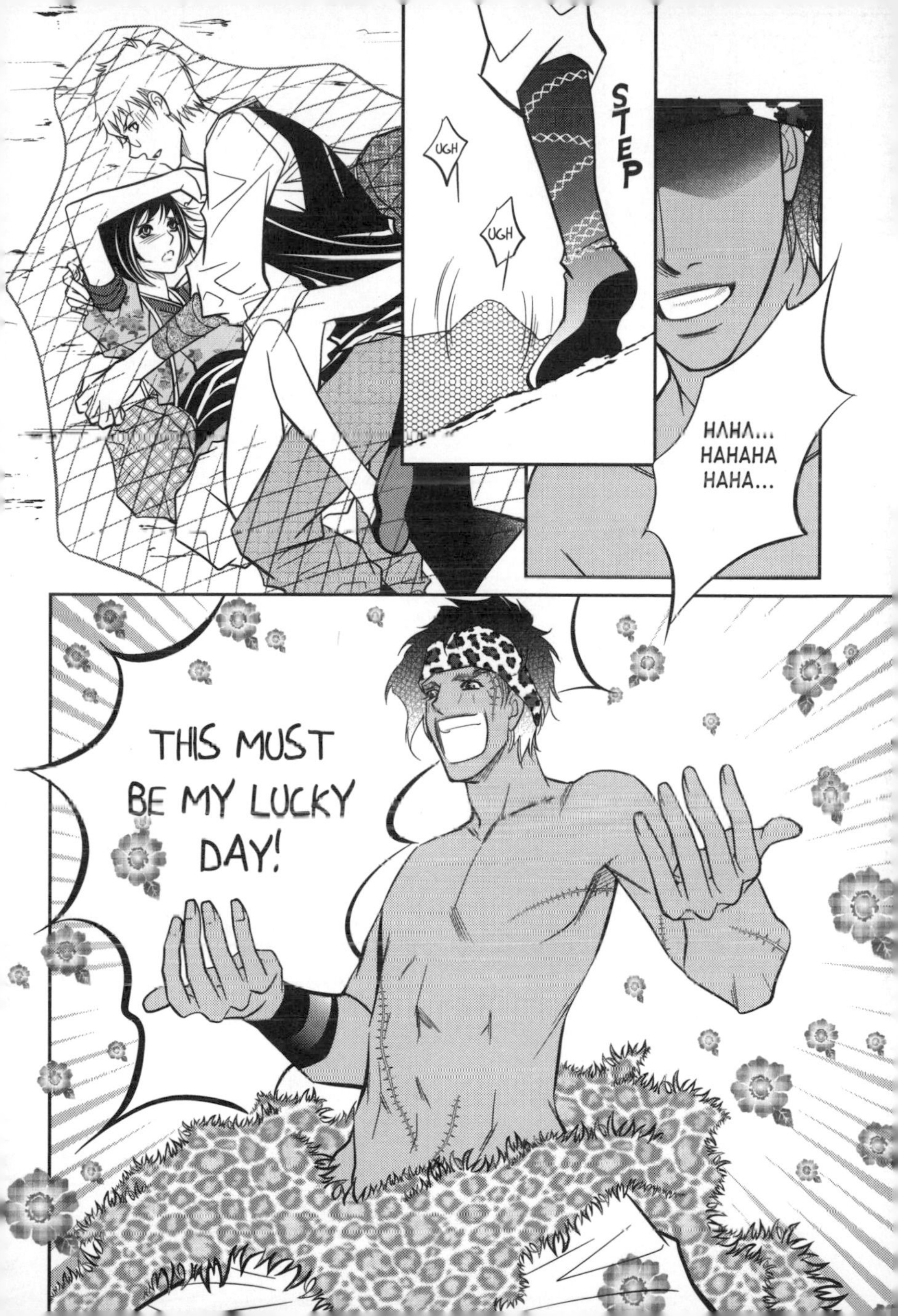
UGH
UGH
STEP
HAHA... HAHAHA HAHA...
THIS MUST BE MY LUCKY DAY!

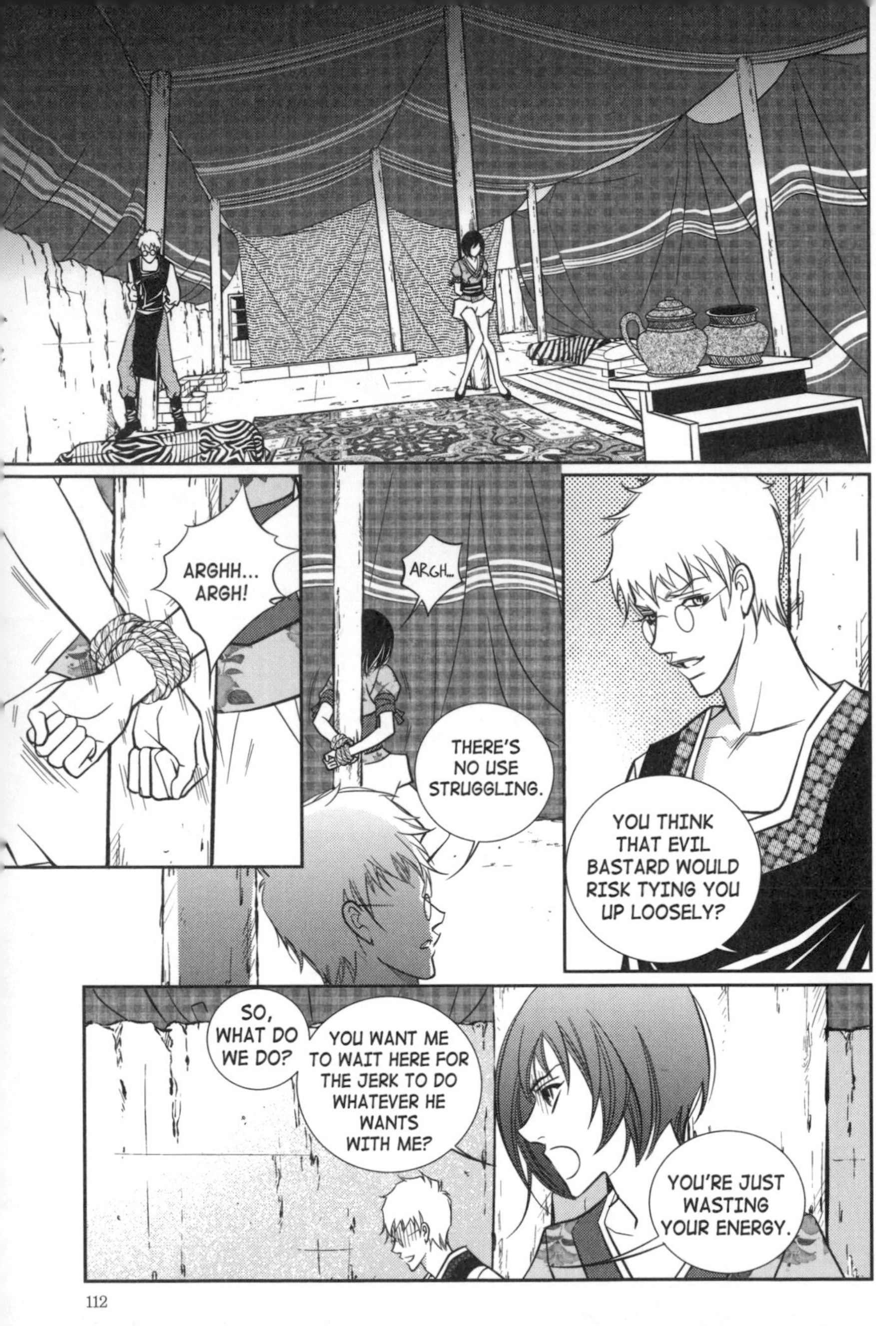
ARGHH... ARGH!
ARGH...
THERE'S NO USE STRUGGLING.
YOU THINK THAT EVIL BASTARD WOULD RISK TYING YOU UP LOOSELY?
SO, WHAT DO WE DO?
YOU WANT ME TO WAIT HERE FOR THE JERK TO DO WHATEVER HE WANTS WITH ME?
YOU'RE JUST WASTING YOUR ENERGY.

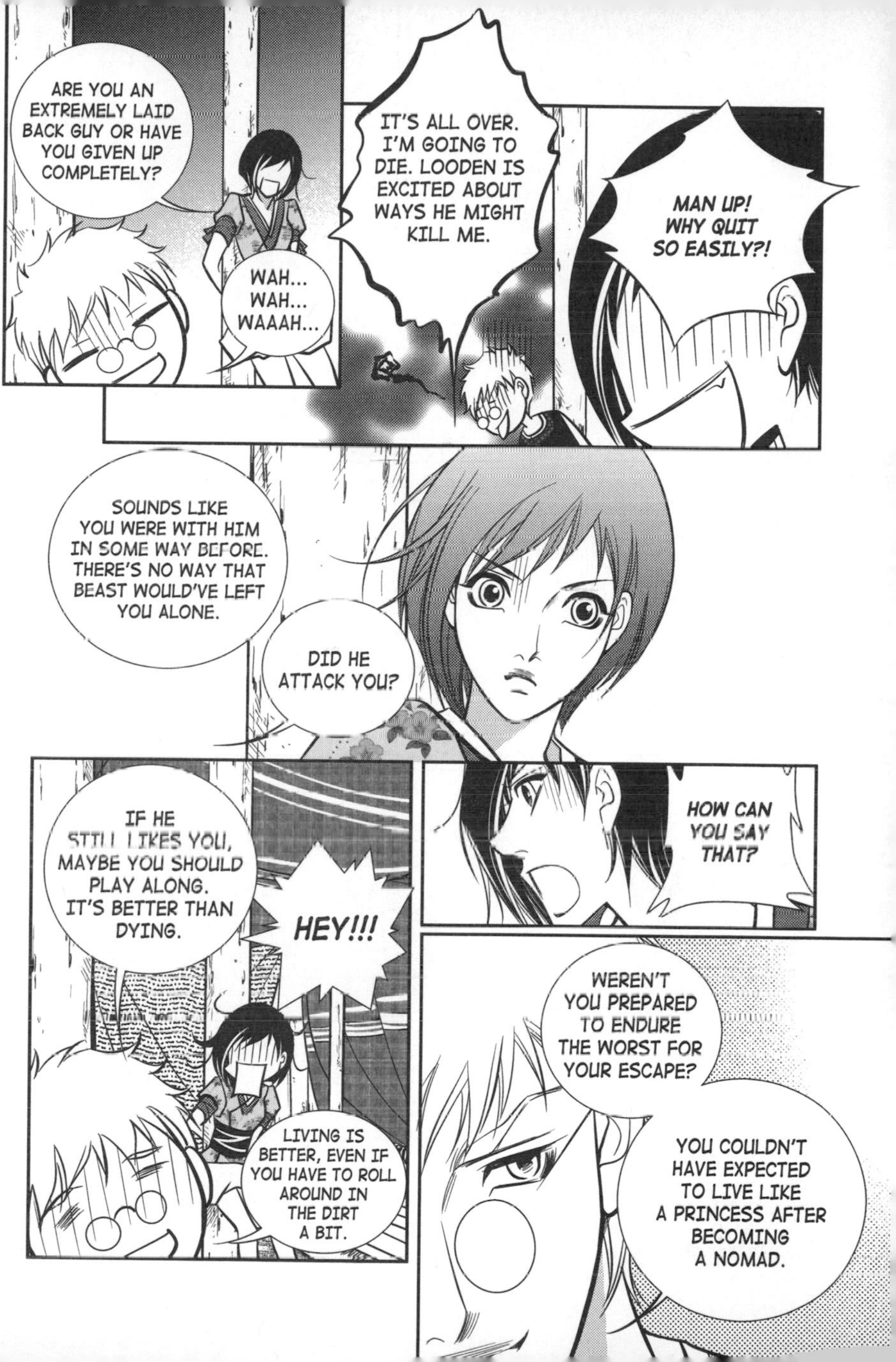
ARE YOU AN EXTREMELY LAID BACK GUY OR HAVE YOU GIVEN UP COMPLETELY?
WAH... WAH... WAAAH...
IT'S ALL OVER. I'M GOING TO DIE. LOODEN IS EXCITED ABOUT WAYS HE MIGHT KILL ME.
MAN UP! WHY QUIT SO EASILY?!
SOUNDS LIKE YOU WERE WITH HIM IN SOME WAY BEFORE. THERE'S NO WAY THAT BEAST WOULD'VE LEFT YOU ALONE.
DID HE ATTACK YOU?
IF HE STILL LIKES YOU, MAYBE YOU SHOULD PLAY ALONG. IT'S BETTER THAN DYING.
HEY!!!
LIVING IS BETTER, EVEN IF YOU HAVE TO ROLL AROUND IN THE DIRT A BIT.
HOW CAN YOU SAY THAT?
WEREN'T YOU PREPARED TO ENDURE THE WORST FOR YOUR ESCAPE?
YOU COULDN'T HAVE EXPECTED TO LIVE LIKE A PRINCESS AFTER BECOMING A NOMAD.

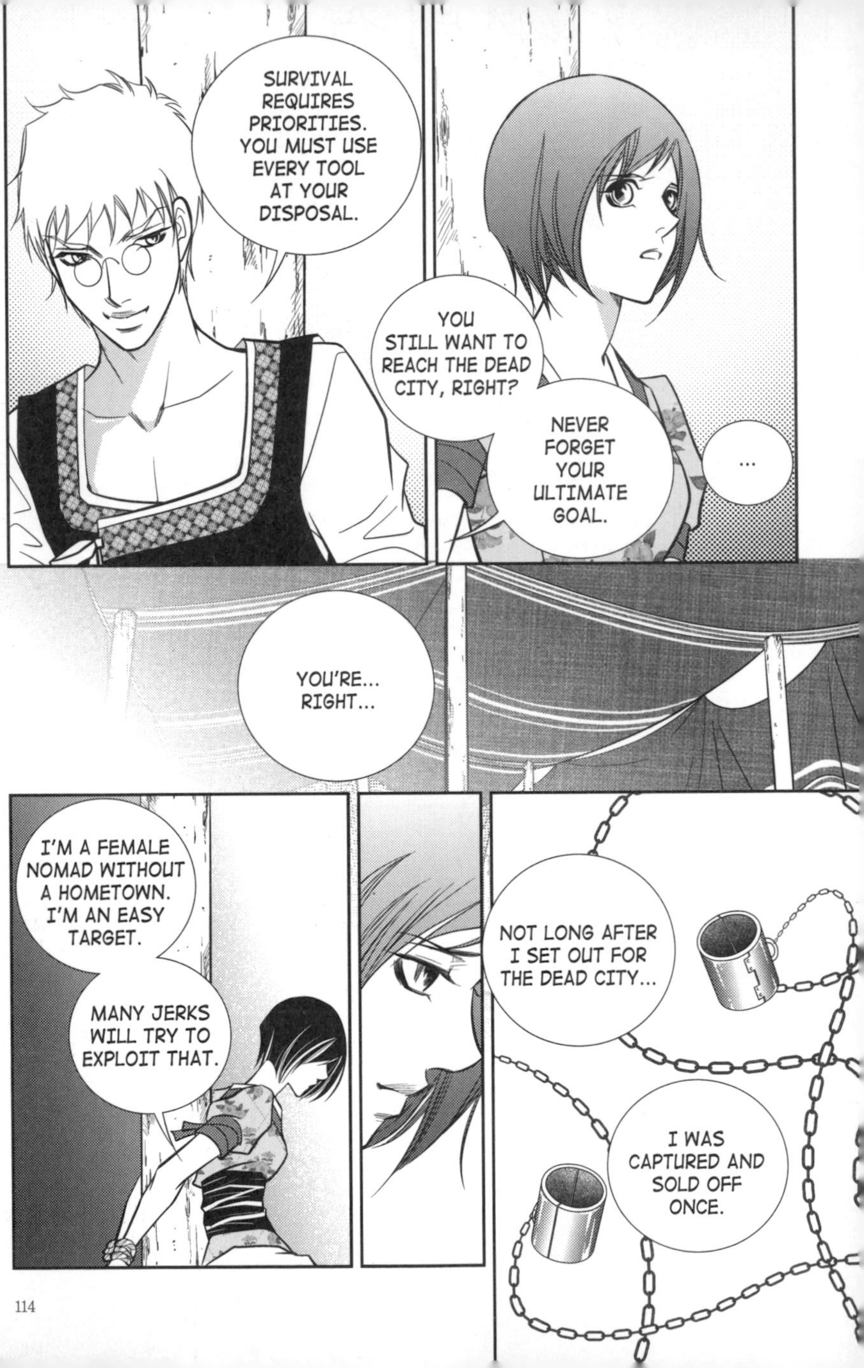
SURVIVAL REQUIRES PRIORITIES. YOU MUST USE EVERY TOOL AT YOUR DISPOSAL.
YOU STILL WANT TO REACH THE DEAD CITY, RIGHT?
NEVER FORGET YOUR ULTIMATE GOAL.
...
YOU'RE... RIGHT...
I'M A FEMALE NOMAD WITHOUT A HOMETOWN. I'M AN EASY TARGET.
MANY JERKS WILL TRY TO EXPLOIT THAT.
NOT LONG AFTER I SET OUT FOR THE DEAD CITY...
I WAS CAPTURED AND SOLD OFF ONCE.

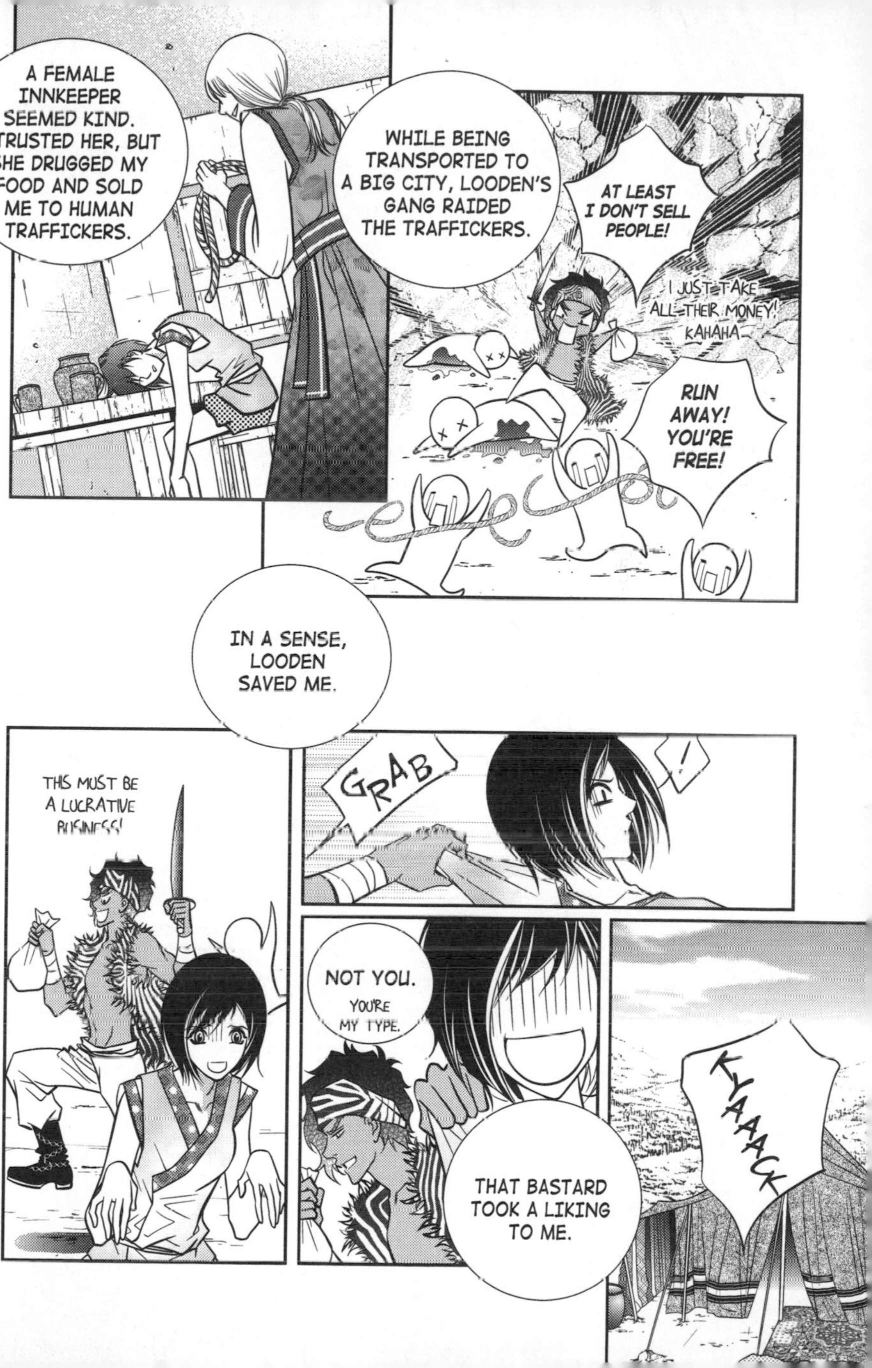
A FEMALE INNKEEPER SEEMED KIND. I TRUSTED HER, BUT SHE DRUGGED MY FOOD AND SOLD ME TO HUMAN TRAFFICKERS.
WHILE BEING TRANSPORTED TO A BIG CITY, LOODEN'S GANG RAIDED THE TRAFFICKERS.
AT LEAST I DON'T SELL PEOPLE!
I JUST TAKE ALL THEIR MONEY! KAHAHA
RUN AWAY! YOU'RE FREE!
IN A SENSE, LOODEN SAVED ME.
THIS MUST BE A LUCRATIVE BUSINESS!
GRAB
!
NOT YOU.
YOU'RE MY TYPE.
THAT BASTARD TOOK A LIKING TO ME.
KYAAACK

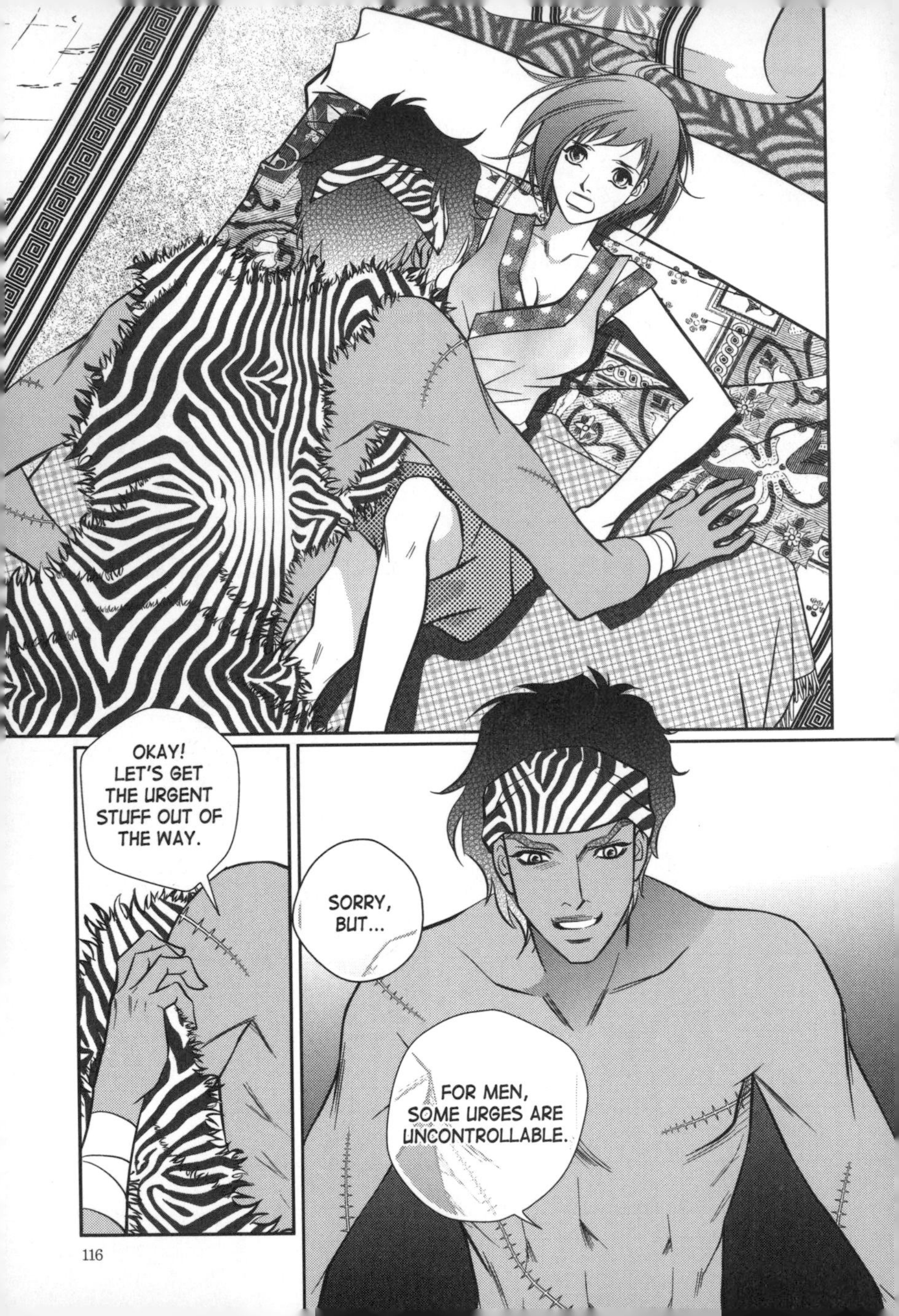
OKAY! LET'S GET THE URGENT STUFF OUT OF THE WAY.
SORRY, BUT...
FOR MEN, SOME URGES ARE UNCONTROLLABLE.

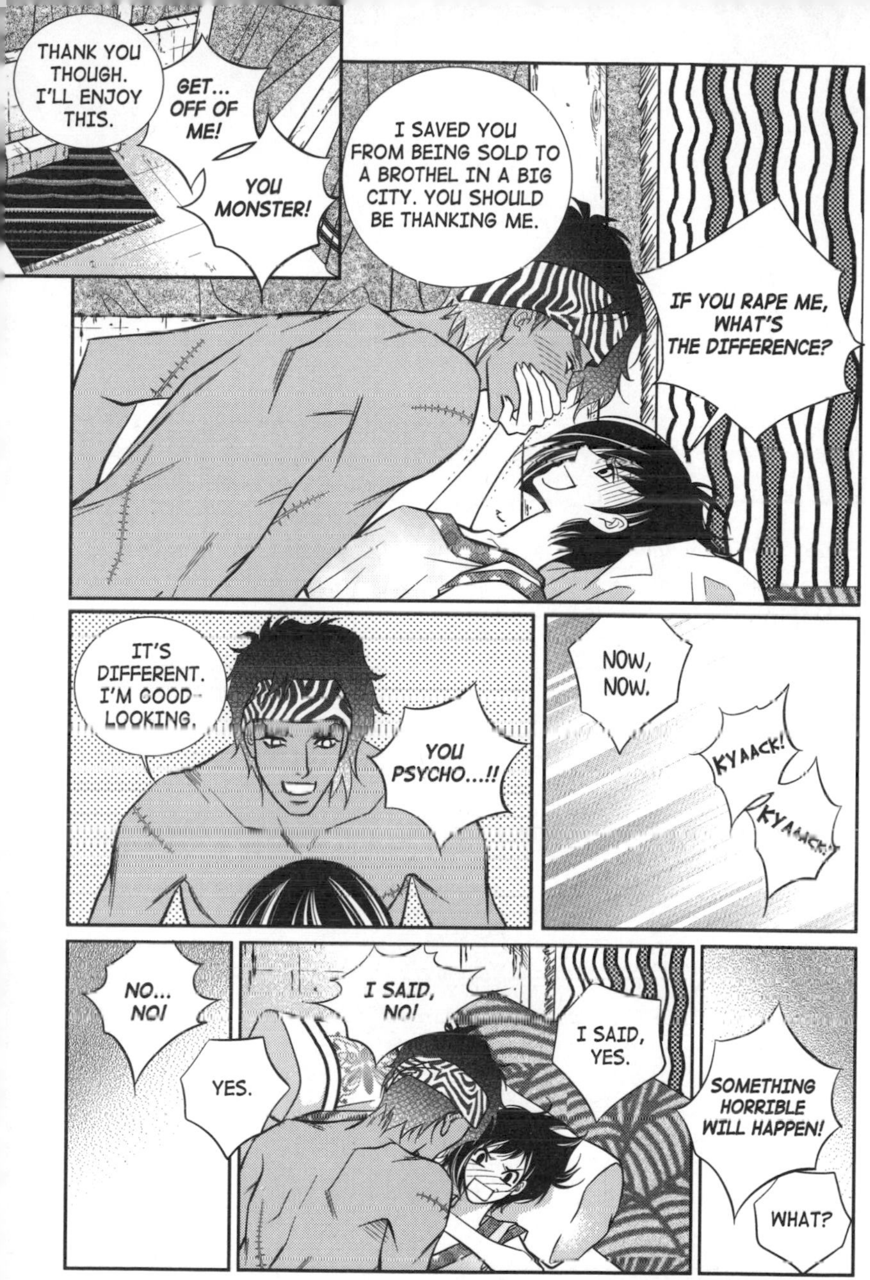
THANK YOU THOUGH. I'LL ENJOY THIS.
GET... OFF OF ME!
YOU MONSTER!
I SAVED YOU FROM BEING SOLD TO A BROTHEL IN A BIG CITY. YOU SHOULD BE THANKING ME.
IF YOU RAPE ME, WHAT'S THE DIFFERENCE?
IT'S DIFFERENT. I'M GOOD-LOOKING.
YOU PSYCHO...!!
NOW, NOW.
KYAACK!
KYAACK!
NO... NO!
YES.
I SAID, NO!
I SAID, YES.
SOMETHING HORRIBLE WILL HAPPEN!
WHAT?

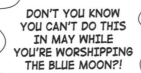

DON'T YOU KNOW YOU CAN'T DO THIS IN MAY WHILE YOU'RE WORSHIPPING THE BLUE MOON?!

HUH?

D-DIDN'T YOUR TOWN ELDERS TEACH YOU? YOU'LL BE CURSED IF YOU DON'T REMAIN ABSTINENT DURING THIS TIME!

REALLY?

HE ACTUALLY BELIEVED THAT?!

TWO YEARS AGO MY GANG WAS BEATEN INTO A BLOODY PULP BY THAT SECURITY TEAM.

THIS IS WHY A MAN CAN'T WALK AROUND IGNORANT.

I DON'T KNOW ANYTHING.

SO, THAT'S WHY IT HAPPENED.

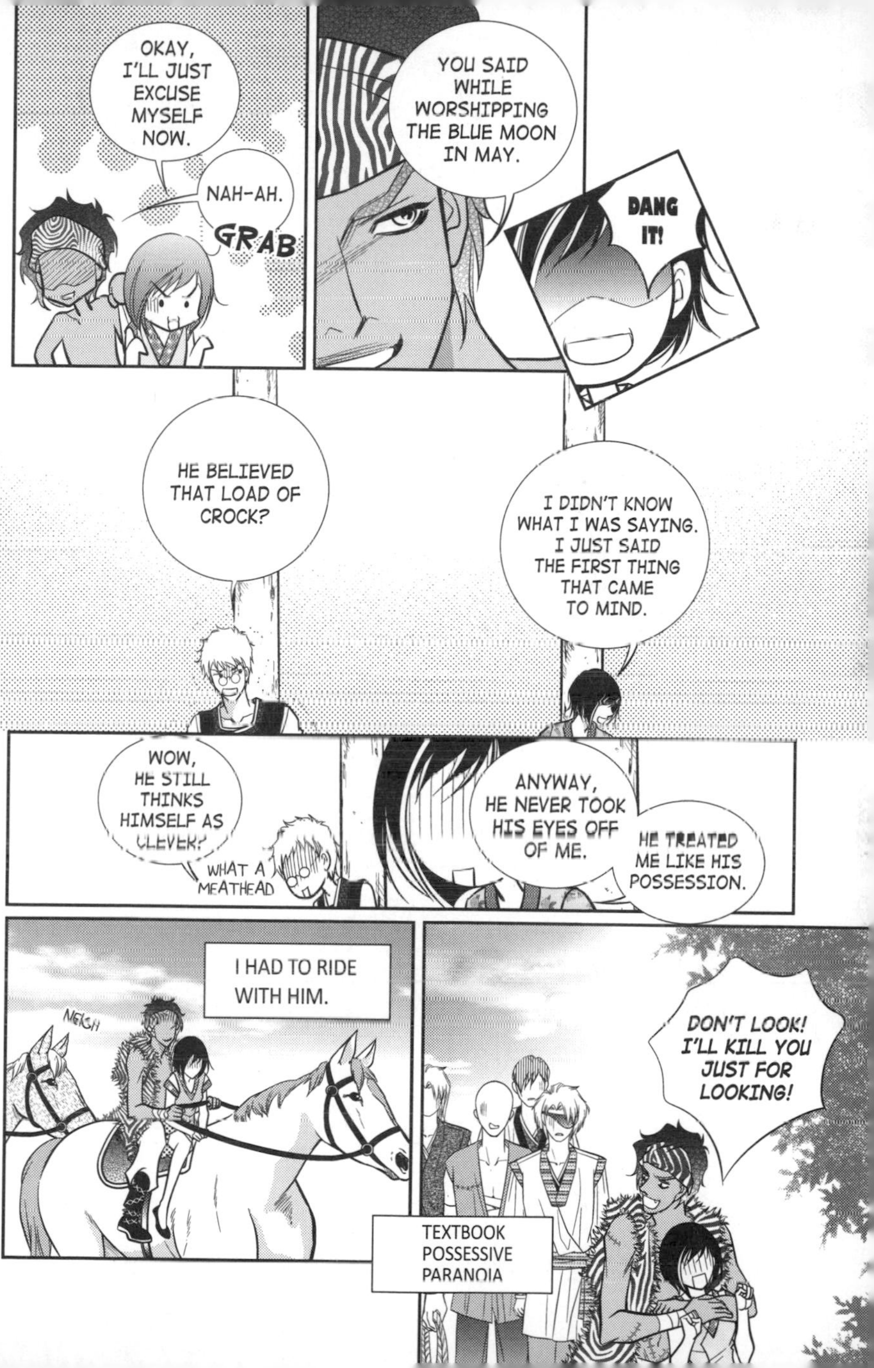
OKAY, I'LL JUST EXCUSE MYSELF NOW.
NAH-AH.
GRAB
YOU SAID WHILE WORSHIPPING THE BLUE MOON IN MAY.
DANG IT!
HE BELIEVED THAT LOAD OF CROCK?
I DIDN'T KNOW WHAT I WAS SAYING. I JUST SAID THE FIRST THING THAT CAME TO MIND.
WOW, HE STILL THINKS HIMSELF AS CLEVER?
WHAT A MEATHEAD
ANYWAY, HE NEVER TOOK HIS EYES OFF OF ME.
HE TREATED ME LIKE HIS POSSESSION.
I HAD TO RIDE WITH HIM.
DON'T LOOK! I'LL KILL YOU JUST FOR LOOKING!
TEXTBOOK POSSESSIVE PARANOIA

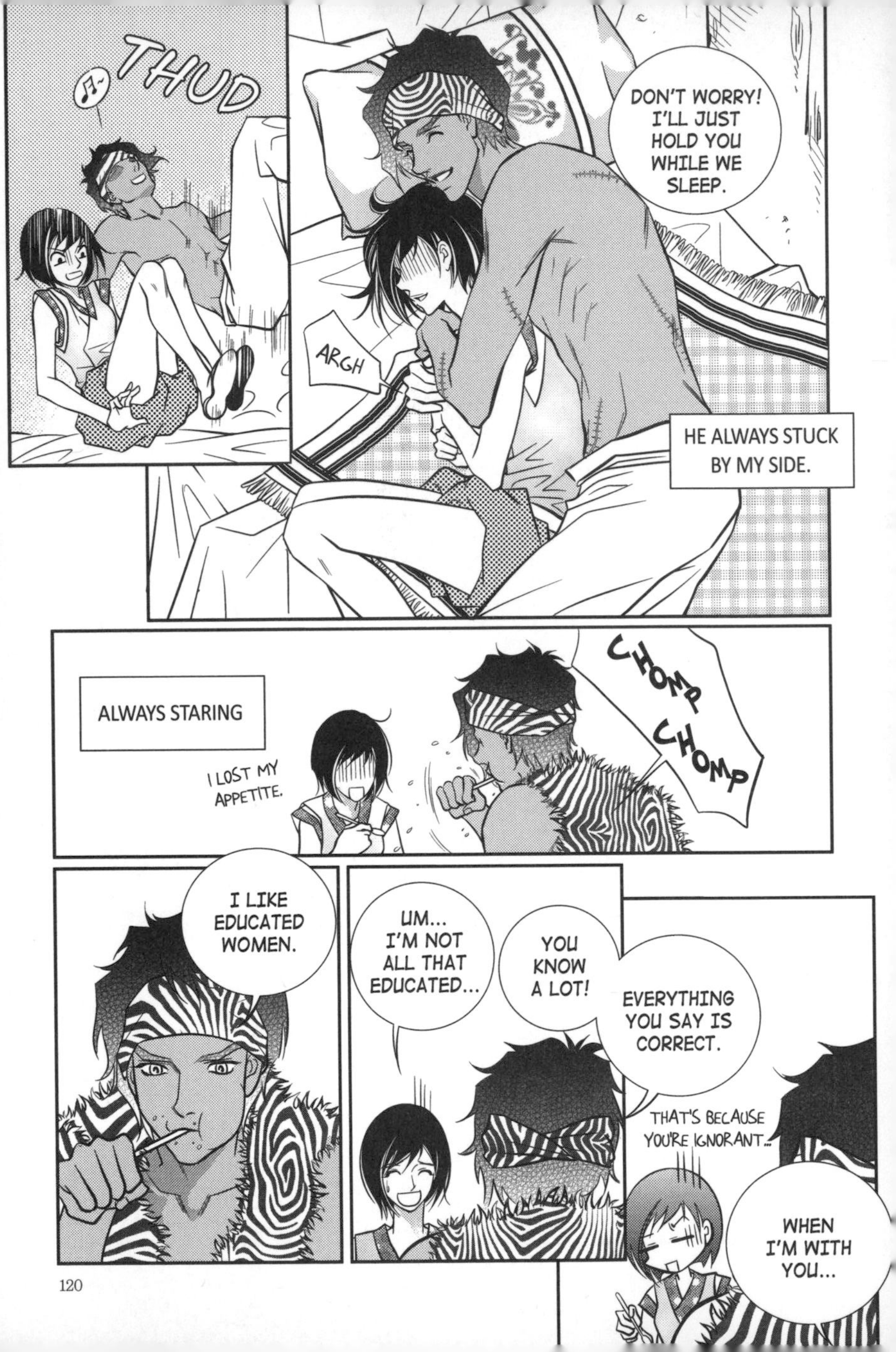
THUD
DON'T WORRY! I'LL JUST HOLD YOU WHILE WE SLEEP.
ARGH
HE ALWAYS STUCK BY MY SIDE.
ALWAYS STARING
I LOST MY APPETITE.
CHOMP CHOMP
I LIKE EDUCATED WOMEN.
UM... I'M NOT ALL THAT EDUCATED...
YOU KNOW A LOT!
EVERYTHING YOU SAY IS CORRECT.
THAT'S BECAUSE YOU'RE IGNORANT...
WHEN I'M WITH YOU...

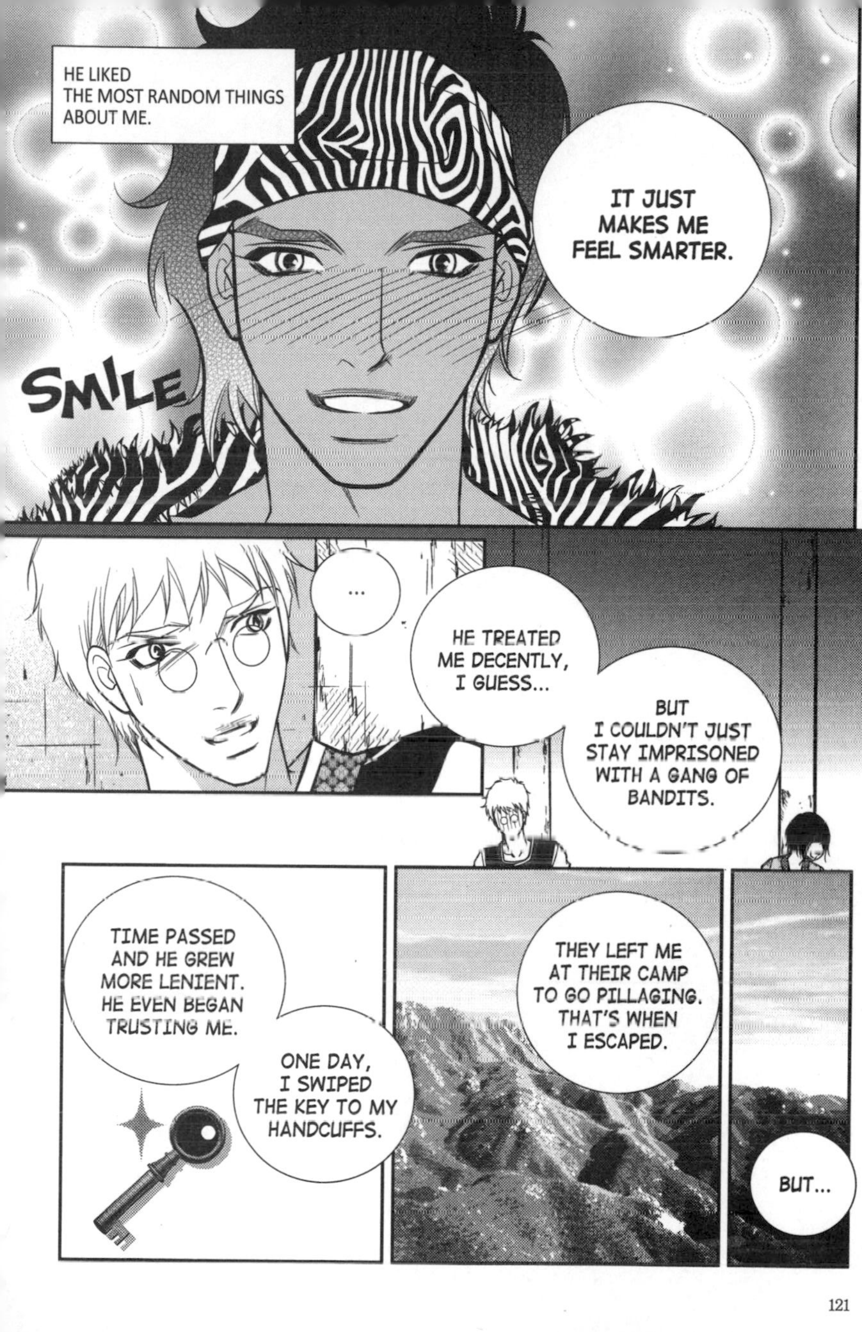
HE LIKED THE MOST RANDOM THINGS ABOUT ME.
IT JUST MAKES ME FEEL SMARTER.
SMILE
...
HE TREATED ME DECENTLY, I GUESS...
BUT I COULDN'T JUST STAY IMPRISONED WITH A GANG OF BANDITS.
TIME PASSED AND HE GREW MORE LENIENT. HE EVEN BEGAN TRUSTING ME.
ONE DAY, I SWIPED THE KEY TO MY HANDCUFFS.
THEY LEFT ME AT THEIR CAMP TO GO PILLAGING. THAT'S WHEN I ESCAPED.
BUT...

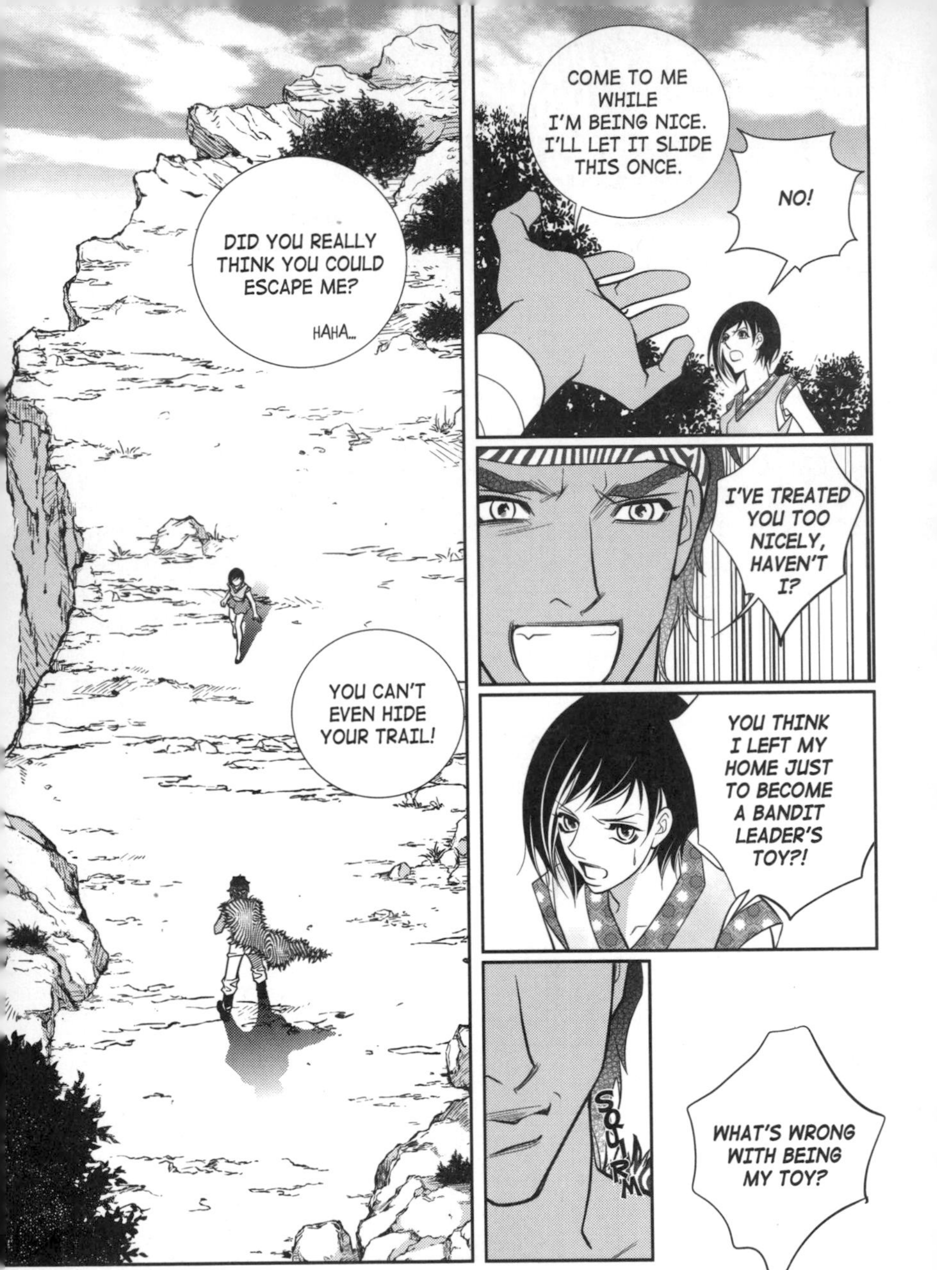
DID YOU REALLY THINK YOU COULD ESCAPE ME?
HAHA...
YOU CAN'T EVEN HIDE YOUR TRAIL!
COME TO ME WHILE I'M BEING NICE. I'LL LET IT SLIDE THIS ONCE.
NO!
I'VE TREATED YOU TOO NICELY, HAVEN'T I?
YOU THINK I LEFT MY HOME JUST TO BECOME A BANDIT LEADER'S TOY?!
SQUIRM
WHAT'S WRONG WITH BEING MY TOY?

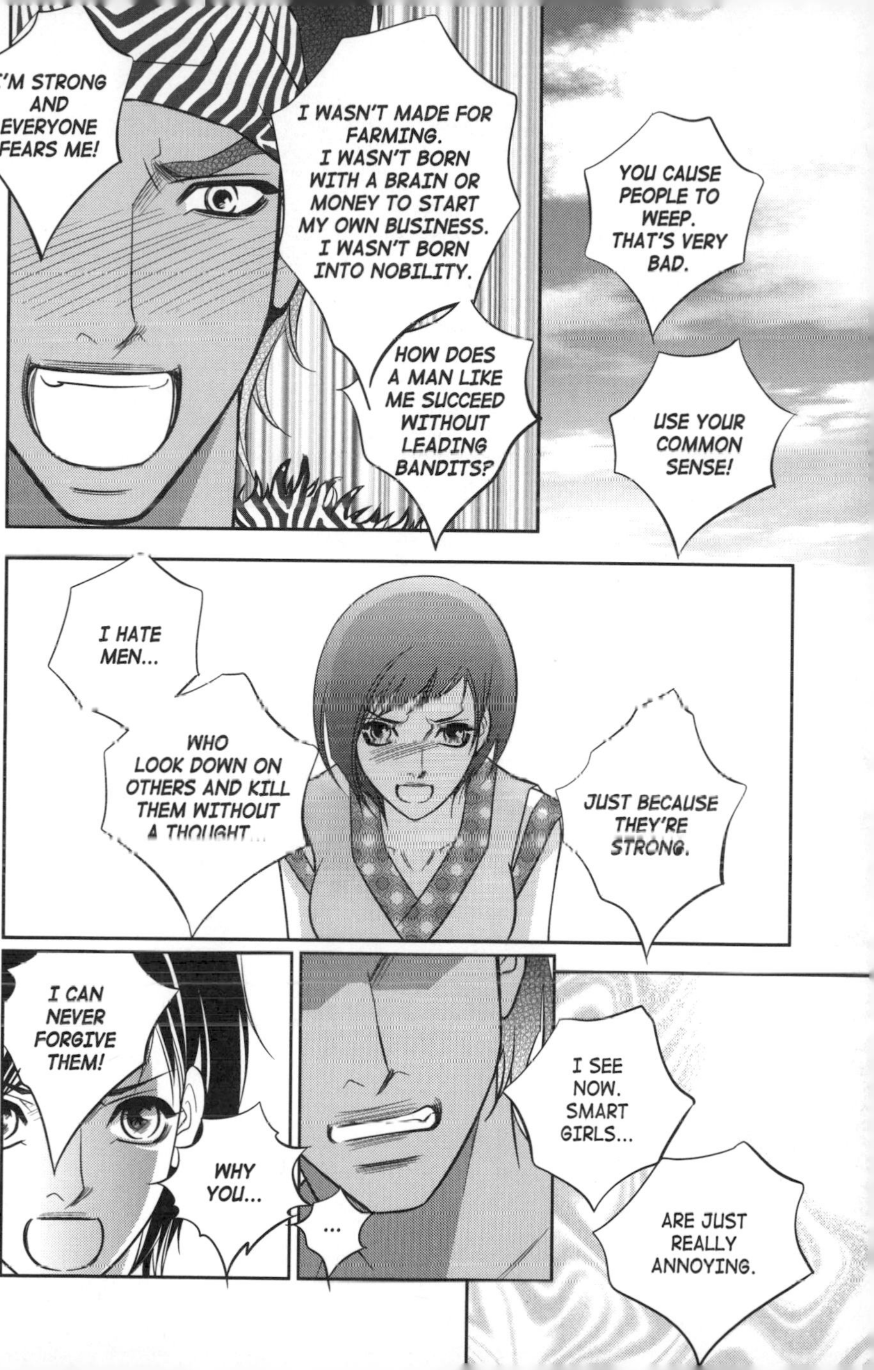

I'M STRONG AND EVERYONE FEARS ME!
I WASN'T MADE FOR FARMING. I WASN'T BORN WITH A BRAIN OR MONEY TO START MY OWN BUSINESS. I WASN'T BORN INTO NOBILITY.
HOW DOES A MAN LIKE ME SUCCEED WITHOUT LEADING BANDITS?
YOU CAUSE PEOPLE TO WEEP. THAT'S VERY BAD.
USE YOUR COMMON SENSE!
I HATE MEN...
WHO LOOK DOWN ON OTHERS AND KILL THEM WITHOUT A THOUGHT...
JUST BECAUSE THEY'RE STRONG.
I CAN NEVER FORGIVE THEM!
WHY YOU...
...
I SEE NOW. SMART GIRLS...
ARE JUST REALLY ANNOYING.

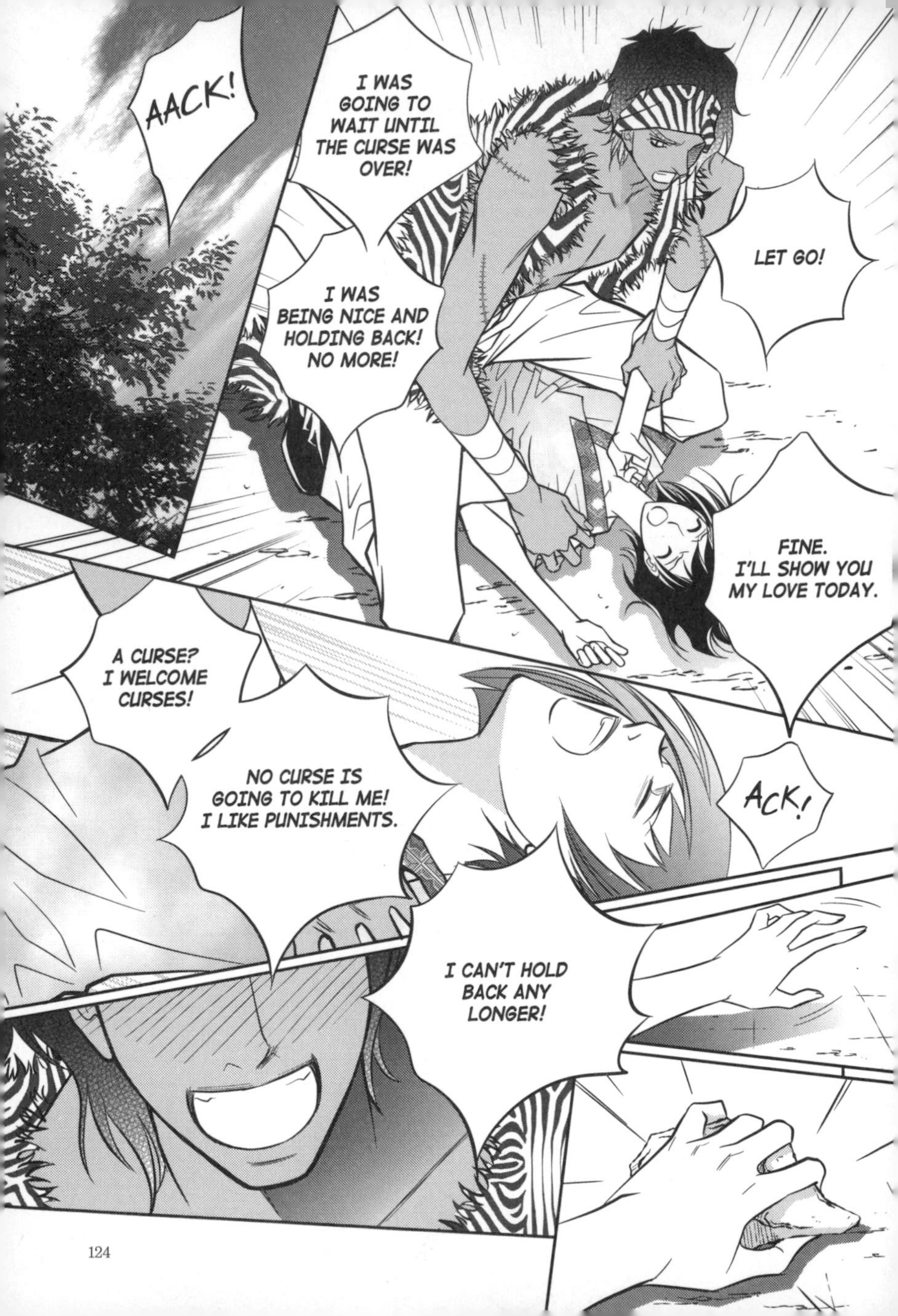
AACK!
I WAS GOING TO WAIT UNTIL THE CURSE WAS OVER!
I WAS BEING NICE AND HOLDING BACK! NO MORE!
LET GO!
FINE. I'LL SHOW YOU MY LOVE TODAY.
A CURSE? I WELCOME CURSES!
NO CURSE IS GOING TO KILL ME! I LIKE PUNISHMENTS.
ACK!
I CAN'T HOLD BACK ANY LONGER!

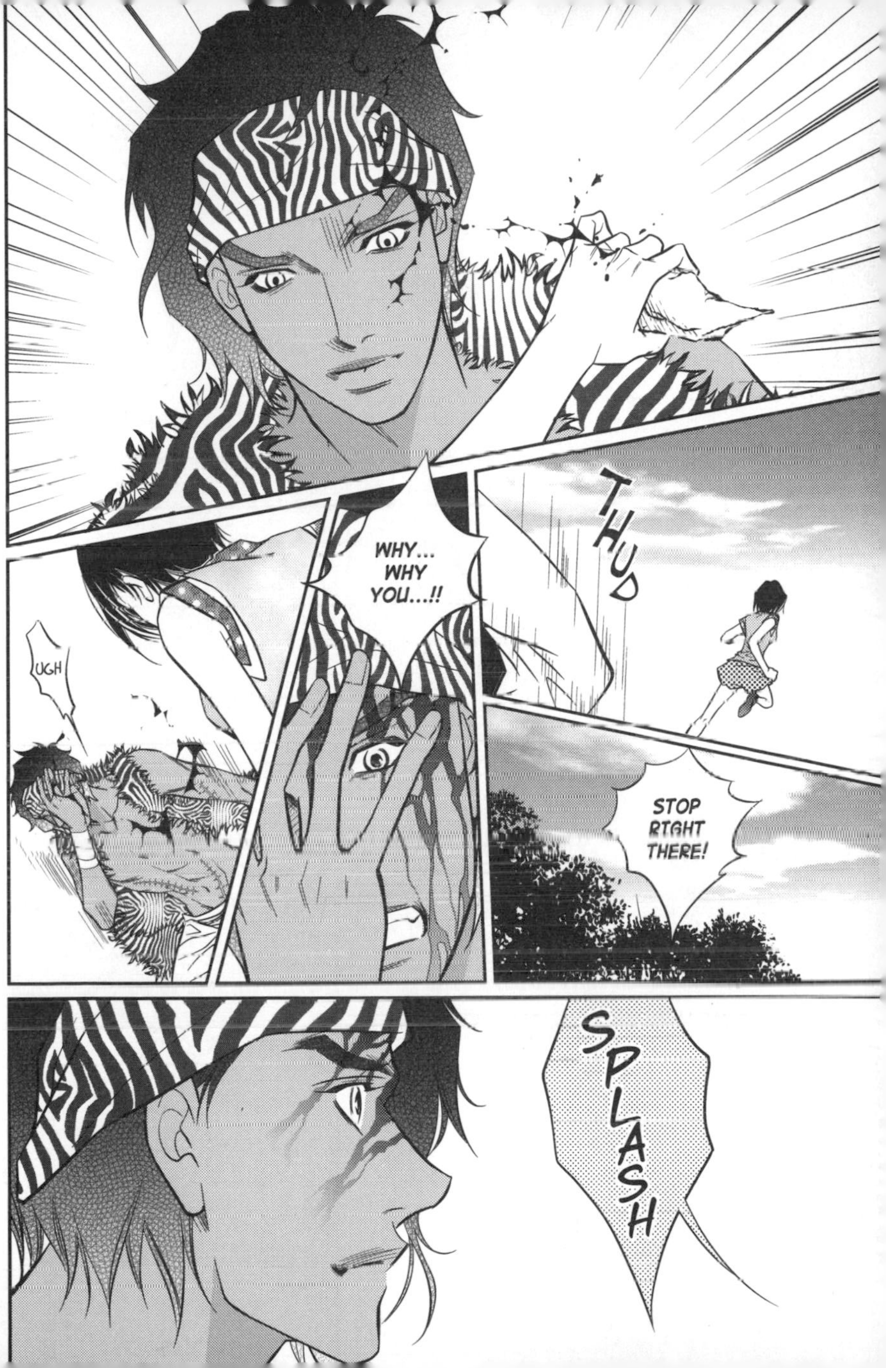
UGH
WHY... WHY YOU...!!
THUD
STOP RIGHT THERE!
SPLASH

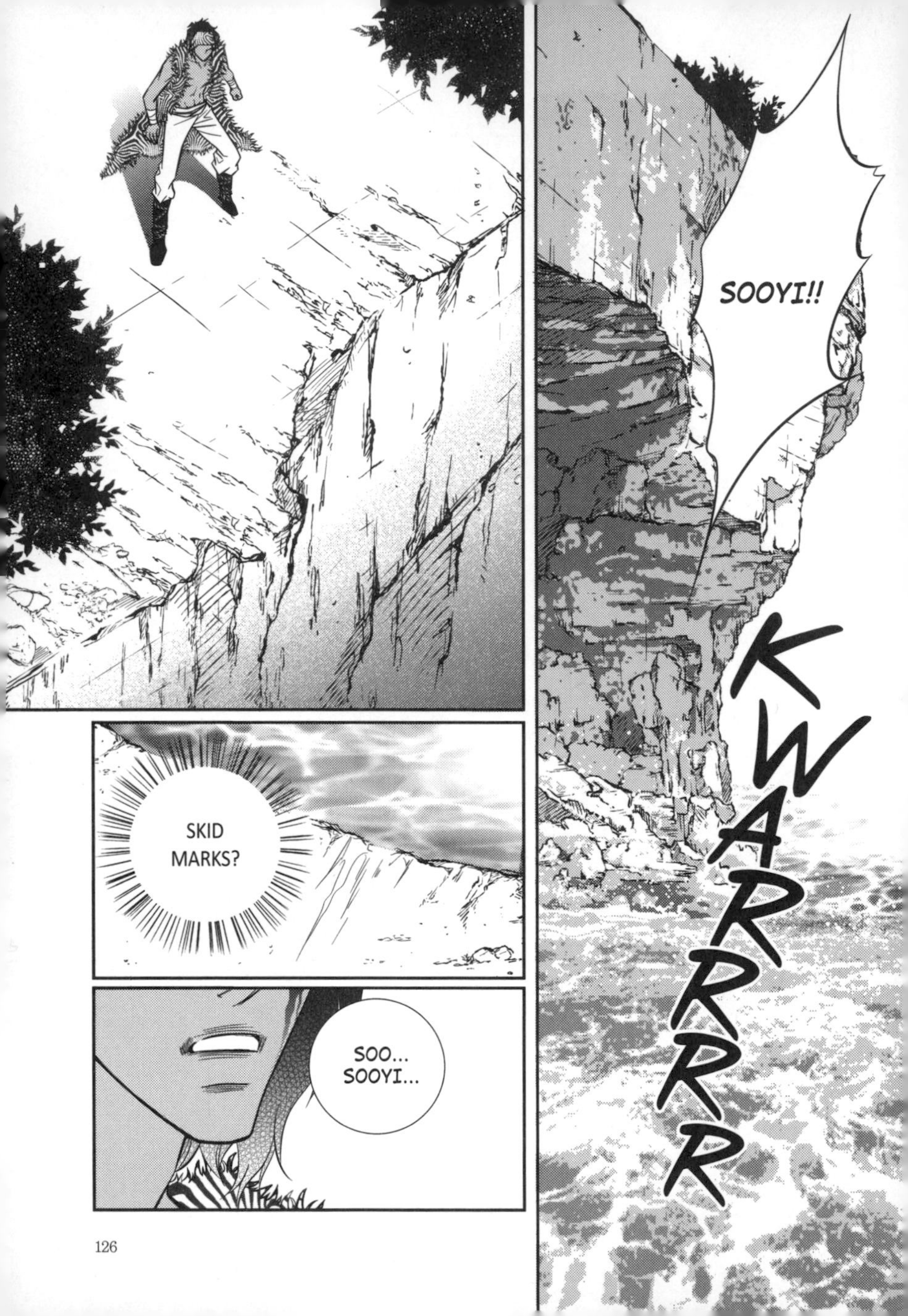
SKID MARKS?
SOO... SOOYI...
SOOYI!!
KWARRRRR

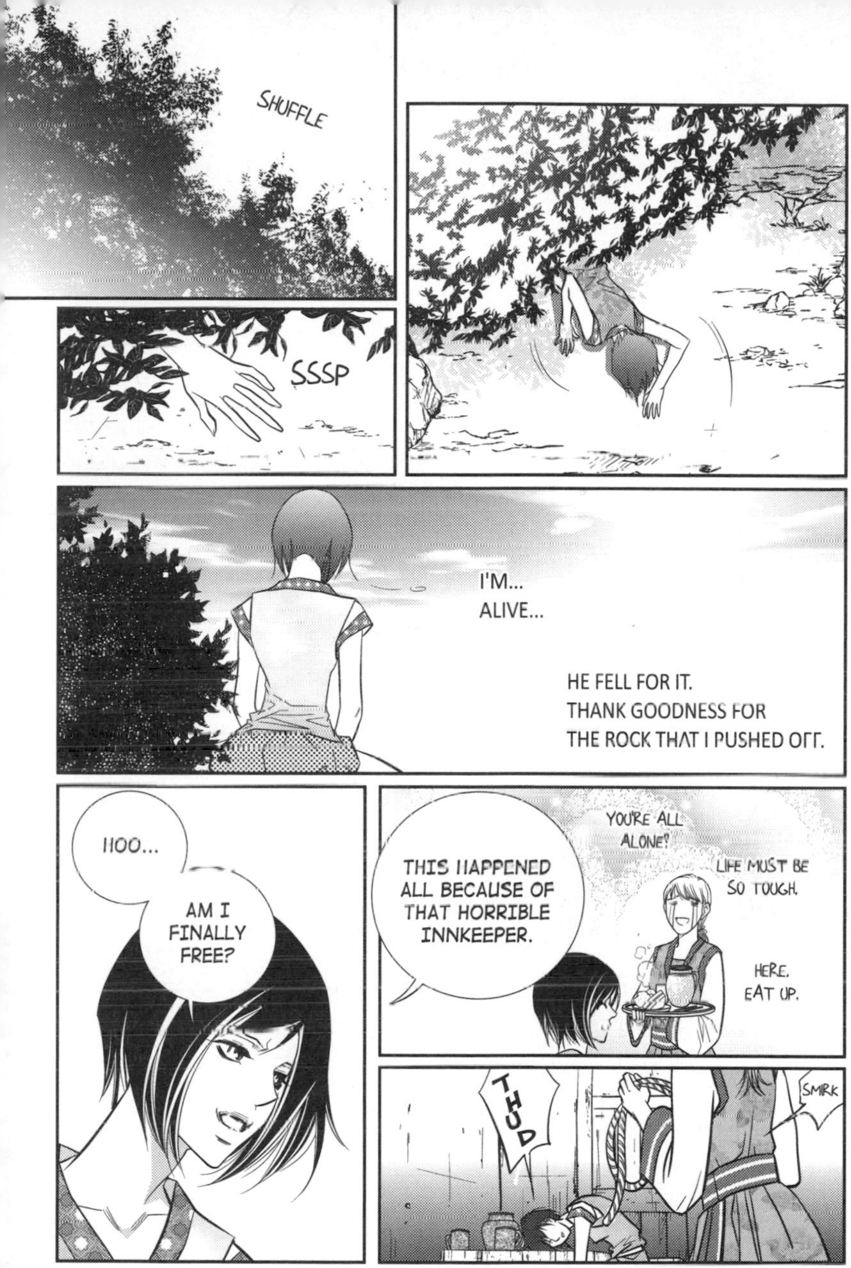
SHUFFLE
SSSP
I'M... ALIVE...
HE FELL FOR IT. THANK GOODNESS FOR THE ROCK THAT I PUSHED OFF.
HOO...
AM I FINALLY FREE?
THIS HAPPENED ALL BECAUSE OF THAT HORRIBLE INNKEEPER.
YOU'RE ALL ALONE?
LIFE MUST BE SO TOUGH.
HERE. EAT UP.
THUD
SMIRK

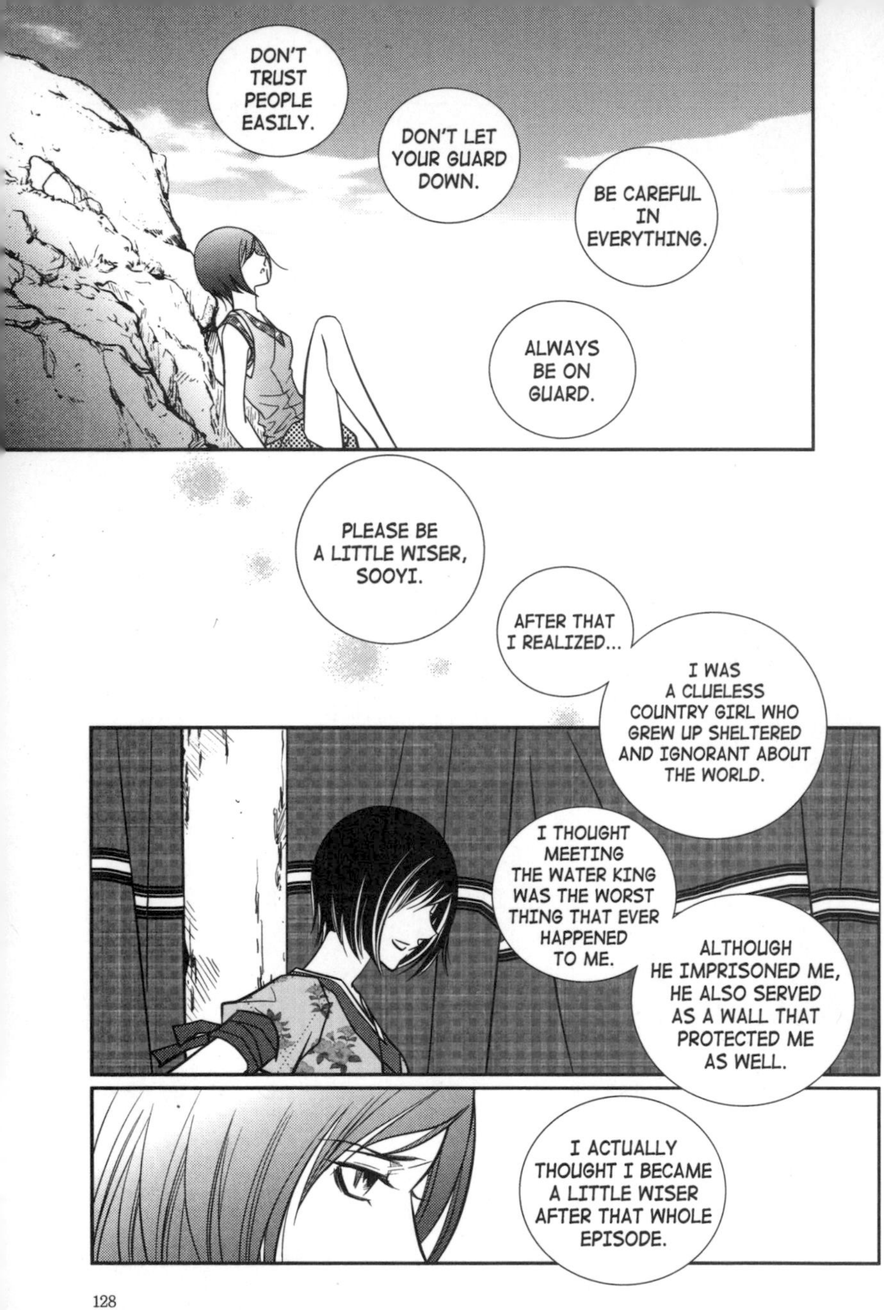
DON'T TRUST PEOPLE EASILY.
DON'T LET YOUR GUARD DOWN.
BE CAREFUL IN EVERYTHING.
ALWAYS BE ON GUARD.
PLEASE BE A LITTLE WISER, SOOYI.
AFTER THAT I REALIZED...
I WAS A CLUELESS COUNTRY GIRL WHO GREW UP SHELTERED AND IGNORANT ABOUT THE WORLD.
I THOUGHT MEETING THE WATER KING WAS THE WORST THING THAT EVER HAPPENED TO ME.
ALTHOUGH HE IMPRISONED ME, HE ALSO SERVED AS A WALL THAT PROTECTED ME AS WELL.
I ACTUALLY THOUGHT I BECAME A LITTLE WISER AFTER THAT WHOLE EPISODE.

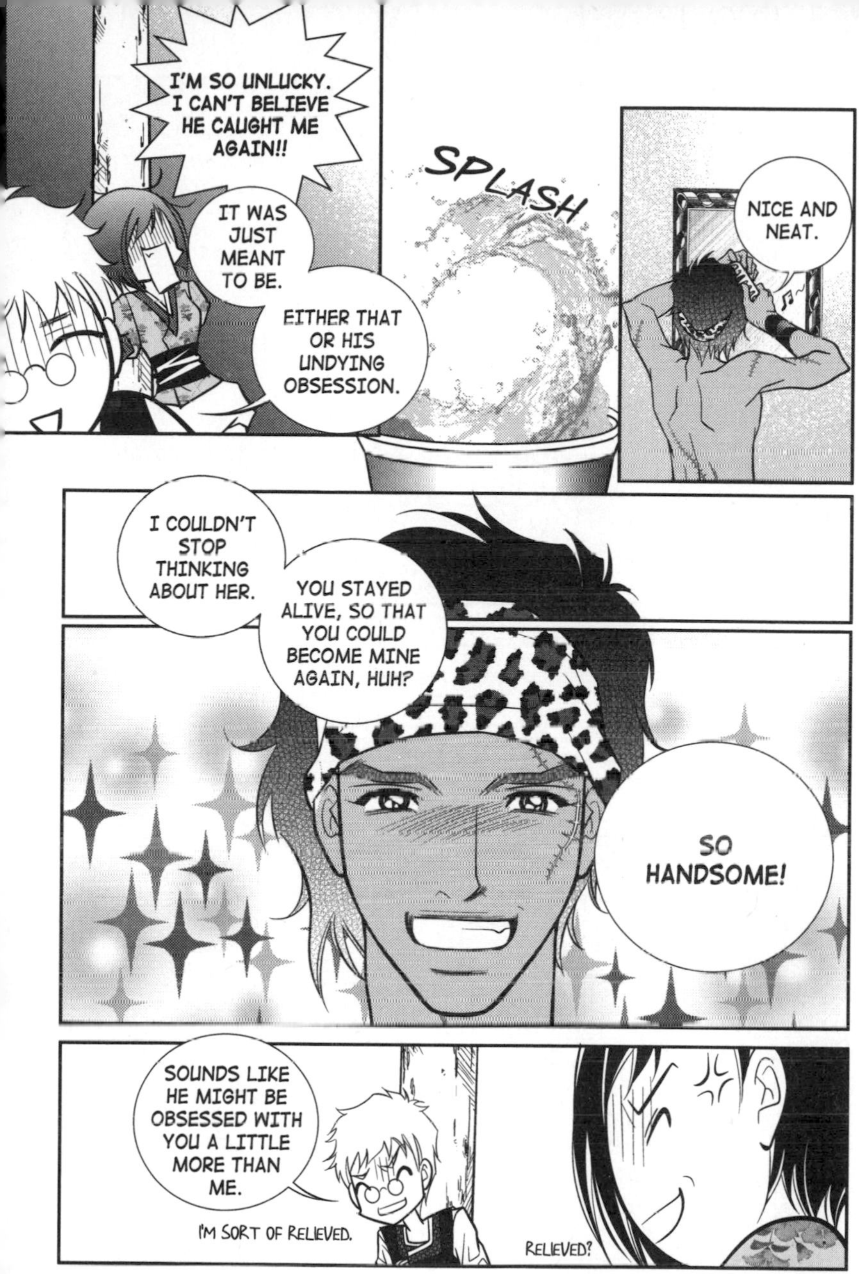
I'M SO UNLUCKY. I CAN'T BELIEVE HE CAUGHT ME AGAIN!!
IT WAS JUST MEANT TO BE.
EITHER THAT OR HIS UNDYING OBSESSION.
SPLASH
NICE AND NEAT.
I COULDN'T STOP THINKING ABOUT HER.
YOU STAYED ALIVE, SO THAT YOU COULD BECOME MINE AGAIN, HUH?
SO HANDSOME!
SOUNDS LIKE HE MIGHT BE OBSESSED WITH YOU A LITTLE MORE THAN ME.
I'M SORT OF RELIEVED.
RELIEVED?

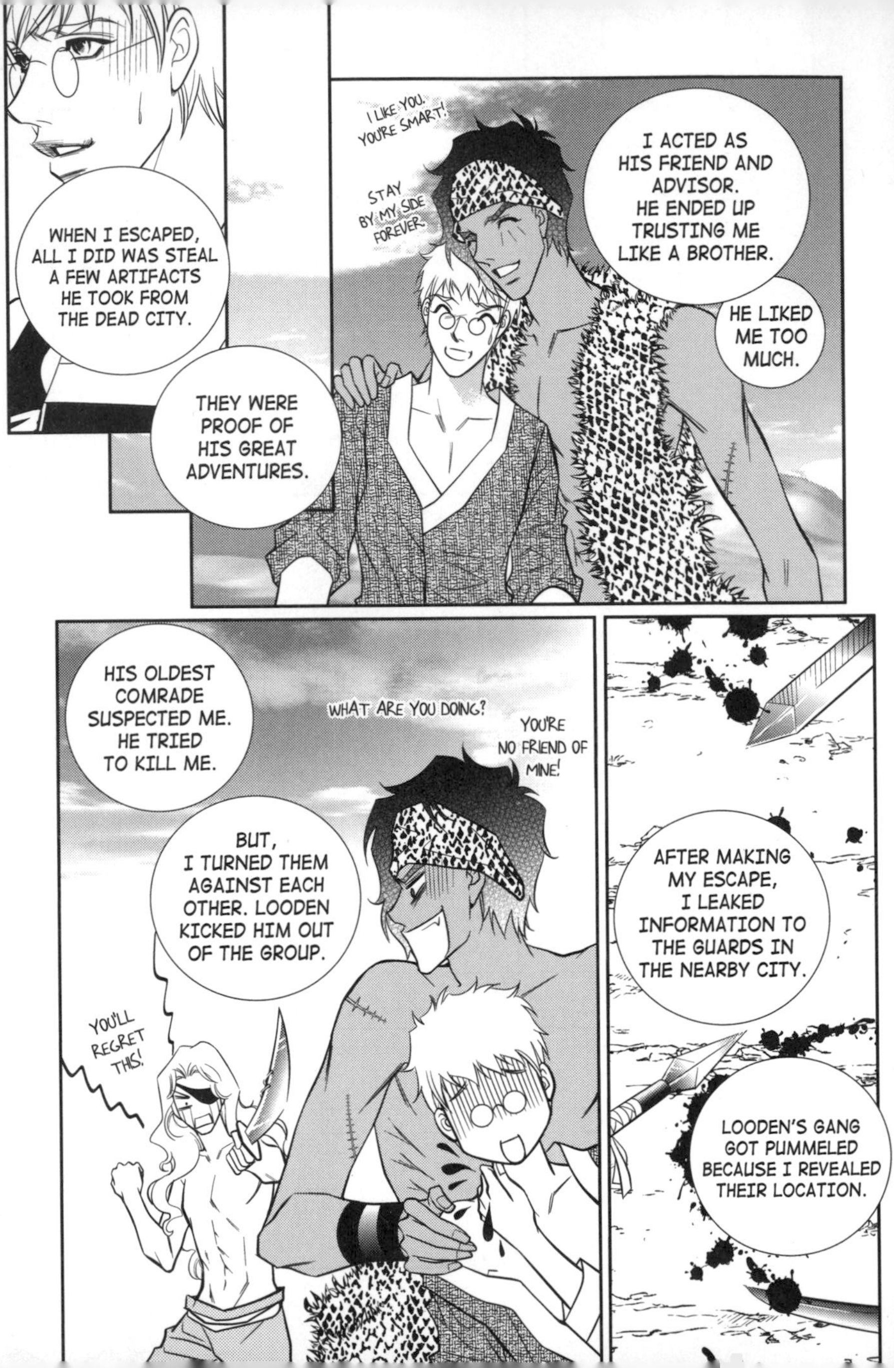
WHEN I ESCAPED, ALL I DID WAS STEAL A FEW ARTIFACTS HE TOOK FROM THE DEAD CITY.
I LIKE YOU. YOU'RE SMART!
STAY BY MY SIDE FOREVER
I ACTED AS HIS FRIEND AND ADVISOR. HE ENDED UP TRUSTING ME LIKE A BROTHER.
HE LIKED ME TOO MUCH.
THEY WERE PROOF OF HIS GREAT ADVENTURES.
HIS OLDEST COMRADE SUSPECTED ME. HE TRIED TO KILL ME.
WHAT ARE YOU DOING?
YOU'RE NO FRIEND OF MINE!
BUT, I TURNED THEM AGAINST EACH OTHER. LOODEN KICKED HIM OUT OF THE GROUP.
YOU'LL REGRET THIS!
AFTER MAKING MY ESCAPE, I LEAKED INFORMATION TO THE GUARDS IN THE NEARBY CITY.
LOODEN'S GANG GOT PUMMELED BECAUSE I REVEALED THEIR LOCATION.

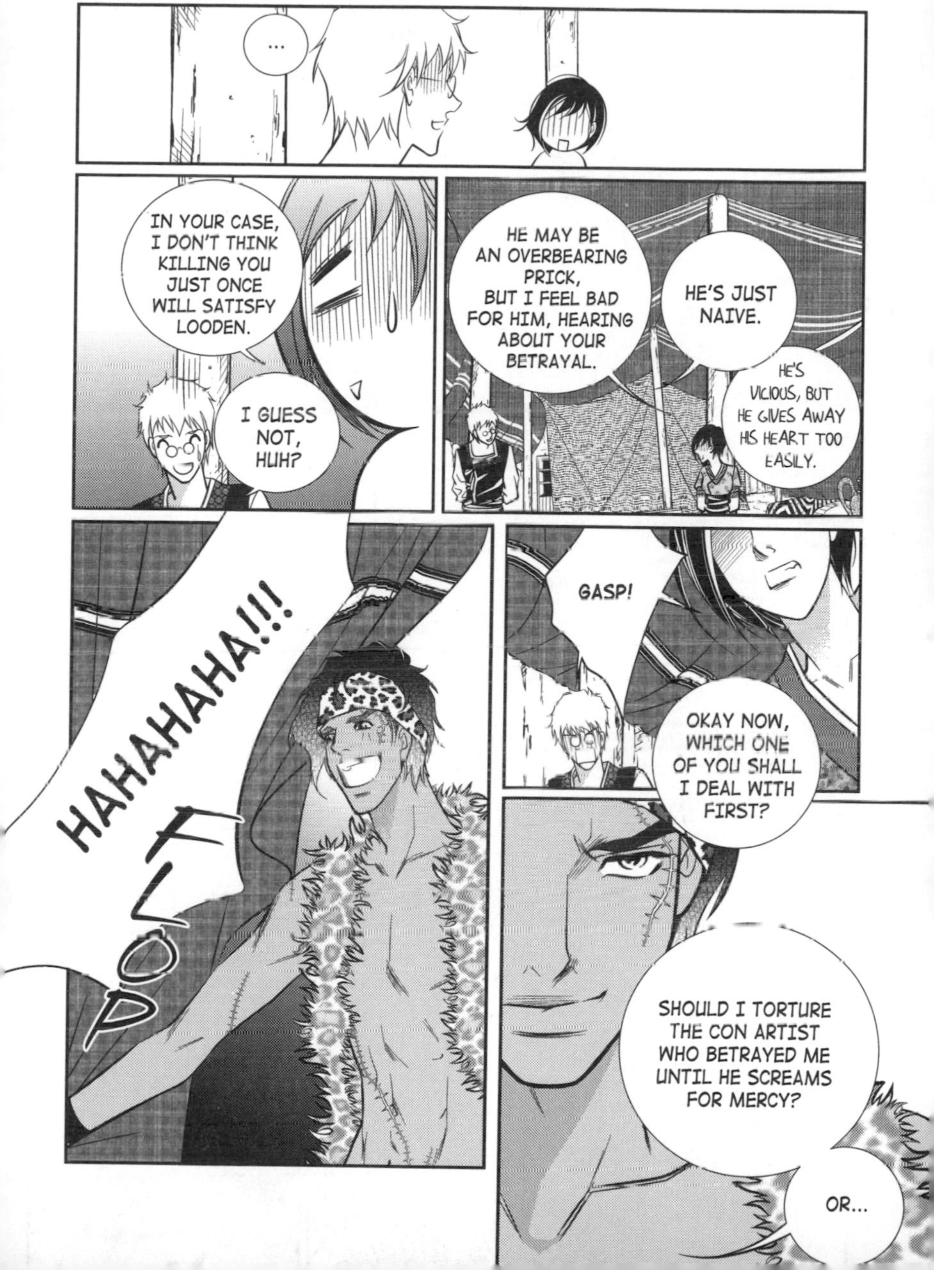
...
IN YOUR CASE, I DON'T THINK KILLING YOU JUST ONCE WILL SATISFY LOODEN.
I GUESS NOT, HUH?
HE MAY BE AN OVERBEARING PRICK, BUT I FEEL BAD FOR HIM, HEARING ABOUT YOUR BETRAYAL.
HE'S JUST NAIVE.
HE'S VICIOUS, BUT HE GIVES AWAY HIS HEART TOO EASILY.
HAHAHAHA!!!!
PLOP
GASP!
OKAY NOW, WHICH ONE OF YOU SHALL I DEAL WITH FIRST?
SHOULD I TORTURE THE CON ARTIST WHO BETRAYED ME UNTIL HE SCREAMS FOR MERCY?
OR...

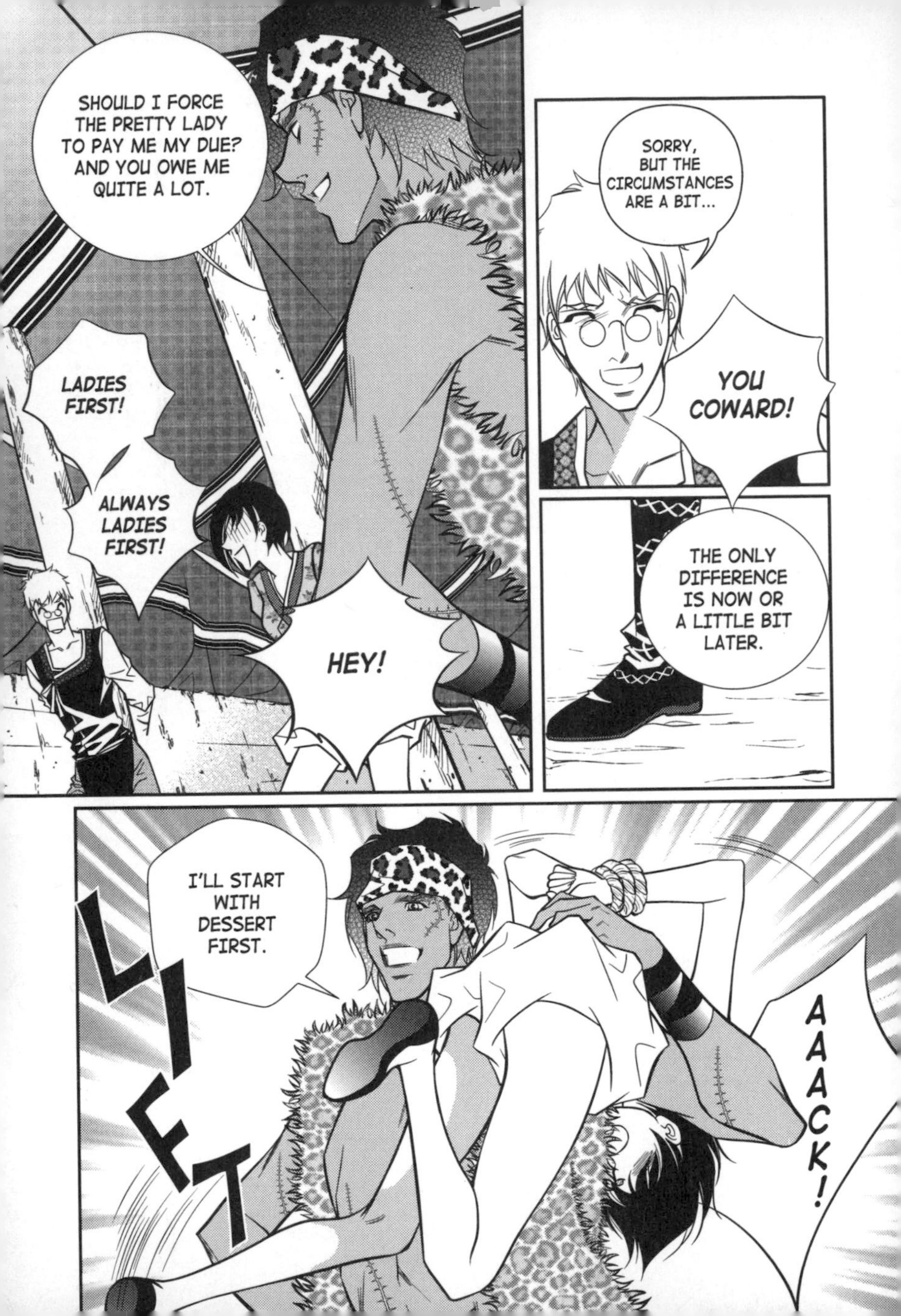
SHOULD I FORCE THE PRETTY LADY TO PAY ME MY DUE? AND YOU OWE ME QUITE A LOT.
LADIES FIRST!
ALWAYS LADIES FIRST!
HEY!
SORRY, BUT THE CIRCUMSTANCES ARE A BIT...
YOU COWARD!
THE ONLY DIFFERENCE IS NOW OR A LITTLE BIT LATER.
I'LL START WITH DESSERT FIRST.
LIFT
AAAACK!

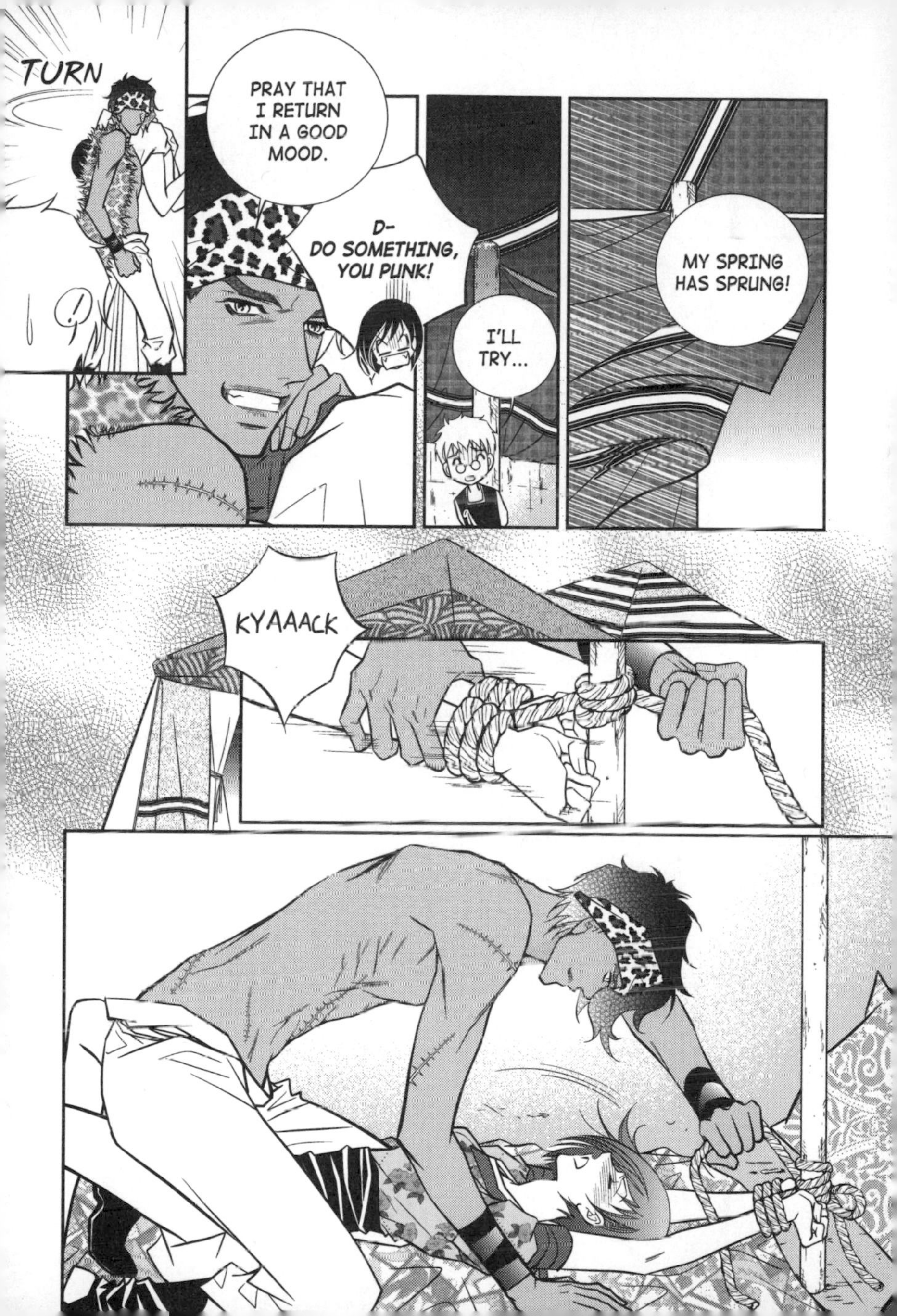

TURN
!
PRAY THAT I RETURN IN A GOOD MOOD.
D- DO SOMETHING, YOU PUNK!
I'LL TRY...
MY SPRING HAS SPRUNG!
KYAAACK

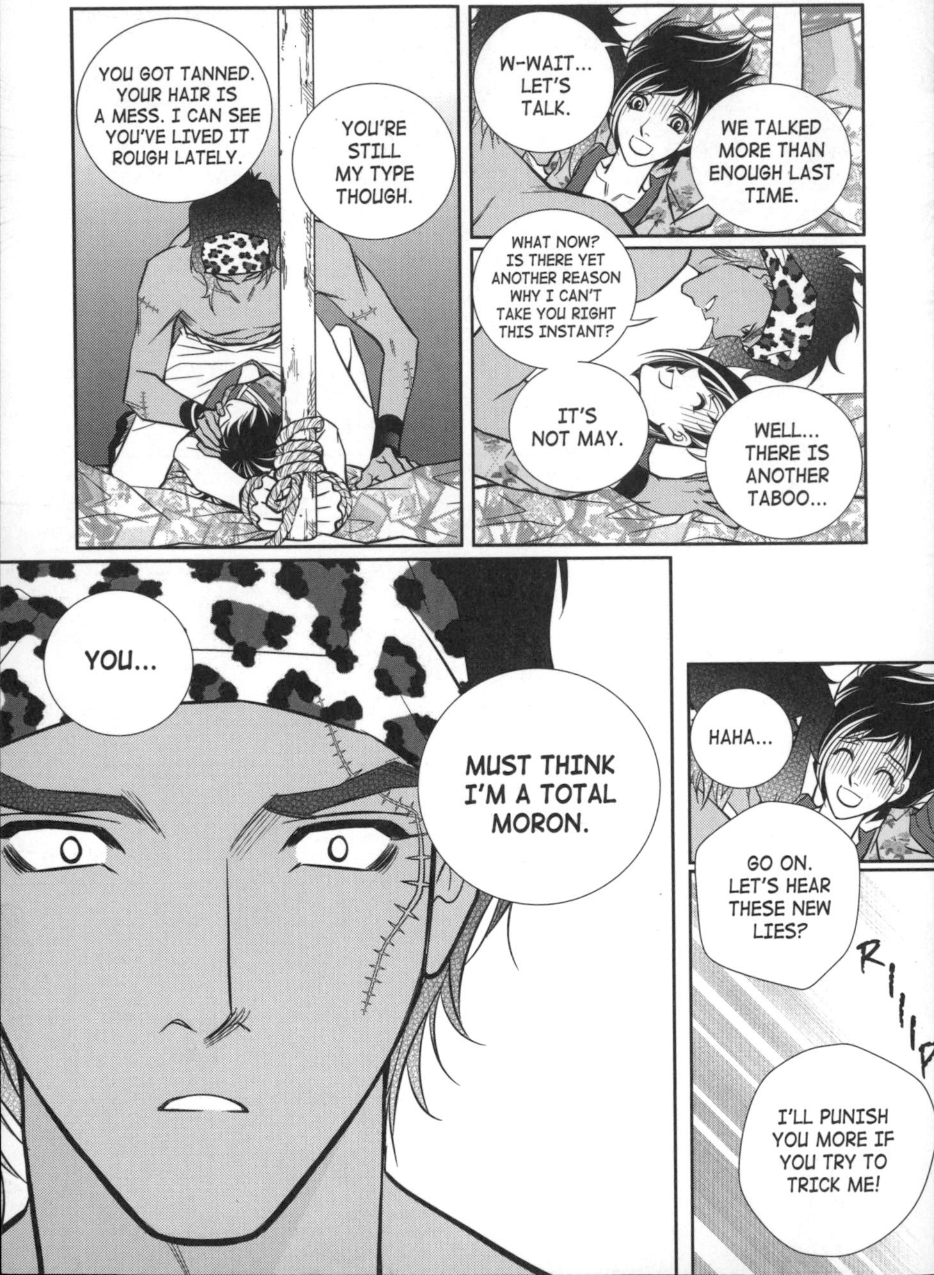
YOU GOT TANNED. YOUR HAIR IS A MESS. I CAN SEE YOU'VE LIVED IT ROUGH LATELY.
YOU'RE STILL MY TYPE THOUGH.
W-WAIT... LET'S TALK.
WE TALKED MORE THAN ENOUGH LAST TIME.
WHAT NOW? IS THERE YET ANOTHER REASON WHY I CAN'T TAKE YOU RIGHT THIS INSTANT?
IT'S NOT MAY.
WELL... THERE IS ANOTHER TABOO...
YOU...
MUST THINK I'M A TOTAL MORON.
HAHA...
GO ON. LET'S HEAR THESE NEW LIES?
RIIIP
I'LL PUNISH YOU MORE IF YOU TRY TO TRICK ME!

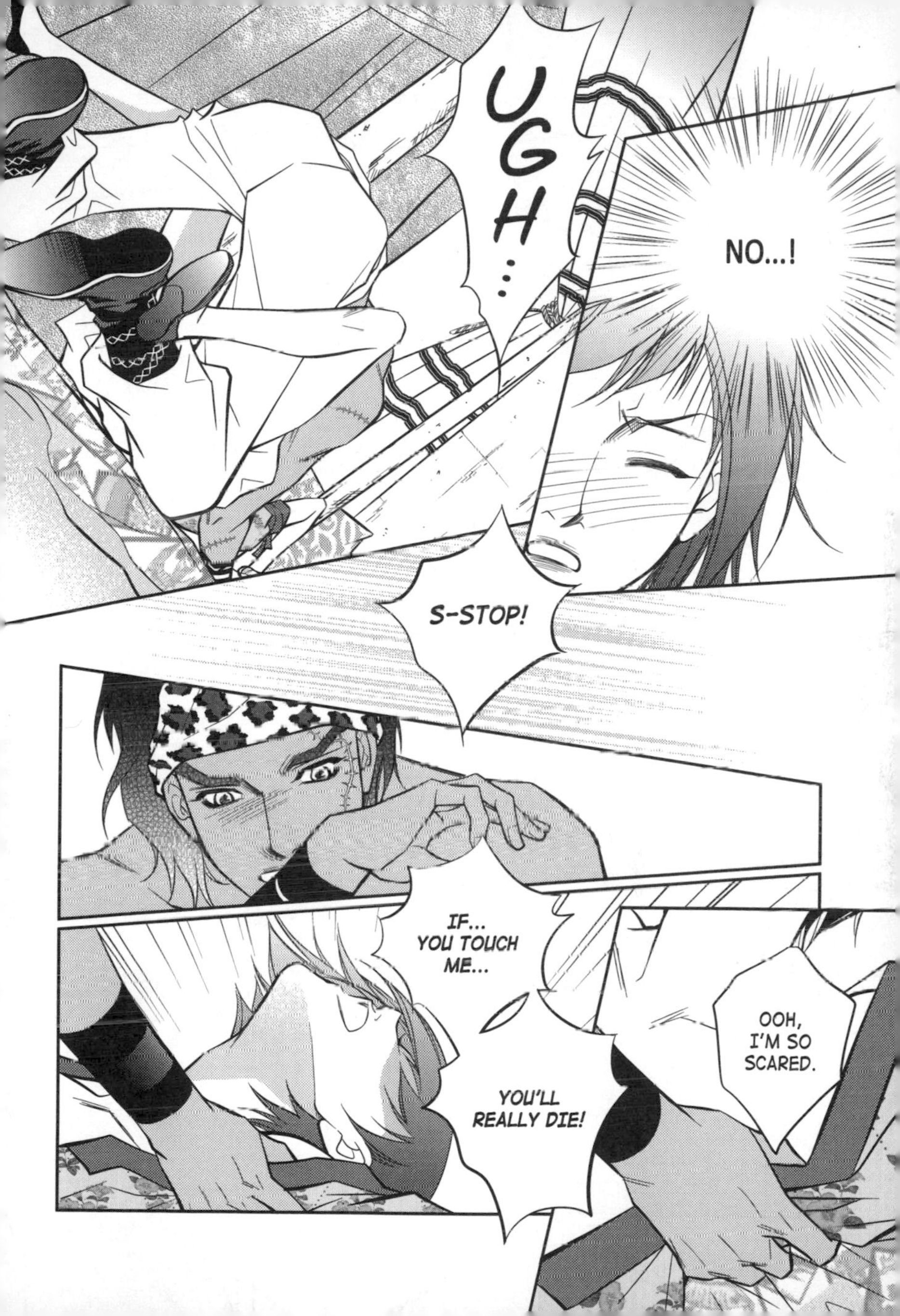
UGH...
NO...!
S-STOP!
IF... YOU TOUCH ME...
YOU'LL REALLY DIE!
OOH, I'M SO SCARED.

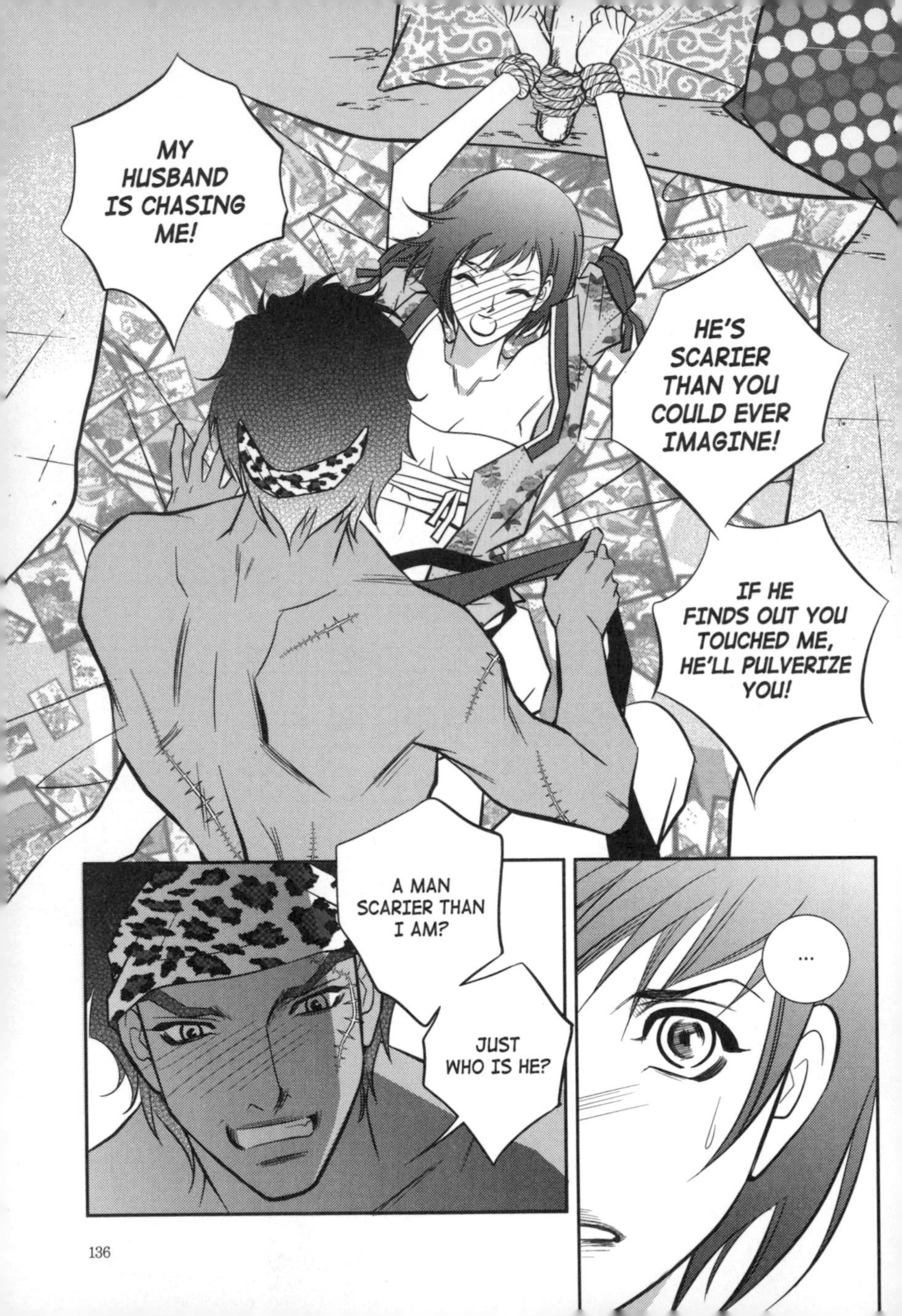
MY HUSBAND IS CHASING ME!
HE'S SCARIER THAN YOU COULD EVER IMAGINE!
IF HE FINDS OUT YOU TOUCHED ME, HE'LL PULVERIZE YOU!
A MAN SCARIER THAN I AM?
JUST WHO IS HE?
...

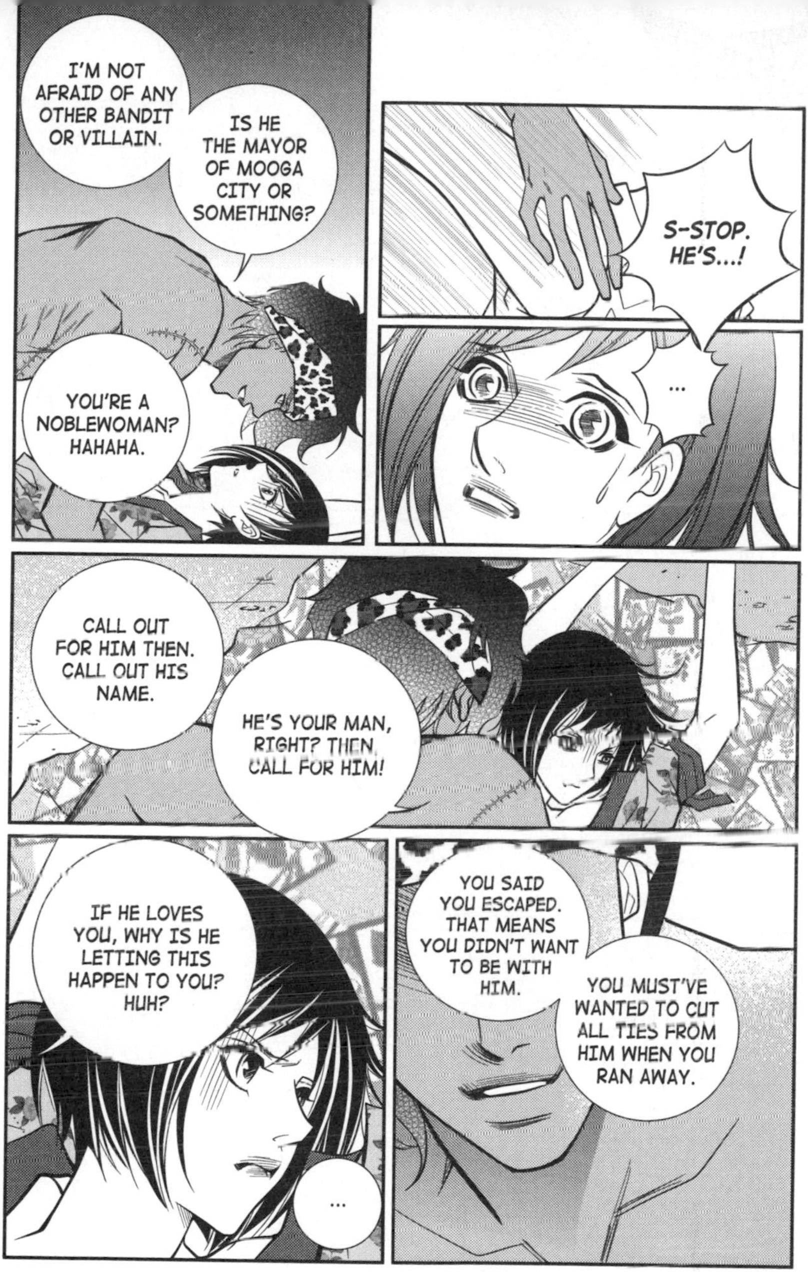
I'M NOT AFRAID OF ANY OTHER BANDIT OR VILLAIN.
IS HE THE MAYOR OF MOOGA CITY OR SOMETHING?
YOU'RE A NOBLEWOMAN? HAHAHA.
S-STOP. HE'S...!
...
CALL OUT FOR HIM THEN. CALL OUT HIS NAME.
HE'S YOUR MAN, RIGHT? THEN, CALL FOR HIM!
IF HE LOVES YOU, WHY IS HE LETTING THIS HAPPEN TO YOU? HUH?
...
YOU SAID YOU ESCAPED. THAT MEANS YOU DIDN'T WANT TO BE WITH HIM.
YOU MUST'VE WANTED TO CUT ALL TIES FROM HIM WHEN YOU RAN AWAY.

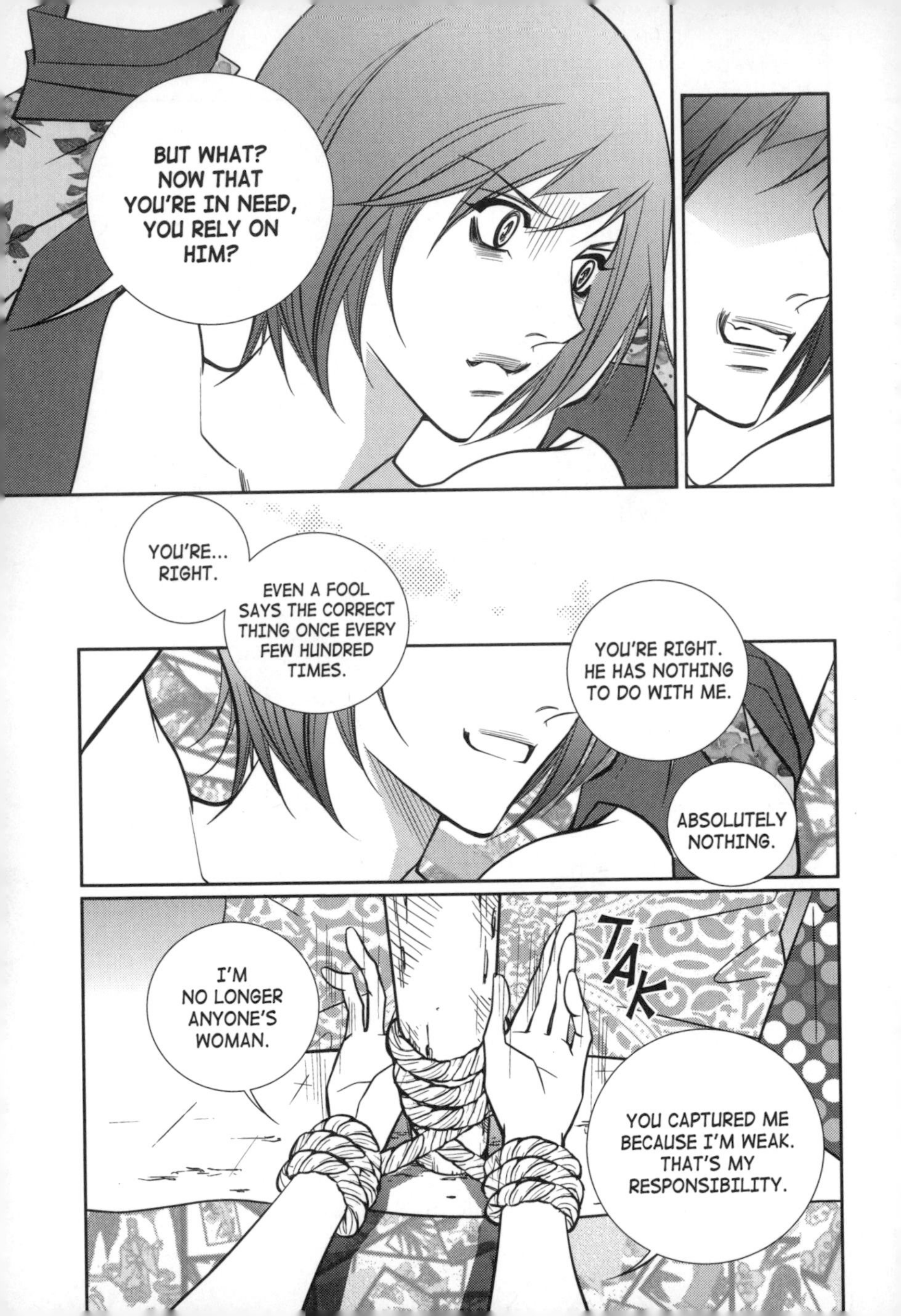
BUT WHAT? NOW THAT YOU'RE IN NEED, YOU RELY ON HIM?
YOU'RE... RIGHT.
EVEN A FOOL SAYS THE CORRECT THING ONCE EVERY FEW HUNDRED TIMES.
YOU'RE RIGHT. HE HAS NOTHING TO DO WITH ME.
ABSOLUTELY NOTHING.
I'M NO LONGER ANYONE'S WOMAN.
TAK
YOU CAPTURED ME BECAUSE I'M WEAK. THAT'S MY RESPONSIBILITY.

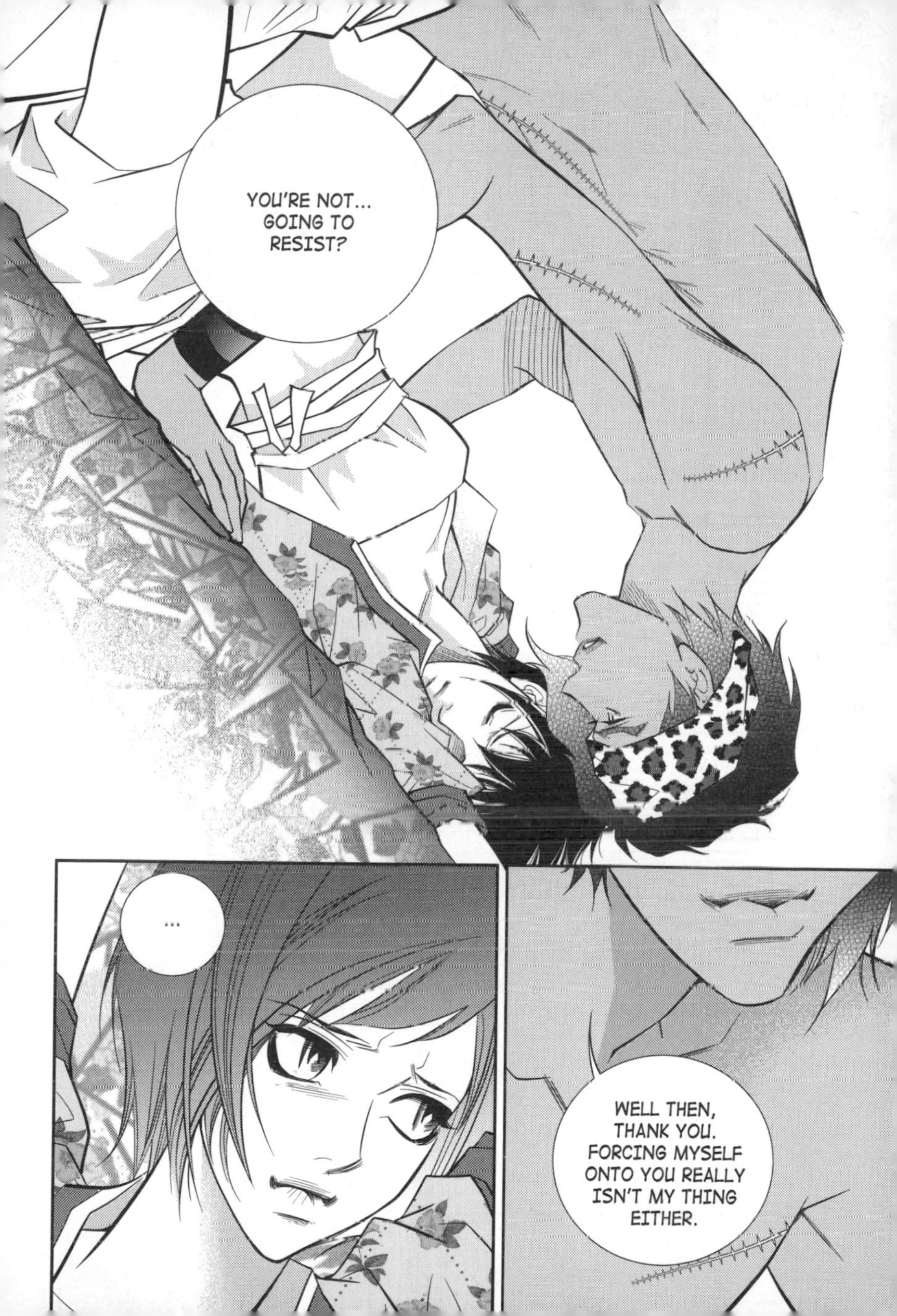
YOU'RE NOT... GOING TO RESIST?
...
WELL THEN, THANK YOU. FORCING MYSELF ONTO YOU REALLY ISN'T MY THING EITHER.

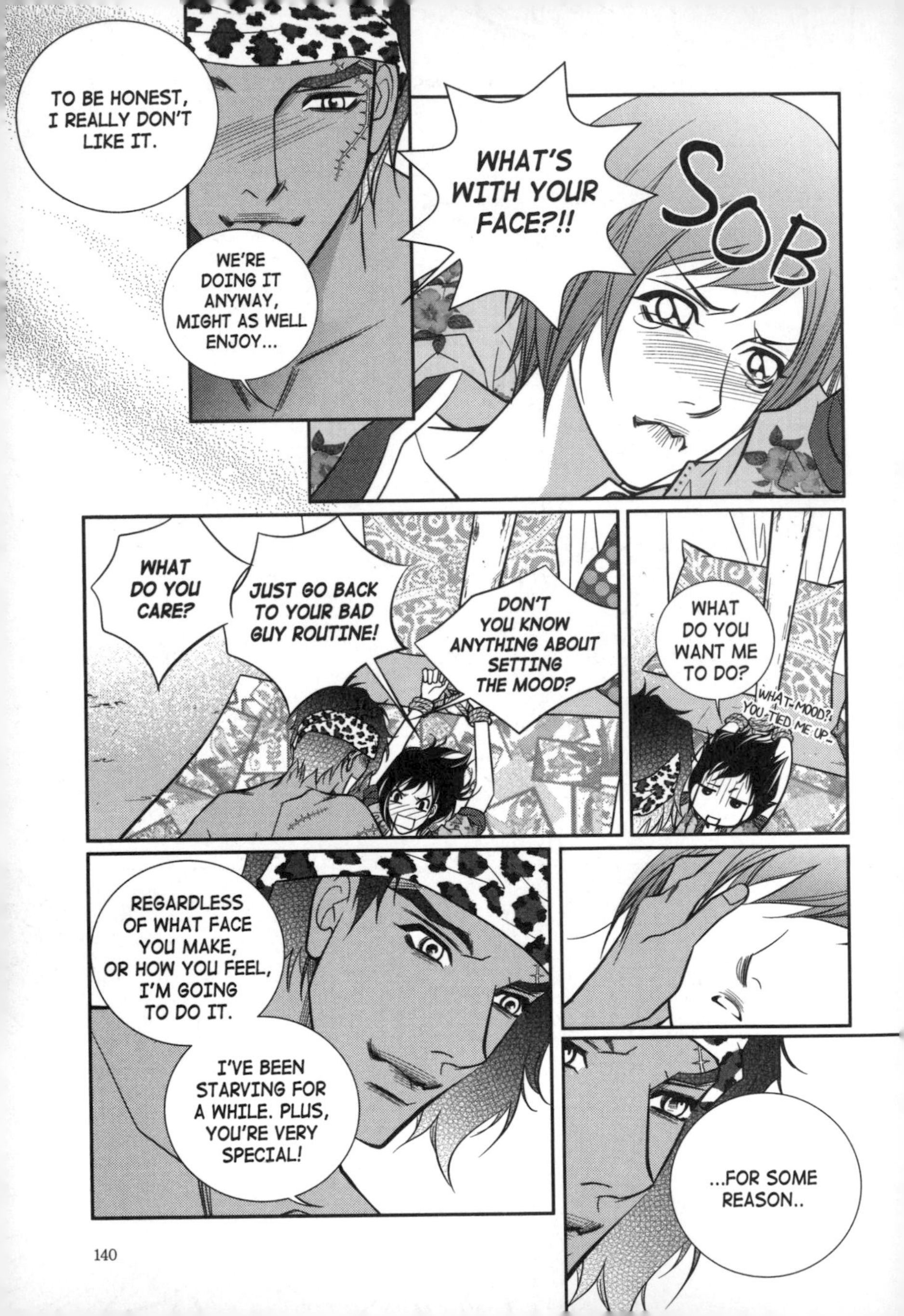
TO BE HONEST, I REALLY DON'T LIKE IT.
WE'RE DOING IT ANYWAY, MIGHT AS WELL ENJOY...
WHAT'S WITH YOUR FACE?!!
SOB
WHAT DO YOU CARE?
JUST GO BACK TO YOUR BAD GUY ROUTINE!
DON'T YOU KNOW ANYTHING ABOUT SETTING THE MOOD?
WHAT DO YOU WANT ME TO DO?
WHAT-MOOD?, YOU TIED ME UP..
REGARDLESS OF WHAT FACE YOU MAKE, OR HOW YOU FEEL, I'M GOING TO DO IT.
I'VE BEEN STARVING FOR A WHILE. PLUS, YOU'RE VERY SPECIAL!
...FOR SOME REASON..

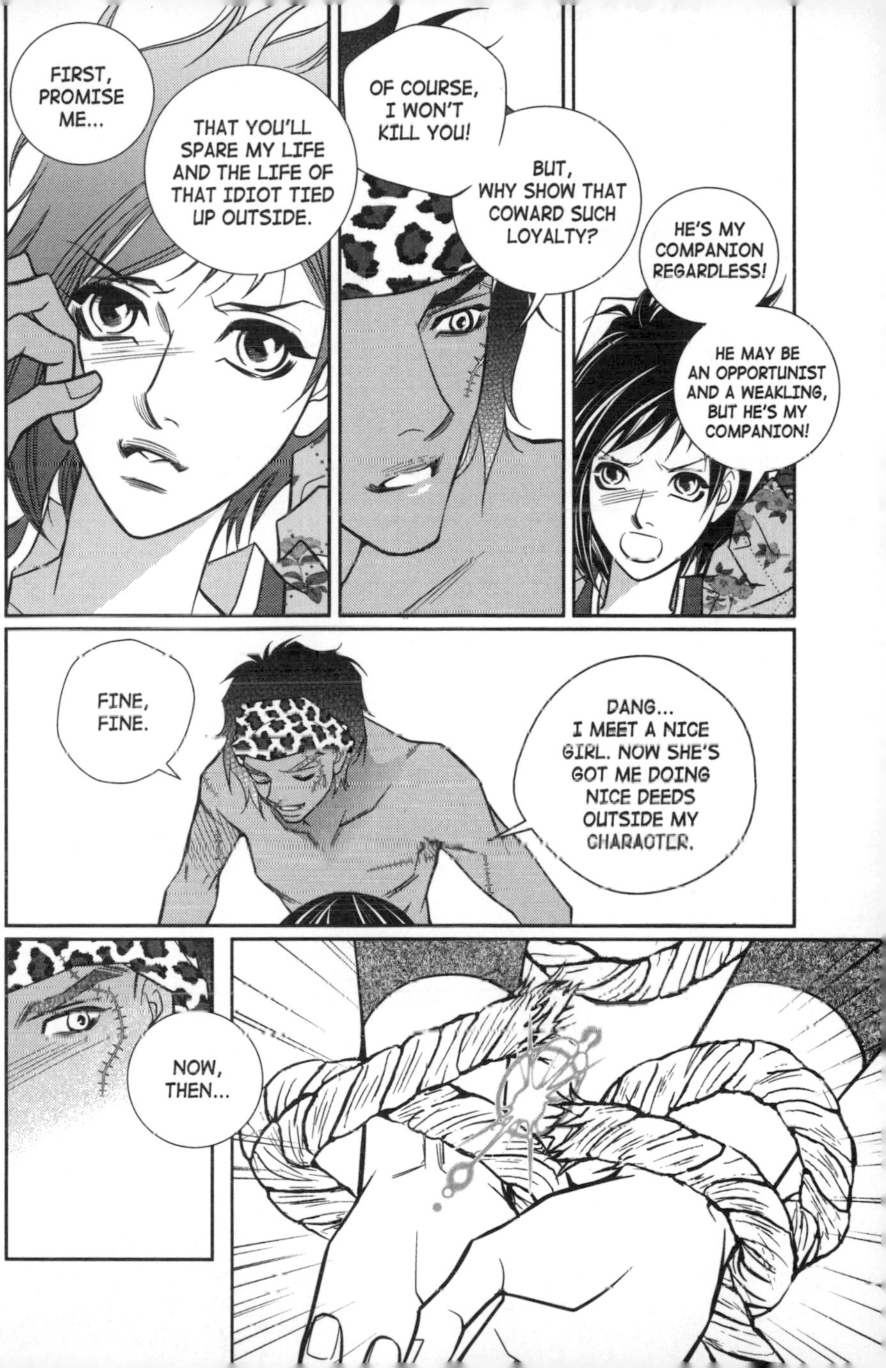
FIRST, PROMISE ME...
THAT YOU'LL SPARE MY LIFE AND THE LIFE OF THAT IDIOT TIED UP OUTSIDE.
OF COURSE, I WON'T KILL YOU!
BUT, WHY SHOW THAT COWARD SUCH LOYALTY?
HE'S MY COMPANION REGARDLESS!
HE MAY BE AN OPPORTUNIST AND A WEAKLING, BUT HE'S MY COMPANION!
FINE, FINE.
DANG... I MEET A NICE GIRL. NOW SHE'S GOT ME DOING NICE DEEDS OUTSIDE MY CHARACTER.
NOW, THEN...

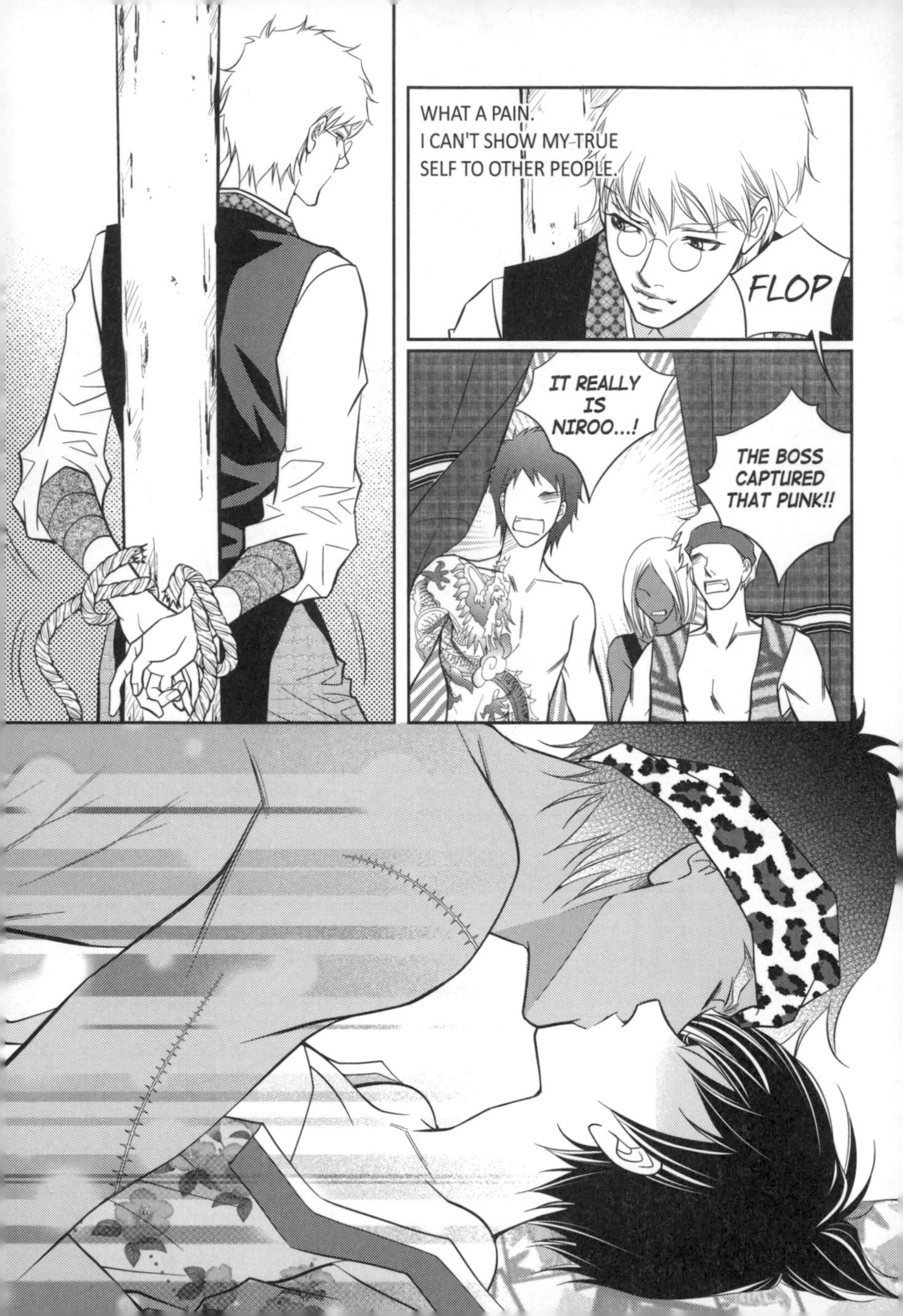
WHAT A PAIN.
I CAN'T SHOW MY TRUE
SELF TO OTHER PEOPLE.
FLOP
IT REALLY
IS
NIROO...!
THE BOSS
CAPTURED
THAT PUNK!!

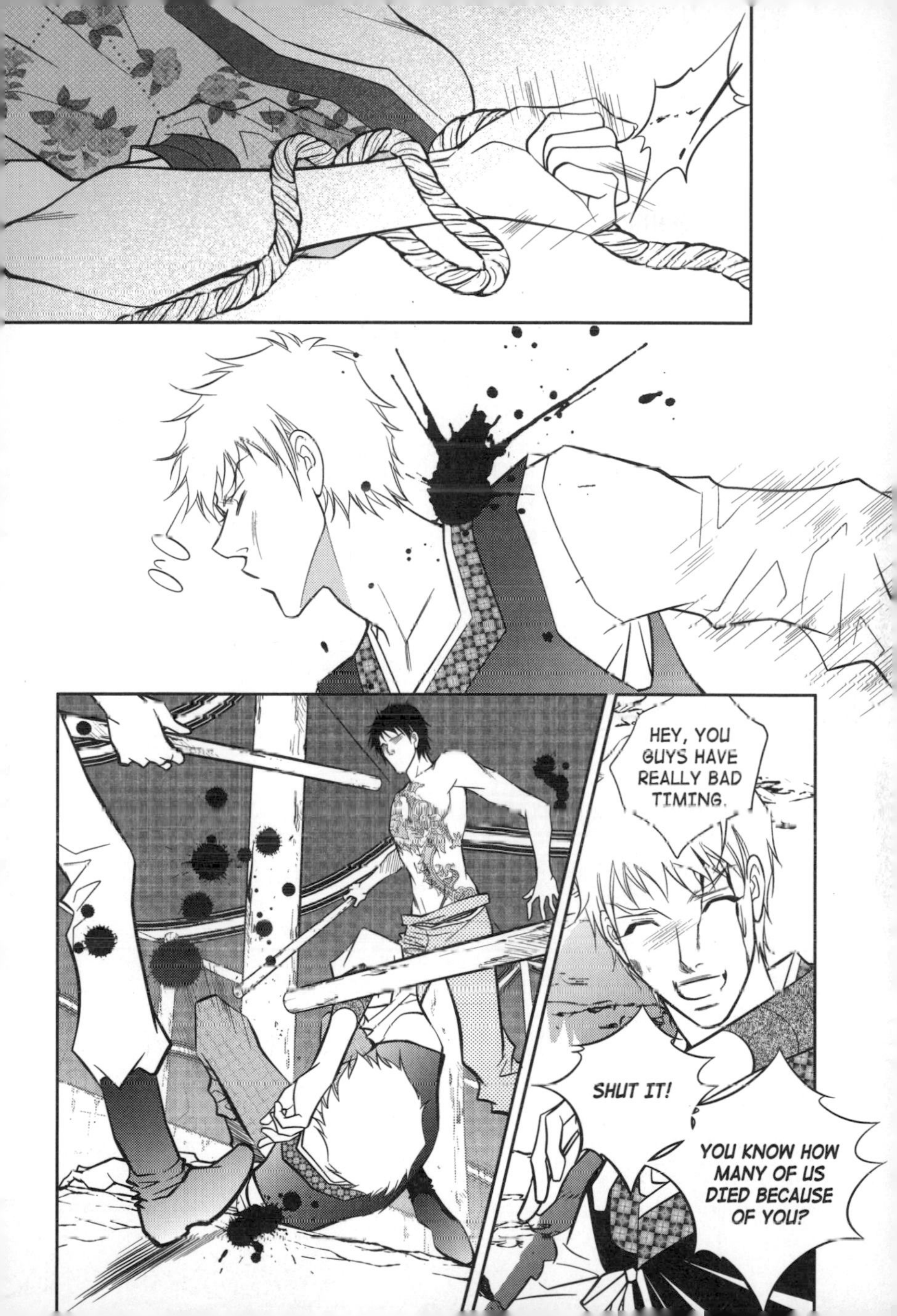
HEY, YOU GUYS HAVE REALLY BAD TIMING.
SHUT IT!
YOU KNOW HOW MANY OF US DIED BECAUSE OF YOU?

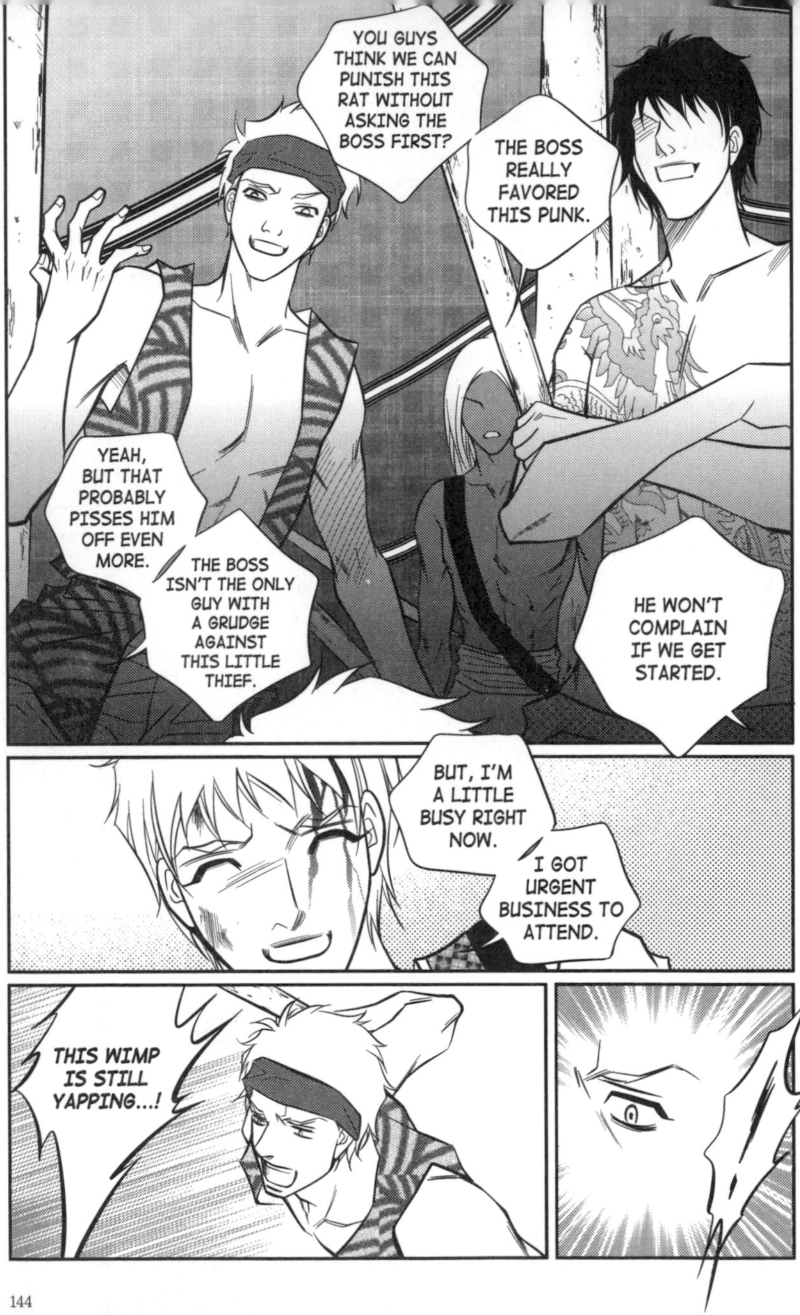
YOU GUYS THINK WE CAN PUNISH THIS RAT WITHOUT ASKING THE BOSS FIRST?
THE BOSS REALLY FAVORED THIS PUNK.
YEAH, BUT THAT PROBABLY PISSES HIM OFF EVEN MORE.
THE BOSS ISN'T THE ONLY GUY WITH A GRUDGE AGAINST THIS LITTLE THIEF.
HE WON'T COMPLAIN IF WE GET STARTED.
BUT, I'M A LITTLE BUSY RIGHT NOW.
I GOT URGENT BUSINESS TO ATTEND.
THIS WIMP IS STILL YAPPING...!

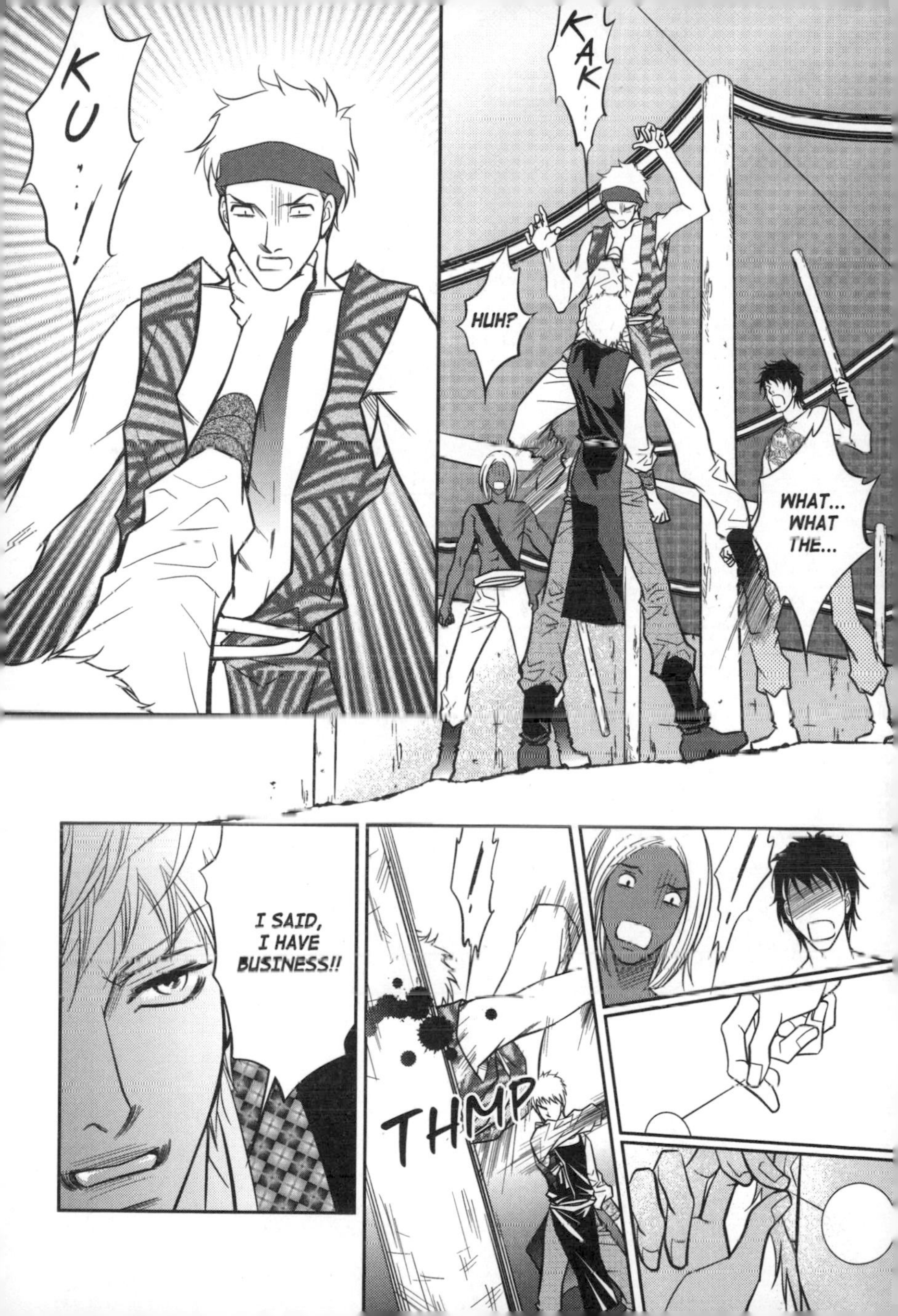

KU...!!
KAK...!
HUH?
WHAT... WHAT THE...
I SAID, I HAVE BUSINESS!!
!
THMP
!

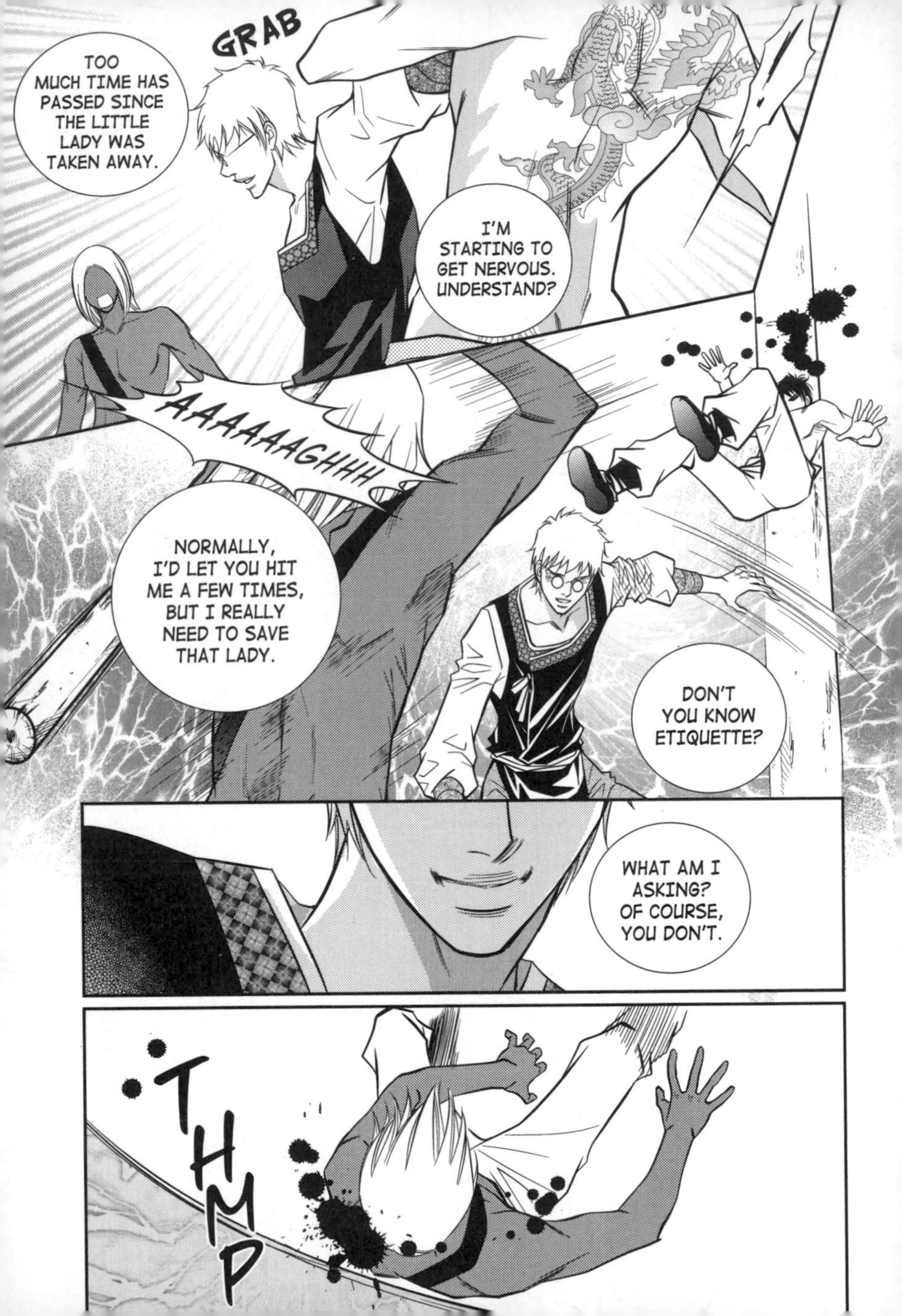
GRAB
TOO MUCH TIME HAS PASSED SINCE THE LITTLE LADY WAS TAKEN AWAY.
I'M STARTING TO GET NERVOUS. UNDERSTAND?
AAAAAAAGHHH
NORMALLY, I'D LET YOU HIT ME A FEW TIMES, BUT I REALLY NEED TO SAVE THAT LADY.
DON'T YOU KNOW ETIQUETTE?
WHAT AM I ASKING? OF COURSE, YOU DON'T.
THMP

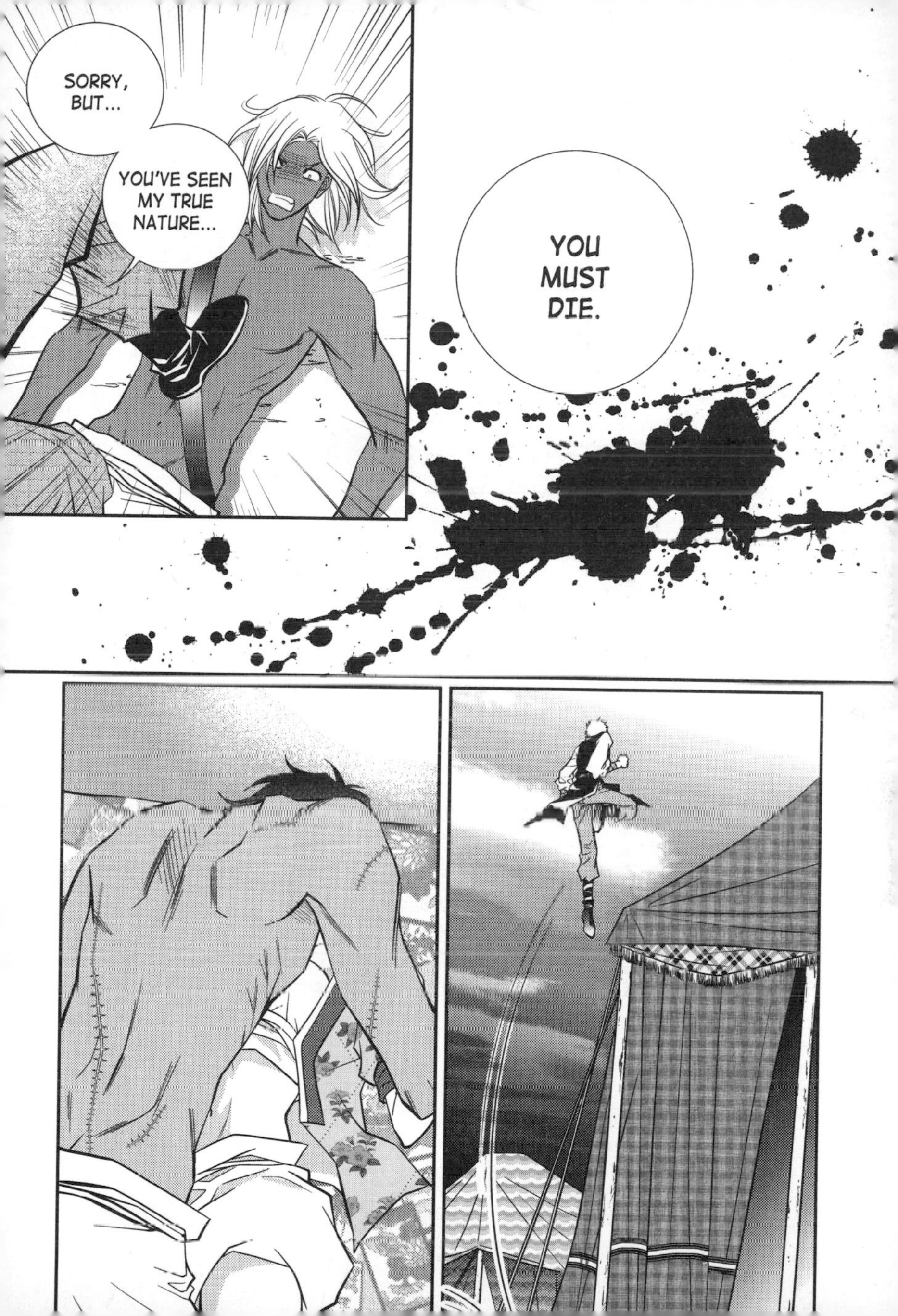
SORRY, BUT...
YOU'VE SEEN MY TRUE NATURE...
YOU MUST DIE.

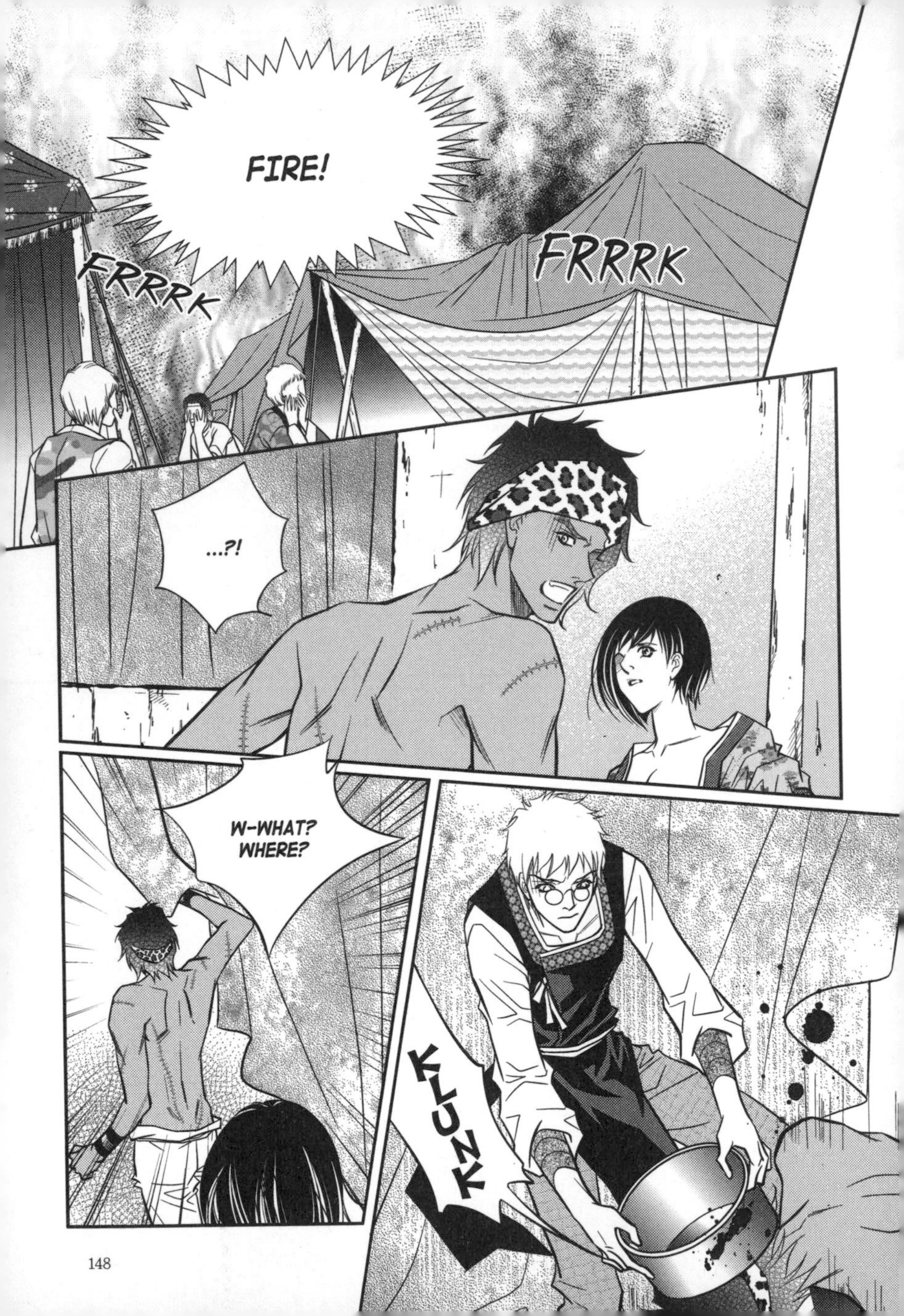
FIRE!
FRRRK
FRRRK
...?!
W-WHAT? WHERE?
KLUNK

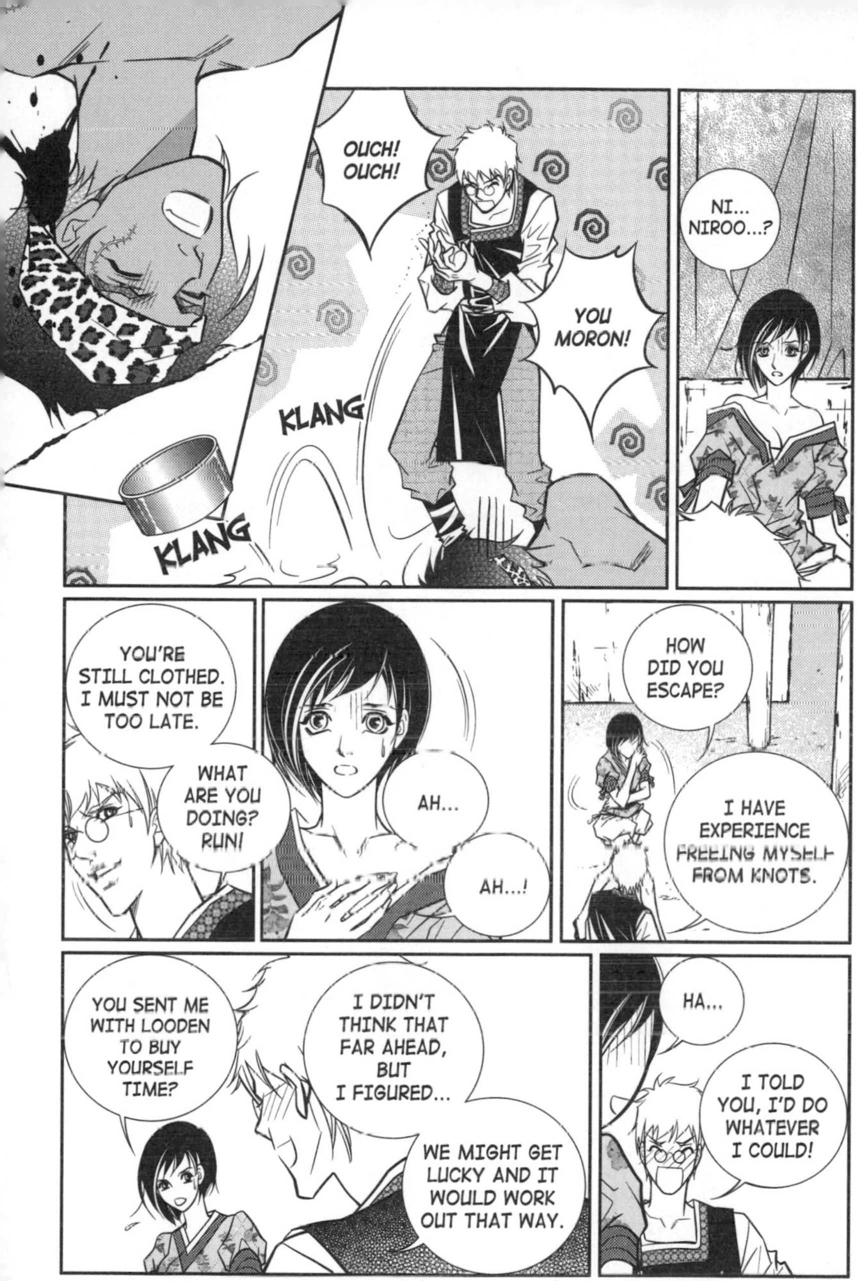
KLANG
OUCH! OUCH!
KLANG
YOU MORON!
NI... NIROO...?
YOU'RE STILL CLOTHED. I MUST NOT BE TOO LATE.
WHAT ARE YOU DOING? RUN!
AH...
AH...!
HOW DID YOU ESCAPE?
I HAVE EXPERIENCE FREEING MYSELF FROM KNOTS.
YOU SENT ME WITH LOODEN TO BUY YOURSELF TIME?
I DIDN'T THINK THAT FAR AHEAD, BUT I FIGURED...
WE MIGHT GET LUCKY AND IT WOULD WORK OUT THAT WAY.
HA...
I TOLD YOU, I'D DO WHATEVER I COULD!

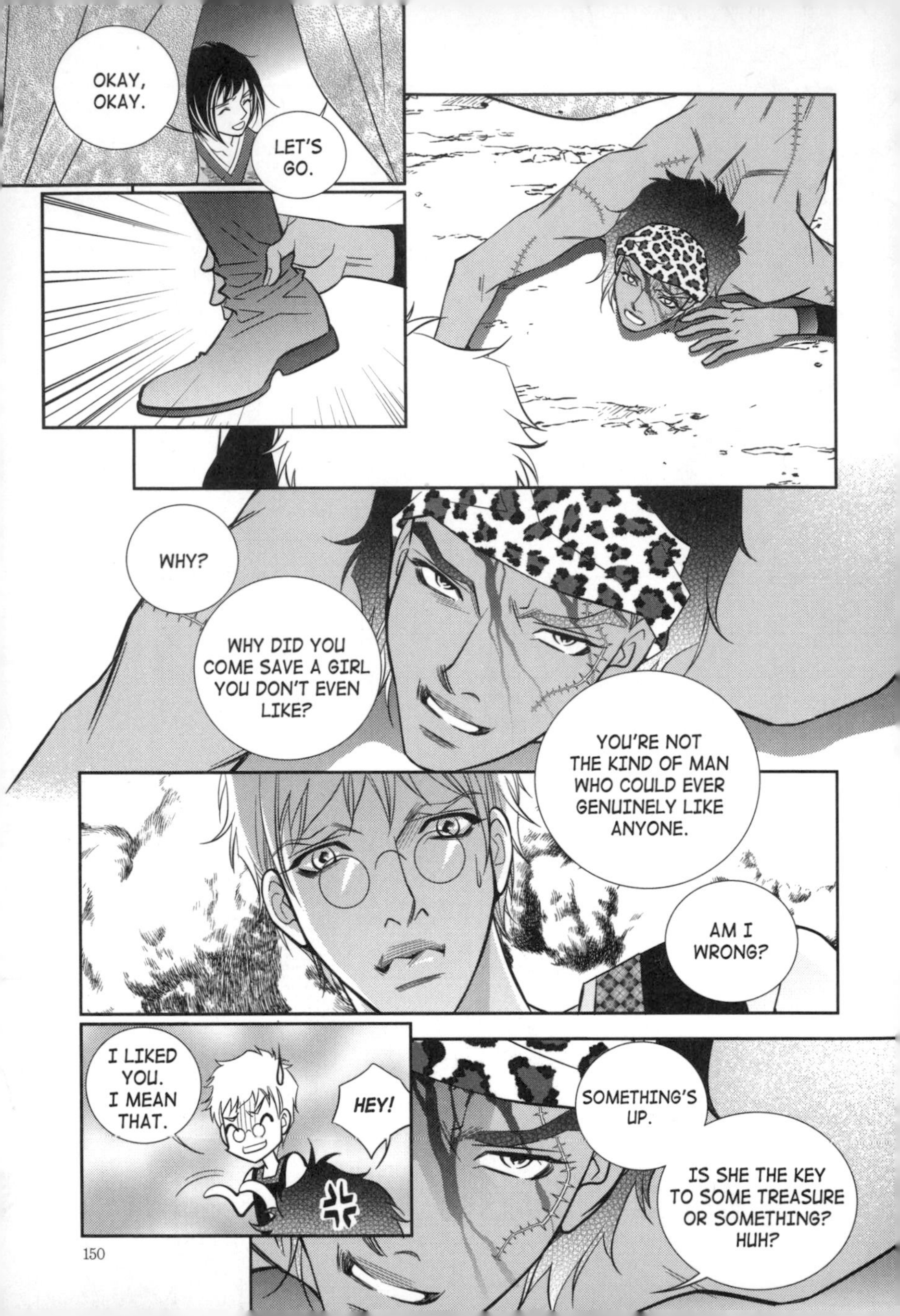
OKAY, OKAY.
LET'S GO.
WHY?
WHY DID YOU COME SAVE A GIRL YOU DON'T EVEN LIKE?
YOU'RE NOT THE KIND OF MAN WHO COULD EVER GENUINELY LIKE ANYONE.
AM I WRONG?
I LIKED YOU. I MEAN THAT.
HEY!
SOMETHING'S UP.
IS SHE THE KEY TO SOME TREASURE OR SOMETHING? HUH?

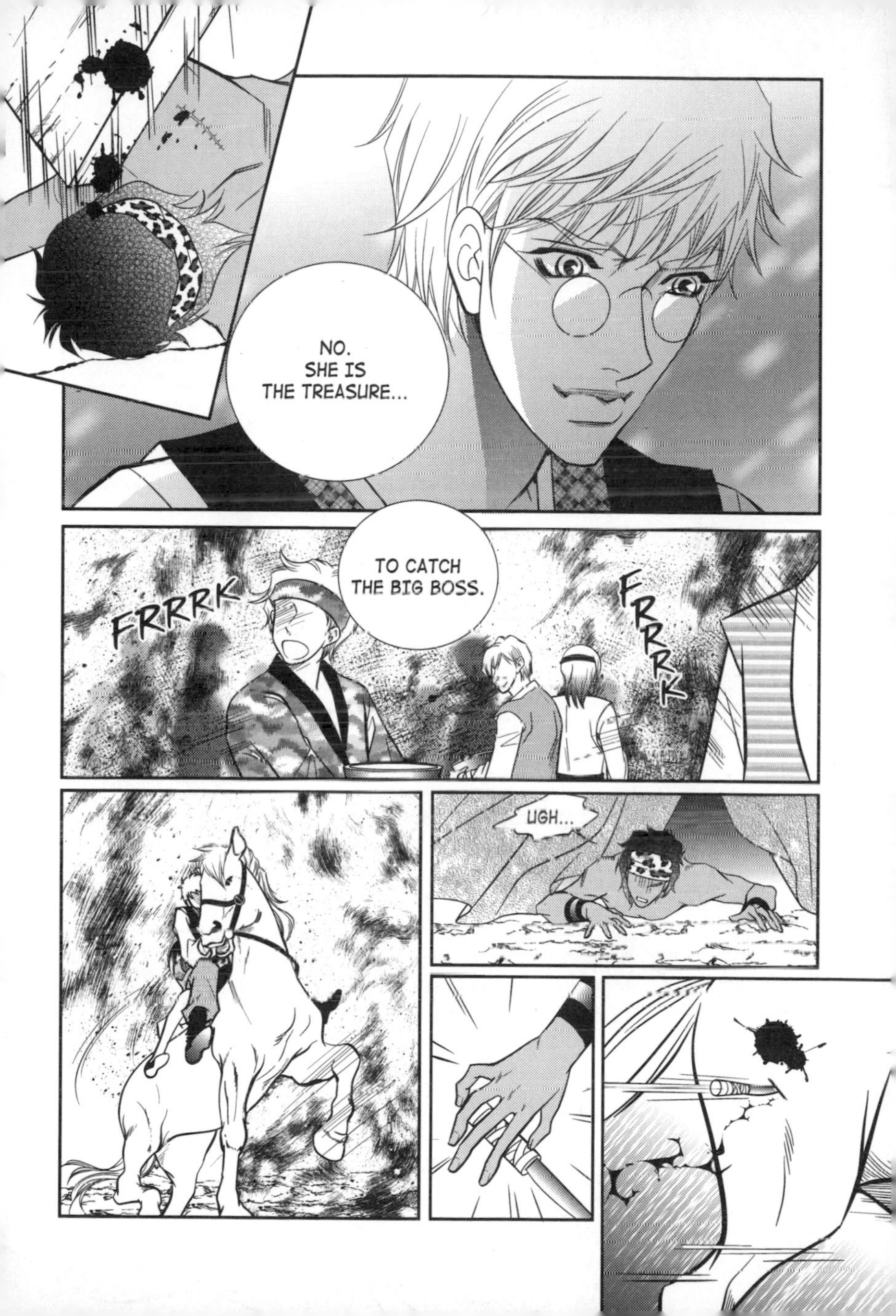
NO. SHE IS THE TREASURE...
TO CATCH THE BIG BOSS.
FRRRK
FRRRK
UGH...

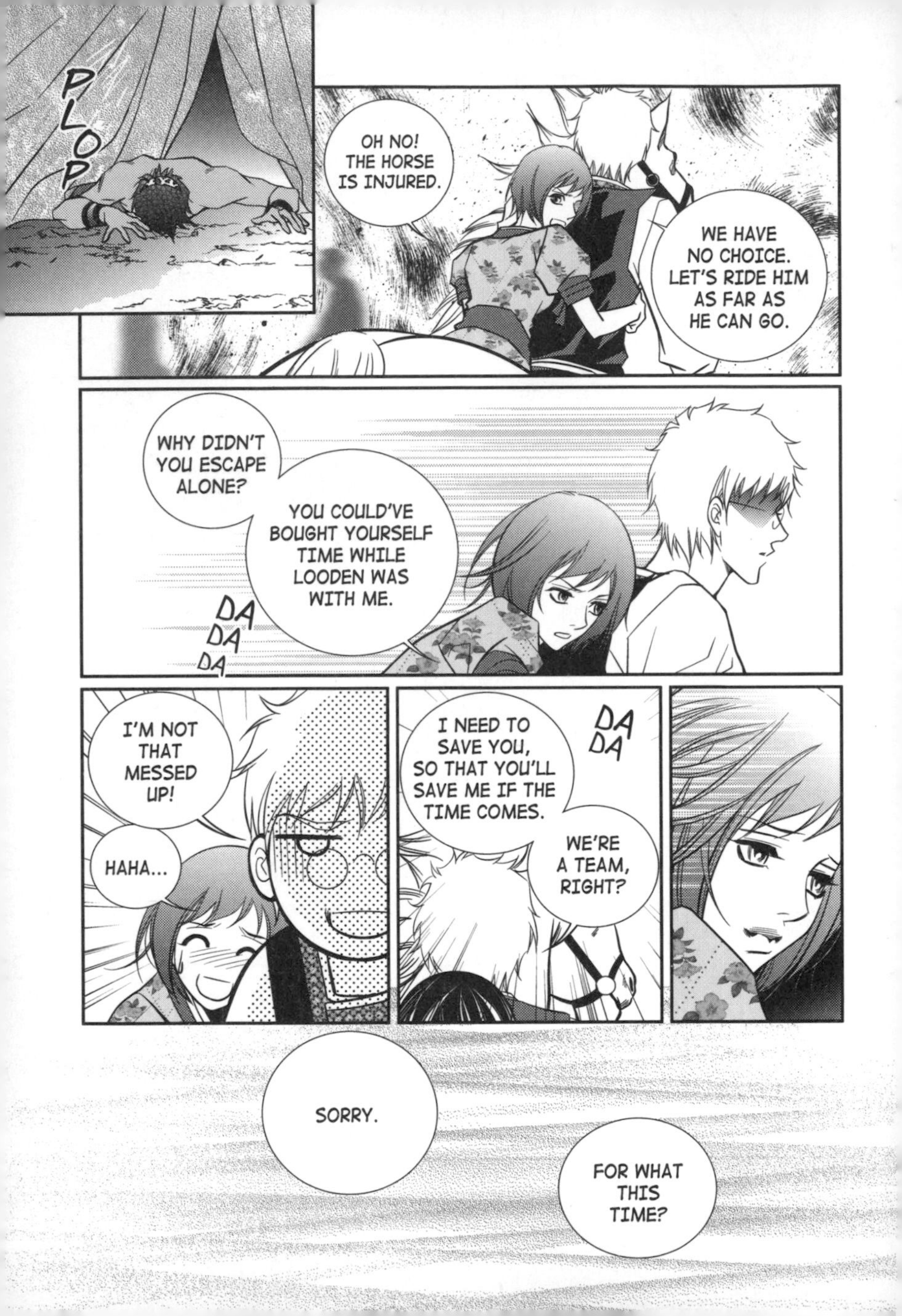
PLOP
OH NO! THE HORSE IS INJURED.
WE HAVE NO CHOICE. LET'S RIDE HIM AS FAR AS HE CAN GO.
WHY DIDN'T YOU ESCAPE ALONE?
YOU COULD'VE BOUGHT YOURSELF TIME WHILE LOODEN WAS WITH ME.
DA DA DA
I'M NOT THAT MESSED UP!
HAHA...
I NEED TO SAVE YOU, SO THAT YOU'LL SAVE ME IF THE TIME COMES.
DA DA
WE'RE A TEAM, RIGHT?
SORRY.
FOR WHAT THIS TIME?

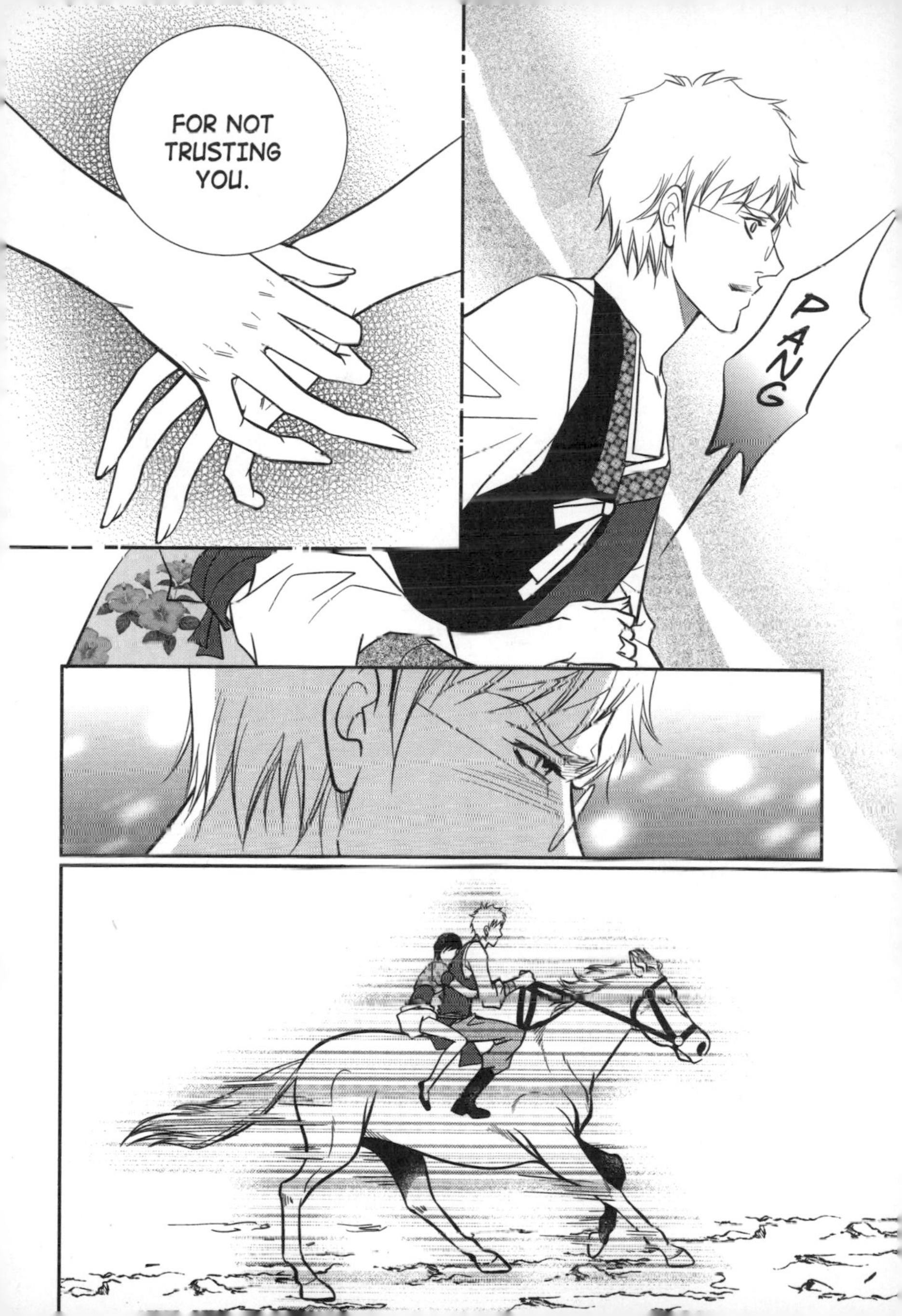
FOR NOT TRUSTING YOU.
PANG

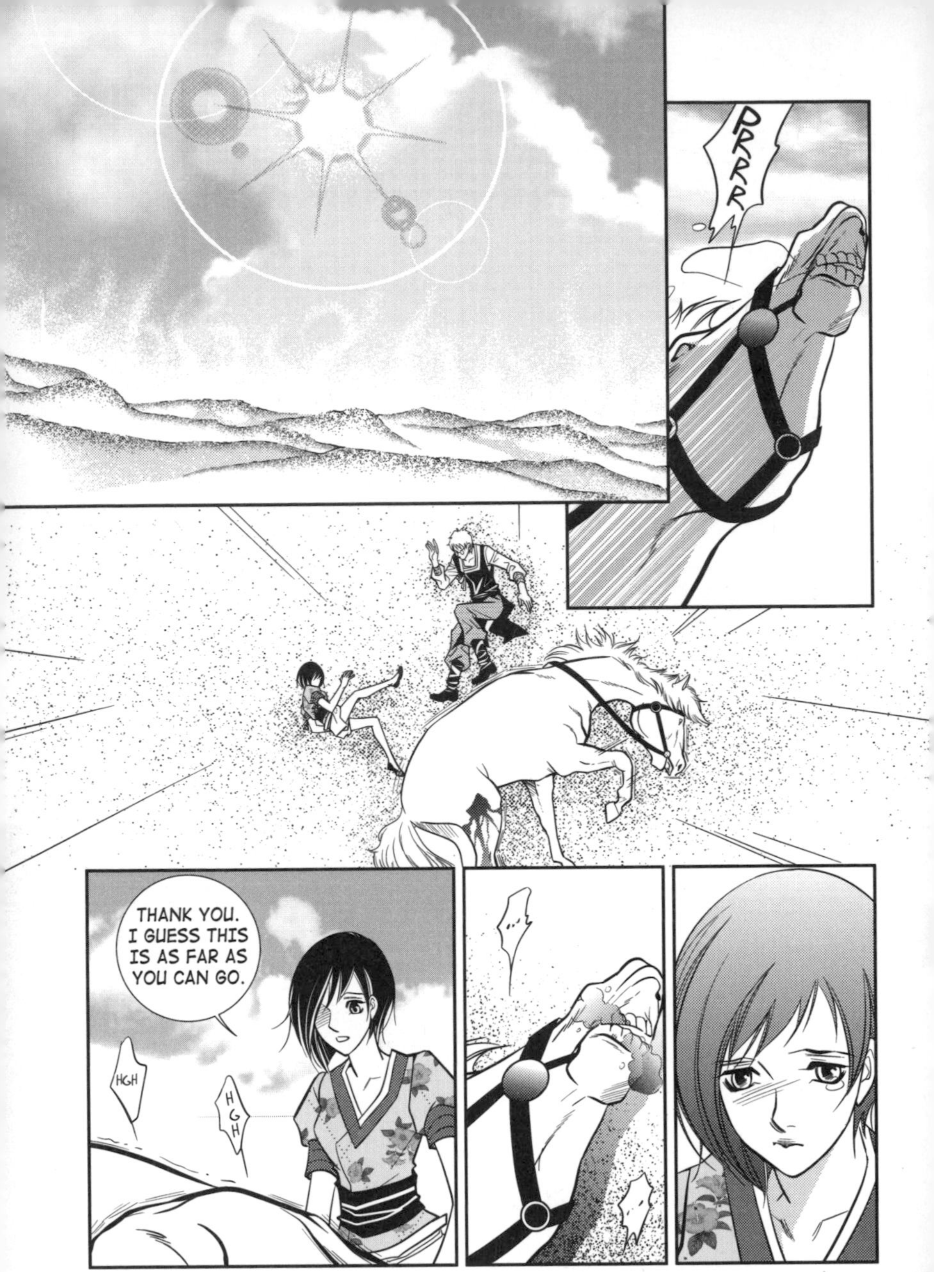
DRRRR
THANK YOU. I GUESS THIS IS AS FAR AS YOU CAN GO.
HGH
HGH
...

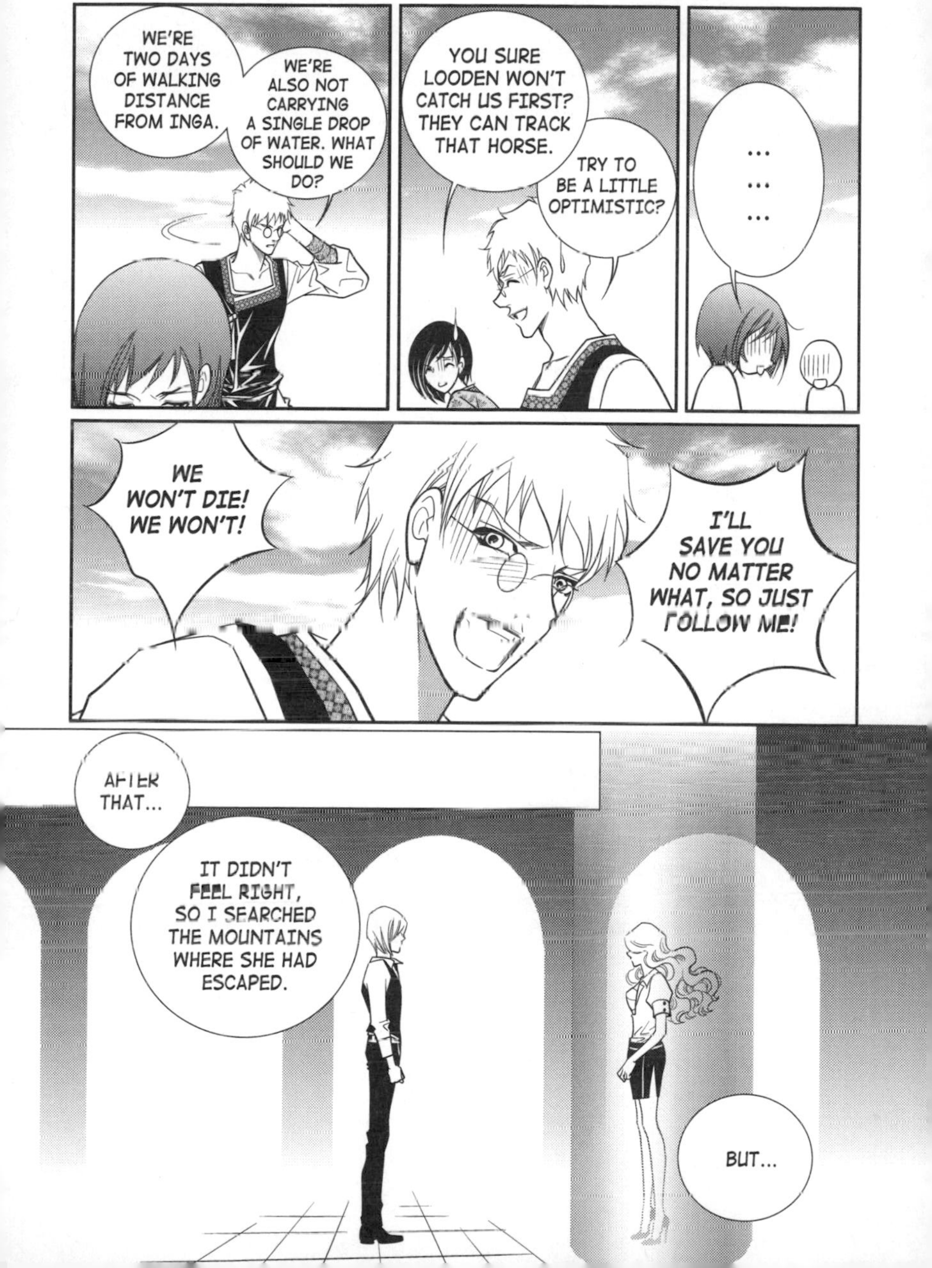
WE'RE TWO DAYS OF WALKING DISTANCE FROM INGA.
WE'RE ALSO NOT CARRYING A SINGLE DROP OF WATER. WHAT SHOULD WE DO?
YOU SURE LOODEN WON'T CATCH US FIRST? THEY CAN TRACK THAT HORSE.
TRY TO BE A LITTLE OPTIMISTIC?
...
...
...
WE WON'T DIE! WE WON'T!
I'LL SAVE YOU NO MATTER WHAT, SO JUST FOLLOW ME!
AFTER THAT...
IT DIDN'T FEEL RIGHT, SO I SEARCHED THE MOUNTAINS WHERE SHE HAD ESCAPED.
BUT...

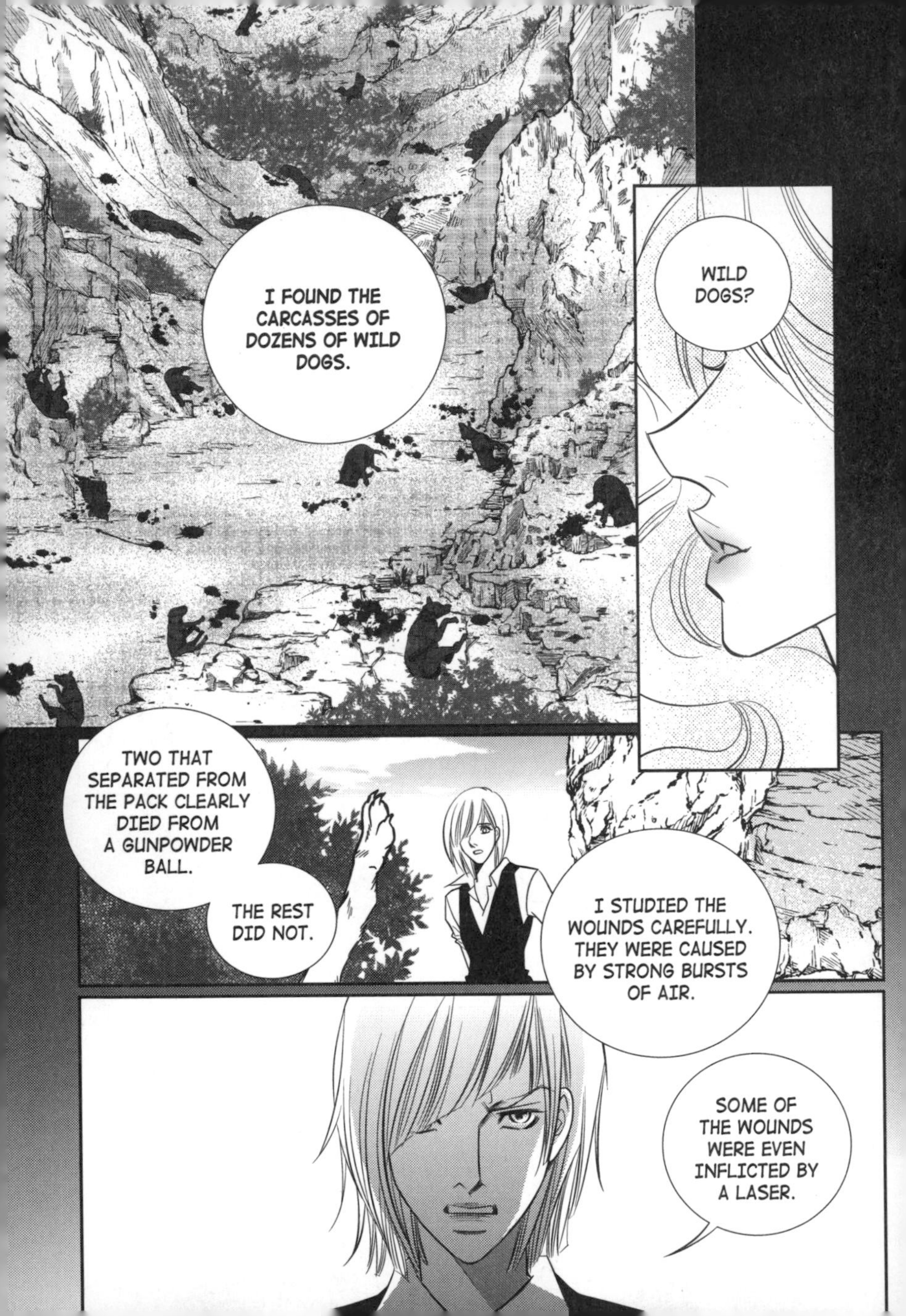
I FOUND THE CARCASSES OF DOZENS OF WILD DOGS.
WILD DOGS?
TWO THAT SEPARATED FROM THE PACK CLEARLY DIED FROM A GUNPOWDER BALL.
THE REST DID NOT.
I STUDIED THE WOUNDS CAREFULLY. THEY WERE CAUSED BY STRONG BURSTS OF AIR.
SOME OF THE WOUNDS WERE EVEN INFLICTED BY A LASER.

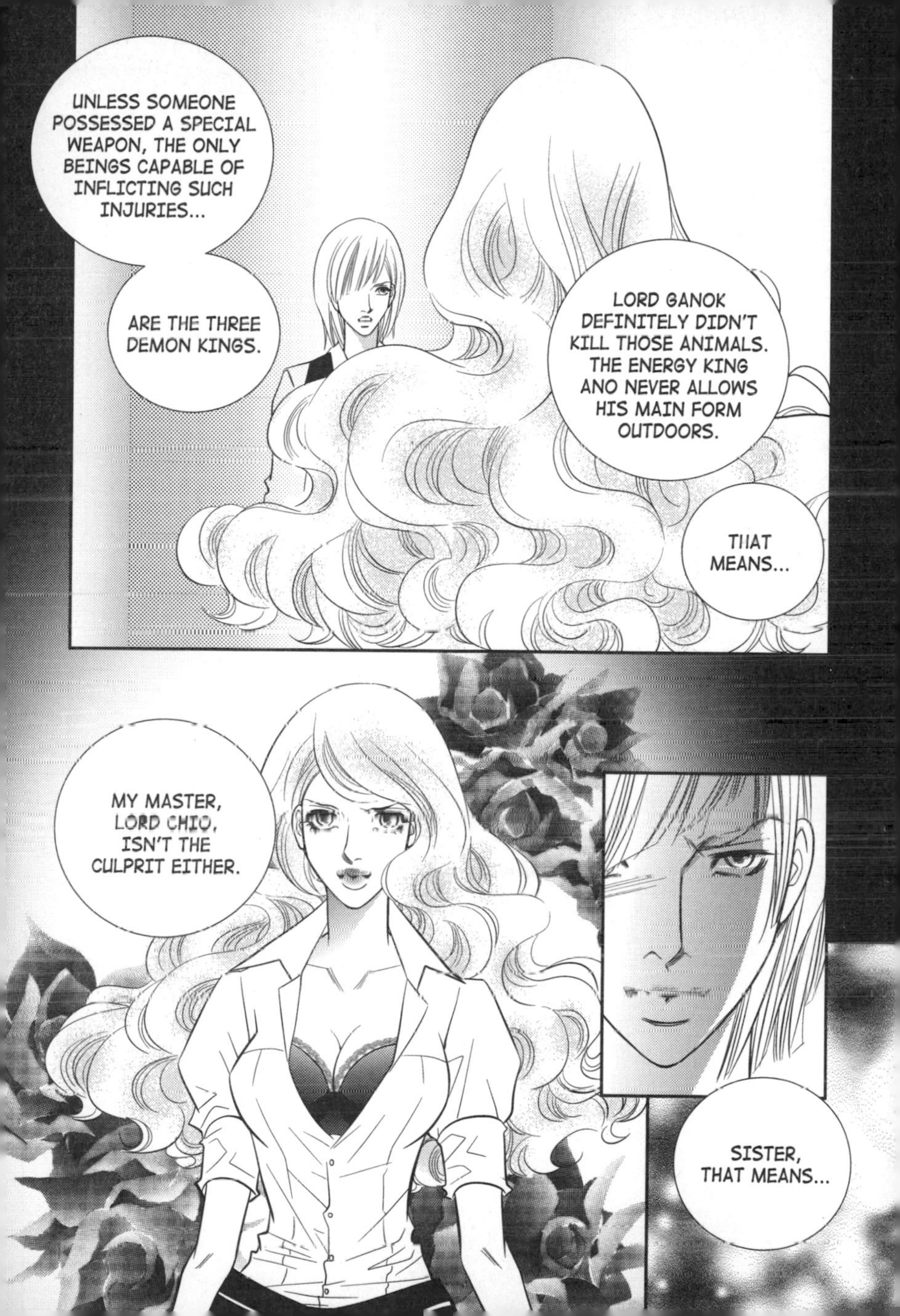
UNLESS SOMEONE POSSESSED A SPECIAL WEAPON, THE ONLY BEINGS CAPABLE OF INFLICTING SUCH INJURIES...
ARE THE THREE DEMON KINGS.
LORD GANOK DEFINITELY DIDN'T KILL THOSE ANIMALS. THE ENERGY KING ANO NEVER ALLOWS HIS MAIN FORM OUTDOORS.
THAT MEANS...
MY MASTER, LORD CHIO, ISN'T THE CULPRIT EITHER.
SISTER, THAT MEANS...

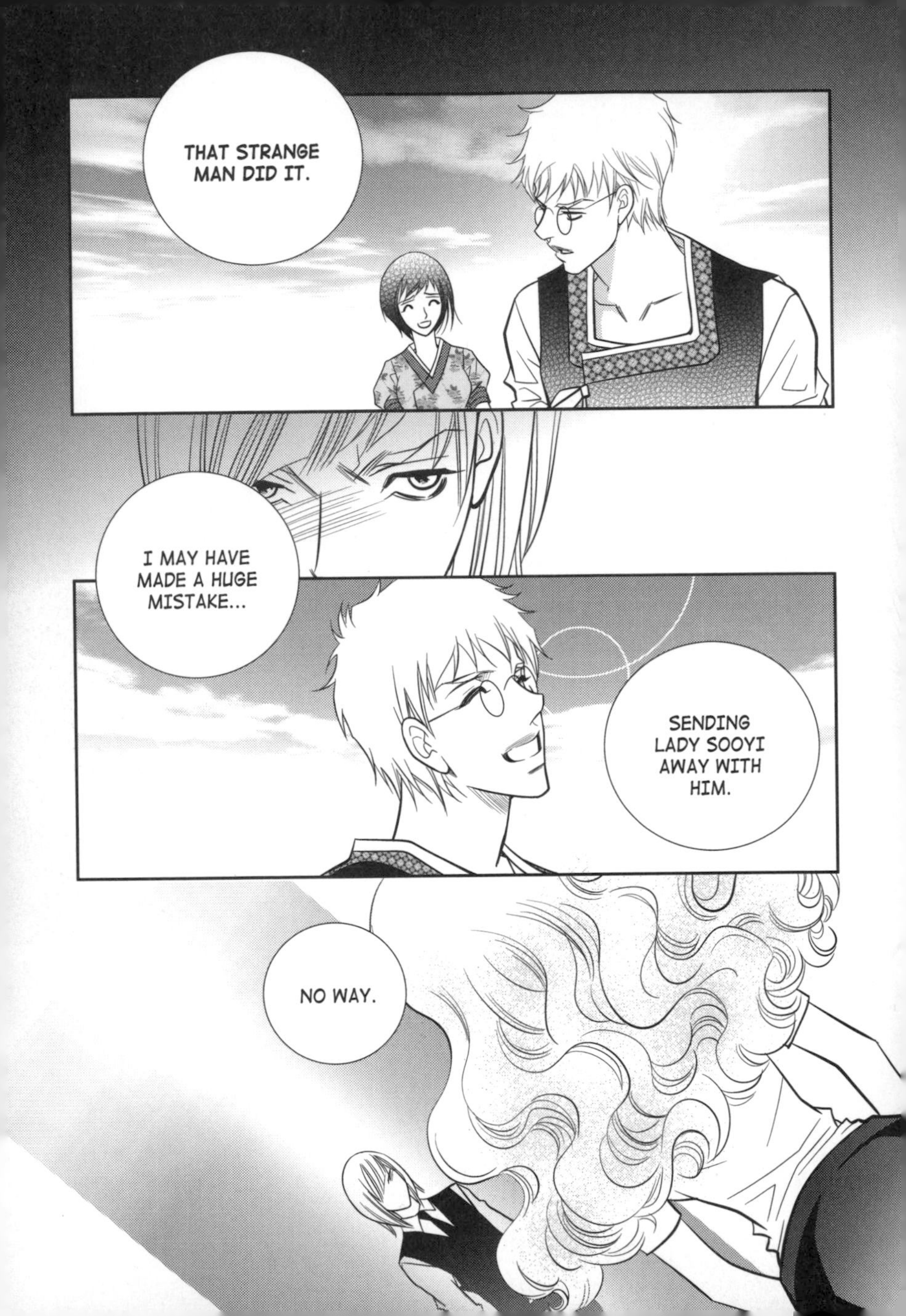
THAT STRANGE MAN DID IT.
I MAY HAVE MADE A HUGE MISTAKE...
SENDING LADY SOOYI AWAY WITH HIM.
NO WAY.

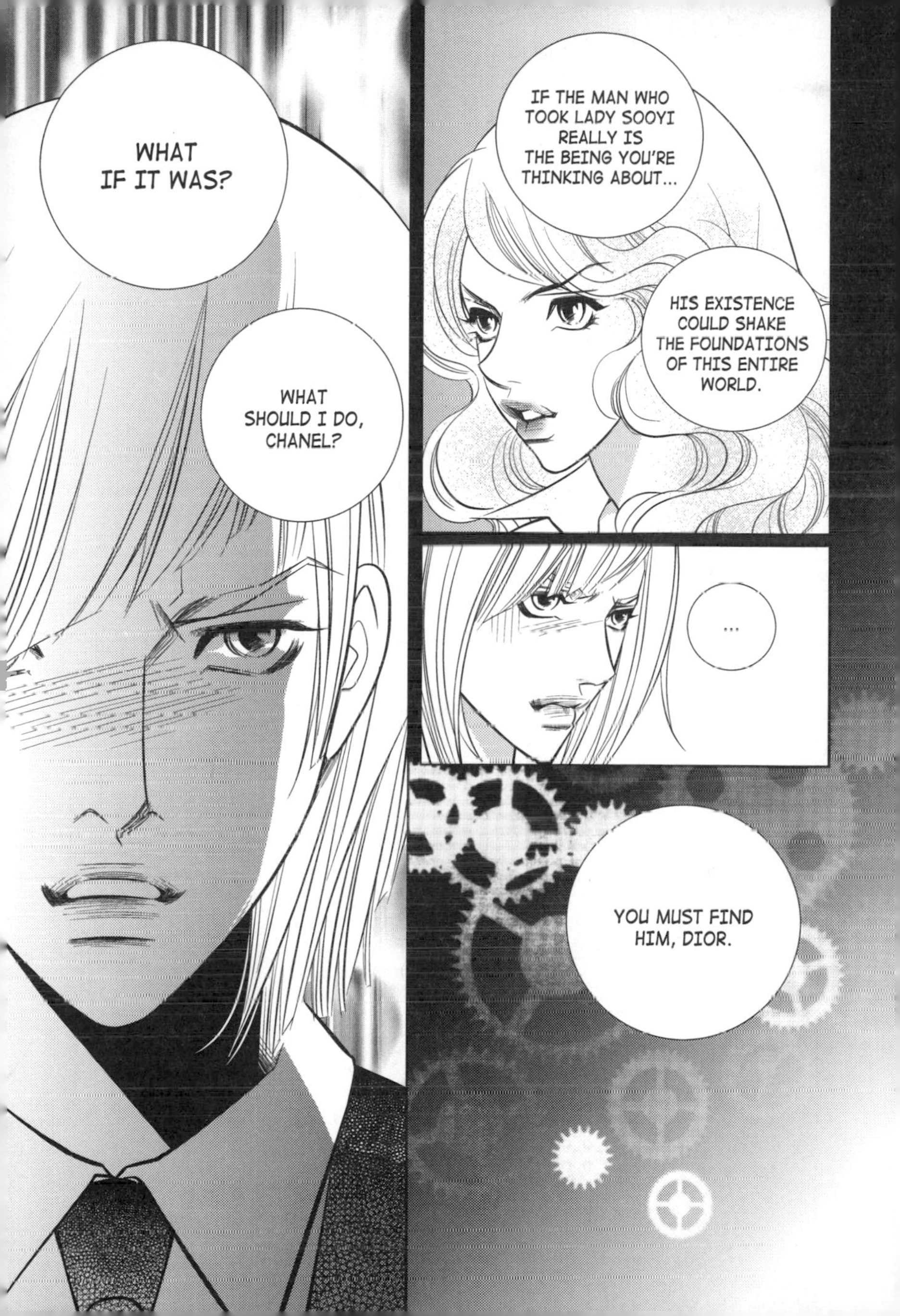
WHAT IF IT WAS?
WHAT SHOULD I DO, CHANEL?
IF THE MAN WHO TOOK LADY SOOYI REALLY IS THE BEING YOU'RE THINKING ABOUT...
HIS EXISTENCE COULD SHAKE THE FOUNDATIONS OF THIS ENTIRE WORLD.
...
YOU MUST FIND HIM, DIOR.

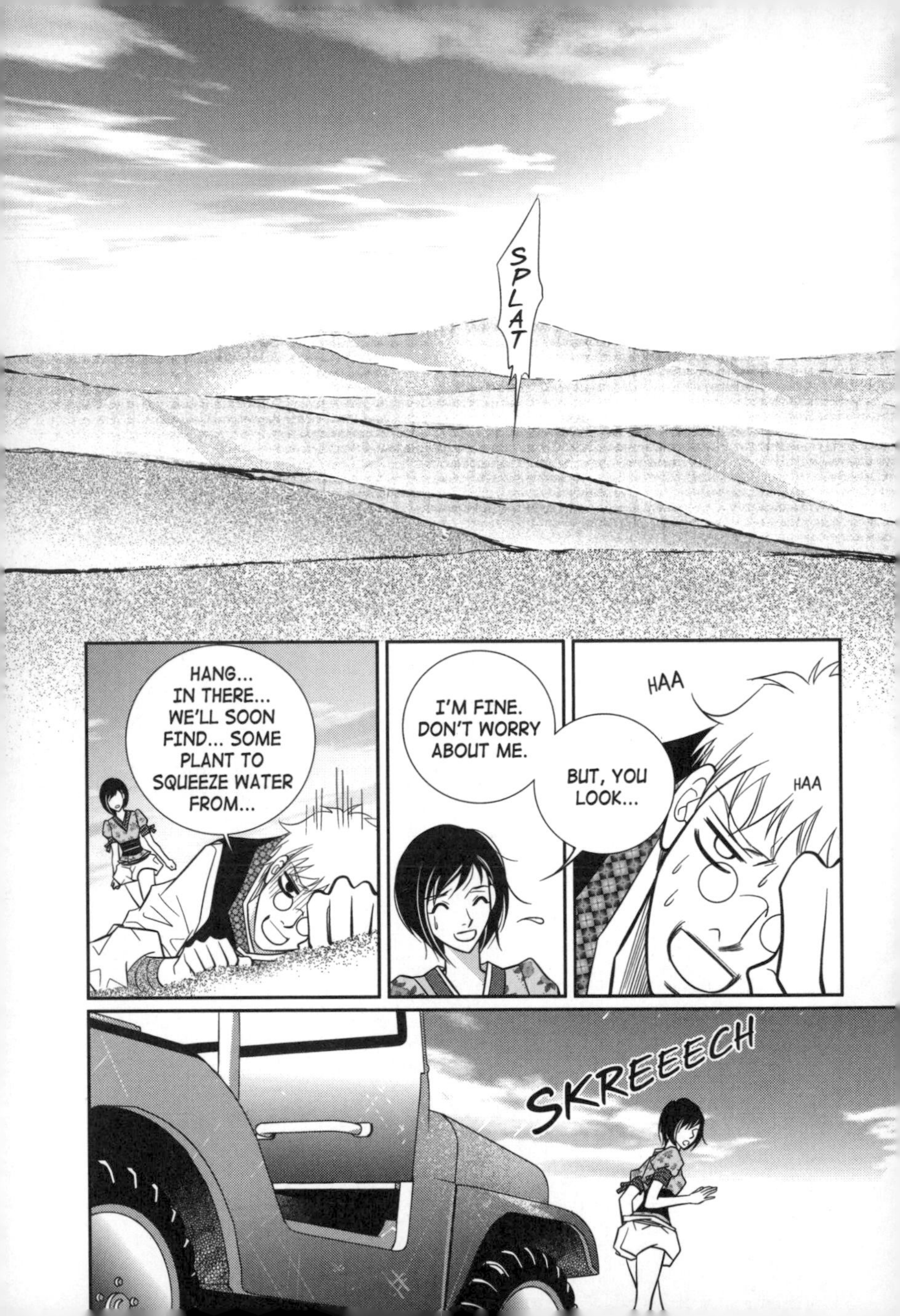
SPLAT
HANG... IN THERE... WE'LL SOON FIND... SOME PLANT TO SQUEEZE WATER FROM...
I'M FINE. DON'T WORRY ABOUT ME.
BUT, YOU LOOK...
HAA
HAA
SKREEECH

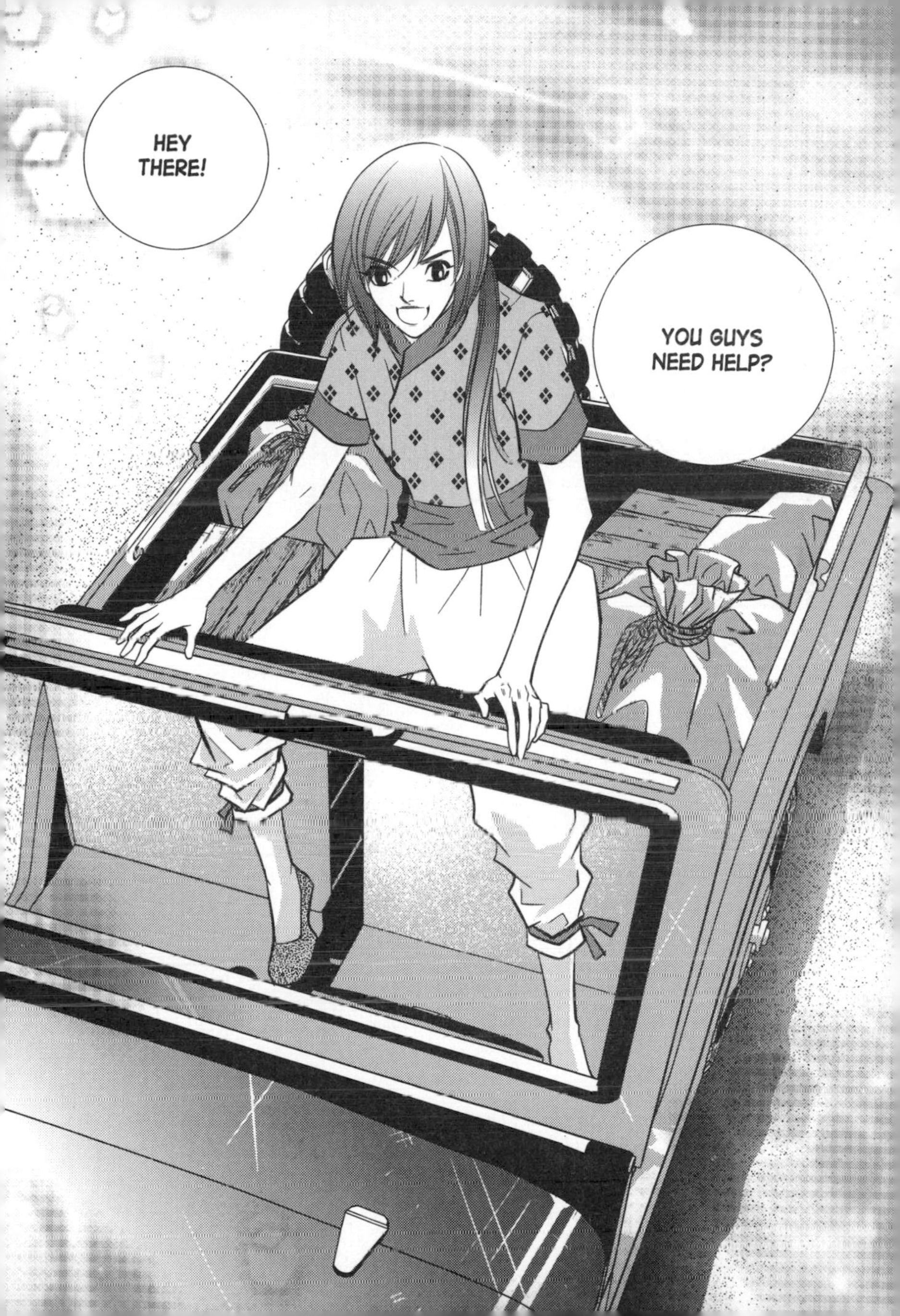
HEY THERE!
YOU GUYS NEED HELP?

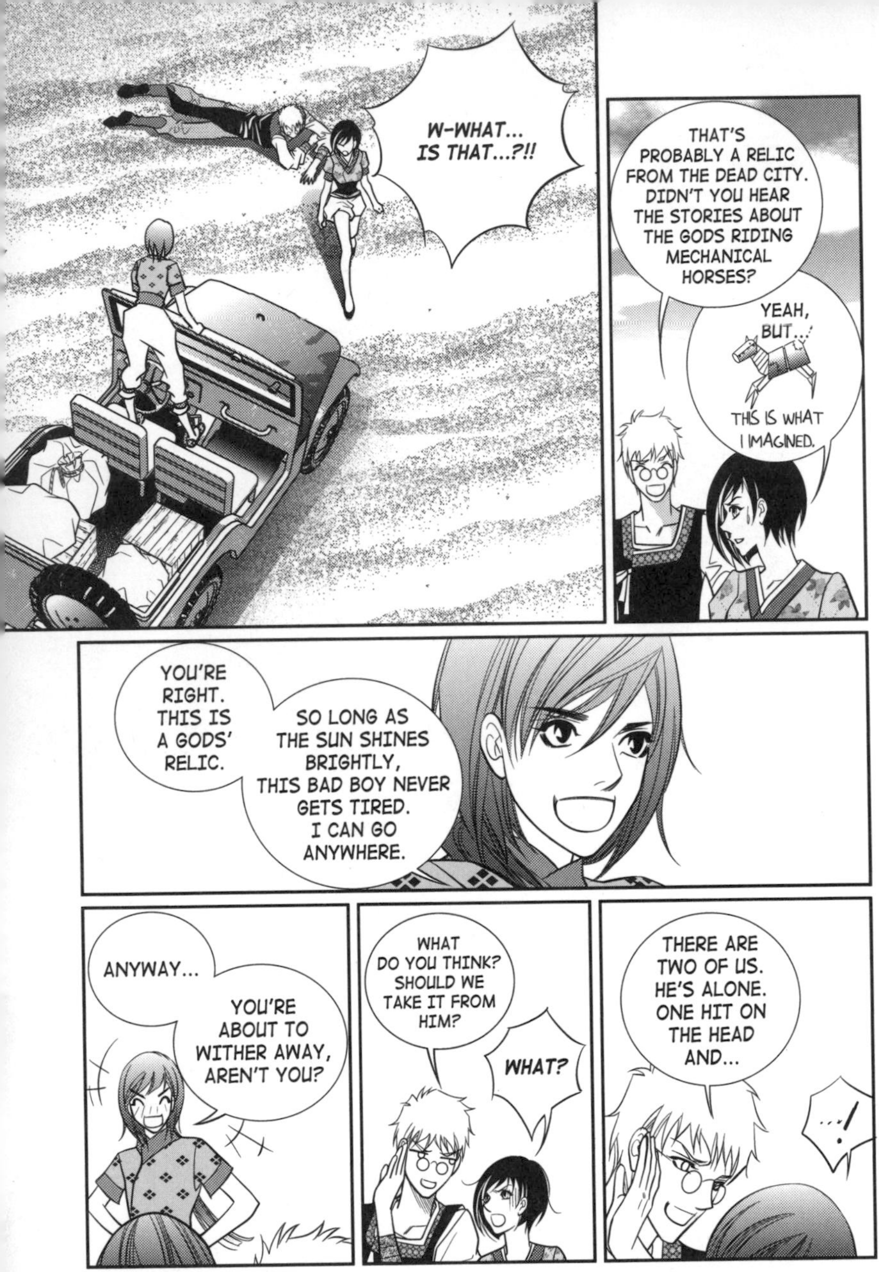
W-WHAT... IS THAT...?!!
THAT'S PROBABLY A RELIC FROM THE DEAD CITY. DIDN'T YOU HEAR THE STORIES ABOUT THE GODS RIDING MECHANICAL HORSES?
YEAH, BUT...
THIS IS WHAT I IMAGINED.
YOU'RE RIGHT. THIS IS A GODS' RELIC.
SO LONG AS THE SUN SHINES BRIGHTLY, THIS BAD BOY NEVER GETS TIRED. I CAN GO ANYWHERE.
ANYWAY...
YOU'RE ABOUT TO WITHER AWAY, AREN'T YOU?
WHAT DO YOU THINK? SHOULD WE TAKE IT FROM HIM?
WHAT?
THERE ARE TWO OF US. HE'S ALONE. ONE HIT ON THE HEAD AND...
...!

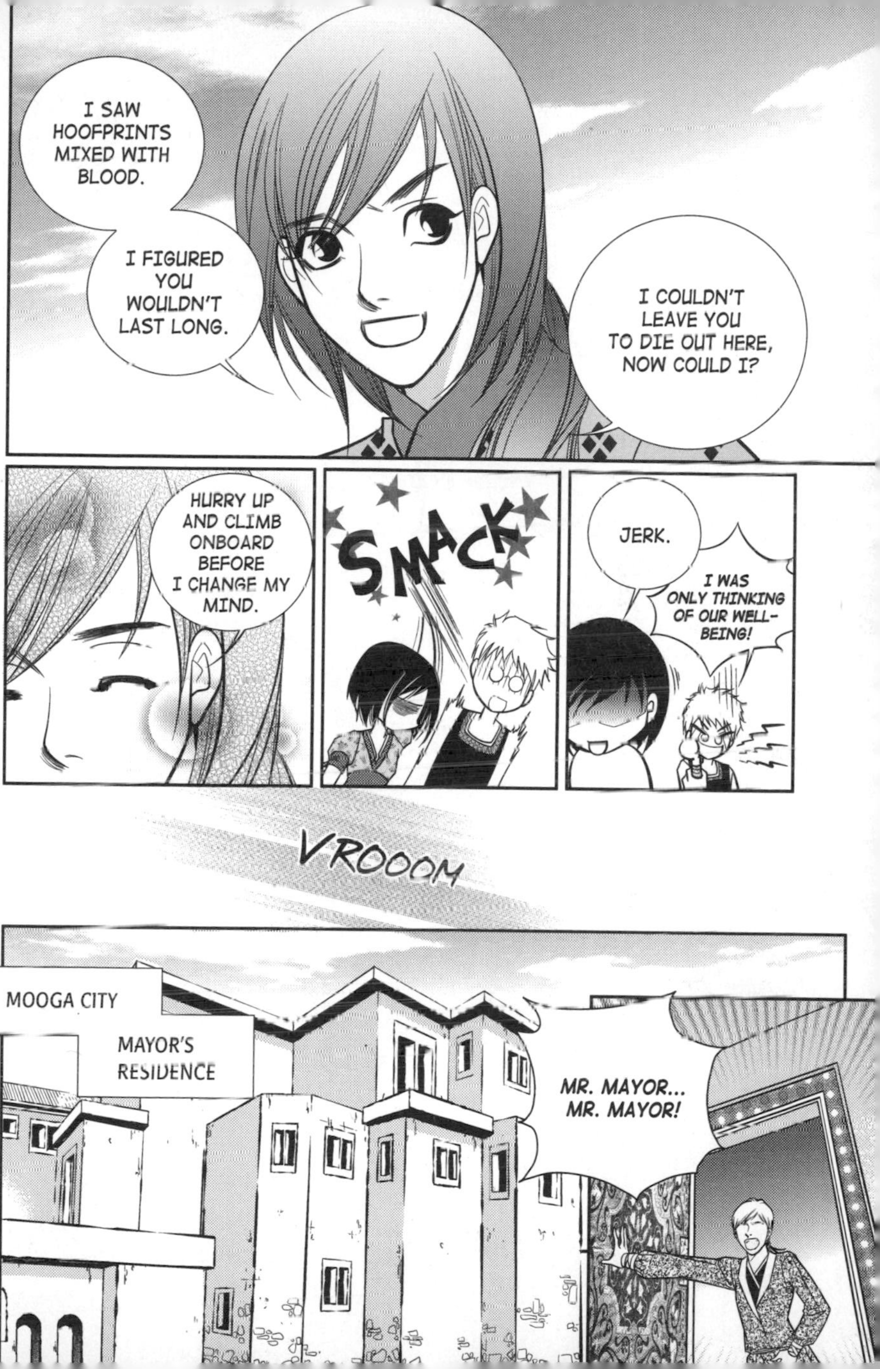
I SAW HOOFPRINTS MIXED WITH BLOOD.
I FIGURED YOU WOULDN'T LAST LONG.
I COULDN'T LEAVE YOU TO DIE OUT HERE, NOW COULD I?
HURRY UP AND CLIMB ONBOARD BEFORE I CHANGE MY MIND.
SMACK
JERK.
I WAS ONLY THINKING OF OUR WELL-BEING!
VROOOM
MOOGA CITY
MAYOR'S RESIDENCE
MR. MAYOR... MR. MAYOR!

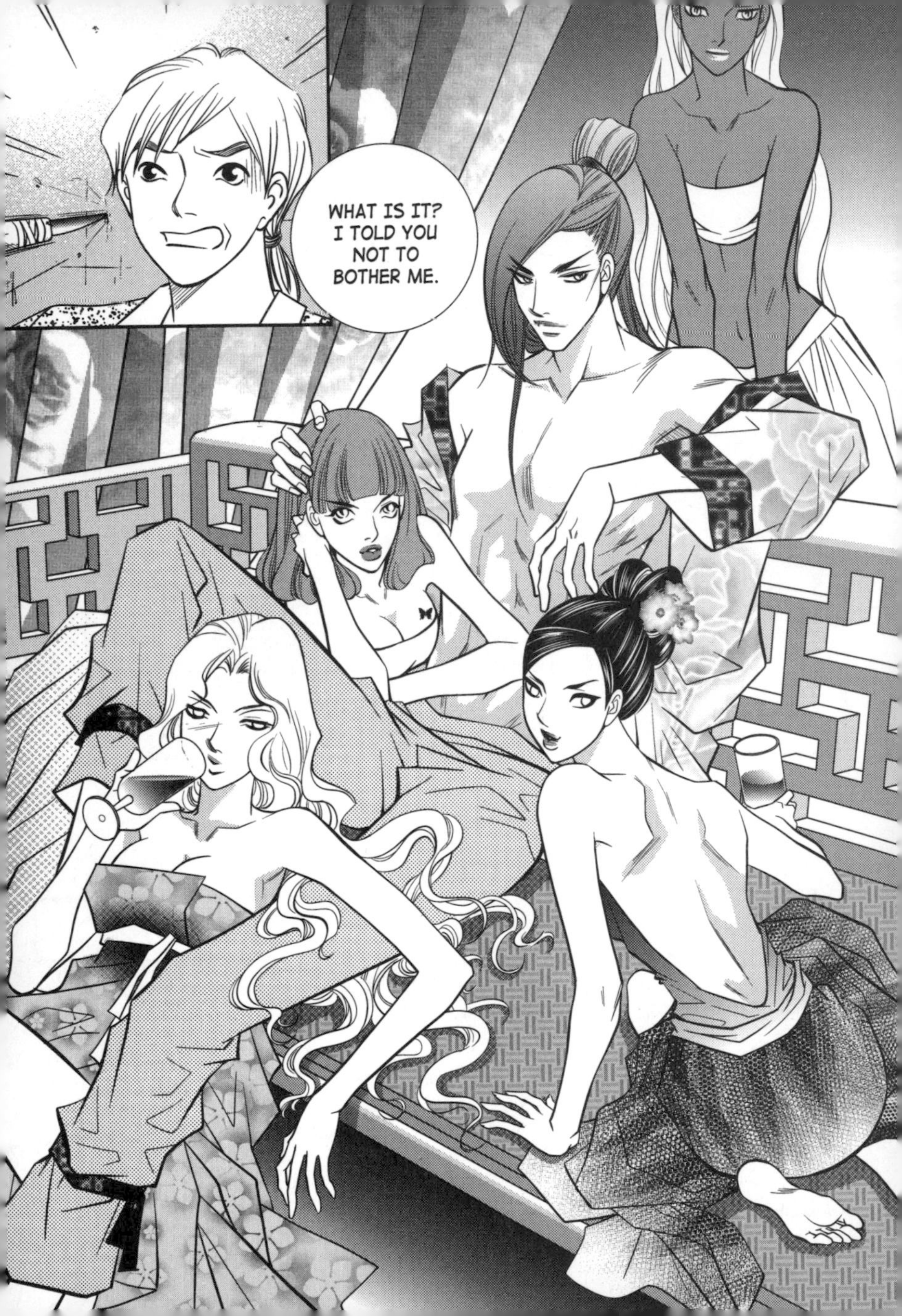
WHAT IS IT? I TOLD YOU NOT TO BOTHER ME.

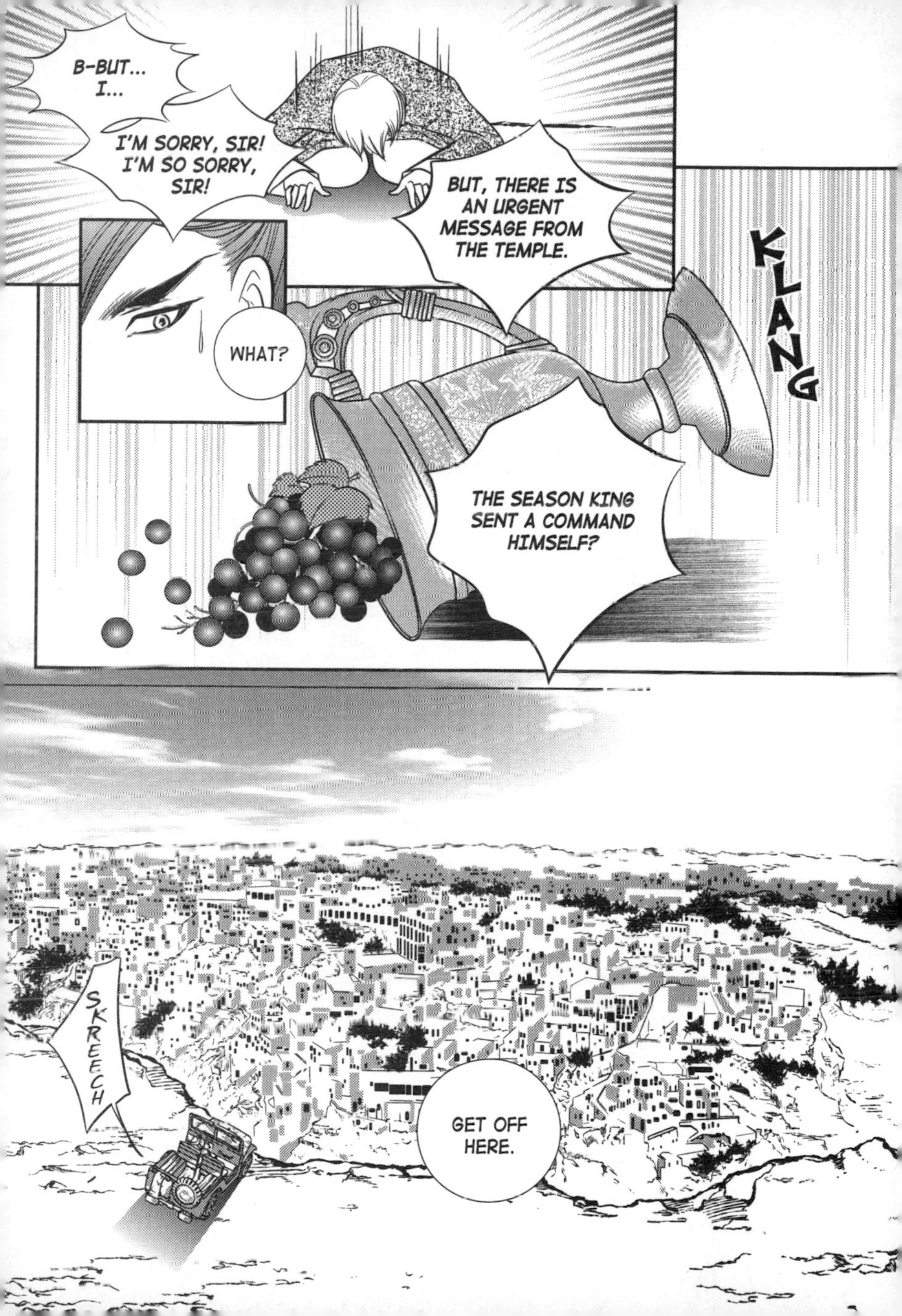

B-BUT... I...
I'M SORRY, SIR! I'M SO SORRY, SIR!
BUT, THERE IS AN URGENT MESSAGE FROM THE TEMPLE.
KLANG
WHAT?
THE SEASON KING SENT A COMMAND HIMSELF?
SKREECH
GET OFF HERE.

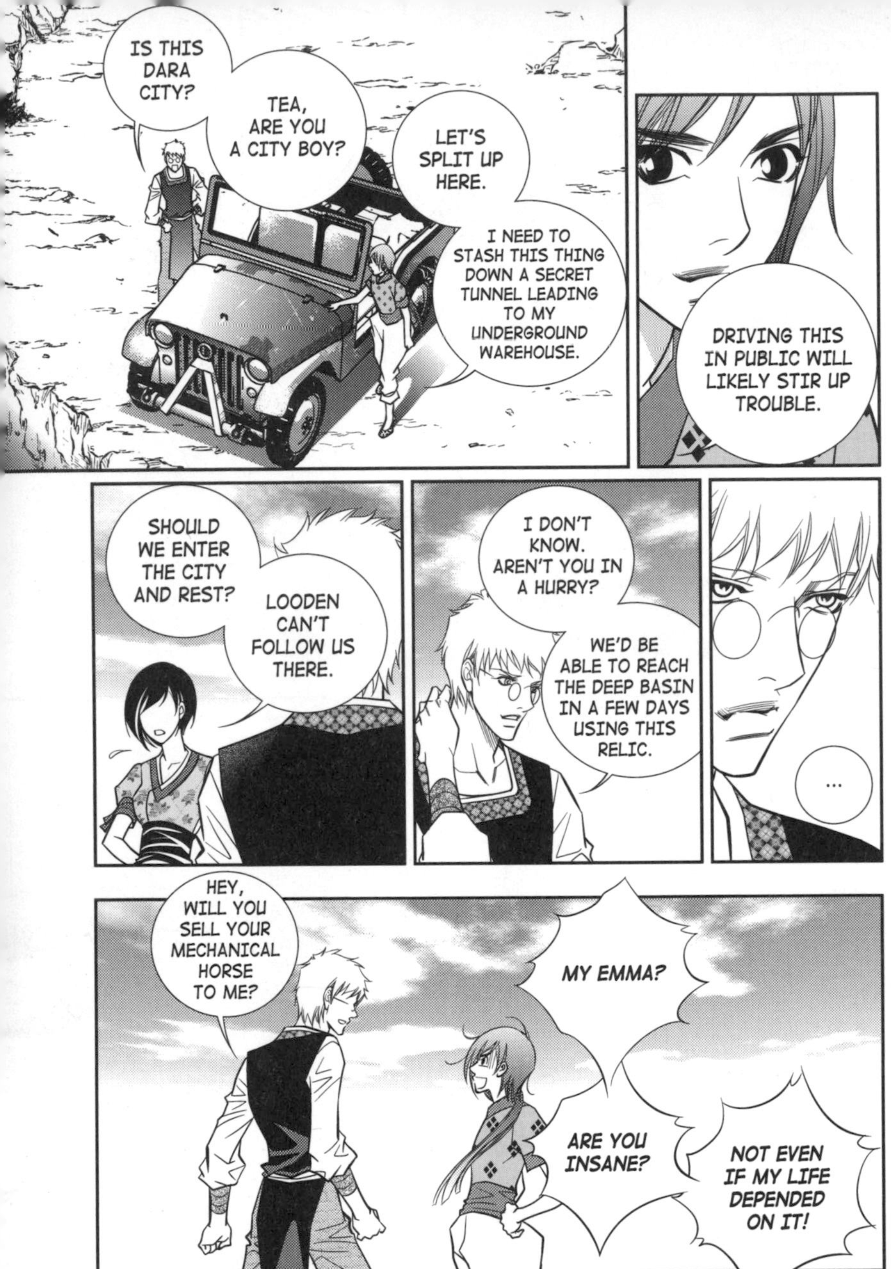
IS THIS DARA CITY?
TEA, ARE YOU A CITY BOY?
LET'S SPLIT UP HERE.
I NEED TO STASH THIS THING DOWN A SECRET TUNNEL LEADING TO MY UNDERGROUND WAREHOUSE.
DRIVING THIS IN PUBLIC WILL LIKELY STIR UP TROUBLE.
SHOULD WE ENTER THE CITY AND REST?
LOODEN CAN'T FOLLOW US THERE.
I DON'T KNOW. AREN'T YOU IN A HURRY?
WE'D BE ABLE TO REACH THE DEEP BASIN IN A FEW DAYS USING THIS RELIC.
...
HEY, WILL YOU SELL YOUR MECHANICAL HORSE TO ME?
MY EMMA?
ARE YOU INSANE?
NOT EVEN IF MY LIFE DEPENDED ON IT!

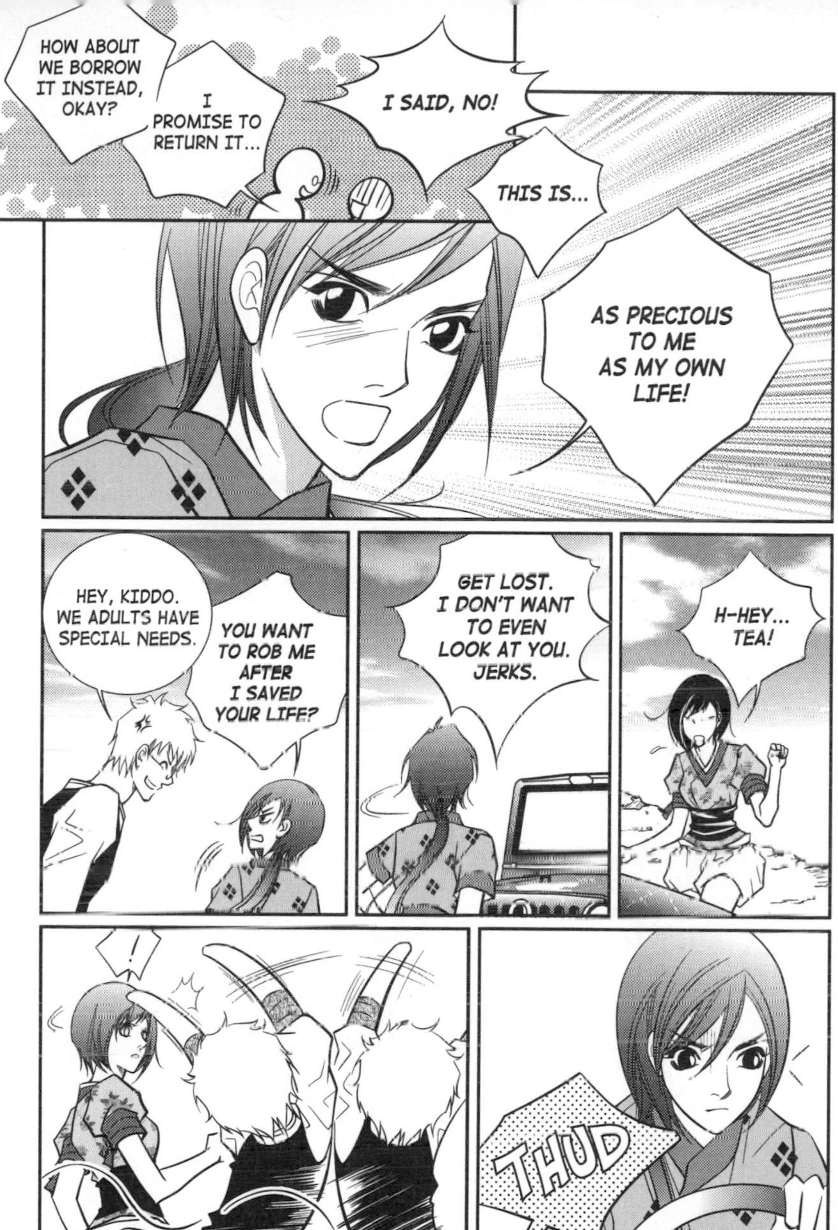
HOW ABOUT WE BORROW IT INSTEAD, OKAY?
I PROMISE TO RETURN IT...
I SAID, NO!
THIS IS...
AS PRECIOUS TO ME AS MY OWN LIFE!
HEY, KIDDO. WE ADULTS HAVE SPECIAL NEEDS.
YOU WANT TO ROB ME AFTER I SAVED YOUR LIFE?
GET LOST. I DON'T WANT TO EVEN LOOK AT YOU. JERKS.
H-HEY... TEA!
!
THUD

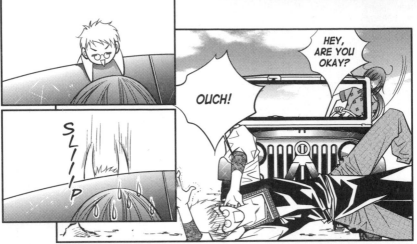

HEY, ARE YOU OKAY?

OUCH!

MY NECK... MY NECK...!

...

YOU CAN'T MOVE?

OH, NO...

GET ON CAREFULLY. I'LL TAKE YOU BACK TO MY HOME FOR NOW.

HE'S PULLING A CON.

HUH?

OUCH... OWWW...

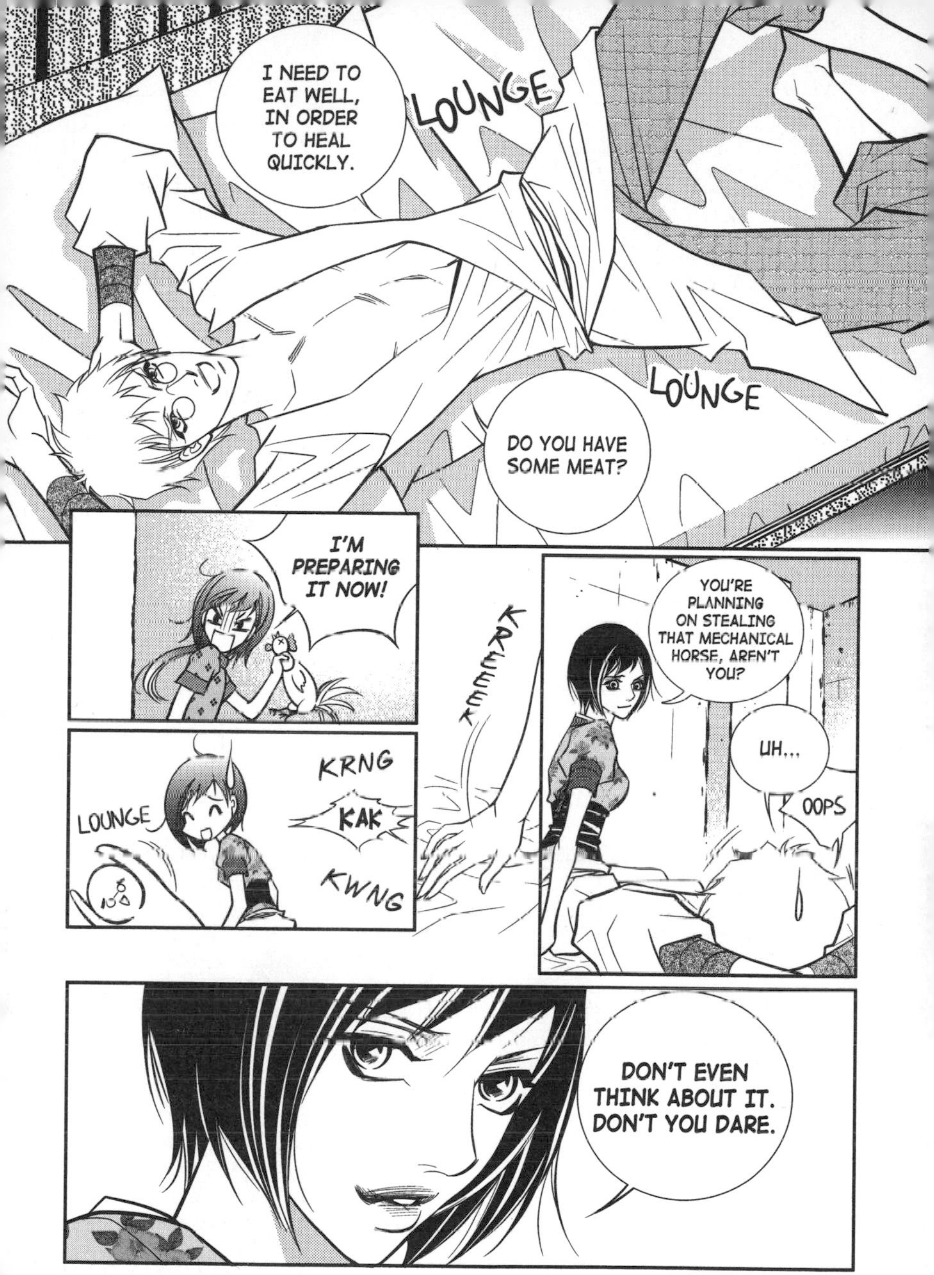

I NEED TO EAT WELL, IN ORDER TO HEAL QUICKLY.
LOUNGE
LOUNGE
DO YOU HAVE SOME MEAT?
I'M PREPARING IT NOW!
LOUNGE
KRNG
KAK
KWNG
KREEEEK
YOU'RE PLANNING ON STEALING THAT MECHANICAL HORSE, AREN'T YOU?
UH...
OOPS
DON'T EVEN THINK ABOUT IT. DON'T YOU DARE.

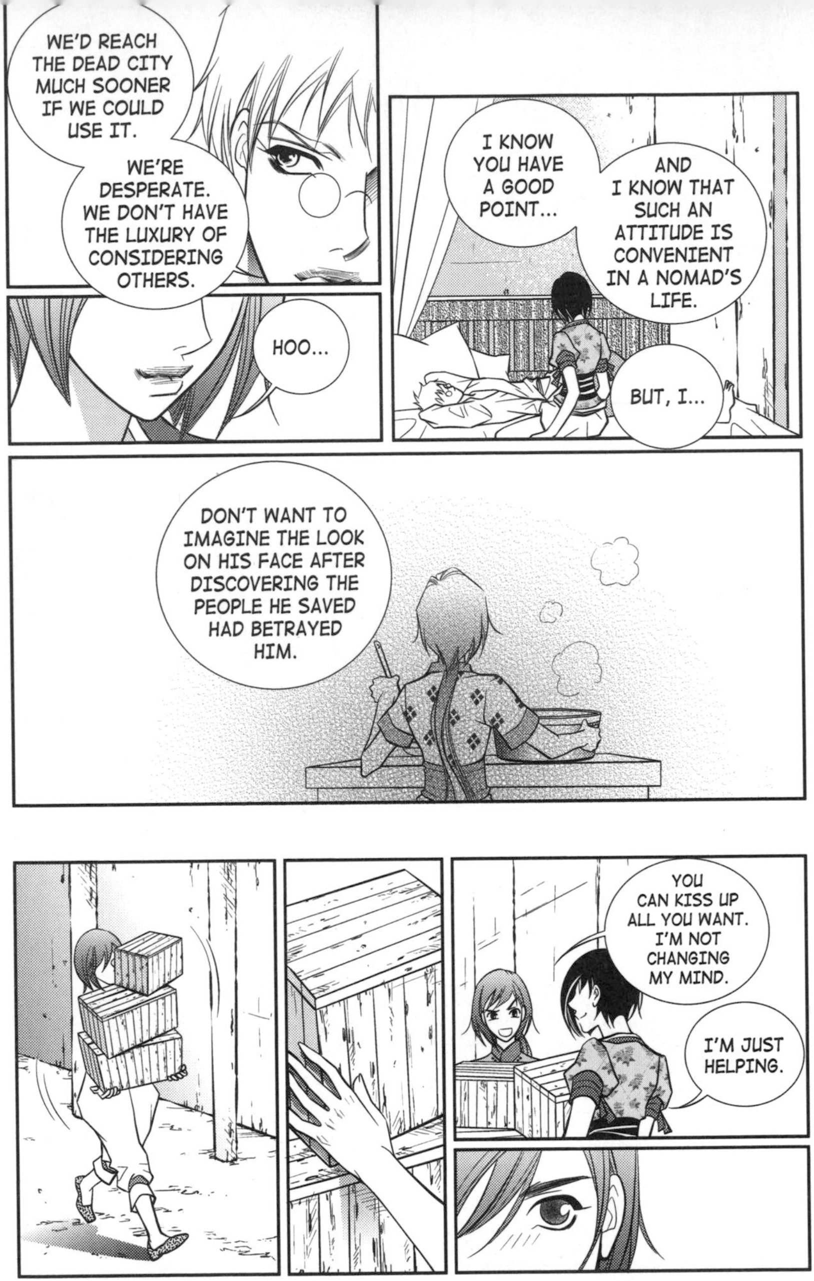
WE'D REACH THE DEAD CITY MUCH SOONER IF WE COULD USE IT.
WE'RE DESPERATE. WE DON'T HAVE THE LUXURY OF CONSIDERING OTHERS.
HOO...
I KNOW YOU HAVE A GOOD POINT...
AND I KNOW THAT SUCH AN ATTITUDE IS CONVENIENT IN A NOMAD'S LIFE.
BUT, I...
DON'T WANT TO IMAGINE THE LOOK ON HIS FACE AFTER DISCOVERING THE PEOPLE HE SAVED HAD BETRAYED HIM.
YOU CAN KISS UP ALL YOU WANT. I'M NOT CHANGING MY MIND.
I'M JUST HELPING.

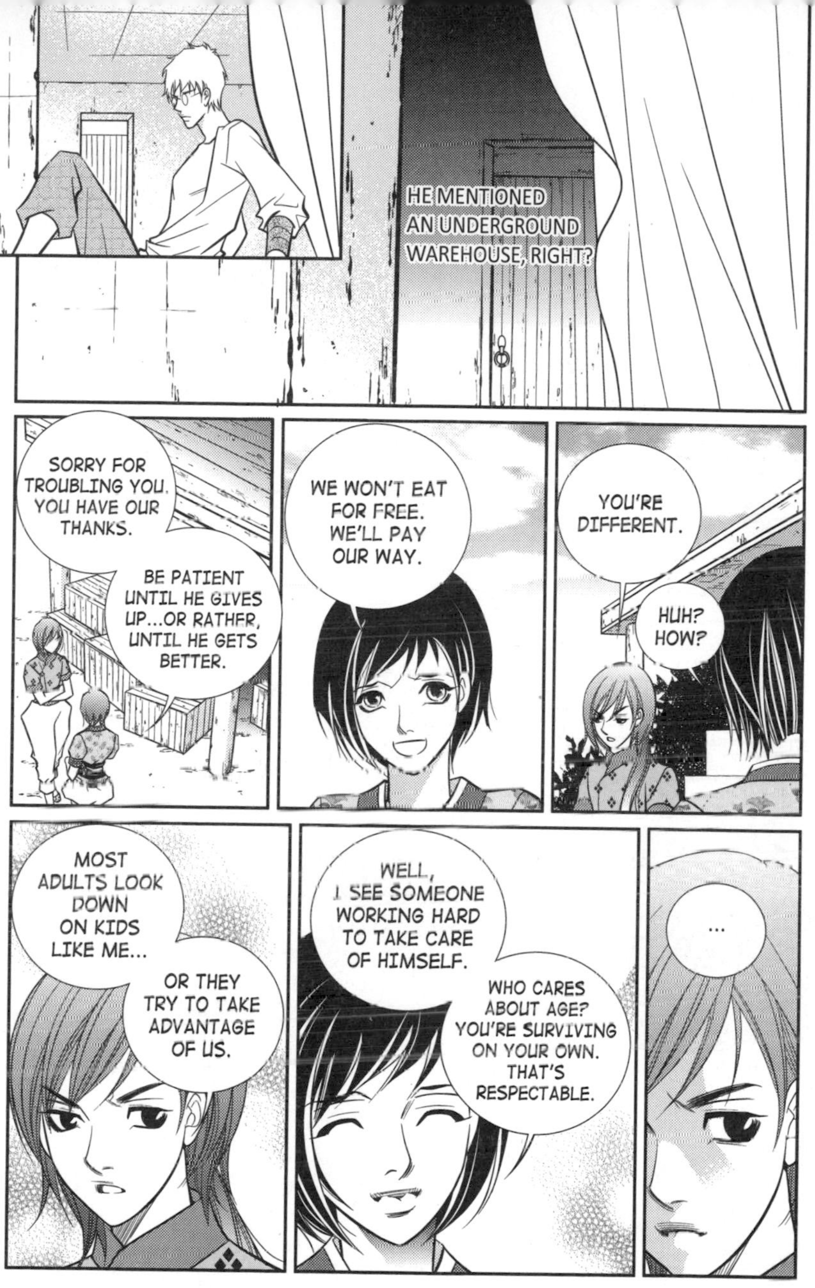
HE MENTIONED AN UNDERGROUND WAREHOUSE, RIGHT?
SORRY FOR TROUBLING YOU. YOU HAVE OUR THANKS.
BE PATIENT UNTIL HE GIVES UP...OR RATHER, UNTIL HE GETS BETTER.
WE WON'T EAT FOR FREE. WE'LL PAY OUR WAY.
YOU'RE DIFFERENT.
HUH? HOW?
MOST ADULTS LOOK DOWN ON KIDS LIKE ME...
OR THEY TRY TO TAKE ADVANTAGE OF US.
WELL, I SEE SOMEONE WORKING HARD TO TAKE CARE OF HIMSELF.
WHO CARES ABOUT AGE? YOU'RE SURVIVING ON YOUR OWN. THAT'S RESPECTABLE.
...

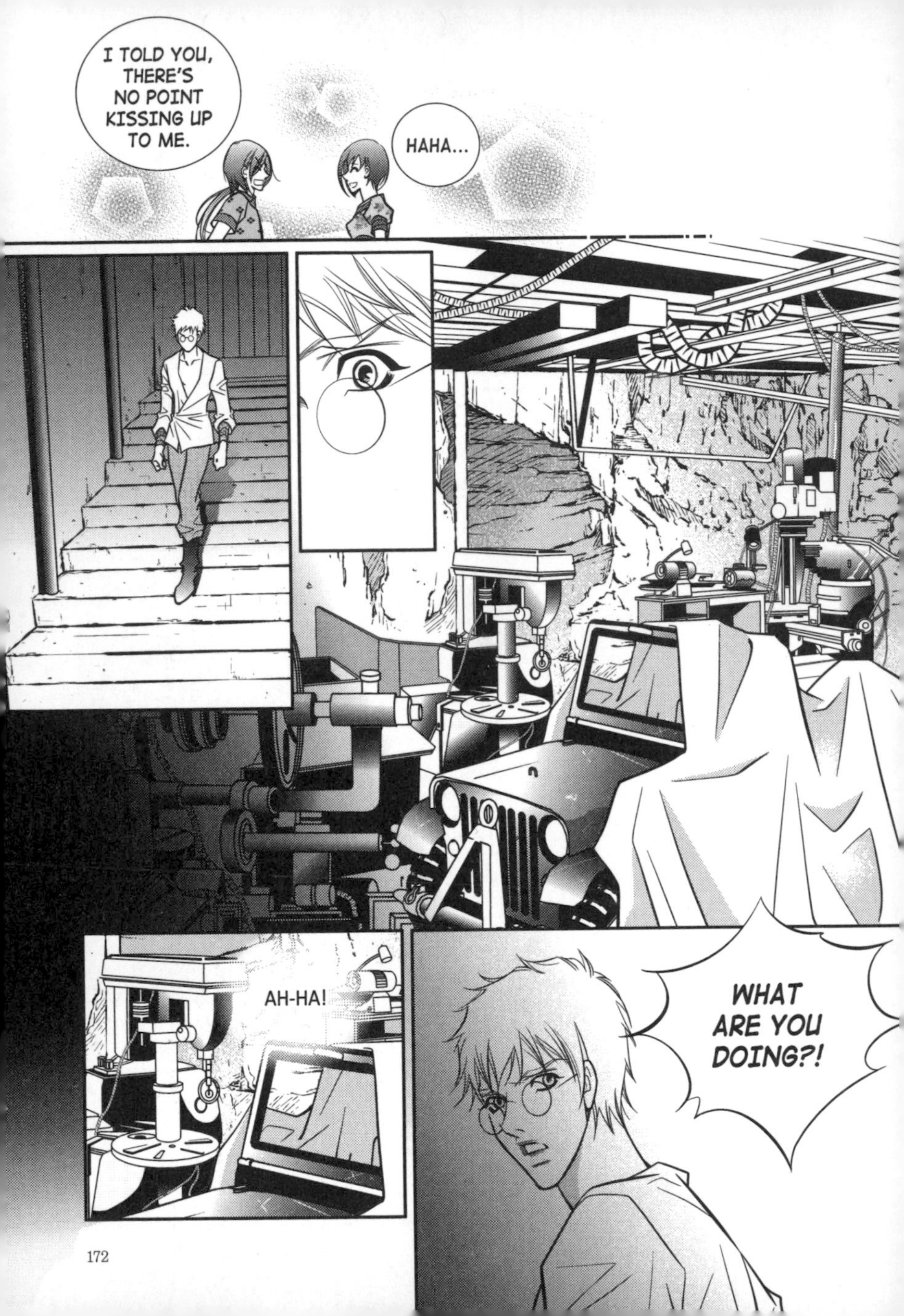
I TOLD YOU, THERE'S NO POINT KISSING UP TO ME.
HAHA...
AH-HA!
WHAT ARE YOU DOING?!

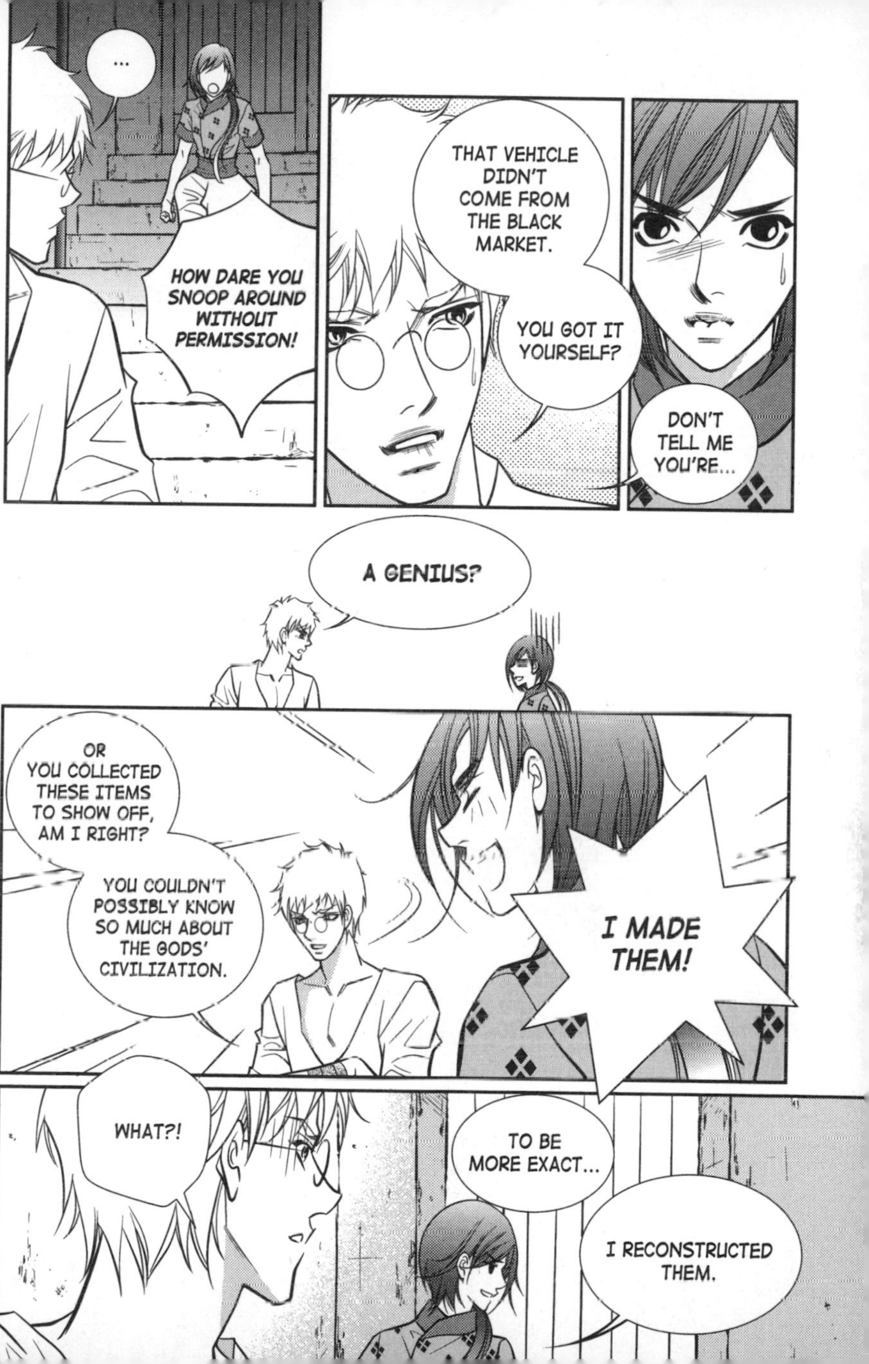
...
HOW DARE YOU SNOOP AROUND WITHOUT PERMISSION!
THAT VEHICLE DIDN'T COME FROM THE BLACK MARKET.
YOU GOT IT YOURSELF?
DON'T TELL ME YOU'RE...
A GENIUS?
OR YOU COLLECTED THESE ITEMS TO SHOW OFF, AM I RIGHT?
YOU COULDN'T POSSIBLY KNOW SO MUCH ABOUT THE GODS' CIVILIZATION.
I MADE THEM!
WHAT?!
TO BE MORE EXACT...
I RECONSTRUCTED THEM.

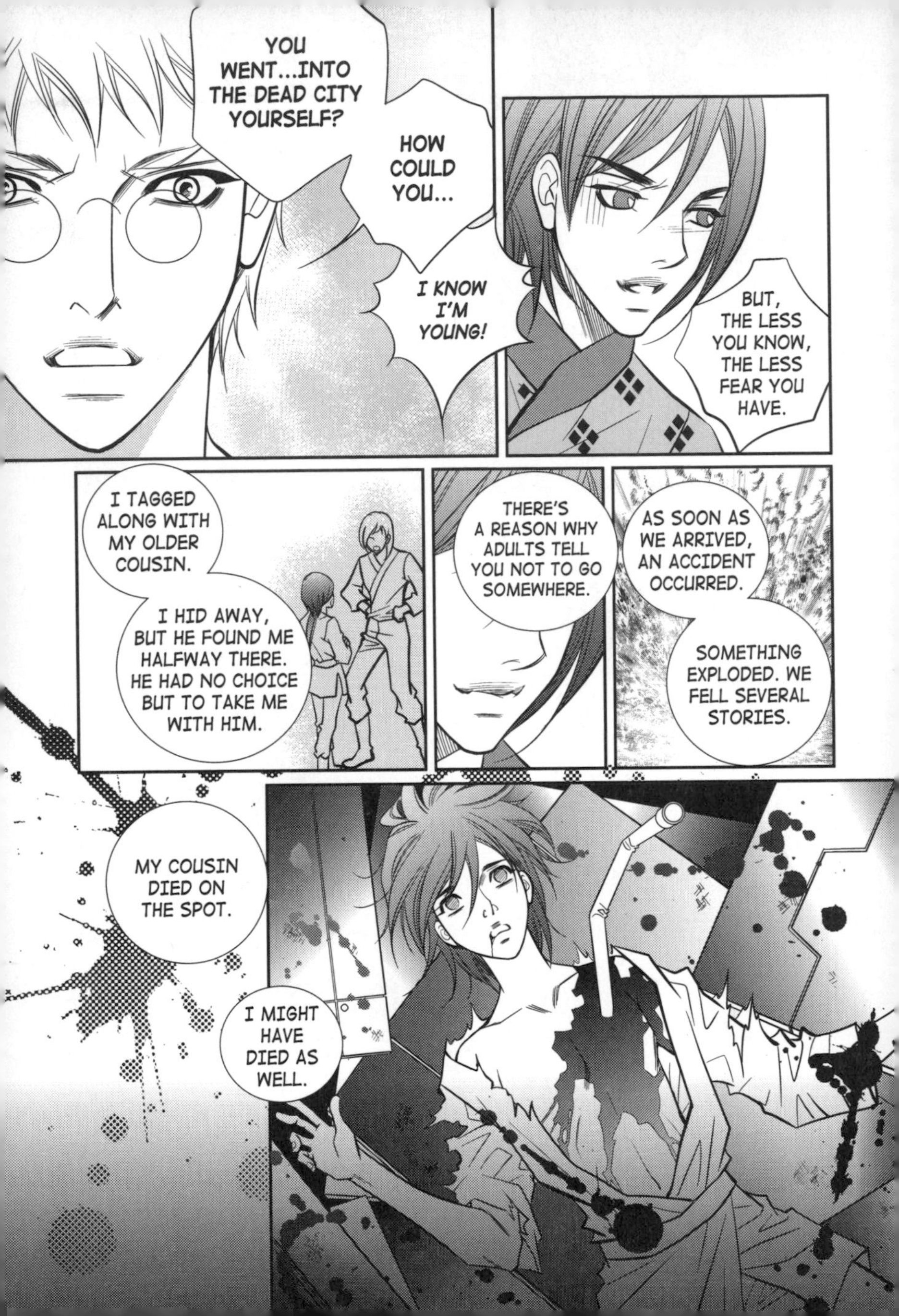

YOU WENT...INTO THE DEAD CITY YOURSELF?
HOW COULD YOU...
I KNOW I'M YOUNG!
BUT, THE LESS YOU KNOW, THE LESS FEAR YOU HAVE.
I TAGGED ALONG WITH MY OLDER COUSIN.
I HID AWAY, BUT HE FOUND ME HALFWAY THERE. HE HAD NO CHOICE BUT TO TAKE ME WITH HIM.
THERE'S A REASON WHY ADULTS TELL YOU NOT TO GO SOMEWHERE.
AS SOON AS WE ARRIVED, AN ACCIDENT OCCURRED.
SOMETHING EXPLODED. WE FELL SEVERAL STORIES.
MY COUSIN DIED ON THE SPOT.
I MIGHT HAVE DIED AS WELL.

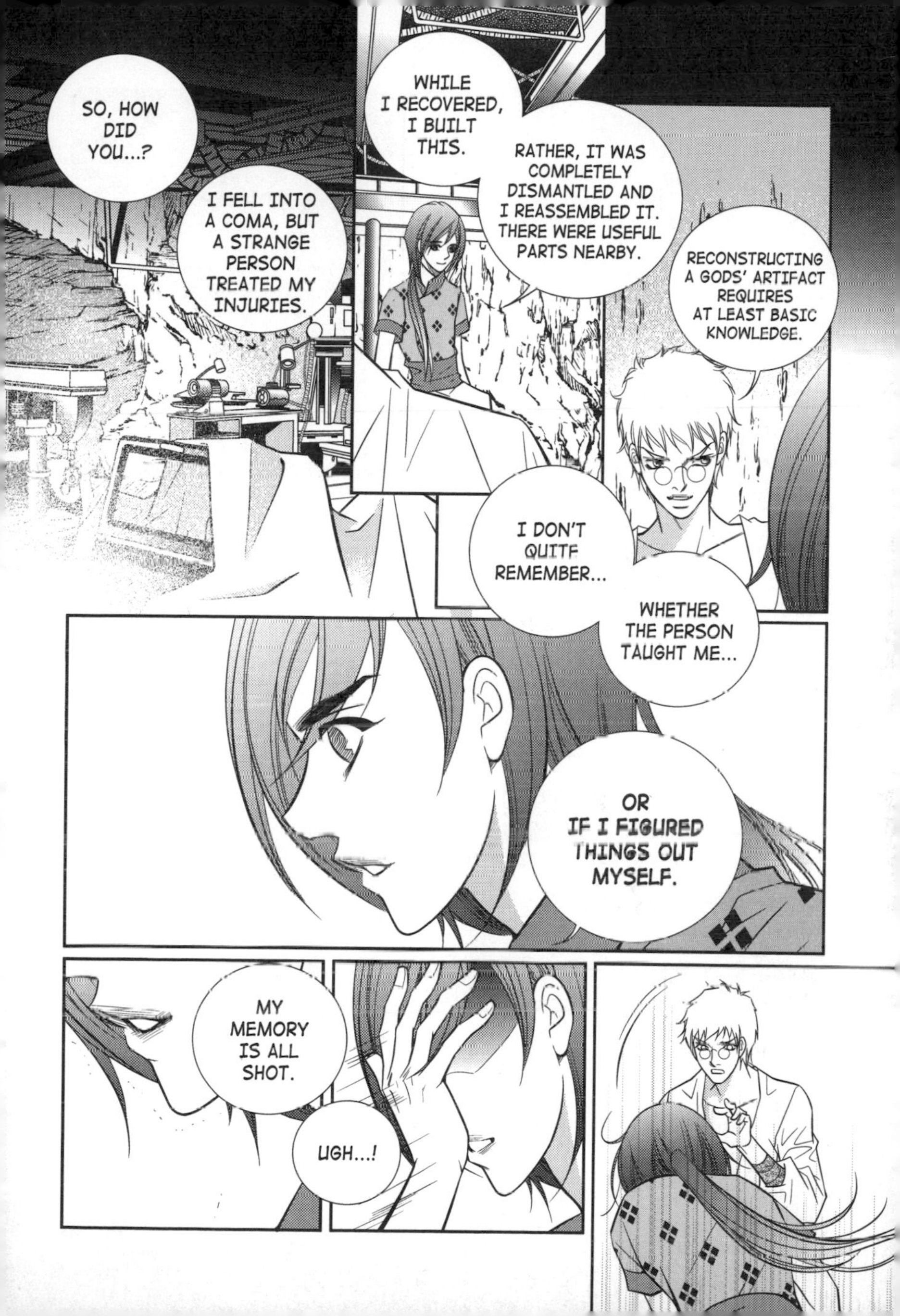
SO, HOW DID YOU...?
I FELL INTO A COMA, BUT A STRANGE PERSON TREATED MY INJURIES.
WHILE I RECOVERED, I BUILT THIS.
RATHER, IT WAS COMPLETELY DISMANTLED AND I REASSEMBLED IT. THERE WERE USEFUL PARTS NEARBY.
RECONSTRUCTING A GODS' ARTIFACT REQUIRES AT LEAST BASIC KNOWLEDGE.
I DON'T QUITE REMEMBER...
WHETHER THE PERSON TAUGHT ME...
OR IF I FIGURED THINGS OUT MYSELF.
MY MEMORY IS ALL SHOT.
UGH...!

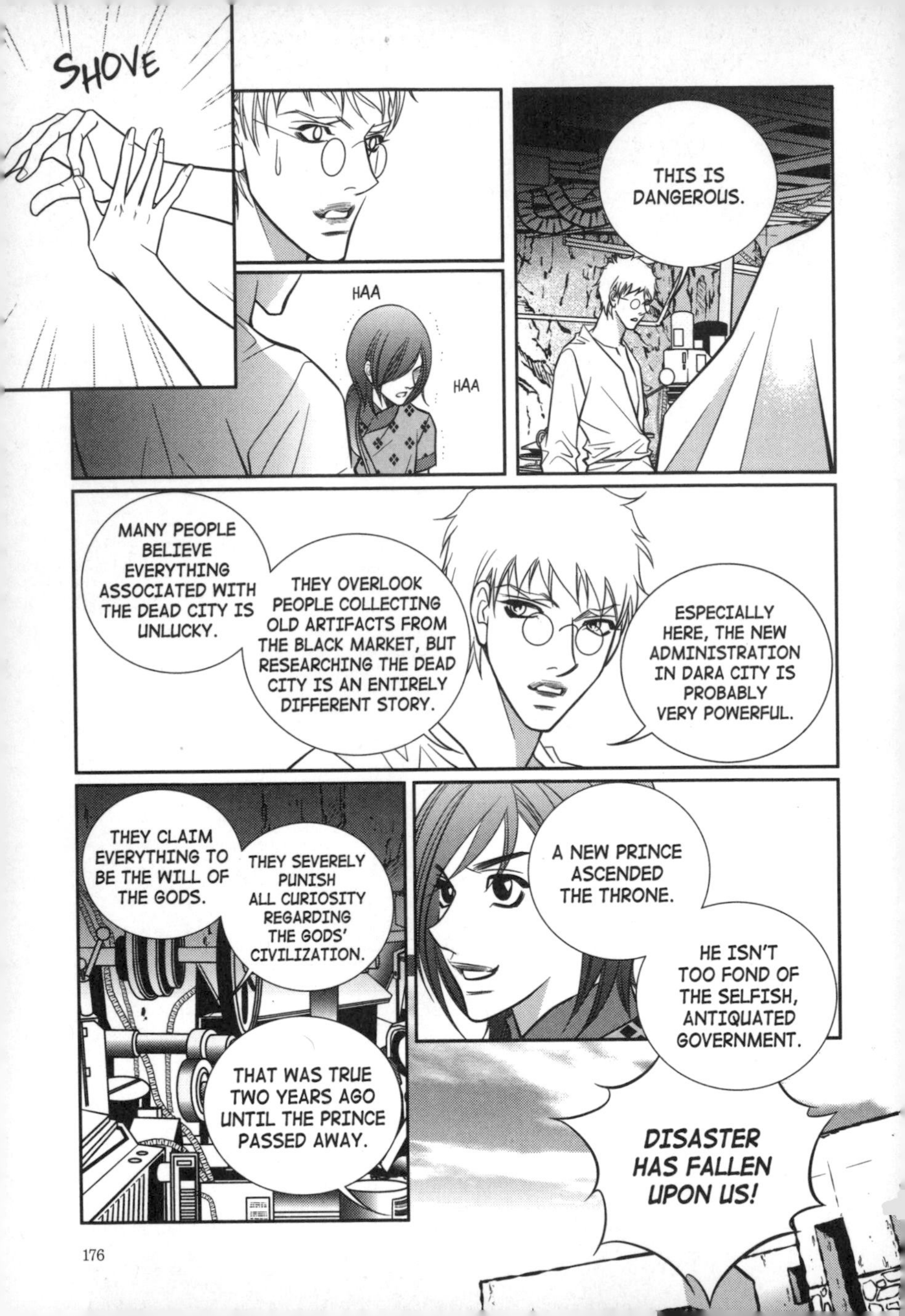
SHOVE
HAA
HAA
THIS IS DANGEROUS.
MANY PEOPLE BELIEVE EVERYTHING ASSOCIATED WITH THE DEAD CITY IS UNLUCKY.
THEY OVERLOOK PEOPLE COLLECTING OLD ARTIFACTS FROM THE BLACK MARKET, BUT RESEARCHING THE DEAD CITY IS AN ENTIRELY DIFFERENT STORY.
ESPECIALLY HERE, THE NEW ADMINISTRATION IN DARA CITY IS PROBABLY VERY POWERFUL.
THEY CLAIM EVERYTHING TO BE THE WILL OF THE GODS.
THEY SEVERELY PUNISH ALL CURIOSITY REGARDING THE GODS' CIVILIZATION.
THAT WAS TRUE TWO YEARS AGO UNTIL THE PRINCE PASSED AWAY.
A NEW PRINCE ASCENDED THE THRONE.
HE ISN'T TOO FOND OF THE SELFISH, ANTIQUATED GOVERNMENT.
DISASTER HAS FALLEN UPON US!

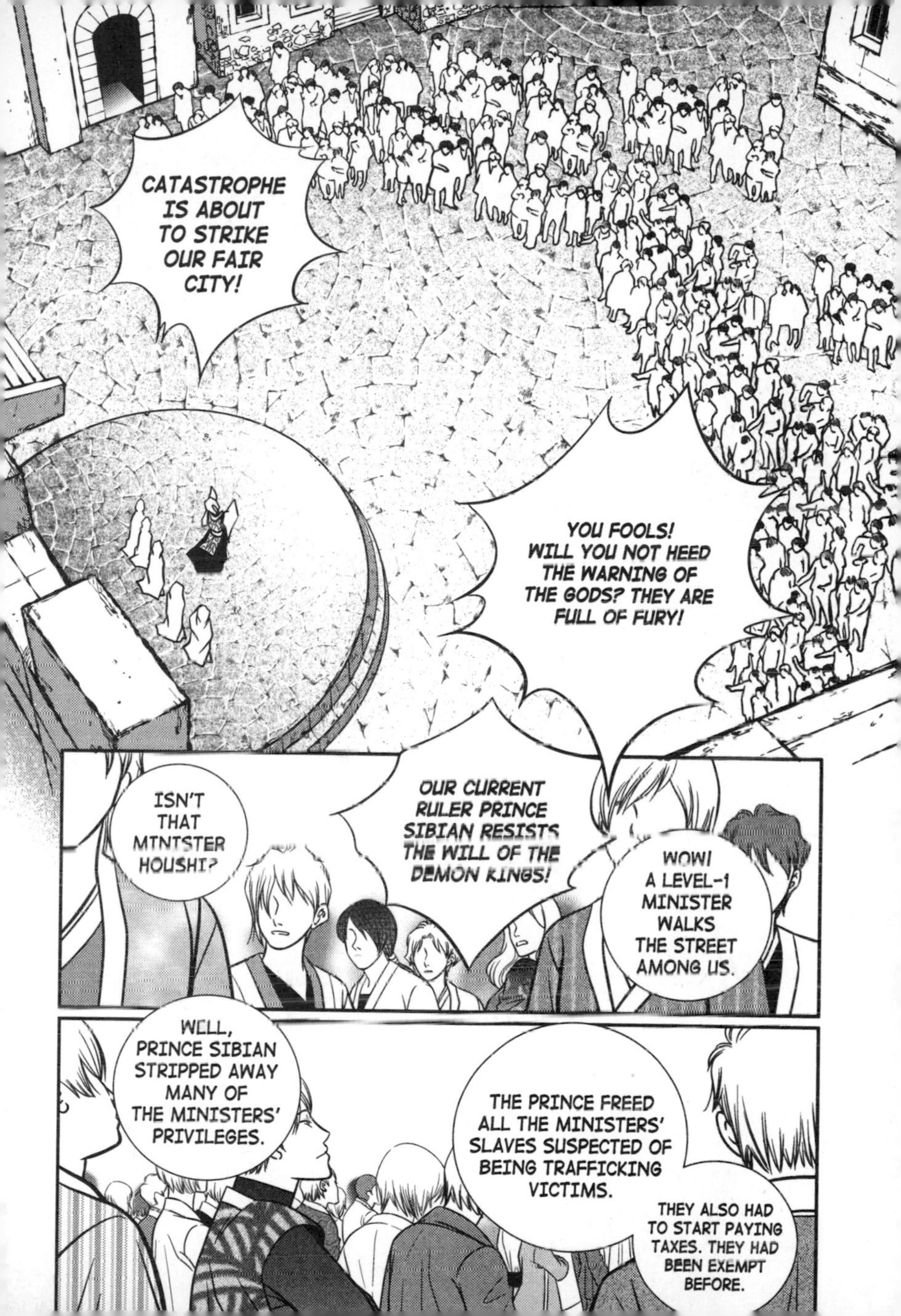
CATASTROPHE IS ABOUT TO STRIKE OUR FAIR CITY!
YOU FOOLS! WILL YOU NOT HEED THE WARNING OF THE GODS? THEY ARE FULL OF FURY!
ISN'T THAT MINISTER HOUSHI?
OUR CURRENT RULER PRINCE SIBIAN RESISTS THE WILL OF THE DEMON KINGS!
WOW! A LEVEL-1 MINISTER WALKS THE STREET AMONG US.
WELL, PRINCE SIBIAN STRIPPED AWAY MANY OF THE MINISTERS' PRIVILEGES.
THE PRINCE FREED ALL THE MINISTERS' SLAVES SUSPECTED OF BEING TRAFFICKING VICTIMS.
THEY ALSO HAD TO START PAYING TAXES. THEY HAD BEEN EXEMPT BEFORE.

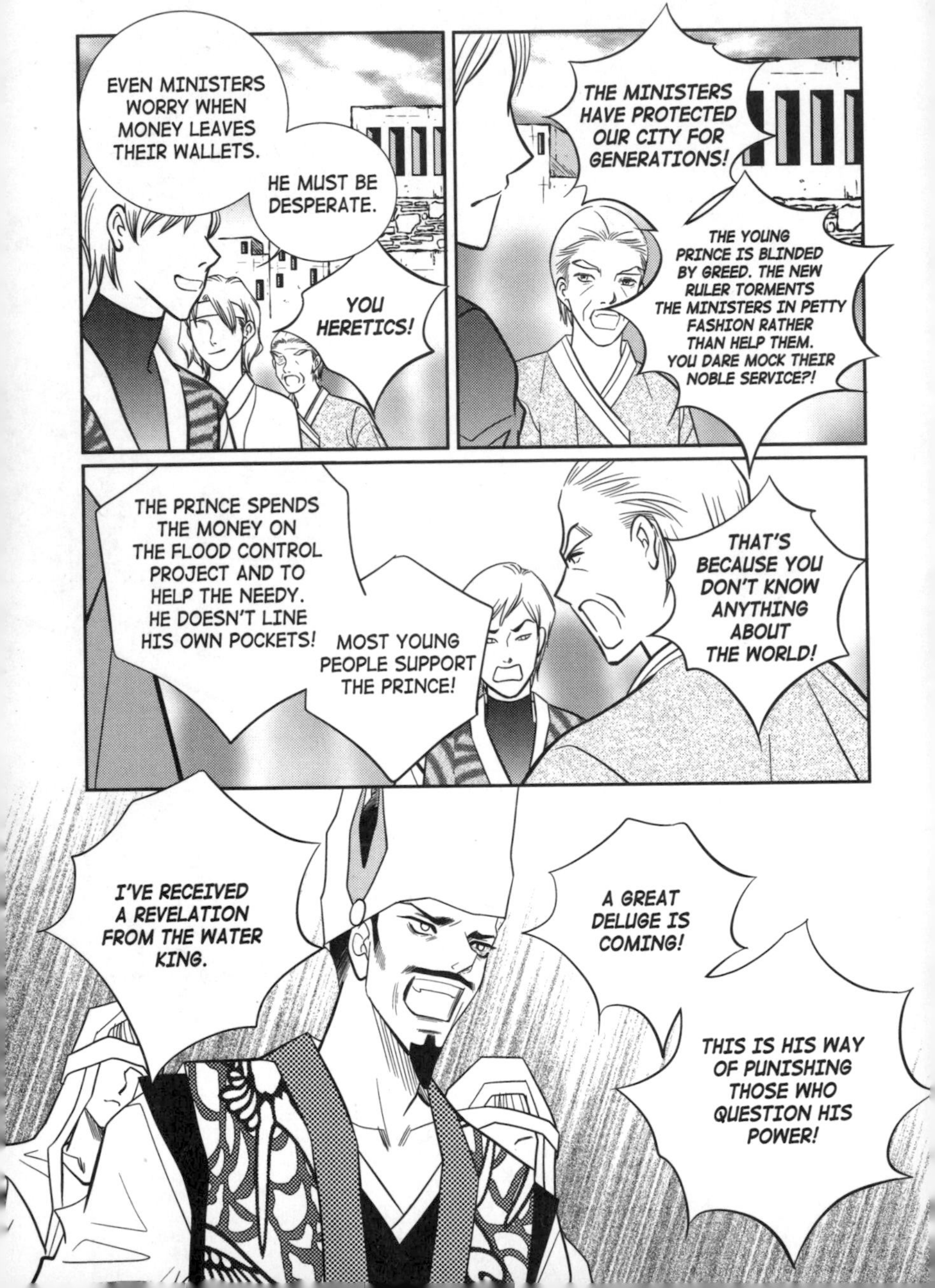
EVEN MINISTERS WORRY WHEN MONEY LEAVES THEIR WALLETS.
HE MUST BE DESPERATE.
YOU HERETICS!
THE MINISTERS HAVE PROTECTED OUR CITY FOR GENERATIONS!
THE YOUNG PRINCE IS BLINDED BY GREED. THE NEW RULER TORMENTS THE MINISTERS IN PETTY FASHION RATHER THAN HELP THEM. YOU DARE MOCK THEIR NOBLE SERVICE?!
THE PRINCE SPENDS THE MONEY ON THE FLOOD CONTROL PROJECT AND TO HELP THE NEEDY. HE DOESN'T LINE HIS OWN POCKETS!
MOST YOUNG PEOPLE SUPPORT THE PRINCE!
THAT'S BECAUSE YOU DON'T KNOW ANYTHING ABOUT THE WORLD!
I'VE RECEIVED A REVELATION FROM THE WATER KING.
A GREAT DELUGE IS COMING!
THIS IS HIS WAY OF PUNISHING THOSE WHO QUESTION HIS POWER!

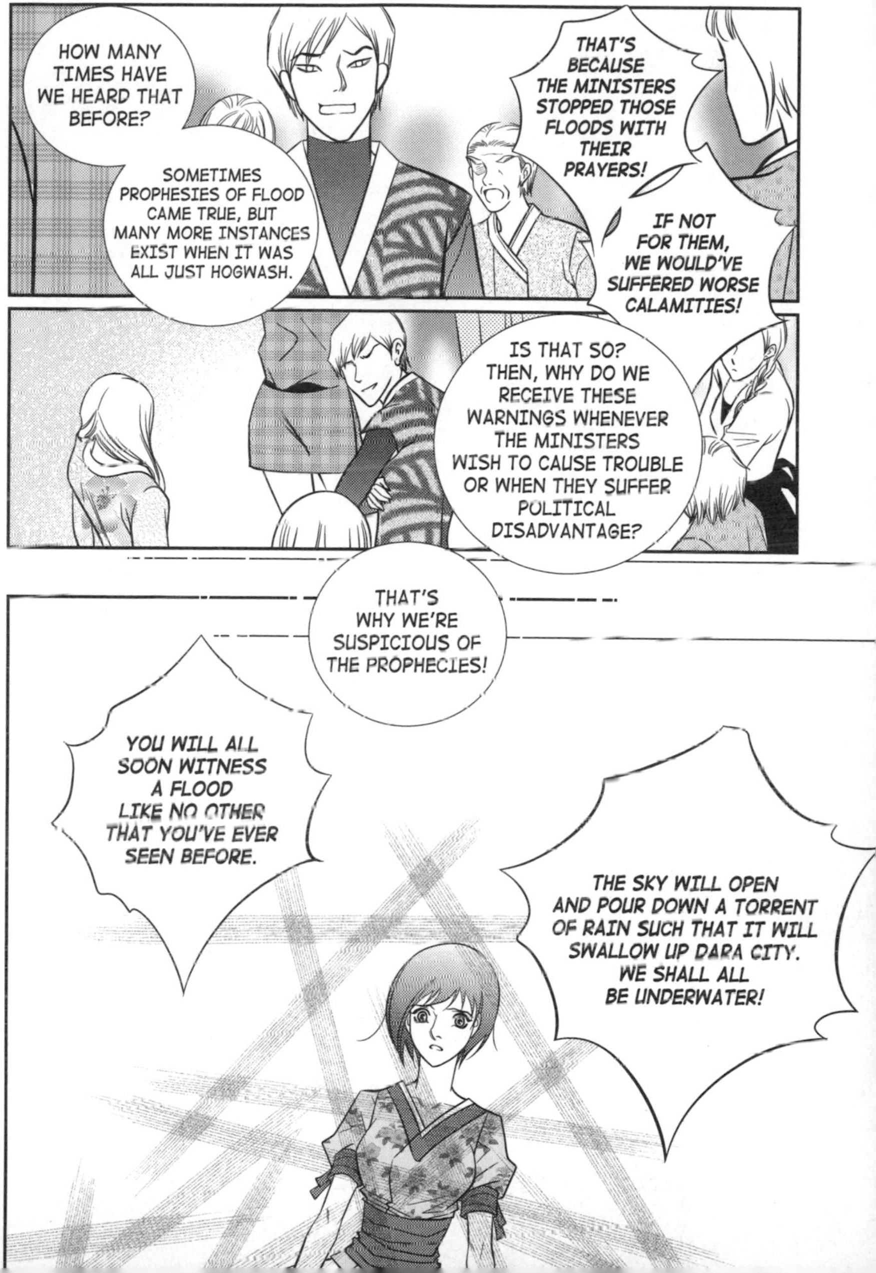
HOW MANY TIMES HAVE WE HEARD THAT BEFORE?
SOMETIMES PROPHESIES OF FLOOD CAME TRUE, BUT MANY MORE INSTANCES EXIST WHEN IT WAS ALL JUST HOGWASH.
THAT'S BECAUSE THE MINISTERS STOPPED THOSE FLOODS WITH THEIR PRAYERS!
IF NOT FOR THEM, WE WOULD'VE SUFFERED WORSE CALAMITIES!
IS THAT SO? THEN, WHY DO WE RECEIVE THESE WARNINGS WHENEVER THE MINISTERS WISH TO CAUSE TROUBLE OR WHEN THEY SUFFER POLITICAL DISADVANTAGE?
THAT'S WHY WE'RE SUSPICIOUS OF THE PROPHECIES!
YOU WILL ALL SOON WITNESS A FLOOD LIKE NO OTHER THAT YOU'VE EVER SEEN BEFORE.
THE SKY WILL OPEN AND POUR DOWN A TORRENT OF RAIN SUCH THAT IT WILL SWALLOW UP DARA CITY. WE SHALL ALL BE UNDERWATER!

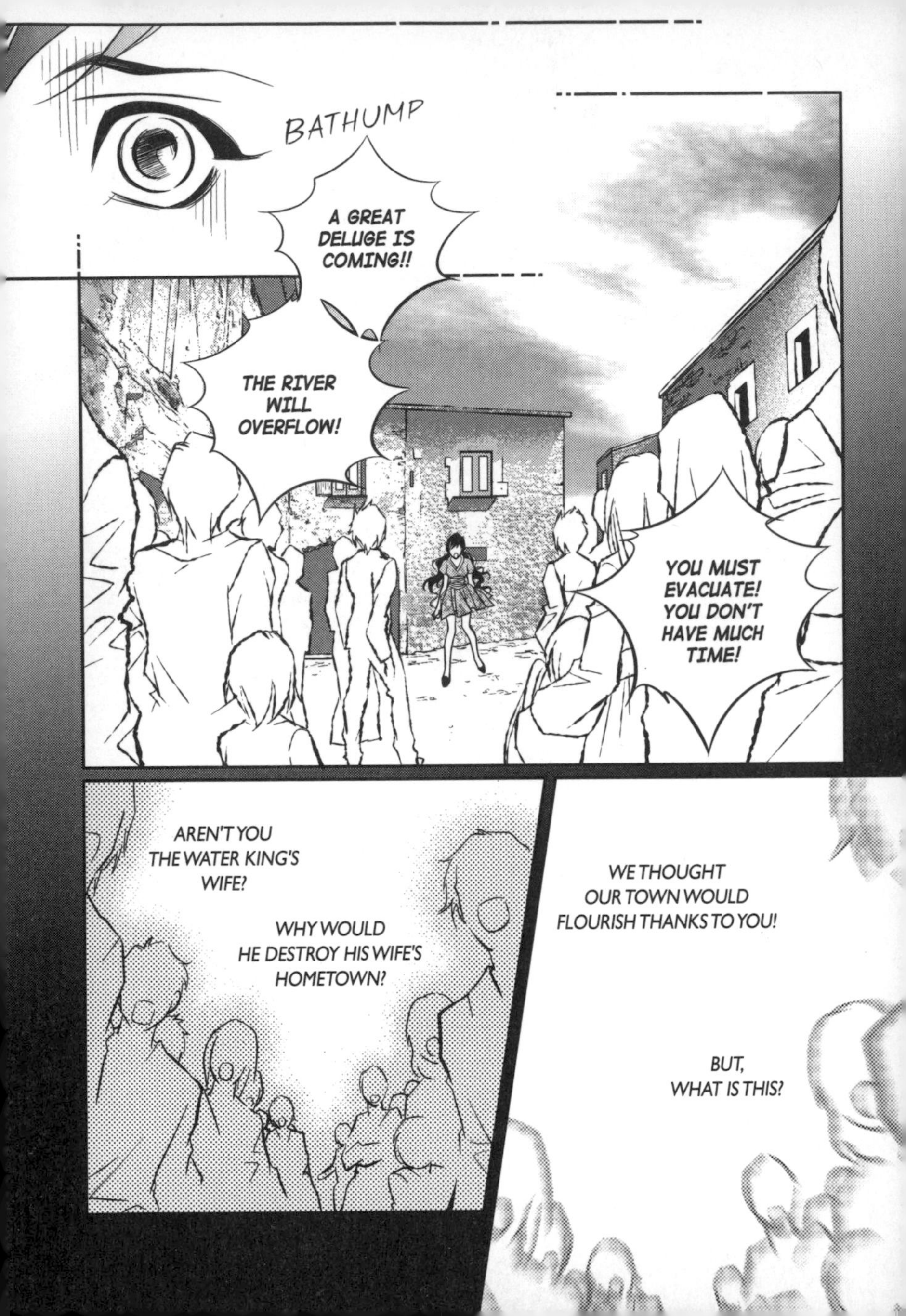
BATHUMP
A GREAT DELUGE IS COMING!!
THE RIVER WILL OVERFLOW!
YOU MUST EVACUATE! YOU DON'T HAVE MUCH TIME!
AREN'T YOU THE WATER KING'S WIFE?
WHY WOULD HE DESTROY HIS WIFE'S HOMETOWN?
WE THOUGHT OUR TOWN WOULD FLOURISH THANKS TO YOU!
BUT, WHAT IS THIS?

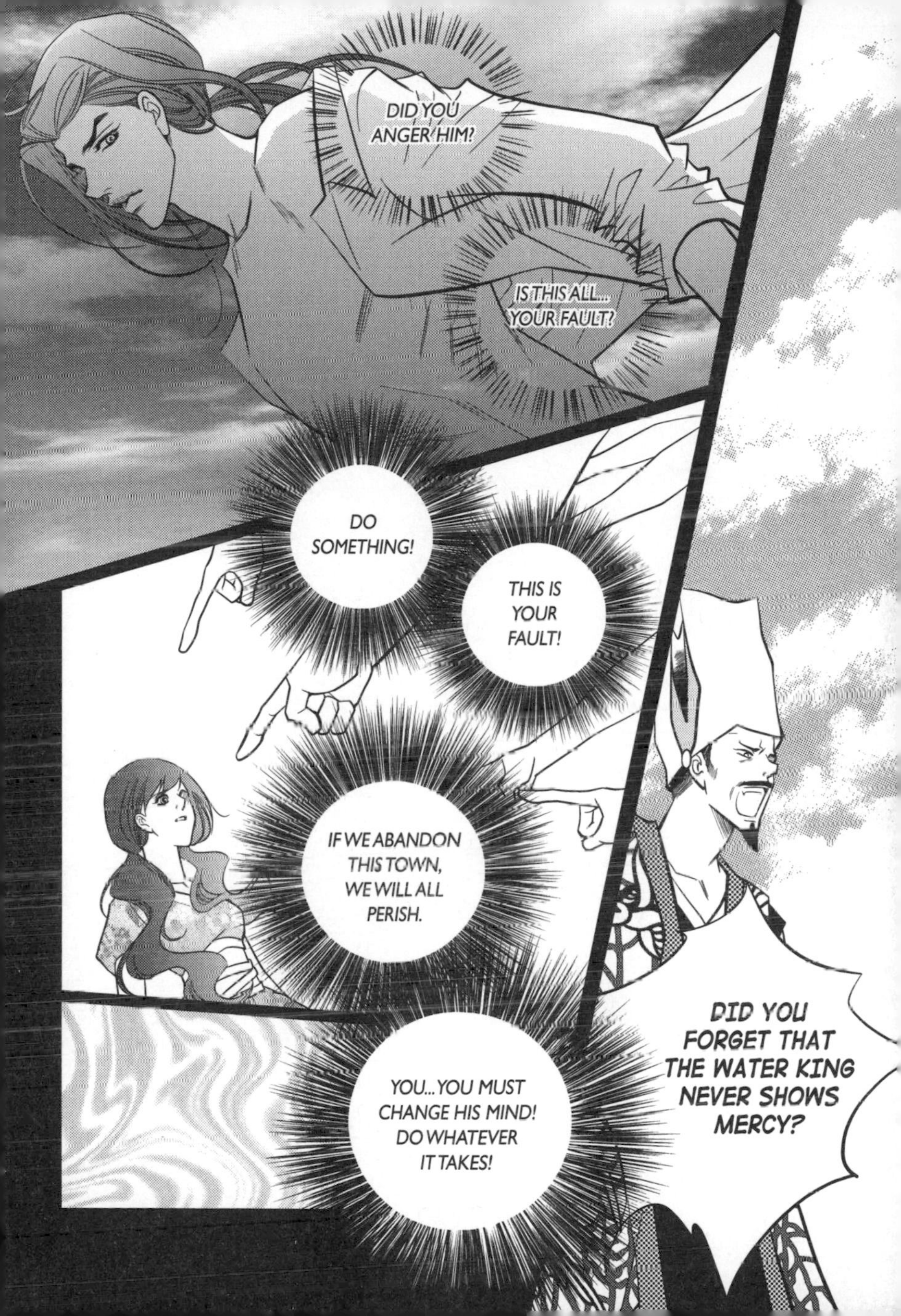
DID YOU ANGER HIM?
IS THIS ALL... YOUR FAULT?
DO SOMETHING!
THIS IS YOUR FAULT!
IF WE ABANDON THIS TOWN, WE WILL ALL PERISH.
YOU...YOU MUST CHANGE HIS MIND! DO WHATEVER IT TAKES!
DID YOU FORGET THAT THE WATER KING NEVER SHOWS MERCY?

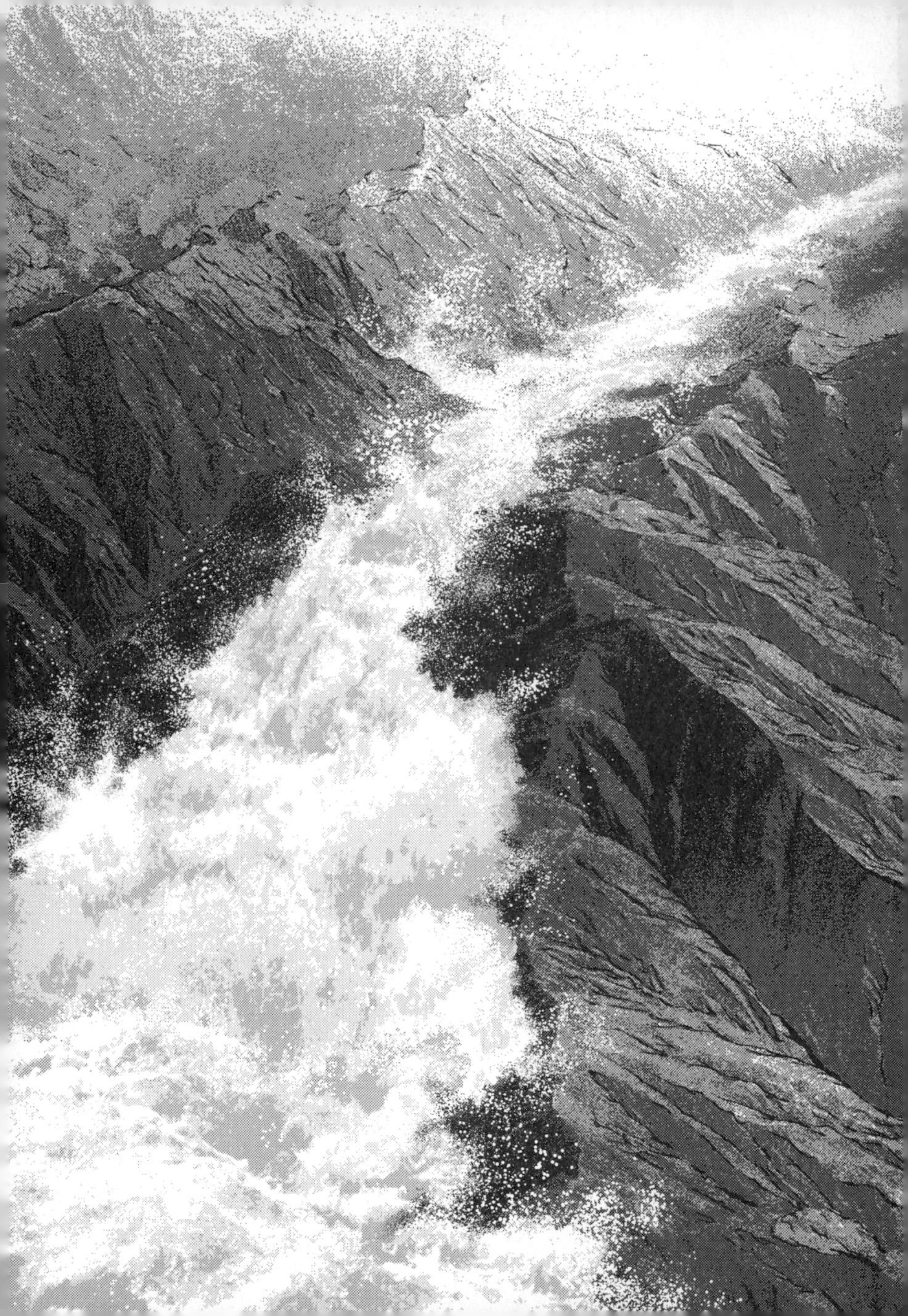

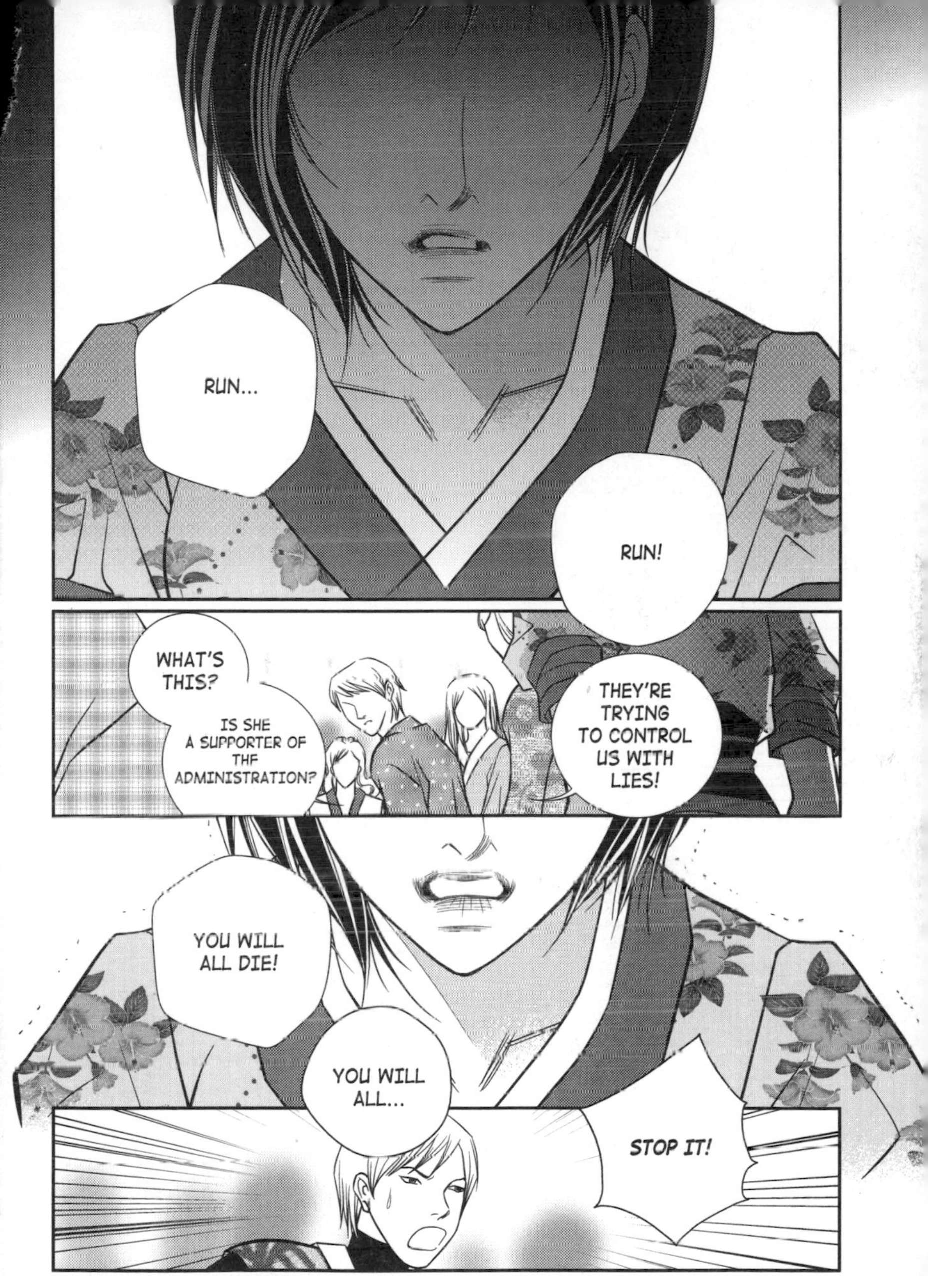
RUN...
RUN!
WHAT'S THIS?
IS SHE A SUPPORTER OF THF ADMINISTRATION?
THEY'RE TRYING TO CONTROL US WITH LIES!
YOU WILL ALL DIE!
YOU WILL ALL...
STOP IT!

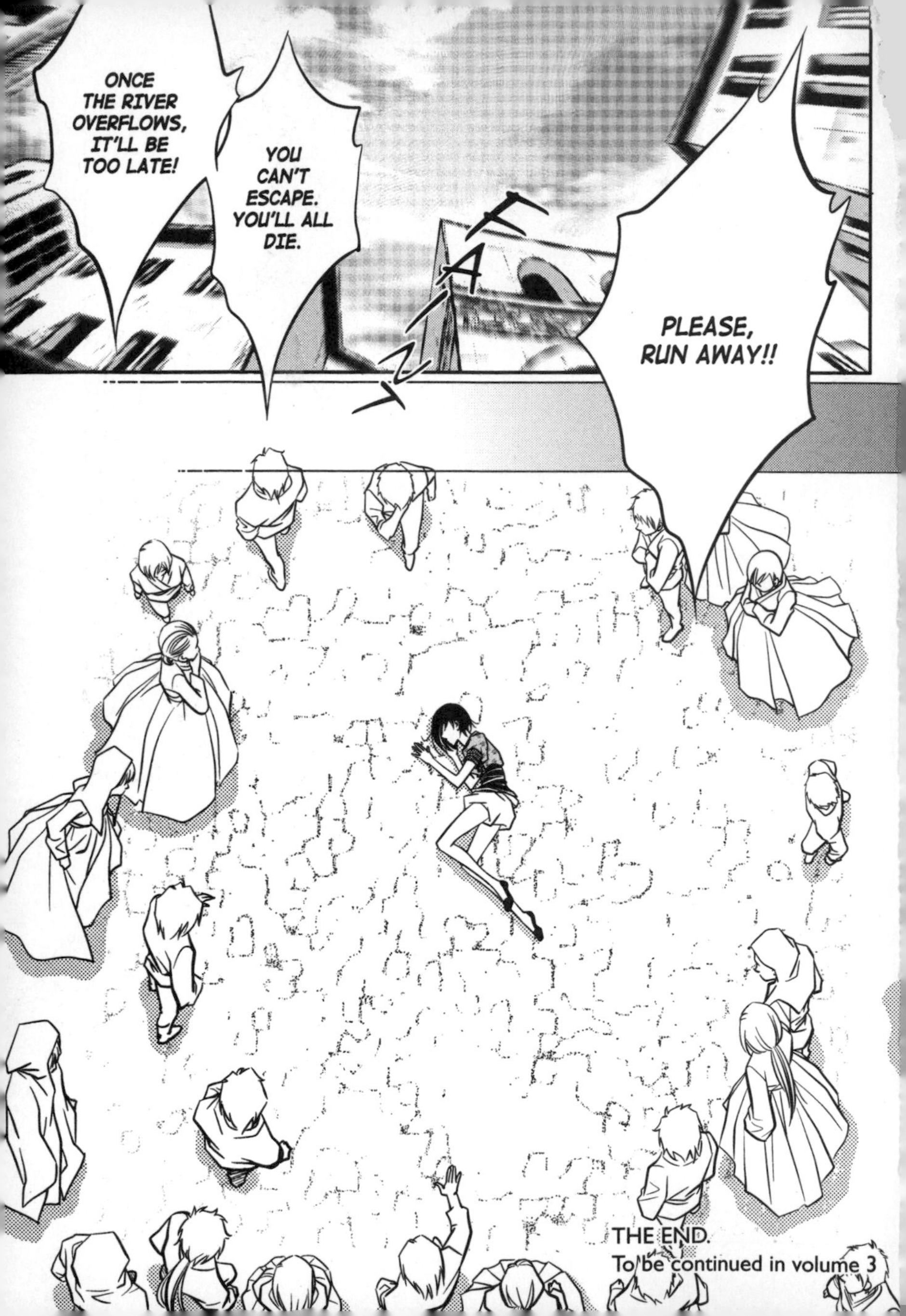
ONCE THE RIVER OVERFLOWS, IT'LL BE TOO LATE!
YOU CAN'T ESCAPE. YOU'LL ALL DIE.
FAINT
PLEASE, RUN AWAY!!
THE END.
To be continued in volume 3